THE HISTORIANS OF
LATE ANTIQUITY

The fourth and fifth centuries AD were an era of religious conflict, political change, and military struggle. The responses of contemporary historians to these turbulent times reflect their diverse backgrounds – they were both Christian and pagan, writing in Greek and Latin, and documenting church and state.

This volume is the first accessible survey of the lives and works of these historians. Chapters 1–12 explore the structure, style, purpose, and nature of their writings. Chapters 13–19 compare and contrast the information they provide, and the views they express, on topics central to the period. These range from historiography, government, and religion to barbarian invasions, and the controversial emperors Julian 'The Apostate' and Theodosius I.

This much-needed introductory work is an invaluable guide and reference tool for the study of late antiquity.

David Rohrbacher is Assistant Professor of Classics at New College of Florida, Sarasota, Florida.

D1452888

THE HISTORIANS
OF LATE
ANTIQUITY

David Rohrbacher

London and New York

First published 2002
by Routledge
11 New Fetter Lane, London EC4P 4EE

Simultaneously published in the USA and Canada
by Routledge
29 West 35th Street, New York, NY 10001

Routledge is an imprint of the Taylor & Francis Group

© 2002 David Rohrbacher

Typeset in Garamond by Taylor & Francis Books Ltd
Printed and bound in Great Britain by TJ International, Padstow,
Cornwall

British Library Cataloguing in Publication Data
A catalogue record for this book is available from the British Library

Library of Congress Cataloging in Publication Data
A catalogue record for this book has been requested

ISBN 0–415–20458–5 (hbk)
ISBN 0–415–20459–3 (pbk)

CONTENTS

CONTENTS

ACKNOWLEDGEMENTS

Many people aided me in the writing of this book. I thank Richard Stoneman and Catherine Bousfield at Routledge for their patience. The completion of the manuscript was aided by a grant from the Division of Sponsored Research at the University of South Florida. Thanks are also due to Holly Barone, Ed Foster, and the staff at interlibrary loan at New College of Florida and the University of South Florida, the Department of Classics and Ancient History at the University of Durham, Anne Ankers and the staff at Hatfield College, my colleagues in the Department of Classics at the University of Tennessee, Knoxville, and the staff at interlibrary loan at the University of Tennessee, Knoxville, my colleagues and students at New College of Florida, Michael Clater and the staff of the library at Clearwater Christian College, Katherine Maynard, Leo Allen, Jared and Casey Wilson, Julie Hayward, Donn D'Alessio, and my mother and father. This book, like so many other things, suffers from the absence of the discriminating eye of my father-in-law, Paul Latowsky, who passed away during its preparation.

I owe an incalculable debt to my wife, Anne, who edited the manuscript and suffered with me through its creation. I dedicate this book to her, with thanks and love.

ABBREVIATIONS

Amm.	Ammianus of Marcellinus
Aug.	Augustine of Hippo
cod.	*codex* (book)
Cod. Th.	*Codex Theodosianus* (Theodosian Code)
comm. ad Ezech.	*Commentarium ad Ezechiel* (Commentary on the book of Ezechiel)
comm. ad Zach.	*Commentarium ad Zachariam* (Commentary on the book of Zachariah)
dem. evang.	*Demonstratio Evangelica* (The Proof of the Gospel)
ep.	*epistula* (letter)
Eun.	Eunapius
Eus.	Eusebius of Caesarea
Eut.	Eutropius
Fest.	Festus
fr.	*fragmentum* (fragment)
HE	*Historia Ecclesiastica* (Church History)
hist. relig.	*Historia Religiosa* (History of the Monks)
ILS	H. Dessau, *Inscriptiones Latinae Selectae*
Jer.	Jerome
KG	Kaisergeschichte
Jul.	Julian
or.	*oratio* (oration)
pref.	preface
Ruf.	Rufinus
scr. orig. const.	T. Preger, *Scriptores Originum Constantinopolitianarum*
Soc.	Socrates
Soz.	Sozomen
Sym.	Symmachus
Theod.	Theodoret
Vell. Pat.	Velleius Paterculus
Vic.	Aurelius Victor
vir. ill.	*De Viris Illustribus* (On Illustrious Men)
Zos.	Zosimus

INTRODUCTION

Interest in late antiquity has increased dramatically in recent decades, and the profusion of scholarly work on the subject shows no sign of abating. The scope of "late antiquity" itself has undergone an expansion both chronologically and geographically. Events as early as the second and as late as the tenth centuries have been described as "late antique," as have events in the histories of Iran, Africa, and Arabia. This book takes a comparatively restricted view of the term "late antique," treating only what seems still to be the core of the late antiquity, the fourth and fifth centuries in the Roman empire. During these two centuries, the empire became Christian, and the political unity of the Mediterranean was sundered by the end of imperial rule over the western provinces. (Useful modern introductions to the period include Jones 1964, 1966; Brown 1971; Cameron 1993a, 1993b; Bowersock *et al.* 1999.)

Scholarly interpretations of the transformations which took place during late antiquity have been altered by the continual accumulation of new sources of information, such as new archaeological exploration and analysis. Just as important as the new data, however, have been changes in attitude and perspective. What had once been seen only as a melancholy time of "Decline and Fall" is now more likely to be celebrated for its new and innovative approaches to religion, art, and culture. Modern judgements on late antiquity are certain to be influenced by modern sentiments about Christianity, empire, and multiculturalism. This study seeks not to pass new judgement on this complex period, but to better illuminate how it was perceived by those living and writing at the time.

1

The Roman empire in the fourth and fifth centuries: political history

The later empire must be considered in the light of the events of the third century, and, more specifically, the events of the years between the murder of Alexander Severus in 235 and the accession of Diocletian in 284. The degree to which the political and economic instability of the period impinged upon the life of the average citizen of the empire has been disputed. Nevertheless, several aspects of the so-called "crisis of the third century" are worthy of note. The rise to power of a new, aggressive, and westward-looking dynasty in Persia, the Sasanians, resulted in major military losses on the eastern frontier. This threat may have emboldened or enabled enemies on other frontiers, who struck repeatedly during this period. The military crisis was exacerbated by a political crisis, which saw approximately two dozen emperors serve in a mere fifty years, almost every one assassinated or killed in civil war. Military and political turmoil was joined by an economic meltdown, as frequent debasement of the currency led to massive inflation and the virtual demonetization of the empire.

The emperor Aurelian (270–5) restored the unity of the empire and made some economic reforms, but was assassinated after five years in office. The reign of the reforming emperor Diocletian, who came to power ten years later, is more often considered a major turning point in imperial history. During Diocletian's reign, the Persians were soundly defeated and the empire remained generally at peace. In what appears to have been an attempt to establish clear lines of succession, and thereby to reduce the prevalence of civil war, Diocletian established a system of government called the Tetrarchy. The emperor selected two senior and two junior emperors, known as "Augustus" and as "Caesar." It was expected that the *Caesares* would one day succeed the *Augusti*, and select *Caesares* of their own. Emperors by this time had long ceased to reside at Rome, and the four tetrarchs tended to be in constant motion along the frontier with their *comitatus*, their administrators and bodyguard. Diocletian doubled the number of provinces of the empire by subdivision, which allowed imperial functionaries to more efficiently control their smaller jurisdictions, and he also revamped the system of taxation after an empire-wide census. Diocletian was the first emperor to fully embrace the regal and absolutist stylings of a Hellenistic or Persian king, and the late empire is sometimes called the Dominate after the new title for the Roman emperor, *dominus* or lord. Diocletian's restoration of order to the empire through the use of an enlarged army and an increasingly autocratic and bureaucratic style of administration set the tone for the governments of the next two centuries.

The tetrarchic system was one of Diocletian's reforms which did not long outlast its inventor, as the tetrarchs and their relatives fell into a series of bloody civil wars shortly after Diocletian's abdication in 305. When the smoke cleared, it was Constantine I who emerged as sole emperor in 324. In addition to Constantine's momentous conversion to Christianity, about which more will be said below, the emperor ratified and extended many of Diocletian's reforms. In particular, he successfully restored a gold currency to the empire after Diocletian's failed attempts at monetary reform, in part thanks to the massive confiscation of gold from pagan temples toward the end of his reign. Constantine was also responsible for the founding of "New Rome," Constantinople, the eastern capital which grew rapidly in size and importance in the fourth century.

Constantine died in 337 and was succeeded by three sons, Constantine II, Constans, and Constantius II. The brothers divided the empire among themselves, but soon came into conflict. Constantine II was killed while invading Constans' territory in 340, and Constans was killed by a usurper, Magnentius, in 350. As Constantius headed west to avenge his brother, he appointed his nephew Gallus as Caesar in the east in 351. Magnentius was defeated in 353, and shortly thereafter Gallus was recalled to the imperial court and put to death, perhaps as punishment for the violence he had provoked during food shortages at Antioch. Continuing incursions along the Persian frontier demanded Constantius' presence in the east, and the emperor therefore appointed his other nephew, Julian, as Caesar in 355 and sent him to Gaul. After successfully restoring order to the province, which had suffered during the usurpation of Magnentius when Constantius had encouraged barbarian attacks, Julian was raised to the rank of Augustus by his troops. Constantius' refusal to accept this promotion meant war, but before the eastern and western armies could seriously clash Constantius died of a fever in November 361 and Julian became sole ruler of the empire.

Julian had been secretly a pagan for years, and his sudden rise to power allowed him to reveal his religious beliefs and to attempt to reverse the legal and social benefits which Christianity had accumulated under the rule of Constantine and his sons. His religious policies generally fell short of full persecution but were calculated to remove privileges from the church and to impose certain burdens upon Christians. Christians reacted with fear and fury, pagans with joy and triumph. In 363 Julian mounted a full-scale invasion of Persia which proved to be a miserable failure, and the emperor was killed during the retreat.

After Julian's death, military leaders in an emergency meeting selected a Christian, Jovian, as the new emperor. Jovian died after less than eight months in office, and was replaced in February 364 by Valentinian I, who ruled the western half of the empire and appointed his brother, Valens, to rule the eastern half. Procopius, one of Julian's relatives, attempted to restore the Constantinian dynasty but was quickly crushed by Valens in 365. When Valentinian was ill in 367, he prepared for his succession by naming his 8-year-old son Gratian as Augustus. As soon as Valentinian died in a fit of anger while receiving a barbarian embassy in 375, his ministers quickly named his second son, the 4-year-old Valentinian II, as Augustus. This move, which may have been designed to ensure the loyalty of the western armies, was grudgingly accepted by Gratian, and the child remained under the protection of his mother, Justina, in northern Italy.

Valentinian I had spent his reign fighting along the Rhine, and his generals were kept busy by disturbances in Britain and Africa. Valens fought the Goths inconclusively in the 360s and fended off plots and suspected plots against him by a series of harsh trials which sparked complaints of judicial excesses. The brothers favored the military and were as a consequence not trusted by senators and other civilians. Both continued the policy of religious toleration toward paganism which Jovian had pronounced after the death of Julian.

After attacks by the Huns in 376, a tribe of Goths petitioned Valens for permission to settle inside the empire. After the request was granted, the migration went disastrously wrong, and Roman confusion and corruption led the Goths to rise in revolt. The attempt by Valens to put down the revolt in a battle on 9 August 378 near Adrianople led to his death and the destruction of the eastern army. The Goths had free rein throughout the Balkans for several years until a peace was made under the leadership of Gratian's new partner as Augustus, the Spaniard Theodosius I. The settlement has been frequently seen as a turning point in imperial history, since for the first time barbarians were settled inside the empire as allied troops who would retain their political sovereignty.

In August 383, the general Magnus Maximus was proclaimed emperor in Britain, and Gratian was murdered by his troops. Italy,

Pannonia, and Africa remained loyal to Valentinian II, who was now 13 and still under the thumb of his mother Justina. In 387 Maximus invaded Italy, and Theodosius in response moved west and defeated the usurper in 388, having left the east in the control of his older son Arcadius. Theodosius returned to Constantinople in 391 after sending Valentinian II to Gaul with the Frankish general Arbogast. Conflict between Arbogast and Valentinian II led to the emperor's suspicious death, officially a suicide, in 392. Arbogast then raised Eugenius, an obscure schoolteacher, to the throne. Theodosius returned to the west and defeated Arbogast and Eugenius at the Frigidus river in September 394, but died a few months later. He left two sons, the 17-year-old Arcadius in the east and the 10-year-old Honorius in the west. The empire, which had briefly been unified under the sole rule of Theodosius I, would never be so again.

At the death of Theodosius I, the western army was under the control of the general Stilicho, who acted as regent for the child Honorius. Stilicho's claim that Theodosius, on his deathbed, had also granted him regency over the eastern emperor Arcadius may or may not have been true, but it poisoned relations between the two halves of the empire during Stilicho's lifetime. The Gothic leader Alaric played off this mistrust by being alternately allied with and inimical toward the west. In addition to Gothic attacks, which culminated in Alaric's sack of Rome in 410, the west suffered from a major German invasion in 405 under the leadership of Radagaisus and a further breach of the Rhine in 406–7. After Stilicho's assassination in 408, the west saw a succession of usurpations in Britain and Gaul. After the death of Alaric in 411, Honorius' general Constantius put down the usurpers, and Spain and Gaul were pacified through a combination of military reconquest and the hiring of barbarian peoples as federate armies. Britain, however, was never reconquered, and was lost to imperial control forever. Honorius' sister Galla Placidia married Constantius in 421 and the two had a son, Valentinian III. Constantius died at the end of the year and Galla Placidia withdrew to Constantinople with her son after a quarrel with Honorius. When Honorius died without an heir in 423, the eastern government supported the claims of his nephew, the baby Valentinian III, and sent an army to kill John, the official who had been proclaimed Augustus. Valentinian III was named Augustus at Rome on 23 October 423.

Power in the east after Theodosius' death remained in civilian control, with the brief ascendancy of the praetorian prefect Rufinus followed by the domination of the eunuch Eutropius. The rebellion of the Gothic federate Gainas in 399 resulted in the execution of Eutropius but Gainas and the Goths were put down and civilian government continued under the prefectures of Aurelian and Anthemius. On Arcadius' death in May 408 his 6-year-old son Theodosius II was named Augustus. Theodosius II was brought up by his pious and forceful sister Pulcheria, who was influential in policy matters. After the emperor's marriage in 421 to Aelia Eudocia, the empress, too, became a powerful force at court. The palace eunuch Chrysaphius succeeded in disgracing Eudocia and her friend Cyrus of Panopolis after 441 and maintained a powerful role in government until his execution after Theodosius' death in 450.

Barbarian attacks troubled the empire throughout the fifth century. In 441 Theodosius II dispatched an army to aid Valentinian III in an unsuccessful attempt to dislodge Gaiseric and his Vandals from Africa. Rua and then his successor as king of the Huns, Attila, took advantage of these difficulties by demanding tribute from the eastern emperor and by devastating the Balkans and Thrace when payment was deemed insufficient. After the death of Theodosius the new eastern emperor, Marcian, refused to continue to pay subsidies to the Hunnic empire. Attila turned his attention to the west, where the sister of Valentinian III, Honoria, unhappy with the marriage that had been arranged for her, offered herself in marriage to Attila. Attila came with his army to collect his bride, but the Huns were checked in Gaul in 451 by Aetius, the chief general and power behind the throne of Valentinian. A Hunnic invasion of Italy in 452 was unsuccessful, and after the death of Attila in 453 the Hunnic empire swiftly disintegrated.

The position of Marcian, the military officer who succeeded Theodosius II to the throne, was legitimated by his marriage to the previous emperor's sister Pulcheria. Marcian was succeeded after his death in 457 by Leo. Both emperors seem to have reached the throne through the influence of the general Aspar, but Leo came to favor another general, Zeno, and eventually had Aspar assassinated in 471. His reign was most notable for a disastrous attempt to drive the Vandals from Africa and for conflict with the Goths under their leader, Theodoric Strabo. At Leo's death in 474, the eastern empire was insolvent and threatened by Gothic power in the Balkans.

Valentinian III was assassinated in 455, having ruled for thirty years. After several short-lived emperors took the throne, the German general Ricimer supported as emperor Majorian (457–61) and, after executing Majorian, Libius Severus (461–5). The nominee of the eastern emperor Leo, the general Anthemius, next held office (467–72). The Roman army in this period ceased controlling Africa, Spain, and most of Gaul, and when the German officer Odoacer came to power in Italy, he neglected to appoint a western emperor and instead sought confirmation of his own power directly from the eastern emperor Zeno. When Zeno refused this recognition, Odoacer ruled with the title *rex*, or king, which was also used by the other German kings on what had once been Roman territory.

The Roman empire in the fourth and fifth centuries: religious history

Christianity was despised by pagan and Jew alike in the first centuries after the ministry of Jesus of Nazareth. Although technically illegal, most emperors sought to minimize prosecutions or persecutions which could lead to false accusations or general unrest. Christians continued to win converts gradually throughout the third century, and their growing numbers provoked two great persecutions, under the emperor Decius (250–1) and Valerian (257–60). Christians across the empire were forced to sacrifice to the gods or be martyred, and the persecution inspired many heroic acts of resistance as well as many more prudent acts of flight or surrender. Valerian's defeat and capture by the Persian king was considered divine vengeance by Christians, and his successor Gallienus restored property to the church and instituted a policy of religious toleration which would last for forty years.

Diocletian was a firm believer in the traditional gods, and considered Jupiter and Hercules, represented by himself and his colleague Maximian on earth, to be protectors of the empire. In February 303 the emperor published an edict intended to destroy the corporate life of Christianity, demanding that churches be destroyed, sacred books be burned, and that Christians lose their offices and legal rights. In the summer the emperor further commanded that Christian bishops be arrested and forced to sacrifice. The persecution was broadened still further under the leadership of the Caesar Galerius, who in 304 demanded that all Christians sacrifice or face death. After the abdication of Diocletian and Maximian in 305, their successors continued to pursue anti-Christian measures.

After years of persecution, however, the dying Galerius had a change of heart, and in 311 published his famous "Edict of Toleration," which returned Christianity to the neutral position it had held before 303. The edict was not accepted by all of the rulers of the Roman state. But in October 312, as the emperor Constantine marched on Rome against Maxentius, he saw in the sky a cross of light with the message, "In this conquer." The emperor credited the Christian God with his victory over Maxentius at the Milvian Bridge. In an alliance with the emperor Licinius, Constantine promulgated the Edict of Milan, which proclaimed freedom of religion throughout the empire. The degree to which Constantine understood the Christian religion at that time is uncertain, but his benefactions to the church were significant, including the exemption of clergy from duties and the showering of wealth upon churches in the west. In only a decade, Christianity had been transformed from an object of persecution to the favored religion of the Roman state.

The granting of privileges to the Christians made the definition of Christianity a much more significant source of strife. The fourth and fifth centuries were wracked with doctrinal disputes fueled by various mixtures of ideological, political, and economic motives. In order to consider these disputes fairly it is essential to avoid retroactively imposing later notions of orthodoxy upon earlier thinkers. It was out of the doctrinal controversies that the implications of various theological positions eventually came to be understood, and orthodoxy came to be constructed.

The relationship between God the Father and Jesus the Son was a frequent subject of debate in the fourth century. On the one hand, common sense and the Greek philosophical tradition would suggest that the Father was in some way greater than or existed prior to the Son. To emphasize too strongly the singularity of God ran the risk of not thoroughly disassociating Christianity from Judaism, which was an attractive alternative to Christianity in the cities of the east. Also, an emphasis on the human and therefore subordinate aspect of Jesus was necessary to underscore the pain that Jesus suffered on the cross. A fully divine Jesus would not seem to have undergone much of a sacrifice on behalf of mankind. On the other hand, there were strong reasons for emphasizing the essential unity of Jesus and the Father. A too-human Jesus might be assimilated with the many pagan stories of demigods and heroes. The greatness of God's sacrifice could only be emphasized by underlining Jesus' divinity. Without a Son whose power was fully divine, how could human sins be forgiven?

Arius was a priest of Alexandria who came into conflict with his bishop, Alexander, over the nature of the relationship between the

Father and the Son. Because, on the one hand, we do not know exactly what Arius taught, and on the other, we can be certain that he did not teach all of the many different things which he was accused of inspiring, the often-used term "Arianism" is not very useful for describing a theological position. It was, instead, used to smear theological opponents, few of whom would have been likely to describe themselves with the word. In some cases, the historian can substitute the more neutral term "homoiousian" and its counterpart "homoousian." The first term, which includes the letter "i," refers to the belief that the Father and Son are of "like" substance, and can refer to a number of theological positions which deny what would eventually become the orthodox belief that the Father and Son are of the "same" substance.

A major church council or "synod" met at Nicaea in northern Asia Minor in May 325, not only to discuss the dispute between Arius and Alexander but to solve various other controversies which divided Christians. Constantine was himself present and played a major role in the debates, eventually winning nearly unanimous assent to the Nicene Creed, which held that the Father and Son were "of the same substance." Constantine's relationship with the church served as a model for later emperors. The emperor was frequently involved in church controversies, but had no official role in the church itself, and was liable to be criticized by clergy should he intervene too aggressively. Constantine's rhetoric constantly proclaimed the virtue of unity in the church, but new conflicts and further rounds of synods to dispute them were the norm throughout late antiquity.

Theological disputes often became quite heated and on many occasions resulted in bloodshed and even massacres. At stake were not only fervently and sincerely held religious beliefs, but also the right to possess and use valuable church real estate and the ability to distribute major amounts of patronage in the forms of jobs and charitable donations. In the fourth century, church historians concentrate on the activities of the "Arians" or homoiousian parties, who were the established church during the reigns of the homoiousian emperors Constantius II and Valens. Athanasius (299–373) was the most indefatigable champion of Nicene Christianity, and church historians tend to take his apologetic writings at face value. Numerous times Athanasius was forced to flee his bishopric in Alexandria for safety in the west. Eastern and western bishops tended to be divided over Christological disputes, with the east favoring homoiousian formulations and the west the Nicene homoousian formula. The two halves of the empire, which would go their own ways politically in the fifth century, were already distrustful of each other in theological matters in the early fourth century.

The spread of monasticism throughout the fourth century was particularly strong in the east. Monasticism could take the form of communal living in accordance with a rule, such as the thousands of monks who lived in communities organized by Pachomius in Egypt. In the Syrian desert one could find individual monks, "athletes for Christ," who underwent severe and sometimes bizarre privations in an attempt to become closer to God. Simeon Stylites, for example, spent forty-five years on a pillar, where the curious and the powerful came for advice and help.

In the fourth century, Christian emperors granted benefits to Christian clergy and favored Christians in other ways, but did not move to outlaw the beliefs of the pagans of the empire. Constantine suppressed a few temples where ritual prostitution was practiced, for example, but did little to disturb most temple buildings. Although he legislated against animal sacrifice, this seems to have been ineffectual, since similar legislation was still being passed under Theodosius. Nevertheless, the removal of imperial patronage from pagan cult, the transfer of wealth and attention to church building and the clergy, and the increased prestige of a religion associated with the imperial house must have encouraged conversion. By the end of the fourth century, especially under the rule of Theodosius I and his sons, a harder line began to be taken against paganism. Much of the violence against pagan temples and shrines in these years was not orchestrated by the emperor, who sometimes actually tried to intervene against the mobs of monks who sought to demolish the dwelling places for demons which remained in their midst. Imperial legislation against paganism appears then to have followed rather than created the wave of popular religious violence directed against the remaining public symbols of the ancient gods.

While ordinary pagans thought of religion in terms of sacrifice and ritual, intellectual pagans studied Neoplatonism. Plotinus and his successors had elaborated upon Plato's system by seeing reality as composed of a series of levels, from the highest level of the One or Unity, down to the level of Mind, and then the level of Soul. The theurgists were Neoplatonists who had integrated cult with philosophy. By means of certain rituals, theurgy allowed the philosopher to ascend toward the One. This form of late antique Platonism influenced Christian philosophers as well.

It is impossible, of course, to say whether people in late antiquity were more "spiritual" or "religious" than those of other ages. The impact of Christianization can be seen more directly, however, in transformations of the landscape and in changes in the rhythms of daily life. In the cities, the church had supplanted the temple and, in some places, the synagogue. The patron and local magnate was likely to be a bishop. Christian preaching and the celebration of Christian festivals and rituals were displacing other forms of oratory and entertainment. The holy man or monk was more prevalent and powerful in the countryside than the waning pagan shrines. While, with hindsight, we are able to see where the process of Christianization was heading, we should not allow our knowledge to blind us to the lack of certainty contemporaries felt in the face of rapid religious change. The very definition of orthodoxy and of paganism was forged in these centuries by the ideological and political controversies of the day.

The historians of late antiquity: an overview

Ancient history is a prose narrative of past events which is true (on the nature of ancient history see Fornara 1983; Woodman 1988). By late antiquity, many centuries of history-writing had both defined the genre by example and had revealed many possible ways in which prose narratives about the past could be written. The historians treated in this volume provide a broad spectrum of ways in which classical traditions of literature were transformed to create new types of truthful narratives about the past.

The category of *classicizing* historians includes Ammianus Marcellinus, Eunapius, Olympiodorus, and Priscus (Blockley 1981; Baldwin 1981). Blockley points to the broad diversity of this group of historians (1981: 86–94). Nevertheless, he shows that these authors all purposely drew attention to the connections between themselves and works of classical antiquity. They write in a self-consciously elevated and rhetorical style, which reveals their traditional education in the classics.

The category of *breviaria* includes Aurelius Victor, Eutropius, and Festus (den Boer 1972; Malcovati 1942). These are short works which provide a summary of historical events. Despite their brevity, these works allowed their authors some margin for individual style and for commentary and interpretation on the events they describe. Because these three authors used the same basic source for their information about the history of the empire, investigation of the ways in which they differ can shed light on their differing purposes and values.

The category of *ecclesiastical* or *church history* includes Rufinus, Socrates, Sozomen, and Theodoret (Momigliano 1990; Downey 1965; Markus 1975; Chesnut 1986). This genre was invented by Eusebius of Caesarea, and all four of the church historians discussed here begin their work where Eusebius' history left off (on Eusebius, see Grant 1980; Barnes 1981; Chesnut 1986). The later church historians grapple with Eusebius' legacy in different ways. All include in some fashion the material which Eusebius' introduction states will be treated in his own ecclesiastical history: the names of famous Christian bishops and leaders, the fight against heretics, pagans, and Jews, and the accounts of those who were martyred (Eus. *HE* 1.1.1–2). But the successor church historians found different answers to questions concerning the style in which to present the material, the purpose served in continuing Eusebius' work, and the proper treatment of secular material in religious history.

The category of *apologetic history* includes Orosius. His unusual work uses history as a weapon to prove his theological points by means of a blend of secular historiography, Eusebian triumphalism, and biblical numerology. While classicizing historians demonstrate the continuing links between late antiquity and the Greco-Roman tradition, Orosius' historical work demonstrates the formal innovation and rethinking of values that are equally typical of late antiquity.

The format of the book

The first section (chapters 1–12) treats each historian individually, presenting what is known of his life and then describing the nature of his historical work. Appended to each chapter is a citation of the Greek or Latin text of the author, and any available English translations. The second section (chapters 13–19) is dedicated to discussions of the opinions of the historians on certain significant themes. The first chapter of this section, chapter 13, explores late antique historians' uses of speeches and documents, and the ways in which they assert their credentials and abilities as historians. Chapter 14 treats the historians' approach to certain novel elements of late antique governance, including the sacralization of the emperor, the bureaucracy, and legal and economic topics. Chapter 15 explores the extent to which historians link themselves to the distant past of the Roman state and how they interpret this period. Chapter 16, on religion, investigates the historical treatment of paganism, of Christian conflict, of Judaism, and of monasticism.

Chapter 17 explores the image of the barbarian, including Goths, Huns, and Persians. Two concluding chapters consider the historians' presentations of two important and controversial emperors of late Roman empire, Julian and Theodosius I. These chapters should help the reader to better understand the strengths, aims, and biases of the late antique historians. They also reveal the sorts of information that are presented in late antique history, and serve as an introduction for the reader to some fascinating topics in late antique history and society.

1

AMMIANUS MARCELLINUS

Life

We know a good deal about the life of Ammianus Marcellinus, who frequently appears in his own history. The complex mixture of Greek and Latin culture with which he was imbued, and his participation in some of the most important events of his time, provided him with the essential background for the creation of his monumental work, the *Res Gestae*.

Ammianus says that he was an "adolescens" (*Res Gestae* 16.10.21) in the year 357. This term generally is applied to those under the age of 30, which suggests that he was born in the late 320s or early 330s. His birthplace was almost certainly the Syrian city of Antioch, one of the most important cities of the empire in the fourth century (Liebeschuetz 1972). This Antiochene heritage helps to explain his surprising decision to write in Latin rather than in Greek, even though he describes himself as a Greek at the conclusion of the work (31.16.9) and frequently glosses Greek words with a comment like, "As *we* call it ... " (e.g. 20.3.11). In the Antioch of his youth, Latin would have been a familiar language. The emperor Constantius II used Antioch as his base during a series of wars against the Persian empire throughout the 340s, and the city was filled with Latin-speaking soldiers and bureaucrats.

Indeed, given what we can reconstruct of Ammianus' early career, it is not unlikely that he was raised in a Latin-speaking family (Matthews 1989: 71–80). Ammianus served as *protector domesticus*, a military staff assistant (Trombley 1999). Some men reached this position through long years of service, but Ammianus was still a young man when he became *protector*, which suggests that he received his rank through family connections. His father had probably been a soldier (Barnes 1998: 58–9), and was perhaps even the Marcellinus who served in the powerful position of *comes Orientis* in 349 (Gimazane 1889: 24–7). Ammianus several times complains about the unfair burdens placed upon the municipal elite, who were increasingly compelled to perform onerous duties as members of the *curia*, or city council (22.9.12, 25.4.21; Thompson 1947a). Ammianus may have derived exemption from such service from his father's position in the imperial service as well as from his own military profession (Barnes 1998: 58–9). The general under whom Ammianus served as *protector*, Ursicinus, had a home in Antioch (18.4.3), and Ammianus' service as *protector* may have been an apprenticeship under a family friend. Appointment to the position of *protector* required the ritual of *adoratio purpurae*, prostration before the emperor and the kissing of his purple robe (Avery 1940), and Ammianus probably performed this ritual while Constantius II was still in Antioch, and therefore before 350.

We can extract some suggestive information about Ammianus' youth from remarks scattered throughout his work. He describes himself as *ingenuus* and therefore accustomed to ride rather than walk (19.8.6); the word implies a reasonably high social status. In 359, he tells us, he stayed at the home of a certain Jovinianus, who was the satrap of the Armenian province of Corduene (18.6.20–1). Jovinianus had developed a love of Roman literature during his youth, which he spent as a hostage in the eastern empire. Perhaps the two met in school. The acquaintanceship reveals a bit of the cosmopolitan nature of the Antioch of Ammianus' childhood.

This traditional account of Ammianus' birthplace and background, outlined by E.A. Thompson (1947a) and augmented by John Matthews (Matthews 1989, esp. 67–80), has come under attack in recent years (Barnes 1993a, 1998; Fornara 1992a; Bowersock 1990b). Some scholars have denied that Ammianus was born in Antioch and have suggested in its place some other city of the Greek east. Most revisionists pay particular attention to a letter of the Antiochene orator Libanius to "Marcellinus" (*ep.* 1069), which had long been believed to be addressed to the historian. The letter congratulates its recipient on the success of his recent readings at Rome and was written around 392. In reviews of Matthews' work, Bowersock (1990b) and Barnes (1993a) both suggest that this letter addressed to Marcellinus was not written to our Ammianus Marcellinus but rather to another holder of that common name. Bowersock goes so far as to claim that "the assumption [of Ammianus' Antiochene origins] is based solely upon the identification of the recipient of [the] letter ... as the historian Ammianus

Marcellinus" (1990b: 247). Both reviewers were influenced by the work of Fornara (1992a), who similarly argued that Libanius' Marcellinus cannot be the historian, and that our understanding of Ammianus and his background should be reconsidered, as this letter is the "singular pillar" holding up the traditional account.

It is, however, incorrect to suggest that the letter of Libanius is the sole evidence linking Ammianus with Antioch. Matthews and Sabbah respond to the revisionists with numerous other pieces of circumstantial evidence (Matthews 1994; Sabbah 1997). Several passages praise the city (14.8.8, 22.9.14). Ammianus identifies himself with the Antiochenes during the reign of Valens several times (29.1.24, 29.2.4). In addition, there is his acquaintance with Jovinianus (18.6.20–1), the home which his patron Ursicinus had in Antioch (18.4.3), and the reference to the Antiochene Hypatius as "our" Hypatius, "praiseworthy from his youth" (29.2.16). Ammianus also knew Syriac, the native language of Antioch, a point made by Matthews that is accepted by one of his critics (Barnes 1998: 56). Barnes also recognizes Ammianus' "profound knowledge" of the city (1998: 60). None of this evidence is decisive, but it is very suggestive.

Fornara argues that the tone and diction of the letter of Libanius to Marcellinus would be appropriate if Libanius were addressing a young orator, but would be wholly unsuitable in a letter to an old historian (1992a: 331–8), and Barnes agrees that "Libanius' tone precludes his [addressee's] identification as the historian Ammianus Marcellinus" (1998: 57–8). Both Barnes and Fornara provide a Greek text and English translation of the words of Libanius, as does Matthews (1994), to which the interested reader may turn. This writer is simply not convinced that the tone of the letter demands any such conclusion. Moreover, altering the identity of the letter's recipient demands one to accept a very impressive coincidence. The letter is dated to 392 because of its position in Libanius' collection and its mention of the recent death of his son and of a former student. The latest datable events alluded to in Ammianus' work include the consulship of Neoterius (26.5.14) in 390 and the death of Petronius Probus (27.11.2) around 390. In addition, Ammianus lavishly praised the Serapeum of Alexandria as a building which would last eternally (22.16.12), a comment unlikely to be made after its destruction in 391 (Matthews 1994: 254). Ammianus Marcellinus, then, who might have been circumstantially considered to be a native of Antioch, completed his history around 391. Within a year, critics suggest, Libanius was writing a letter to a completely different Marcellinus of Antioch, giving readings from a prose work to great acclaim. Surely it is most economical to identify the recipient as the historian.

Toward the beginning of the surviving text of the *Res Gestae*, Ammianus reveals that in 353 he had been a member of Ursicinus' staff and was traveling with the general from Nisibis in Mesopotamia to Antioch, where Ursicinus was to serve as a judge for treason trials being orchestrated by the Caesar Gallus (14.9). The emperor Constantius had decided to remove Gallus from power, Ammianus tells us, and was persuaded by his advisors of the dangers of leaving the popular Ursicinus alone in the east, unchecked by a member of the imperial family (14.11.1–3). In 355, Ammianus was at the court of Constantius II at Milan, where, he claims, constant intrigue was being directed against Ursicinus (15.2.1–6). Trouble arose in Gaul, where the general Silvanus had been forced into revolt against the emperor (Hunt 1999; Drinkwater 1994; den Boer 1960; Balducci 1947). The emperor selected Ursicinus and Ammianus for the unenviable task of gaining the confidence of the usurper and then assassinating him. They succeeded in these goals, befriending Silvanus and then paying soldiers to murder him as he sought refuge in a church (15.5.27–31). After Silvanus' death, Ursicinus took over his position as general in Gaul, although technically he remained assigned to the eastern frontier (Frézouls 1962). This allowed Ammianus to witness the early successes of the young Julian described in the sixteenth book of his history. Although Marcellus was sent as a successor to Ursicinus in 356 (16.2.8), Ursicinus was ordered to remain, and was only summoned by the emperor to Sirmium in northern Italy in the summer of 357 (16.10.21), with Ammianus remaining in his retinue.

Leaving Sirmium, Ursicinus returned to his old position as *magister equitum* in the east. In 359, however, the general Sabinianus arrived bearing imperial letters which demanded the recall of Ursicinus to court (18.6.1). As Ursicinus and Ammianus were returning to Italy, they were met in Thrace by other imperial messengers ordering their immediate return to the eastern front (18.6.5). Ammianus saw these events as manifestations of the incompetence and malice of Constantius and his court, and blamed the increase in Persian aggressiveness on their discovery that Ursicinus had been replaced by the inferior Sabinianus (18.6.3–4). Ammianus also considered the return of Ursicinus to the east to be part of a cunning plot by the general's enemies at court, allowing them to blame him for any failures of a campaign directed by Sabinianus, while exempting him from praise should the campaign be successful (18.6.6). The truth is surely more charitable to the emperor. Ursicinus' recall appears to have been demanded in order to replace the recently executed western general Barbatio, and his return to the east a necessity given the increasing Persian hostilities (Matthews 1989: 40–1).

Ammianus' involvement in the Persian invasion of 359 makes for an exciting story (18.6.8–19; Paschoud 1989b). Ursicinus and Ammianus set out for Nisibis, a city in Mesopotamia, to help prepare it for a siege, but found that they had arrived too late. Smoke from enemy encampments was already visible along the horizon. Two miles from Nisibis, the party came upon an 8-year-old boy who had been abandoned by his panicked mother in the flight from the city. Ammianus was ordered to return the boy to the city, and, surrounded by Persian cavalry, he barely missed being caught up in the siege himself. The swiftness of his mount enabled him to outrun his pursuers and to reach Ursicinus and his companions, who were pasturing their horses, unaware of the proximity of the enemy. Ammianus urged them to flee, but the risk of detection remained high due to the full moon and the level terrain. As a decoy, they attached a lantern to a mule and sent it to their left while they themselves headed for the mountains on the right. The party entered a wooded area which the inhabitants had abandoned. There they discovered a Roman soldier who admitted, under harsh questioning, to being a deserter and Persian spy. After providing the party with information about the enemies' movements, he was put to death. From there the party hastened to the city of Amida, where scouts brought them information about the Persian advance hidden in the scabbard of a sword and couched in deliberately obscure language, which has only recently been fully understood (Blockley 1986).

It was then decided that Ammianus would go to Corduene to gather more information about Persian troop movements from Jovinianus. At Corduene he claims to have seen the massive Persian army on the move (18.6.20–3). After determining the course of the army, Ammianus returned to Roman territory and made his report. Orders came down to remove peasants from their land and to burn the fields to limit the enemies' fodder (18.7.1–3). As Ammianus and his party quickly destroyed several bridges to prevent the enemy from crossing, the carelessness of certain Roman cavalrymen allowed a Persian contingent to attack. Ammianus narrowly escaped and took refuge in Amida, which was filled with refugees and with farmers who had been participating in an annual fair nearby (18.8). Ammianus was then shut up inside the walls of Amida for seventy-three days while the Persian king Shapur besieged the city. Ammianus' account of the siege (19.2–8) "is one of the high points of his narrative and a classic passage in Roman historical narrative," according to Matthews (1989: 58). The city finally fell to Shapur, but the delay forced by the protracted siege left the Persians unable to capitalize on the victory. Ammianus himself slipped out of a gate with two companions when he recognized that the fall was imminent (19.8.5). Their escape was not without incident, but eventually, with the help of a captured runaway horse, they made their way to the Armenian town of Melitina, where they met up with a general whom they accompanied to Antioch (19.8.6–12).

The fall of Amida had repercussions for Ursicinus' career, and, one must imagine, for Ammianus' as well. An investigation at court into the reasons for the fall led to intrigue against the general, who from frustration blamed his troubles on the emperor's excessive deference to the palace eunuchs (20.2). As a result, Ursicinus was forced into retirement, and Ammianus disappears as an actor in his history for several years. He may have left the military when his sponsor did, or performed more mundane duties. A letter from Libanius to former students in Tarsus, written in 360, could possibly refer to Ammianus. In Barnes' translation (1998: 61), Libanius writes, "to judge from the dress [of the man bearing this letter] he is enlisted in the army, but in fact he is enrolled among philosophers; he has imitated Socrates despite having gainful employment – the fine Ammianus" (*ep.* 233).

After the revolt of Julian and the death of Constantius, the new emperor headed east to prepare for a renewed Persian campaign. Ammianus frequently discusses Julian's recruitment of personnel for his new administration, and presumably Ammianus himself came out of retirement to rejoin the military when the emperor arrived at Antioch in 363. Ammianus reappears in the narrative just before the Roman army invaded Persian territory. He describes the crossing of the river Abora and then includes himself among the men who saw, ominously, the tomb of the third-century emperor Gordian, a military hero who was treacherously killed (23.5.7). The invasion of Persia was a dreadful failure, and Julian was killed. Ammianus records the difficult and dangerous retreat of the army, and the cession of the city of Nisibis to the Persians by the new emperor, Jovian. Ammianus' last use of the first person occurs at 25.10.1 ("we came to Antioch"), and this suggests that he did not proceed on to Constantinople with Jovian (Matthews 1989: 13).

During the next twenty years Ammianus must have traveled to gather information for his history and continued to compose his work. He claims personal familiarity with a few places which he must have visited during this time: Greece (26.10.19), Egypt (22.15.1), and the Black Sea (22.8.1), for example. He was in Antioch during the treason trials which Valens held in 370 and 371, and he describes the terror that gripped the city in book 29 of the work. Material for the earlier books of the *Res Gestae* could most easily be collected in the east, but proper coverage of Valentinian's reign required the historian to head west. Ammianus writes with satirical anger about the expulsion of foreigners from Rome during a food crisis (14.6.19). If he was among those expelled, he would have had to be in the city by 383 or 384 at the latest.

At Rome, Ammianus probably collected information about Valentinian's campaigns on the Rhine, events in Rome itself, and affairs in North Africa. His complaints directed against a few senators, whom he accused of being unworthy of their proud heritage, have often led modern scholars to imagine him as bitter and alone. Such an analysis misinterprets the satirical persona which the historian has created in these passages and ignores the non-senatorial circles in which Ammianus probably traveled (Cameron 1964; Matthews 1989: 465–6). He integrated the new information he gathered into the work up to around 390. This suggests that Ammianus gave public readings from his work in 390 or 391, in time for details to reach Libanius in the east within a year. No further notices of his life or work remain.

Work

The extant text of the *Res Gestae* stretches from book 14 to book 31. The first books were lost at an early stage in the transmission of the manuscript. Book 14 begins in 353 and describes the last year of the life of the Caesar Gallus. Books 15 and 16 describe the rise of Julian as Caesar and his successful campaigning in Gaul, despite the attempts of the emperor Constantius II to obstruct his nephew. Books 17 and 18 alternate between Julian's military success in Gaul and Constantius' failure in the east. Book 19 is largely devoted to the siege of Amida by the Persian king Shapur, which ends in Roman defeat.

In book 20, Julian is pronounced Augustus by his troops, and Constantius refuses to recognize his claim of equality. In book 21, the two armies begin their march and prepare for war, but Constantius dies of illness in October 361. In book 22, Julian, now sole ruler of the empire, continues east to Constantinople and Antioch, distributing patronage and establishing his position. He withdraws state support from Christianity and flaunts his paganism. At the end of book 22, Julian prepares for a major invasion of Persia, the subject of books 23 and 24. In book 25 the emperor is killed and the army manages its hasty retreat under the leadership of the newly chosen emperor Jovian, who is forced to sign an unfavorable peace treaty with Shapur. The book ends with the death of Jovian from smoke inhalation in 364.

Book 26 begins with a preface that suggests that Ammianus is now moving up to "the boundaries of our own time." The book covers the selection of Valentinian as emperor, his selection of his brother Valens as co-emperor, and Valens' suppression of the revolt of Procopius, a cousin of Julian. Book 27 describes the military activities of Valentinian in the west and Valens in the east. Book 28 treats western events in Rome, Britain, and North Africa, particularly cases of unfair prosecutions and corruption, and book 29 begins with parallel events in the east, where Valens oversaw a number of trials for treason and magic. The narrative then turns back to the west to treat the campaigns of Valentinian and the successful suppression of the African rebel Firmus by the general Theodosius, the father of the future emperor. Book 30 begins with eastern affairs as Valens and Shapur vie for control of Armenia. The scene shifts west, to the successful campaigning of Valentinian, who then dies of a stroke in 375. His son is elevated to the throne, despite his youth (he is 4 years old). Finally, book 31 is an almost continual narrative of how the admission of a group of Goths into the Roman empire turned into a disaster, culminating in the Battle of Adrianople and the death of Valens in 378.

We know from the last sentence of the *Res Gestae* that the work began with the accession of Nerva in 96. The extant eighteen books cover the period from 353 to 378, for an average of less than a year and a half for each book. The earlier books clearly must have been narrated in far less detail than the books which survive. The first thirteen covered 257 years, for an average of about twenty years per book. The point at which the work shifted from severe compression to full and detailed narrative cannot be known, but Matthews (1989: 27) estimates that if it occurred at book 11 with the accession of Constantius in 337, the ten earlier books would have covered an average of twenty-five years per book, and if it occurred earlier, say in the seventh book with Constantine's defeat of Licinius in 324, the first six books would have covered an average of forty years per book.

The disparity between the lost portion and the surviving portion of the work, both in their scope and in the research methods necessary for their writing, once led some scholars to suggest that Ammianus was the author of two entirely separate works. Adherents to this theory argued that the first work covered the period from Nerva to perhaps the accession of Constantine, and the second work, of which we possess the second part, would have covered the period from Constantine to Adrianople with the sustained level of detail found in the surviving books. This theory is generally not accepted by scholars today. Careful study of the parts of the extant books which refer back to events of the lost books (Barnes 1998: 213–17; Frakes 1995; Gilliam 1972) reveals almost no information about that ill-recorded period that we do not already know from other sources, suggesting that the coverage could not have been especially detailed. Similarly, some important information about the second and third century, of the sort which would presumably have been covered in a full and detailed account, is provided in the surviving part of the work apparently for the first time. Moreover, some of the formulas used to refer back to lost material that would have been in the supposed first work are identical to formulas used to refer to material that would have been in the supposed second work. One might think that different terminology would be required when directing the reader to an entirely separate work than would be used to remind the reader of an episode related earlier in the book at hand.

Even the portion of the work that remains is quite unbalanced in the density of its coverage. Books 15 to 19 treat about six years of events in the careers of Constantius and Julian, dedicating approximately the same amount of space to each ruler at a rate of only slightly more than a year per book. The treatment of Julian as sole ruler in books 20 to 25 covers about four years in six books, at a rate of only two-thirds of a year per book. The last six books, however, cover fifteen years, at a rate of two and a half years per book. The figure of Julian is central to Ammianus' project, and his coverage of even the near-contemporary reigns of Valens and Valentinian is sketchy compared to the space allotted to the Apostate. It is not difficult to imagine, then, that Ammianus could have covered

earlier centuries only in outline form. Just as his treatment of
Constantius, Jovian, Valentinian, and Valens is largely intended to
make Julian shine brighter by contrast, so the lost books may have
served largely to provide models and themes of past heroism that
would recur in the Julian narrative.

Barnes has recently suggested that the manuscript numeration of
the *Res Gestae* is incorrect, and that the original work contained
thirty-six, not thirty-one, books (1998: 28–31). He points out that
thirty-one is an unusual and unwieldy number of books, that some
ancient historians, such as Tacitus, arranged their material in
hexads, and that the eighteen surviving books of Ammianus do in
fact divide fairly well into groups of six. He postulates the
following book division: 1–6, Nerva to Diocletian (96–305); 7–12,
Constantine (306–37); 13–18, Constantius' rise to sole power
(337–53). He further argues, less convincingly, that this increase in
books would remove a "very real difficulty," that "Ammianus
cannot have compressed his history of the Roman empire from 96
to 353 into a mere thirteen books" (1998: 28). Under Barnes' more
elegant arrangement of books, however, the first six still cover
Roman history at the rapid rate of thirty-five years per book. The
part of the *Res Gestae* which Ammianus wrote without the benefit of
living sources must have been superficial under any arrangement. A
parallel may perhaps be seen in the extremely rapid survey of three
centuries of history which begins the *New History* of the Greek
historian Zosimus (Blockley 1975: 12).

Although we regrettably lack the preface to the entire work,
Ammianus has provided us with two prefaces to smaller sections of
his work, at the beginning of the fifteenth and the twenty-sixth
books. The first of these serves to introduce the ten books of the
history in which Julian plays a part (15.1.1). In it, Ammianus
describes his historical method: he has put the events in order, and
has related what he himself witnessed and what he learned from
careful questioning of those who were involved in the events. This
method will not change, but his presentation will. He promises to
write both more carefully and more expansively, and dismisses in
advance the complaints of those who might claim that he is being
long-winded or tedious.

The preface to book 26 (26.1.1–2) is also concerned with
presentation rather than method. Whereas previously Ammianus
had defended his decision to include more detail than the audience might want, as he turns away from Julian and toward more
recent history, he defends his omission of information for which

his audience might clamor (Fornara 1990). His explanation for limiting detail in the last six books is twofold. First is a glancing reference to avoiding "the dangers which often touch upon the truth," perhaps invoking the political or social dangers which accurate reporting about the near past could stimulate. Ammianus expresses more concern, however, about the danger of inviting the grievances of contemporaries who complain of neglect if even the most trivial details are omitted. He lists the emperor's dinner conversation, the punishment of some common soldiers, the names of some minor forts, and the names of those who greeted the urban praetor, as examples of the kind of trivial matters whose omission draws complaints, and claims that Cicero (in a letter no longer extant) suggested that these sorts of complaints explain why many historians have not published accounts of their own day.

The last three sentences of the work (31.16.9) form an epilogue, beginning with this important sentence: "I, a soldier once, and a Greek, have presented these events, from the principate of Nerva up to the death of Valens, so far as I was able, never knowingly having dared to corrupt a work professing the truth by omission or by falsehood." Ammianus then encourages younger and more learned men to pick up where his history has concluded, suggesting that, if they should do so, they should write in "higher style," a reference perhaps to panegyric and perhaps simply to his own classicizing style of history, in contrast to *breviaria*, biographies, and chronicles (Blockley 1998).

"A soldier once, and a Greek," are words which have lent themselves to many interpretations (Barnes 1998: 65–78; Matthews 1989: 452–72; Classen 1972; Tränkle 1972; Heyen 1968; Stoian 1967). Ammianus' reference to himself as a soldier has been taken apologetically, as a "mere" soldier who dared to create such a rhetorically elaborate and learned history. But it is probably best understood as a proud statement, which underscores his first-hand knowledge of events and places him firmly in the tradition of the great Roman historians for whom participation in political life and public affairs was a necessary source of their authority as writers. Despite his military experience, however, Ammianus' descriptions of battles and warfare owe more to rhetorical tradition than to specialized knowledge, even if military historians judging in the context of the rhetorical tradition have usually been favorable to Ammianus' presentation (Austin 1979; Crump 1975). A recent study of Ammianus' digression on siege engines, for example, finds that the historian has relied on written sources rather than first-hand information (23.4; den Hengst 1999).

Ammianus' use of the term "Graecus" is even more controversial. If "soldier" is understood as apologetic, a mere soldier, then "Greek" might be understood in the same way, as a mere Greek having ventured upon a major work in Latin. Yet it is preferable to concentrate upon the almost paradoxical contrast between the words soldier and Greek, words which reveal the two distinctive qualities Ammianus brings to the writing of history: on the one hand, the soldier, the man of action and involvement, and on the other, the Greek, the learned scholar and master of literature. This sense of "Greek" comes out clearly in Ammianus' reference to the historian Timagenes, whom he describes as a Greek "in diligence and language" (15.9.2). Clearly the term has a cultural as well as a linguistic significance in Ammianus' epilogue as well. "Graecus" may also have a religious meaning, if we understand Ammianus to be translating the Greek "Hellene," which often means "pagan."

Ammianus' blending of Greek and Latin culture throughout his work is one of the most intriguing features of the *Res Gestae*. For a Greek to choose to write in Latin is surprising in itself, despite the fact that Latin was in many ways the language of Ammianus' own world and the world of the army and the court portrayed in the *Res Gestae*. Ammianus reinforces his connections to Latin historiography in several ways. The choice of 96 as the starting point for a history that primarily covers fourth-century events must be understood as an attempt to link his own work to the work of Tacitus, which concludes in that year. Indeed, given that Tacitus' *Annals* and *Histories* were read as a single work in thirty books in late antiquity (according to Jerome in *comm. ad Zach.* 3.14), perhaps Ammianus' choice of thirty-one books represents a conscious attempt to supersede his predecessor. Ammianus' work alludes to other Roman historians, especially Sallust, in numerous places, and also demonstrates particular fondness for Cicero (Fornara 1992b: 427–38). In contrast, Ammianus shows a surprisingly poor knowledge of Athenian oratory in his comments on the subject, and his claim of direct knowledge of Herodotus and Thucydides may be doubted (Fornara 1992b: 421–7). Ammianus shows great interest in the city of Rome and the narrative returns regularly to events there, although the city no longer played an important role in the fourth-century empire. This anachronistic attention to the city perhaps served to emphasize his links to early Latin historiography where the city played a central part. Ammianus shows his reverence toward the city in his account of the visit of the emperor Constantius to Rome in 357 (16.10; Matthews 1989: 231–5; Classen 1988; Duval 1970; Klein 1979). The city is the "home of empire and all the virtues," and its temples, stadiums, and forums are portrayed as divine and exalted (16.10.3; Harrison 1999). Ammianus' Greek background is also constantly on display. His identification with the Greek language is evident in the numerous passages where he glosses Greek terms with the first person plural, such as his discussion of "nighttime visions, which we call 'phantasies'" (14.11.18; den Boeft 1992: 12). Certain linguistic peculiarities of the *Res Gestae* can best be explained with the understanding that the author is "thinking in Greek." Den Boeft explores the high frequency of participial use in Ammianus, a phenomenon associated with Greek, and the absence of the historical infinitive, a construction peculiar to Latin that might have been particularly difficult for a Greek-speaker to use comfortably (den Boeft 1992). Ammianus' choices of accentual *clausulae*, the rhythmic endings to phrases and sentences, are especially striking. Stephen Oberhelman studied 104 prose works written between AD 200 and 450 and found that Ammianus' use of *clausulae* was a unique blend of a Greek rhythmical system refined by the appropriation of certain features common to republican historians like Sallust and Livy (Oberhelman 1987). Other "Grecisms" in Ammianus' style are discussed by Barnes (1998: 65–71).

One aspect of the *Res Gestae* that seems more in keeping with the Greek historiographical tradition than the Latin is Ammianus' extensive use of formal digressions. Ammianus is unmatched by any historian, save Herodotus, in the percentage of his work that is digressive, and in the sheer variety of the subject matter in his digressions (the exact number of digressions is variously enumerated by Cichocka 1975; Emmett 1981; Barnes 1998: 222–4). Ammianus provides a wide sweep of geographical, ethnographical, scientific, philosophical, and religious information. Many of Ammianus' digressions appear in the section of the work dedicated to Julian, where their presence serves a narrative function, both in enlarging the proportion of the history in which Julian is the central character and, in the case of digressions like those on Gaul and Persia, in emphasizing the vastness and importance of the lands he set out to conquer.

In his geographic digressions, Ammianus provides information derived both from written sources and from personal observation, as the digression on Gaul indicates. In a discussion of the origin of the

Gauls, Ammianus credits Timagenes (15.9.2) for his information, and he also cites Sallust as a source for Caesar's campaigns in Gaul (15.12.6) as well as alluding to Caesar's *Bellum Gallicum* in a reference to the original "tripartite" division of Gaul (15.11.1). Yet he also mentions that Aventicum was an important city at one time "as its partially destroyed buildings even now demonstrate" (15.11.12), and his references to the character of the Gauls have sometimes been thought to rely upon personal observation. "A group of foreigners will be unable to contain one of them in a fight if he calls his wife in, as she is much stronger than him," he claims, adding that Gallic women will kick and punch like a catapult (15.12.1). In addition to Gaul and Persia, Ammianus provides extensive geographic information on Thrace, Oriens, the Black Sea, and Egypt.

Ammianus is the only ancient historian to offer extensive digressions on scientific matters (den Hengst 1992). These digressions include information on earthquakes, tidal waves, plagues, eclipses, the rainbow, meteors, comets, and the bissextile day. Den Hengst is surely correct in including in the scientific category the "religious" digressions, such as those on divination and on the *genius*, as these are also explanations of the natural world as Ammianus understood it. Scientific digressions, like geographic digressions, often serve a narrative purpose. Ammianus describes ominous natural phenomena, such as eclipses and comets, which occur at significant points in the action, and his digressions force the reader to stop and to reflect upon these turning points. An egregious example is the digression on eclipses, inspired by an eclipse which Ammianus suggests foreshadowed the elevation of Julian to the rank of Augustus. The historian uses the digression to put the celestial mark of approval upon Julian's elevation, an approval so desperately desired that, it appears, Ammianus simply invented an eclipse which did not really take place (20.3; Barnes 1998: 102–6).

Digressions in Ammianus may also have a moralizing purpose. There are many ethnographic digressions, including passages on the Gauls (15.12.1–4), Persians (23.6.75–84; Teitler 1999), Saracens (14.4.1–7), Huns, and Alans (31.2.1–25; King 1987), to which one might add the scattered comments on eunuchs (especially 14.6.17, 16.7.8–10, 18.4.5; Tougher 1999), who are treated as a race apart. Ammianus' treatment of non-Romans in his digressions is very much in keeping with traditions of ancient historiography. The bizarre and primitive habits of the barbarian (for example, the Huns do not cook meat, but merely heat it by a day's ride under a saddle) are contrasted with the civilized behavior of the Romans. On the other hand, the barbarian often possesses some traits, such as loyalty and fighting ability, which the effete Roman has lost. This use of ethnographic digressions as an opportunity for the historian to comment upon contemporary *mores* is not uncommon in ancient historiography.

Ammianus' satirical and moralizing "Roman digressions" are, by contrast, a striking innovation (14.6 and 28.4; Rees 1999; Salemme 1987; Kohns 1975; Pack 1953). In the course of a discussion of Orfitus' prefecture of Rome, Ammianus describes how the city was wracked by riots inspired by wine shortages (14.6.1). The digression which follows is introduced as an explanation for why Ammianus' descriptions of events at Rome concern nothing but "riots, taverns, and worthless things" (14.6.2). The historian attributes Rome's success to a partnership between Virtue and Fortune, a union which enabled the Romans to expand from a single city to a worldwide empire. Rome, the personified city, has now retired, passing on its power and responsibility to the emperors, who serve as its heirs. And although the ancient assemblies no longer rule the city, Rome is revered and admired throughout the world (14.6.3–6; Matthews 1986).

This idyllic picture of Rome is marred, however, by the fickleness and licentiousness of a few inhabitants who do not respect the magnificence of their native city. Ammianus' criticism of these Romans centers upon traditional satiric concerns: they prance in overly luxurious clothes (14.6.9), they boast of their wealth (14.6.10), and they offer hospitality to gamblers and gossips but not to the learned (14.6.14), for they prefer music and dance to serious scholarship (14.6.18). He has words of criticism for the Roman plebeians as well, who are obsessed with gambling, and are normally to be found either gaping at the chariot races or snorting unpleasantly over a dice game (14.6.25–6). Ammianus' account of the city prefecture of Ampelius in 371–2 (28.4.3–5) provides further opportunity for the historian to digress in a satirical vein. Again the nobles are reproached for directing their hospitality toward charioteers and parasites (28.4.10–12) and for hating learning like poison (28.4.14). They are also legacy-hunters (28.4.22), arrogant (28.4.23), and superstitious (28.4.24). Commoners are again scorned for their obsession with races and shows (28.4.29–32) and for stuffing themselves with loathsome food (28.4.34).

Various attempts have been made to interpret these unprecedented derisive digressions. Ammianus' criticisms have often been linked to particular bad experiences he himself may have undergone at Rome. Both digressions do place great emphasis on the abysmal hospitality offered by the city elite (14.6.12–15, 28.4.10–13, 17). The hosts prefer gamblers, musicians, and loudmouths to learned men because of their ignorance. Libraries have been shut up like tombs (14.6.18), and the only reading that these men do is of the satirist Juvenal and the scandalous biographer Marius Maximus (28.4.14). Ammianus is also critical of the attitude of the Romans toward foreigners. While in the old days, noble Romans kindly welcomed foreign travelers of high birth, now they only have time for the childless and unmarried (14.6.22), and the common people are now wont to chant in the theater that visitors ought to be driven from the city (28.4.32). These complaints come together in Ammianus' account of the expulsion of foreigners from the cities during a time of food shortages (14.6.19–20). Ammianus says that "not so long ago" foreigners who were students of the liberal arts were driven from the city, while scandalously unmarried dancing girls and their attendants remained behind. This expulsion is usually dated to 383 (Symm. *ep.* 2.7). Since Ammianus may well have been affected by this expulsion, and since we would certainly expect him to have experienced Roman hospitality and to include himself among the learned foreign visitors to the city, it may be that we see in these digressions a reflection of Ammianus' personal pique.

The digressions may also be examined for what they tell us about the composition and expectations of Ammianus' audience. His exaggerated lampooning of the senatorial aristocracy suggests that senators did not dominate his audience. Instead, we can best under-stand the satirical digressions as pitched toward an audience of bureaucrats and soldiers like Ammianus himself, perhaps some of those who were associated with the visit of Theodosius to Rome in 387 and who would transmit news of the history to Libanius on the return to the east (Matthews 1989: 8–9). They would have shared his difficulties with the hospitality of local aristocrats, and may have shared the Greek contempt for their hosts' lack of learning. It is noteworthy that Ammianus in several places parodies the Romans as soldiers *manqués*. He jokes that the Romans who must travel a bit to reach their summer homes believe that they have thereby rivaled the conquests of Alexander the Great (28.4.18), and he says that they arrange their household slaves and staffs – eunuchs, cooks, weavers – as if they are an army on the march (14.6.17, 28.4.8). In another passage, it appears (the text is uncertain) that Ammianus presents a retired soldier who cleverly deceives his gullible Roman audience (28.4.20). These sorts of criticisms might be judged particularly amusing by an audience familiar with soldiering.

Despite Ammianus' claim to be speaking about only "a few" of the Romans, and his obvious use of satiric exaggeration, readers of the Roman digressions have sometimes taken at full value Ammianus' portrait of Roman life. The passages fit particularly well into interpretations of the fall of Rome which blame the collapse on the decadence of a once-great people. But this passage, like the rest of the *Res Gestae*, must be approached with a more sophisticated eye. Despite Ammianus' portrait, fourth-century Rome was still a vibrant and intellectually exciting city, as numerous other sources reveal. While Ammianus has a reputation for balance and accuracy, these passages reveal his willingness to use exaggeration and outright slander to make a point. Traditional respect for Ammianus' reliability has been eroded in certain areas by modern studies which focus on the ways in which his work is marred by tendentiousness and partisanship.

Several features of the *Res Gestae* encourage the reader to trust in Ammianus' good faith and honesty. His prefaces declare his careful historical method and his devotion to the truth, although such declarations are conventional and employed by many of the historians of the period. After all, he also declares that he "will never depart intentionally from the truth" as he begins his outrageous Roman digression (14.6.2). Ammianus' comments on the emperor Julian more effectively support his claim of an even-handed approach. The emperor is, on the one hand, clearly the hero of the work, and when Ammianus begins to describe Julian's campaigns in Gaul he warns that, although he will always tell the truth, the account will seem almost like a panegyric (16.1.3). Julian is favorably compared with the great emperors of the past, such as Titus, Vespasian, Trajan, and Marcus Aurelius (16.1.4). Digressions describe Julian's many outstanding qualities (e.g. 16.5) and at his death his virtues are laid out as in a formal encomium (25.4.1–15). Nevertheless, despite the open partisanship of parts of his narrative, Ammianus provides the reader with several critical comments on the emperor's career and character. Julian was "superstitious rather than truly religious" (25.4.17), given to excessive sacrificing and foolish dependence on untrustworthy diviners. He was also too populist and too often undignified in his conduct as emperor (25.4.18), as he demonstrated when he leapt out of his seat in the senate of Constantinople to embrace the philosopher Maximinus

(22.7.3), or when he dismissed every one of the attendants from the palace (22.4.1–2). Ammianus also criticizes several of Julian's laws, such as the school law which forbade Christians to teach the pagan classics (25.4.20), and the curial laws which attempted to press more people into service in their local government (22.9.12, 25.4.21).

Ammianus shows this same willingness to provide a mix of favorable and unfavorable material in his obituary treatments of other emperors. At the death of each, he presents their virtues and vices in turn. Although his narrative accounts of the reigns of Constantius II, Valentinian, and Valens are broadly critical, in their obituaries Ammianus includes some positive judgements as well. Constantius was dignified, careful as an administrator, and temperate and abstinent in his personal life (21.16.1–7). Valentinian successfully fortified and defended the Rhine, and had military success on other western frontiers (30.7.5–11). Valens was a just and prudent administrator who restored public buildings and successfully resisted unfair attempts on the public purse (31.14.1–5). These obituary evaluations are, however, typically more negative than positive, and even the positive comments are often laced with sarcasm, as in this comment on Constantius' artistic pretensions: "He was a diligent striver after culture, but he was dissuaded from rhetoric because of his dull mind, and when he turned to the more difficult art of writing poetry, nothing worthwhile resulted" (21.16.4). That Constantius never ate fruit during his life is also curiously brought forth as an example of his merits (21.16.7). Yet Ammianus' willingness to provide any exculpatory information at all about his "bad" emperors can be seen as an attempt at fairness.

Ammianus' treatment of Christianity also has been cited as evidence of his fairness (Hunt 1985, 1993). Although Ammianus was a pagan, the *Res Gestae* is free from the virulent contempt for Christianity often found in the work of other fourth-century writers. Indeed, Ammianus occasionally makes references to Christianity which can be interpreted positively, such as his description of Christianity as a "simple and complete religion" (21.16.18), his praise of provincial bishops (27.3.15), and his reference to the "glorious death" of Christian martyrs (22.11.10). This moderate tone is, however, often undermined by more subtle attacks on Christianity (Barnes 1998; Elliott 1983).

Other motives have also undermined the impartiality of Ammianus' history. Ammianus was, unsurprisingly, a partisan supporter of his patron Ursicinus, and he presents him in a favorable light (Matthews 1989: 34–47; Thompson 1947a: 42–55; Blockley 1969, 1980a). He tries to excuse Ursicinus' participation in the trials under Gallus in 354 by claiming that Ursicinus sent secret letters to Constantius describing the corruption and begging for aid (14.9.1). These letters and the excesses of these trials may have provided the impetus for Constantius' recall and execution of his nephew later in the year (14.11). From this point on Ammianus depicts the relationship between Constantius and Ursicinus as fueled by the emperor's paranoia and his lamentable susceptibility to court gossip. We might be more willing to see Constantius' behavior as evidence of the prudence required of a late Roman emperor in dealing with a popular subordinate. Ammianus suggests that the dispatch of Ursicinus to put down Silvanus was a fiendish trick of the emperor to ensure that he would rid himself of at least one of his troublesome generals (15.5.19). We receive from Ammianus a thrilling narrative of this event, which emphasizes the fear and isolation felt by Ursicinus, Ammianus, and their small party, the cynicism and corruption at the court of Constantius, and the regrettable end of the general forced into rebellion. Ammianus begins by convincing us of the innocence of Silvanus, in order that he might blacken the character of Constantius, and ends by convincing us of Silvanus' guilt, in order that he might excuse the murder orchestrated by Ursicinus and Ammianus himself (Hunt 1999). Ammianus' manipulations and inconsistencies make it clear that he has shaded the truth. It is, for example, impossible that Silvanus could have been in full revolt when Ursicinus' party headed to Gaul, and yet Ursicinus could plausibly have pretended to be unaware of the usurpation upon his arrival (Drinkwater 1994). After the murder of Silvanus, Ursicinus must have remained in Gaul as Silvanus' replacement for the next two years (Frézouls 1962), but Ammianus makes little mention of it. Perhaps Ursicinus played a discreditable role in the trials of the associates of Silvanus that followed his fall (15.6; Matthews 1989: 81–3). In addition, the historian wishes to stress the disorder in Gaul when Julian became Caesar, in order to emphasize the magnitude of Julian's accomplishments, without blaming this disorder on Ursicinus.

Ammianus' portrait of Julian contains some similarly partisan coloring. In Gaul, his Julian is a brilliant and eager young general, whose struggle against the meddling and ill will of Constantius' advisors in Gaul culminates in a triumphant success over the Alamanni at the Battle of Strasbourg in 359 (16.2–5, 16.11–12). In fact, it appears that Julian overstepped the bounds of his command, and that Ammianus has greatly exaggerated the importance of Strasbourg, a battle which Julian seems to have needlessly provoked in pursuit of glory (Blockley 1977; Drinkwater 1997; Matthews 1989: 87–93, 299–301). Ammianus also provides the authorized version of the elevation of Julian to Augustus, describing it as completely forced by the spontaneous revolt of the soldiers (20.4), although there is reason to suspect that Julian may not have been as completely uninvolved as Ammianus claims. Julian's invasion of Persia in 363 takes up books 23 to 25. The tone is epic and increasingly ominous, as the early success of the expedition is followed by more and more disquieting signs of looming failure. The army finds itself trapped deep within Persian territory and Julian, fatally wounded, spends his last hours in Socratic contemplation. Ammianus so obscures his account of the invasion with literary artifice that Julian's ultimate goals remain unclear. By portraying Julian as an Achilles-like hero, doomed to die while performing glorious deeds, Ammianus is able to avoid addressing Julian's responsibility for the tremendous military disaster. Ammianus also attempts to shift the blame for the disaster off of Julian, finding fault both in the past, by suggesting that Roman hostilities with Persia actually dated back to the greedy behavior of the emperor Constantine (25.4.23; Warmington 1981) and, in the future, by his condemnatory account of the actions of Jovian, Julian's successor.

Ammianus' account of the reign of Jovian is much more detailed than our other accounts, and unique in several regards (25.5–10; Lenski 2000; Heather 1999a; Barnes 1998: 138–42). While other sources claim that Jovian was well respected and the unanimous choice of the army after the death of Julian, Ammianus suggests that Jovian was little known. Ammianus omits discussion of the probable role played by Jovian's pious Christianity in making him a viable candidate for the throne. He subtly attempts to portray Jovian as an illegitimate emperor by emphasizing the poor fit of his purple imperial robes (25.10.14) and the ill-omened crying of his son during the emperor's consular ceremony (25.10.11). The reader is everywhere encouraged to share the reaction of the Roman soldiers who, Ammianus claims, at first cheered wildly when they misheard the name "Julian" when Jovian's name was announced, and then burst into tears when they realized that Julian was indeed dead and Jovian had replaced him (25.5.6). The historian unfairly saddles Jovian with the responsibility for the defeat, although he was compelled to surrender Nisibis to Shapur in return for safe passage of the army out of Persia. Ammianus improbably claims that, prior to Jovian's shameful capitulation, Shapur was frightened, the omens predicted a Roman victory, and the army could easily have made it home safely. It also seems that Ammianus deliberately neglects to mention Jovian's policy of religious tolerance in order to avoid having anything praiseworthy to say about the emperor (Heather 1999a: 112–14).

Ammianus is also unfavorable toward the emperors Valentinian and his brother Valens. He provides less detail about their reigns in comparison with his treatment of Constantius and Julian, and his treatment suffers from his lack of personal involvement in most of the events. Valentinian's various campaigns against the Alamanni make up a large part of Ammianus' account of his reign, and scholarly dispute over the nature and success of these campaigns has influenced scholarly evaluation of Ammianus' treatment of the emperor. Ammianus has been condemned for his insufficient appreciation of the emperor's successes, presumably downgrading Valentinian in order to better vaunt the military success of Julian (Paschoud 1992), but he has also been criticized for his excessive approbation of the emperor's military successes, presumably exaggerating Valentinian's conquests in order to inflate the threat posed by Germans in the west and thus emphasize the successes of Julian in the 350s (Drinkwater 1999). In either case, Ammianus uses language carefully to contrast the skillful handling of military affairs by Julian with the rash mistakes of Valentinian (Seager 1996). Valentinian is also repeatedly portrayed as a particularly cruel and savage emperor with a quick temper (27.7.4–9, 29.3, 30.8.1–7). He frequently put officials to death for minor offenses, as when he had a page beaten to death for losing control of a hunting dog, or when he executed the maker of a breastplate because of an error in the weight. Ammianus also claims that he kept two man-eating bears in cages near his bedroom with the charming names of Innocence and Goldflake. Valens is portrayed as ineffectual and a mere tool of his brother (Tritle 1994). He was "unskilled in liberal or military arts" (31.14.5). His faults led to his death and the loss of his army at Adrianople, which Ammianus blames on his decision, inspired by envy, to attack the Goths at Adrianople prematurely to prevent his nephew Gratian from bringing aid and receiving the credit for the victory.

Ammianus holds the administrations of both Valens and Valentinian responsible for the magic and treason trials that he describes in great detail (28.1, 29.1–2; Matthews 1989: 209–26;

Zawadski 1989; Elliott 1983: 148–58; Blockley 1975: 104–22; Funke 1967). At Rome, imperial agents, in particular the acting prefect Maximinus, directed a wave of prosecutions against aristocrats. Senators were tried and on some occasions executed for magic, adultery, and poisoning. Ammianus' account relies heavily on atmospherics, emphasizing the dread that all nobles felt ("all were stunned by the atrocities," 28.1.14) and the ruthlessness of the prosecutors ("Maximinus poured out the ferocity naturally fixed in his cruel heart, like beasts in the amphitheater do," 28.1.10). Ammianus does not, however, claim that the convicted nobles were innocent, and in several cases he admits their guilt. Nevertheless, the prosecutions at Rome seem not to have targeted a connected conspiracy, unlike those at Antioch under the reign of Valens. Ammianus himself was probably present for this wave of trials. In this case, some of those prosecuted appeared to have been participating in magical rites which were judged by imperial law to be treason. In one case, a magical tripod was used to determine who would succeed Valens as emperor. When the device marked out the letters theta, epsilon, omicron, and delta, the conspirators began to plot with a certain imperial official named Theodorus, whom they assumed would become the next emperor. The reader of the *Res Gestae* recognizes, of course, that the tripod had successfully predicted the succession of the emperor Theodosius. Theodorus and his co-conspirators were put to death, and while Ammianus approves of the prosecution of those truly responsible for plots against the legitimate emperor, he deplores the prosecutorial excesses that followed, in which innocents were convicted for benevolent uses of magic, such as healing charms and family horoscopes. The ghosts of those put to death in this purge, Ammianus tells us, terrified many in the east by shrieking funeral laments at night, an omen of the coming death of Valens at Adrianople (31.1.3).

The whole of the last book is devoted to events surrounding the Battle of Adrianople in Thrace in 378. Vicious behavior by Roman officials turned the crowd of Gothic refugees into a hostile army which overcame Valens and his men. The victorious Goths failed in an attempt to lay siege to Adrianople and joined with Huns and Alans in an unsuccessful attempt on Constantinople. Ammianus digresses to describe similarly calamitous events in Roman history, such as the invasion of the Cimbri in the fourth century BC, the German wars in the time of Marcus Aurelius, and the wave of invasions of the third century AD (31.5.10–17). This disaster, he pessimistically suggests, is worse than those, since in those days the higher moral character of the Romans allowed them to recover, whereas contemporary Romans are weakened by licentiousness and decay. But the last action of the history presents a more optimistic tone, as the general Julius cleverly entices the Goths in the east to gather and has them massacred. This "prudent" plan, Ammianus says, saved the east from serious dangers (31.16.8).

Ammianus writes with a striking and unusual style (Fontaine 1992; Blockley 1998; Roberts 1988). Some of the oddness of his speech can perhaps be attributed to Latin being his second language. Ammianus' language, however, is mostly the result of a purposeful attempt to create an elevated style which mixes Ciceronian Latin with the disjointed syntax of earlier historians like Sallust and Tacitus, the arresting visual imagery of contemporary Roman art and theater, and the technical vocabulary found in contemporary panegyric and government documents.

Rather than providing a smooth, flowing, plot-based narrative, Ammianus often leaves the reader with startling and memorable images, such as the confrontation between the city prefect Leontius and the huge redhead Peter Valvomeres (15.7), famously explored by Erich Auerbach (Auerbach 1957 [1946]: 43–67; cf. Matthews 1987; Barnes 1998: 11–16), or the triumphal entrance of Constantius II into Rome (16.10; MacMullen 1964; Klein 1979; Classen 1988). In his picture of Constantius, he carefully describes the gleam of the armor and the snapping of the colorful banners of the emperor's attendants, and he focuses on Constantius himself, who demonstrates his regal nature by remaining completely motionless as the shouts of the crowds echo around him.

Ammianus' extensive use of historical *exempla* is especially noteworthy (Blockley 1975: 157–67, 191–5). There are more than a hundred instances in the *Res Gestae* where Ammianus uses quotations or examples drawn primarily from ancient Greek or Roman history to underscore his point, often a moral one. While the surviving fragments of Eunapius show frequent use of *exempla*, no extant historian of antiquity uses this device nearly as often as Ammianus. Constantius supposedly plotted to have Ursicinus killed, just as corrupt Nero had his loyal general Domitius Corbulo assassinated (15.2.5). The general Barbatio would certainly not have slandered Julian so often to Constantius had he been aware of the advice Aristotle gave to Callisthenes on his way to meet Alexander the Great (18.3.7). Worthless, untrained lawyers chatter ignorantly in court like Homer's Thersites (30.4.15). Valentinian dramatically increased the number of executions, which "is the last remedy sought by the pious soul in difficult times, as the outstanding Isocrates says" (30.8.6). Ammianus uses Roman *exempla* more than Greek (Blockley 1975 calculates a ratio of seven to three), and he uses republican *exempla* more than imperial ones. Ammianus presents a vision of history which is continuous and cumulative through his use of these *exempla*, constantly weighing the actors in his history against those of the past. Gallus, roaming through the taverns of Antioch at night, is emulating the loathsome act which Gallienus is said to have performed at Rome (14.1.9), Constantius persecuted his subjects based on the most slender of evidence, falling woefully short of standards set by Marcus Aurelius (21.16.11), but Julian surpassed even Alexander the Great in his ability to go without sleep (16.5.4–5). The effect is to elevate the tone of the work by situating every contemporary event in the long and glorious history of the past. Julian is thus not only great, but is comparable to the greatest rulers of all time, and other figures are not only tyrannical, but comparable to the greatest tyrants of history.

Ammianus makes frequent use of the phraseology of Livy, Sallust, Tacitus, Vergil, Cicero, and other Latin writers, sometimes with specific reference to the context from which the allusions are drawn, but often simply to imbue his work with the language of his illustrious predecessors. Just as *exempla* place the events of his history within the context of the heroic past, so his allusions set his own historical work in the venerable context of Latin historiography. This is made particularly clear in his reflections on Julian's attempt to storm the city of Pirisabora (24.2.9–22). Julian recalled, claims Ammianus, that Scipio Aemilianus, accompanied by his historian Polybius, was likewise repelled in an attempt on Carthage. When Ammianus claims that Julian's deed was nevertheless bolder and more heroic than that of Scipio, he elevates both Julian over Scipio and himself over Polybius.

Ammianus has a strong predilection for violent imagery and diction (Seager 1986: 43–68). Figures frequently burn, seethe, or swell with madness or cruelty. Savagery, excess, and arrogance are common. Ammianus' frequent use of the word "immanis," "monstrous," is instructive (Seager 1986: 5–7, 14–15). The word, rarely used by Tacitus, is used in late antique panegyric almost exclusively of barbarians. Ammianus, however, applies the word to barbarian and Roman alike, as he frequently does with other words meaning "fierce" or "savage." The comparison of humans, both foreign and Roman, to animals is another commonplace in

Ammianus. Arbitio lies in wait for Ursicinus like a snake in a hole (15.2.4), Constantius' eunuch chamberlain Eusebius sends forth his eunuch subordinates like a venomous snake stirring up its young (18.4.4), and Valens reacts to acquittals in treason cases with savage madness, like a beast in the amphitheater who sees someone escape from its grasp (29.1.27). In several places, Ammianus speaks with a matter-of-fact tone about killings in which he participated – that of Silvanus (15.5.31) and of the Persian deserter who, accosted and threatened by Ammianus and Ursicinus, divulged some information about troop movements and was then quickly killed (18.6.16). Ammianus' cold-blooded attitude emerges throughout the *Res Gestae* in his use of dehumanizing metaphors and imputations.

The investigation of the sources which Ammianus drew upon in composing the *Res Gestae* is a threefold task. The historian required written sources for the composition of the lost books that dealt with events before living memory, and both written and oral sources for the main narrative of the surviving books to flesh out the material he witnessed himself. Finally, the digressions also derived from separate sources.

Of course we cannot determine with certainty the sources of the lost books, but the use of the back references in the surviving books can suggest some possibilities. The Greek sources for this period, Dio Cassius, Herodian, and Dexippus, were rich and, one might think, promising sources for Ammianus' purposes, but it does not appear that Ammianus made much use of them. If Ammianus had used Herodian as a major source for the years 180–239, for example, one would not have expected the numerous divergences between the two historians found even in the surviving books (Brok 1976/7). Studies of Ammianus' attitudes toward the emperors of the earlier period suggest that he followed the Latin rather than the Greek tradition (Gilliam 1972; Stertz 1980). For example, Ammianus' references to the emperor Hadrian are hostile (22.12.8, 25.4.17, 30.8.10) and critical of him for excessive superstition. This appears to have been the position of the Latin biographer Marius Maximus, but not that of Dio, who is reported to have said that Hadrian was popular with soldiers and Greeks (70.1.3; Stertz 1980: 502–3). It seems likely that Ammianus depended upon the lost third-century Latin history known as the *Kaisergeschichte*, the lost Marius Maximus, and other lost and generally inferior Latin works as the primary sources for his earlier books.

Ammianus' digressions were generally based upon written sources, even in many cases where one might expect the historian to use his first-hand knowledge. The digression on siege engines is one example where the historian has gone to the reference books rather than into the field (23.4; den Hengst 1999). Similarly, Ammianus' longest digression, on Persian history, religion, and geography, draws far more from written sources than from his own experience (23.6; Drijvers 1999; den Boeft 1999; Teitler 1999). Ammianus seems to favor Latin sources even in cases where Greek sources would provide richer and more accurate information, although he sometimes writes in such a way as to imply that he has consulted the Greek. Thus, his digression on rhetoric is based on Cicero's *Brutus* and on Aulus Gellius, but he quotes Demosthenes as if at first hand (30.4; Fornara 1992b: 425–6). Some scientific digressions can also be traced to Latin sources, such as the passage on earthquakes which also comes from Gellius (17.7; den Hengst 1992). An exception has been found in the digression on Neoplatonism, a subject particularly dear to Ammianus, where Barnes has demonstrated that Ammianus was familiar with the original Greek (1998: 76–7; 21.14.5).

For the period chronicled in the surviving part of the *Res Gestae*, Ammianus had few contemporary histories to draw upon. Although he mentions both Aurelius Victor (21.10.6) and Eutropius (29.1.36) as actors in his work, their abbreviated accounts could provide little useful information for his detailed narrative. Both may have provided information orally to Ammianus, however. It remains a debated question whether Ammianus drew upon the first edition of the *History* of Eunapius of Sardis for some information concerning Julian's Persian invasion (Fornara 1991; Chalmers 1960; Matthews 1989: 163–79; Barnes 1976: 265–8; Elliott 1983: 222–41; Paschoud 1980b). Ridley (1973) compares the accounts of the Persian invasion in Zosimus, who is dependent on Eunapius, with that in Ammianus. The two accounts differ markedly, with each preserving details not found in the other. It remains possible, however, that in several places Ammianus used Eunapius to provide information which he himself was unable to witness (Matthews 1989: 169–75). Ammianus' use of such lost works as the *Annales* of Nicomachus Flavianus or the historical work of Magnus of Carrhae is sometimes suggested, but impossible to prove.

Ammianus probably drew upon other quasi-historical documents, such as the account of the Battle of Strasbourg which Eunapius tells us was written by Julian himself (*fr.* 17), and perhaps even the memoirs written by Julian's companion Oribasius which Eunapius used (*fr.* 15). Ammianus also demonstrates his familiarity with some other works of Julian, such as the *Misopogon*, the unusual diatribe the emperor wrote against the people of Antioch (22.14.2).

A major documentary source for Ammianus appears to have been *relationes*, documents written by imperial functionaries for official purposes (Sabbah 1978: 115–217). Documents of this type which survive include the official correspondence between Pliny the Younger and the emperor Trajan and, nearly contemporary with Ammianus, the letters of Symmachus to the emperors from when he served as prefect of the city of Rome. A few passing remarks suggest that these reports were accessible to the historian. After Julian's success at Strasbourg, Ammianus complains that Constantius tried to take the credit for the victory, and claims that records exist in the public archives which preserve this unwarranted boasting (16.12.70). Describing the unfair prosecutions under Maximinus, Ammianus pauses to point out that there were so many evils that even the material from the public archives would not suffice to describe them all (28.1.15). After Ammianus reproduces the letter written by Julian to Constantius explaining his usurpation, he adds that a second, harsher private letter was also written, which he was unable to inspect. Sabbah suggests that the first letter was available in the public archives, the second only in the personal papers of the emperor (1978: 135–6). Ammianus is vague, and we cannot be certain what sort of records he could inspect or where and when he could inspect them, but given the existence and apparent accessibility of such archives, one might expect that Ammianus would have made regular use of this kind of information. Indeed, there are numerous passages in the *Res Gestae* which seem to have been derived from such records. Ammianus' account of events in Africa during the reign of Valentinian, for example, makes several references to *relationes* which the historian has almost certainly seen himself (28.6; Warmington 1956). The level of detail in this account, including many obscure names and records of several embassies, suggests that Ammianus had the equivalent of the official dossier in front of him as he wrote. The account of the campaigns of Theodosius the Elder in Britain (27.8, 28.3) also bears the marks of official reports (Sabbah 1978: 172–3).

Much of Ammianus' material which is not derived directly from his personal experience must have been drawn from interviews with those who had participated in the events recounted. The potential number of informants is very large: fellow *protectores* and other military companions, friends and associates of Ursicinus or Julian, officials whom he could have met at Antioch, at Rome, or else-

where. Ammianus' lavish praise for Alypius, a victim of the persecution of Valens at Antioch, suggests that he knew him, and
perhaps therefore used him as a source for his account of the
rebuilding of the temple in Jerusalem, which Alypius supervised
during the reign of Julian (23.1.2–3). His profuse praise for the
eunuch Eutherius may also indicate an informant. Eutherius had
served the imperial court since the reign of Constantine, had an
"excellent memory," and had retired to Rome (16.7). He undoubtedly could have provided Ammianus with vast amounts of
information about events at court. Praetextatus was another official
who may have been a source for the historian. After relaying several
anecdotes concerning the acts of Julian at Constantinople,
Ammianus tells us that Praetextatus was present for all these events
(22.7.6). This Praetextatus, who served later as prefect of Rome,
was appointed governor of Greece by Julian, and surely was the
source for Ammianus' information.

The *Res Gestae* is distinguished by its wild profusion of detail,
and Ammianus was the author of the most colorful, readable, and
elegant history of the fourth century. The *Res Gestae* is the product
of an attempt not only to revive the grand style of history which
had lain dormant in the Latin-speaking world for two centuries, but
also to surpass previous histories with the addition of *exempla* drawn
from all of ancient history and with the addition of digressions
covering every facet of ancient knowledge. While modern readers
may not find the relentless moralizing or the encyclopedic detail
entirely to their liking, Ammianus' colossal ambition cannot be
denied. Ammianus' diction and imagery provide a scathing portrait
of a squalid and violent age. His evidence must be approached with
caution, since his distaste for Christianity and partisanship for
Julian have resulted in subtle but systematic distortion.
Nevertheless, the *Res Gestae* remains the essential source for the
reconstruction of the history of the later fourth century, and stands
out among late antique histories as one of the enduring creations of
antiquity.

Text and translation

Latin text edited in two volumes by W. Seyfarth (1978), Teubner.
English translation of entire work in three volumes by J.C. Rolfe
(1935), Loeb edition, and of most of the work by W. Hamilton
(1986), Penguin.

2

AURELIUS VICTOR

Life

The life of Sextus Aurelius Victor has been comprehensively limned by H.W. Bird in several works (Bird 1975, 1984: 5–15, 1994: vii–xi. See also Nixon 1971; den Boer 1972: 19–20; Dufraigne 1975: ix–xv). Victor tells us that he, like the emperor Septimius Severus, was born in the country, the son of a poor and uneducated father (20.5). Several pieces of evidence suggest that he was from Africa. He treats the African emperor Septimius Severus favorably and at great length (20), he includes a digression on a relatively minor event in the African town of Cirta (40.28), and he refers to Carthage as *terrarum decus* (40.19), the "glory of the world" (Bird 1984: 128 n. 2). He was probably born around 320, since he held the position of consular governor of Pannonia Secunda in 361, and his humble background would have prevented him from rising more rapidly through the imperial service (Bird 1975: 49). Victor may have been in Rome from 337 to 348. It has been suggested that his remark on the unhappiness of the people of Rome in the year 337 over the burial of Constantine at Constantinople (41.17) might be evidence of his presence in the city, as might his comment on the lack of celebrations at Rome to mark the eleven hundredth anniversary of the city (28.2), although neither of the passages demands such an interpretation (Bird 1975: 50).

In 361, when the usurping emperor Julian prepared for the looming campaign against Constantius II, he met Victor at Sirmium in northern Italy, and he urged the historian to join him at Naissus in modern-day Serbia (Amm. 21.10.6). Sirmium was an important center of the imperial administration in the fourth century, serving as an imperial residence as well as the headquarters for both the governor of Pannonia Secunda and the praetorian prefect for Illyricum (Bird 1984: 8–9). Victor must have been in imperial service for some time before 361, beginning perhaps as a *notarius*, or scribe, a common position for those of humble birth (Teitler 1985; Jones 1964: 572–5), or perhaps, given his detailed knowledge of somewhat trivial affairs around the empire, in the *scrinium epistolarum*, the department which drafted replies to petitions from local authorities (Bird 1984: 7–8). At Sirmium, Victor presumably served under the praetorian prefect Anatolius, whom he praises for his skill in managing the system of public post-roads (13.5–6; cf. Amm. 19.11.2–3). Victor's frequent mention of taxation, particularly toward the end of the book and often with personal comments appended, leads Bird to suggest that he likely served as a financial officer under the prefect (Bird 1984: 9–10).

Ammianus tells us (21.10.6) that Julian made Victor governor of Pannonia Secunda, a promotion which included membership in the senate and the elevated rank of *clarissimus*, and also honored him with a bronze statue. Julian's usurpation was risky, and he would certainly have been pleased to have gained the allegiance of any high-ranking civil servant, especially one whom Ammianus describes as "worthy of emulation because of his temperance." But the special honor of the statue may suggest that it was Victor's literary accomplishment that had caught Julian's eye. Bird points out that Victor's moralizing tone and excoriation of the tax collectors would have matched Julian's predilections, although his complaints about the military might not have coincided as well with the views of the emperor (Bird 1984: 12). The length of Victor's term in office is unknown, but he must have left before 28 May 365, when another governor is attested (Bird 1984: 12).

In addition to the governorship, Victor held the position of prefect of the city of Rome, under the emperor Theodosius I. His holding of the prefecture is clear both from Ammianus (21.10.6) and from the inscription on the base of a statue which Victor himself dedicated to the emperor (*ILS* 2945). This prestigious position was highly sought after and therefore generally held for a limited tenure. Victor seems to have served from the end of 388 until the summer of 389 (Bird 1984: 13–14). Victor's whereabouts in the more than twenty-five years which intervene between the holding of these two offices is unknown. He likely held some other office, perhaps the proconsulship of Africa (Bird 1984: 12–13).

Work

The *Historiae Abbreviatae*, commonly known as the *De Caesaribus*, survives only in two late manuscripts, bound with two other short works which were falsely attributed to Victor. Of the three *breviaria*, or abridged histories, investigated here, Victor's work was the first published, and in many ways it is the most ambitious and most original.

The history covers the period from the reign of Augustus to the reign of Constantius. Victor probably began writing in 358, to judge from his mention of the earthquake in Nicomedia (16.12) which occurred in August of that year. Near the end of the book, Victor says that Constantius had been ruling as Augustus for twenty-three years, which implies a date of publication after September 360 (42.20). The last section of the book is rather curious. Victor first lavishes the emperor Constantius with praise, but then ends the work with a pair of sentences which sharply criticize Constantius' selection of advisors and subordinates. Bird has suggested that the early panegyrical remarks on the emperor marked the original ending to the work, and the more critical remarks were added after the outbreak of civil war between Constantius and Julian in the summer of 361 (Bird 1994: xi).

The major, perhaps sole, written source for Victor's history was the work known as "Enmann's Kaisergeschichte," or the *KG*. The *KG*, which is no longer extant, was first inferred by Alexander Enmann on the basis of similarities between Victor, Eutropius, and the *Historia Augusta* (Enmann 1884; see also Cohn 1884; Barnes 1970, 1976, 1978: 90–7; Bird 1973, 1989; Burgess 1993). Its influence has since been detected in Festus, Jerome, the anonymous *Epitome de Caesaribus*, Ausonius, and Ammianus Marcellinus, among others. Victor and Eutropius share a similar selection of facts and several errors in their descriptions of the imperial period, particularly the third century. Because Victor's treatment is more thorough than that of Eutropius, but precedes Eutropius in date of publication, the two must depend upon a common source, the *KG*.

Given the number of fourth- and fifth-century histories which depend upon it, the *KG* must have been one of the few Latin sources to cover the third and early fourth centuries. It seems to have covered the period from the beginning of the empire, around 30 BC, up to at least the Constantinian period, around 340, and maybe up to the reigns of Constantius and Julian in 357. The work cannot have been particularly long, or the similarities between Victor and Eutropius would not have been so obvious. The author demonstrates a particular interest in usurpers. It has been suggested that the *KG* should be identified with the lost historical work of Eusebius of Nantes, which served as a source for a (lost) series of poems on usurpers written by Ausonius in the 380s (Burgess 1993).

Victor took the dry narrative of the *KG* and expanded it with the addition of moralizing commentary and stylistic flourishes. Neither addition has been well received by modern critics. Unlike the sober and flowing narrative of Eutropius, who follows the *KG* more closely in his imperial section, Victor frequently speaks in the first person in complex and sometimes puzzling asides. In diction and in syntax, Victor is greatly dependent upon the historian Sallust, who was one of the primary authors taught in the schools of late antiquity. Sallust's pessimistic moralism fits well with Victor's historical approach, but unfortunately Victor is no Sallust and his work is often affected and artificial (Bird 1984: 90–9). Victor was also familiar with the works of Tacitus, and the introduction to the *De Caesaribus* purposefully recalls the opening section of Tacitus' *Annales*. Tacitus clearly serves as a stylistic model only, however, and not as a historical model, since numerous errors which must derive from the *KG* would have certainly been corrected if Victor had a copy of Tacitus at hand while he wrote.

Victor pauses at certain points in his narrative to impose structure upon the history of the imperial period. Den Boer suggests that this periodization, which mirrors that of modern historians of the empire, is one of Victor's original accomplishments (1972: 28–31). Victor marks important breaks after Domitian, after Alexander Severus, and at the accession of Diocletian. After the assassination of Domitian, Victor remarks that those born in Italy had held the throne up to that point, but afterwards emperors from elsewhere did so as well. "And to me at least … it is perfectly clear that the city of Rome grew great especially through the virtues of immigrants and imported skills" (11.13). Alexander Severus is praised for his intellect, his modesty, and his military and judicial excellence. At the end of his thirteen-year reign, Victor pauses to reflect. The empire had grown enormously between the reigns of Romulus and Septimius Severus, and had reached its peak under Alexander, he claims. Subsequent emperors, more interested in civil wars than wars of foreign conquest, sent the state into decline. "And without discrimination, men good and evil, noble and ignoble, even many barbarians seized power." Fortune, which had previously been restrained by virtue, entrusted power to the least noble and the least educated (24.9–11). Victor casts a mixed judgement on the recovery of the state at the accession of Diocletian. He was "a great man" with a list of accomplishments in military, civil, and religious affairs. He was additionally looked up to as if he were a father, and his character impelled him to abdicate voluntarily. He was not, however, of noble background, and Victor considers his lack of nobility to be the reason for his demand that he be addressed as "Lord" and for his wearing of silk and jewels. Victor adds that those of humble origin often become excessively proud with power, and that nobility is therefore to be preferred in a ruler (39.7).

A general picture of Victor's vision of proper political and social behavior can be derived from his scattered reflections. His approval of nobility, remarked upon in connection with Diocletian, has parallels in other passages. Nerva's choice of Trajan as a successor is judged as particularly good due to Trajan's senatorial status (13.1). Antoninus Pius and Marcus Aurelius (15–16) were equally distinguished because of their noble birth. Victor's criticism of Gallienus partially depends upon that emperor's (purported) removal of senators from military roles (33.34, 37.6). Yet Victor is not a simple apologist for the nobility and the senatorial order. He portrays Vespasian, a man of humble origins, as one of the best of the emperors (9), and conversely asserts that the noble Galba was cruel and murderous (6). Victor saw the weakened state of the senatorial class not as the result of external pressures but as largely self-inflicted. Victor argues that after the assassination of Caligula, the republic might have been restored if only noble Romans were still performing military service (3.14). Again, after the death of Probus, Victor feels that the policy of Gallienus might have been reversed, and senators returned to leadership in the army, if only the nobles cared for something beyond their leisure and their wealth (37.5).

The roles of the army and of the imperial administration are recurring concerns in Victor's work. From the earliest period the army is depicted as barbarized, corrupt, and prone to civil war (Bird 1984: 41–52). The military quartermasters known as *actuarii* receive special criticism in a digression. They are "worthless, venal, cunning, quarrelsome, greedy" (33.13; Bird 1984: 47–8). Victor, a bureaucrat himself, has similar criticism for other imperial bureaucrats. Emperors who reduced taxation and cracked down on corruption receive praise, such as Vespasian, who restored cities ravaged by the civil wars without burdening farmers (9.9) and Aurelian, whose assassination is blamed on his zeal for good government (35.8). He praises Diocletian for his abolition of the *frumentarii*, or grain inspectors, who were notorious "secret police" whom Victor likens to the *agentes in rebus* who performed similar functions in his own day (39.44). To Victor, of course, bureaucratic corruption does not arise from structural causes but from personal ones, as his comments on the reforming prefect Anatolius make clear: "there is nothing good or bad in the state that cannot be changed to the opposite by the character of its rulers" (13.7).

Victor was a pagan, and he favors emperors who worshipped the traditional gods. He praises Augustus for being extremely devoted to religion (1.5), and he thinks that an example of Diocletian's excellence is his restoration of ancient cult (39.45). Hadrian was as pious as Numa Pompilius or an ancient Athenian in his attention to religious cult and his celebration of the Eleusinian Mysteries (14.2). Prodigies also play a role in Victor's history, as when the discovery of female genitals on a pig's abdomen during the reign of Philip predicted the decadence of generations to come (28.4–5). Victor's support of traditional Roman religion seems to derive more from his support of tradition than his support of religion. His traditionalism is clear also in his championing of the classical education which allowed him to progress so far in his own career. He frequently compares emperors to figures from Roman antiquity: Hadrian resembled Numa, Pertinax, the Curii (18.1), and Constantius, Pompey (42.22). He judges emperors based on their cultural attainments and digresses upon this criterion after the death of Vitellius. All the early emperors, he states, had been men of great eloquence and learning, and both character and education should be requirements for holding supreme power (8.8). A similar focus on these two criteria can be found in his reflections on the emperor Didius Julianus, whom he (following the *KG*: Bird 1989) confuses with the legal expert Salvius Julianus. While this man was well educated in the law, his lack of character made him unable to restrain his passions (19). Diocletian and the other tetrarchs were likewise flawed only because of their lack of culture (39.26; Bird 1984: 71–80).

Victor's ambitious attempt to expand the *KG* with his stylized reflections appears to have succeeded in the eyes of one important reader, the emperor Julian, but has found few other champions up to the present day. The difficult style of Victor may have led readers to the easier and far more popular work of Eutropius. Victor's commentary is often trite and flaccid, and it lacks coherence. Victor does serve as an ideal example of a particular type of Roman in the mid-fourth century, one who has risen from rather humble origins to power in the imperial administration, and perhaps for that reason holds conventional and nostalgic views on government and morality. The *De Caesaribus* thus remains as a valuable witness to a view of history and a style of historiography produced by participants in the new class of imperial functionaries.

Text and translation

Latin text edited by F. Pichlmayr (1966), Teubner. English translation by H.W. Bird (1994), Translated Texts for Historians.

3

EUTROPIUS

Life

Eutropius reveals little about his life in his *Breviarium*, but there are numerous references to Eutropius outside of his work. Unfortunately, the name was popular in antiquity, and a biographer must decide which figures who bear it are the historian Eutropius, and which are not (den Boer 1972: 114–15; Capozza 1973: 84–95; Bonamente 1986: 19–45; Bird 1988a: 51–60, 1992: vii–xviii; Hellegouarc'h 1999: vii–xi).

Eutropius' title is given as *magister memoriae* in the dedication of his work, written in 369 to the emperor Valens. Eutropius' statement that he accompanied that emperor in his invasion of Persia in 363 suggests that he had also been a member of the imperial administration under Julian (10.16). The *Suda* describes Eutropius as "an Italian sophist who wrote a historical epitome in Latin and other things." Another source (pseudo-Codinus, in *scr. orig. const.* 1.58, p. 144) suggests that he was "epistolographos," a secretary in charge of correspondence, under the emperor "Constantine," presumably an error for "Constantius." This would imply that Eutropius was (to use the Latin terminology) *magister epistularum* before 361. The fourteenth-century historian Nicephorus Gregoras adds that Eutropius was a contemporary of Valens and Julian, and a pagan.

Eutropius' birthplace is unknown. Although he is referred to in the *Suda* as Italian, and is the author of a work in Latin, he served as *magister memoriae* in the east and has a Greek name. He certainly demonstrates a familiarity with the Greek language (Bird 1988a: 51–2) and perhaps owned property in Asia (Symm. *ep.* 3.53). Most scholars deny that the historian Eutropius is also the Eutropius mentioned by Marcellus Empiricus as a medical writer and native of Bordeaux (*de medicamentis, pref.*), although the identity remains

49

possible. Bonamente (1986: 22–3) points out that there is no evidence of special medical interest or knowledge in the accounts of emperors' deaths in the *Breviarium*.

The following reconstruction of Eutropius' life requires the identification of the historian with the governmental official who is found, without mention of any historical work, in the legal codes and in the letters of Symmachus and Libanius. The identification is perhaps strengthened by our knowledge that the historian served in important positions under both Julian and Valens, and thus possessed the talents and survival skills which would have allowed him to hold other offices and to correspond with important figures of the late fourth century. The reconstruction must still, however, be understood as tentative.

To reach the position of *magister epistularum* before 361 would normally require at least a decade of work as a civil servant. This would place Eutropius' birth, whether in the east or the west, around 320. Scribal duties included the movement of judicial paperwork from the emperor out to the provincial governors and the reception of similar paperwork from the provinces for the emperor. Scribes would also have handled paperwork which concerned army service and appointments and promotions in the civil service (Jones 1964: 575–6). After the death of Constantius, Eutropius continued to serve under Julian. It has been speculated that he may even have been among those higher-ranking officials who met after Julian's death to determine a successor (Bird 1988a: 54). Eutropius' promotion to *magister memoriae* under Valens between 367 and 369 suggests that he avoided supporting the usurper Procopius in 365. The dedication of the *Breviarium* can be understood as an offering of thanks to the emperor for his appointment, and the writing of the *Breviarium* may even be understood as one of Eutropius' duties in his new position.

Ammianus and Libanius refer to a certain Eutropius as proconsul of Asia in 371. If this is the historian Eutropius, his career path would mirror that of the historian Festus, who succeeded Eutropius as *magister memoriae*, wrote his own *Breviarium* in that position, and then became proconsul of Asia. Festus' succession in Asia appears to have been the result of intrigue. When a plot against Valens had been uncovered, Ammianius tells us that Festus attempted to falsely involve Eutropius in the plot. Fortunately, the philosopher Pasiphilus refused under torture to implicate Eutropius, and the proconsul escaped death (29.1.36).

Perhaps the historian Eutropius should also be identified with the Eutropius who moved in important circles in Rome in the late 370s and the 380s. This would suggest that after the death of Valens, Eutropius regained influence in the courts of Gratian and Theodosius. The powerful Roman aristocrat Symmachus corresponded with this Eutropius, in one case attempting to enlist his support on behalf of a governmental position for a protégé. Eutropius would have shared an interest in early Roman history with Symmachus, who was an editor of the works of Livy. This Eutropius was appointed prefect of Illyricum. Numerous laws appear under his name from January of 380 until September of 381. It has been suggested that the laws reveal a merciful character, since some mitigate or remit serious penalties. After his departure from that position, he presumably remained in the east. His correspondence with Symmachus and with Libanius survives from the following decade. In 387, Eutropius received the highest possible honor when he was appointed eastern consul with the emperor Valentinian II as his colleague in the west. He last appears in history as the addressee of a letter from Libanius written in 390 and of letters from Symmachus in the same year.

Eutropius was almost certainly a pagan, but not a militant one. He faults Julian for his overzealous attacks on Christianity, but points out that he refrained from bloodshed (10.16.3). He is guardedly critical in his judgement of Constantine (Bird 1987: 147–8), and he prudently avoids discussion of religion when he treats the other emperors. His correspondence with the pagan Symmachus omits any mention of Christianity, although opportunities were not lacking (Seeck 1883/1984: cxxxii).

Work

The *Breviarium* of Eutropius is divided into ten books and treats Roman history from Romulus to the death of Jovian. The work takes up seventy-one pages in the Teubner edition, as compared to the fifty-two pages Victor uses to cover only the empire. The first book covers the period from the founding of the city to the sack of Rome by the Gauls around 390, and thus covers the same ground as the first five books of Livy. The second book, which ends with the successful conclusion of the First Punic War, covers the same ground as books 6 to 20 of Livy. Book 3 also parallels the structure of Livy's history, concluding with the defeat of Carthage in the Second Punic War, which Livy treated in books 21 to 30. Book 4, however, diverges from the Livian model by concluding with the Jugurthine War, passing quickly over the Third Punic War, and completely omitting the Gracchi from consideration.

The conclusion of the fourth book introduces "the great" Sulla, along with Marius, and their struggle dominates the fifth book. The sixth book features the war between Pompey and Caesar and concludes with Caesar's assassination. Eutropius makes no secret of his preference for Sulla in the fifth book and Pompey in the sixth (Bird 1990: 88). The history was arranged to place the two civil wars in the central books, at the price of a slight imbalance in the fifth book, which is considerably shorter than the rest.

The books which cover the empire end at traditional division points. Book 7 concludes with the assassination of Domitian, which Tacitus and Suetonius had also understood to be a significant historical turning point. To begin the eighth book, Eutropius takes advantage of a coincidence to praise his sponsor by dating the transition from the tyrant Domitian to the noble Nerva during the consulship of Vetus and the emperor's namesake Valens. Book 8 concludes with the death of Alexander Severus, which had been recognized as an important transitional moment by Aurelius Victor as well (Bird 1990: 89) and book 9 begins with Maximinus gaining power. Victor (25.1), and presumably their common source, the *KG*, note that Maximinus was the first emperor to seize power without senatorial consent. Eutropius concludes the ninth book with the voluntary retirement of Diocletian, whom he admires, and thus a book which had begun on an ominous note and which covered a difficult period for the empire ends on an upbeat note. The last book brings the story up to the death of Jovian. Eutropius concludes with words very similar to those with which Ammianus concludes his history: "What remains must be related by a greater pen. We do not now so much pass over them as reserve them for greater care in writing" (10.18.3).

Eutropius' suggestion that contemporary events require the more elevated prose of panegyric emphasizes the plain and unpretentious style of his work (see Santini 1979; Bird 1992: li–liii; Hellegouarc'h 1999: xlvii–liii). In contrast to Aurelius Victor, Eutropius makes few attempts to allude to historical models or to adorn his prose with rhetorical figures. The work appears as the product of a bureaucrat in several ways. Lexically, Eutropius employs many abstract substantives which are commonly found in legal codes and other products of the chancery (Santini 1979: 5–6). The narrative connections, particularly in the first half of the work, are frequently rudimentary. Simple sentences follow upon each other with simple transitional phrases such as "then," "next," or "a little later." The lack of subordination creates a monotonous feel to the syntax, which perhaps reaches its peak in a description of Trajan (8.4) which contains eleven coordinate participles. Eutropius' use and reuse of the same phrases and words increase the monotony of the work. Consider the first phrases of the chapters in the first book, which deal with the Roman kings: "Afterwards, Numa Pompilius became king ... " (1.3.1); "Tullus Hostilius succeeded him" (1.4.1); "After him, Ancus Marcius ... " (1.5.1); "Then Priscus Tarquinius took the throne" (1.6.1); "After him, Servius Tullius took power ... " (1.7.1). Consider as well, also in the first book, the first phrases of the chapters which describe the early republic: "In the second year also ... " (1.11.1); "In the ninth year after the kings were expelled ... " (1.12.1); "In the sixteenth year after the kings were expelled ... " (1.13.1); "In the following year" (1.14); "In the eighteenth year after the kings were driven out ... " (1.15). Eutropius even twice uses the word "exordium," "beginning," artlessly in the very first sentence of the work.

Other elements of the history are formulaic, and thus perhaps typical of a historian who is used to the hackneyed and repetitive writing typical of official documents. He is given to numbers and lists: four wars of Sulla (6.1) and four campaigns of Domitian (7.23.4), four theaters of battle in the Second Punic War (3.13.1), three triumphs in the year 146 (4.14.2) (Hellegouarc'h 1999: xliii–xlv). He dutifully records which emperors were voted divine honors by the senate upon death. His use of the impersonal passive has been seen as typical for a bureaucrat who is trained to write objectively and to see people as cogs in the machinery of the empire (Santini 1979: 9).

Hellegouarc'h emphasizes the difference in style between Eutropius' treatment of the royal and republican periods and his treatment of the imperial period. While the first part is organized in annalistic fashion, the second part is organized biographically (1999: xxii–xxiii). Pompey, Caesar, and Octavian serve as transitional figures in this arrangement, since the sections devoted to them incorporate more biographical information than had appeared in earlier books, but less than would appear in later books. In the last book, where Eutropius draws upon his personal experience to describe contemporary emperors, he provides more detail. The different approaches to the arrangement of the material result from the changing sources upon which Eutropius drew.

Livy, and perhaps an epitome of Livy, is the primary source for the royal and republican sections of Eutropius. The *Suda* (under the entry "Kapiton") describes Eutropius as an epitomator of Livy, and many modern studies have demonstrated the accuracy of this description for the first six books of the work (Capozza 1962/3, 1973; Scivoletto 1970; Ratti 1996: 24). This dependence is clear both in the annalistic structure of the first books and in some of the phrasing and judgements. Eutropius' dependence upon Livy for the history of the royal and republican periods does not, however, result in mere compression and reproduction of the earlier historian's work. Rather, the act of compression lends different emphasis to certain events, and results in the omission of others. Eutropius also brings a distinctly fourth-century approach to his interpretation of the earlier periods. His criterion for evaluating the kings, for example, is colored by their superficial similarities to the autocratic emperors of his own day, and his evaluations of the republican senate and consulship are influenced by his understanding of the vastly different late antique institutions (Capozza 1973).

Book 7, which covers the emperors from Augustus to Domitian, contains information and phrasing which was clearly derived from the biographies of Suetonius. Eutropius included other information, however, which was not found in Suetonius, but which Aurelius Victor also included. These commonalities between Eutropius and Victor, and particularly their shared errors, formed the basis of the hypothesis of their shared source, "Enmann's Kaisergeschichte," or the *KG* (Ratti 1996: 25–30). Although some scholars have denied the existence of this work (which is more fully described in the chapter on Aurelius Victor), the evidence for its existence and influence is substantial. For example, although Eutropius often provides information which is identical to that of Victor, he also occasionally is more accurate or more specific than Victor. Since Victor wrote before Eutropius, it is clear that a shared source could be the only explanation (cf. Ratti 1996: 33–45). The *KG* was arranged biographically, as are Eutropius' books 7–9. Eutropius also seems to mirror the *KG* by including similar details in each biography: the emperor's family background, his personality and actions, the date of his death, the length of his reign, his age at death, and whether he was voted divine honors by the senate (Hellegouarc'h 1999: xxxiii).

While Eutropius seems to have used some other sources beyond Livy and the *KG*, their influence appears to have been limited. The *Breviarium* was presumably written in a quick and workmanlike fashion which did not demand extensive research or pretensions to scholarship. It was, rather, written by a courtier in service to the emperor for official state purposes. Thus it is not surprising to find that one other source upon which Eutropius may have drawn directly or indirectly was the self-promoting testament of the emperor Augustus known as the *Res Gestae Divi Augusti* (Ratti 1996: 47–68).

Eutropius' general approach to history is traditionalist. He favors the senate, the expansion of the empire, and powerful military leaders. A senator himself, the historian emphasizes the wisdom and importance of the senate in his account of the republican period. Of sixteen mentions of the senate in the first four books, for example, fifteen are positive (Bird 1988b: 65). Eutropius also favors Sulla over Marius (5.3–4), and Brutus over Caesar (6.25). In later books, Eutropius judges emperors in part based on their relationships with the senate. The abominable Nero "killed a large part of the senate and was an enemy to all good men" (7.14.1) and Domitian "killed the most noble from the senate" (7.23.2). But during the beneficent reign of Trajan, only one senator was condemned, and the condemnation took place at the direction of the senate itself (8.4). Eutropius' habit of ending many imperial biographies with a notice of *consecratio*, the vote of the senate to confer divinity upon favored emperors after death, may likewise be interpreted as emphasizing senatorial power.

The *Breviarium* of Eutropius focuses almost entirely on military affairs. Both Eutropius and Festus write at the behest of Valens in preparation for a major eastern campaign, and their concentration on military glory in their official works may be compared to the work of Aurelius Victor, who is much more leery of military power. A preoccupation with military success can be seen in Eutropius' diction: Hellegouarc'h counts thirty examples of *triumphare* and twenty-one of *triumphus* in the work (1999: xl). The *Breviarium* lacks significant information on economic, cultural, or institutional history. This helps to explain the almost complete lack of information on the "Struggle of the Orders" which marked the early republic, and the complete erasure of the career of the Gracchi. Republican history is reduced to events which demonstrate the supremacy of the senate and which chronicle the military expansion of the state. Eutropius treats the imperial period in a similar way, judging emperors largely on their military successes. He portrays Augustus primarily as a military conqueror (7.9). By contrast, bad emperors are not warriors, like Caligula, who "undertook a war against the Germans, but after entering Suebia, made no effort" (7.12.2). Eutropius' bellicose attitude is clear in his statement that Trajan widely extended the borders of the empire which, after Augustus, "had been defended rather than honorably enlarged" (8.2.2). He also makes military discipline a prominent theme, perhaps because Valens himself was a severe disciplinarian (Amm. 31.14.1; Bird 1990: 91–2). The conclusion of the work dwells on the humiliation of Jovian's loss of territory in the east, which Eutropius sees as unequalled in more than a thousand years of Roman history (10.17.2). This should be understood as a rallying cry for the looming Persian campaign of Valens, and the final conclusion to the work, "we reserve these matters for a more ornate composition" (10.18.3), looks to a panegyric to praise the emperor's military success to date and predict glory in the campaign to come.

The ideology of the *Breviarium* is wholly conventional, as one might expect from its quasi-official nature, and Eutropius' concerns can be readily paralleled in other fourth-century works. The historian praises good relations between the emperors and the senatorial aristocracy, which may be achieved by emperors who recognize their shared interests with the local and bureaucratic elites. Emperors should be reminded of the need for *civilitas*, the "civility" which restrains them from excessive punishments and encourages them to support the established leadership of the cities (Scivoletto 1970). In turn, aristocrats are encouraged to support the glory of the state and, in particular, glorious military expansion. In a world in constant danger of civil war and of alienation between civilian and military leaders, Eutropius' work draws upon the past in the hope of unifying contemporaries in support of foreign conquest.

Text and translation

Latin text edited by C. Santini (1979), Teubner. English translation by H.W. Bird (1993), Translated Texts for Historians.

4

FESTUS

Life

The brief and impersonal work of Festus contains little information about its author. Festus must have been considerably older than the emperor Valens, the patron of the work, since he refers to himself as very old (30.1; Arnaud-Lindet 1994: vii–viii). Since Valens died in August 378, when he was nearly fifty years old (Amm. 31.14.1), Festus must have been born in the period roughly before 318. In the last sentence of the work, the comments of Festus about a god (*deus*) and a divinity (*numen*) have been interpreted as the words of a pagan distinguishing gracefully between his beliefs and those of the Christian emperor (e.g. Eadie 1967: 9 n. 2). This is not, however, a necessary reading of the words, and Baldwin (1978: 203) provides numerous parallel examples of such panegyrical writing in the fourth century.

Various manuscripts provide the additional information that the author's name was Rufus or, alternatively, Rufius Festus. A single manuscript identifies the author as holder of the position of *magister memoriae*, the same position held by Eutropius. Although this evidence is not conclusive (Baldwin 1978: 199), we do know that a man named Festus served in that position sometime between 365 and 372 (the work itself was written in 369 or 370). Scholars generally identify the historian, whose work was written in 369 or 370, with this imperial official Festus who was from Tridentum, a city in northern Italy.

Festus of Tridentum is mentioned with disgust by three pagans, Ammianus Marcellinus, Libanius, and Eunapius. Ammianus says that he was of lowly birth (29.2.22–8). Ammianus is less interested in Festus himself than in using the historian to further blacken the character of Maximinus, the official whom Ammianus decries for his role in a series of sorcery trials at Rome. Therefore Ammianus praises Festus' early career, when he served as *consularis Syriae* (in 365 or 368) and *magister memoriae* (in 370). When Festus became *proconsul Asiae*, however, Ammianus claims that he fell under the sway of the evil Maximinus. While Festus had at first opposed Maximinus' despotic behavior, Ammianus says, he soon saw it as a means for career advancement and began prosecuting his subjects for sorcery. Among his victims were the philosopher Coeranius and numerous other innocents who, far from practicing malicious magic, were persecuted for simply performing simple charms for their health.

Unlike Ammianus, Libanius does not present a Festus who is corrupted later in his career, but rather portrays him as bloodthirsty from the beginning when he took the position of *consularis Syriae*. Libanius describes him as an idiot and a man who knew no Greek (the two being synonymous for the Latin-loathing Libanius), and accuses him of plotting with Libanius' enemy Eubulus in return for a luxurious feast (*or.* 1.156). Festus managed to disrupt Libanius' public orations, but he failed in his attempt to destroy the orator by connecting him to the supposed crimes of a certain Martyrius. The prosecution of this otherwise unknown man is reminiscent of the prosecutions that Ammianus described as common during Festus' administration as proconsul. Martyrius' weakness for wrestling apparently led him to dabble in magic in an attempt to hinder a competitor, and Libanius claims that Festus, in a private meeting with the emperor Valens, attempted to link both him and the historian Eutropius to this sorcery.

Festus is attacked even more harshly by Eunapius, who portrays him as madman with the soul of a butcher, and a persecutor of pagans (*Lives* 480–1). Eunapius blames Festus for many beheadings, including that of the philosopher Maximus of Ephesus, the friend of Julian. Eunapius also relates the story of the death of Festus, which he claims to have witnessed himself. After leaving office, he married a wealthy woman of Asia, and decided to try to pacify the enemies he had made through his conduct by holding a lavish banquet for nobles and office-holders. After many had agreed to attend his party, Festus made the error of entering the temple of the goddess Nemesis, although he was not a pagan and had punished pagans with death. He described to those in the temple an ominous dream he had had in which his victim Maximus had dragged him by the neck to be judged by Pluto. Although Festus followed the advice of those in the temple and offered prayers to Nemesis, on his way out of the sanctuary he slipped on the pavement and fell on his back, expiring soon after. Eunapius found this end to be a particularly satisfying example of the justice of the gods.

Work

Momigliano claimed that the work of Festus was an epitome of the work of Eutropius (1963: 85–6). He suggested that after the *magister memoriae* of 369, Eutropius, had produced his *Breviarium*, the ignorant emperor Valens found it too complex. Thus, he asked for an abridgement of the abridgement from his *magister memoriae* of the following year. This theory is partly based on the title of the work, which one manuscript preserves as *Breviarium Festi De Breviario Rerum Gestarum Populi Romani* (Eadie 1967: 13). Momigliano, and den Boer following him (den Boer 1972: 173–4), interpreted the title to mean "a *breviarium* of the *breviarium* (of Eutropius)." This is in contrast to the earlier theory of Wölfflin (1904: 72), who interpreted the phrase to mean "the *breviarium* to surpass all *breviaria*," like the phrase "king of kings." Because, on the one hand, Wölfflin's suggestion is linguistically impossible, and on the other, Festus' work is clearly not an abridgement of Eutropius' work, a different explanation for the title is required. One is provided by Arnaud-Lindet (1994: xv). He suggests that the actual name of the work was *De Breviario Rerum Gestarum Populi Romani* ("[book] concerning a summary of the history of the Roman people") and that the first two words were originally added by a copyist after the "incipit" ("here begins the *breviarium* of Festus") and then erroneously considered to be part of the original title. There is thus no reason to adhere to Momigliano's untenable thesis.

At the end of his work, Festus laments his inability to rise to the level of eloquence which a full narrative history of the deeds of Valens would demand. He prays that the gods will grant the fortune necessary for the emperor to subdue Persia in the manner in which he has subdued the Goths. The Gothic victory took place in 369 (Amm. 27.5), so the work must have been published after that date. Mommsen suggested that the work must have been completed in 369 as well, since the list of provinces which Festus provides omits the province of Valentia, which was created in 369 and named for Valentinian. This date is not necessarily certain, however, since scribal error may have caused the name to be lost, or Festus may have used an older list which did not contain the newest division (Baldwin 1978: 197–9). Since Ammianus suggests that Festus was *magister memoriae* in between his service as *consularis Syriae* (either in 365 or 368) and as *proconsul Asiae* (from 372 to 378), it would not be inconsistent with the evidence to imagine the work was composed in late 369, when he succeeded Eutropius in the position.

Festus dedicated his production to the emperor Valens, who had requested its production, as several passages of the work make clear. Various forms of the fulsome address required of court officials to the emperor appear throughout, such as "most glorious emperor" (1.2), "your clemency" (1.1), and "your eternity" (2.1; Eadie 1967: 2 n. 2). It is certain that the intended recipient was the eastern emperor Valens, rather than the western emperor, his brother Valentinian, since in the tenth chapter Festus describes how the eastern provinces fell under "your rule," "sceptris tuis" (10.1). In addition, the victory over the Goths praised by Festus in chapter 30 (30.2) must refer to Valens' recent conquest of Athanaric. No credence need be given to the suggestion that the existence of Valentinian's name at the beginning of one line of the manuscript tradition represents a second dedication; rather, the name is best explained as an incorrect scribal expansion of an original abbreviation "VAL" (cf. Eadie 1967: 3–4).

The work itself is less a summary of Roman history than a piece of official propaganda prepared by the court to lay the foundations for Valens' Persian expedition. A large majority of the work pertains to the history of Roman–Persian relations, and of the part which does not, a majority pertains to Roman foreign policy. In length it is more a pamphlet than a book, and it does not attempt to provide a succinct history of Rome as do the *breviaria* of Victor and Eutropius.

The work was composed very rapidly and the historian used few sources for its composition. Several close linguistic parallels suggest that the information in the republican section of the work was derived from an epitome of Livy, perhaps one which served as a source for the extant *Periochae* of Livy. The abbreviated history of Florus may also have been used. Parallels between Festus, Eutropius, and the *Historia Augusta* in the imperial section of the history reveal that Festus made use of the *Kaisergeschichte*. The numerous errors in the work suggest that Festus was not always careful in using his sources, and that he may also have relied upon his memory for some information (Eadie 1967: 70–98; Arnaud-Lindet 1994: xxi–xxiv).

The work can be divided into an introduction (1), a numerical division by years of all of Roman history into the regal, republican, and imperial periods (2), a quick survey of which provinces were conquered during the three periods (3), the conquest of the western provinces (4–9), the conquest of the eastern provinces (10–13), a history of Roman warfare against Persia (14–29), and a conclusion encouraging Valens' designs against Persia (30).

In the introduction, Festus states that the emperor has requested brevity and that he will therefore proceed in the fashion of money-changers, who express large amounts of small change in smaller numbers of higher-denomination coins (1.1). This is an introduction not so much to the entire work, but rather to the subsequent chapter, in which Festus makes good on his introductory promise to enable the emperor to not read about the past as much as to count it out. The period from the founding of Rome to the accession of Valens comprised 1,117 years. The regal period included 243 years, the consular period 467, and the imperial period 407. He gives the length of rule of each king, the number of consuls who held office in the republican period, and the number of emperors.

Festus again summarizes in the third section, in which he lists which regions had been conquered during each of the three major divisions of Roman history. In chapter 4 he turns to a different task, the listing of each province and the date and circumstances of its absorption into the Roman empire. This signals a shift from the historical arrangement of the second and third chapters to a new geographic arrangement of his material. This also reveals the fundamental difference in structure between the work of Festus and that of Victor or Eutropius. Chapters 4 to 14 of Festus travel roughly clockwise from Sicily and Sardinia to Africa (4), Spain (5), and Gaul (6), then from Crete north through Greece, Illyricum, Pannonia, and Noricum (7), and then east through Asia Minor (11–12), to Cyprus and Egypt (13), and finally to Judaea, Arabia, Mesopotamia, and Armenia (14).

This geographic section is split into a western and an eastern section by Festus' comment in chapter 10 that he now turns to the jurisdiction of Valens. The western and eastern sections are also distinguished by an unusual feature which Festus includes in the former, but not the latter section. After the sketch of the history of the acquisition of each western diocese, Festus provides a list of its provinces. This is the earliest surviving list of its type, and it may represent the only source of information which modern historians find useful in Festus' work. An eastern provincial list is lacking, perhaps because it would have been unnecessary at the eastern court. The purpose of the list has been disputed. Eadie (1967: 170–1) suggests that the list rounds off the discussion of the dioceses of the western half of the empire, to which Festus will not return. Den Boer sees the list as "remarkable" and innovative (den Boer 1972: 197). The list, which fits in well with the unadorned nature of the first half of the work, emphasizes the geographic arrangement of chapters 4–9. By presenting the magnitude of Roman strength and conquests in the west, perhaps it is meant to suggest that war in the east is the logical and inevitable result of the growth of Roman power (cf. Peachin 1985).

After describing the western Roman conquests in a geographically clockwise spiral which concludes in the east, Festus turns to a historical summary of Roman–Persian relations. The introduction to this section (15.1) suggests the instructions Festus had received from Valens. "I know now, illustrious prince, where your purpose leads. You assuredly seek to know how many times Babylonian and Roman arms clashed, with what fortunes the javelin contended with the arrow." Festus' use of "Babylonian" for "Persian," and his synecdoche of the Roman *pila*, the typical javelin of the Roman infantryman, and the Persian *sagitta*, the arrow of the Persian cavalryman, are examples of his intermittent attempts at high style. He goes on to state that the Persians will emerge only rarely as victors in his account, and that the Romans would often win because of their superior virtue.

Festus' account of Roman policy in the east is too minimalist to shed much light on his opinions or beliefs. Contrary to what one might expect from the official nature of Festus' account, the narrative mostly provides the unadorned facts. A slightly higher estimate of casualties inflicted by Pompey (16; Eadie 1967: 129) than those found in other sources, and the possible invention of a Persian delegation to Constantine to head off a threatened invasion (26; Arnaud-Lindet 1994: 34 n. 190), are exceptions which prove the rule by their triviality. In discussing the campaigns of Lucius Verus, the younger co-emperor of Marcus Aurelius who had great success in the east, one might expect Festus to exploit the parallels with his patron, Valens, also a junior emperor. Perhaps the slightest hint of this can be seen in Festus' reference to Marcus and Verus as "pariter Augusti," "equally emperors." This stress on the equality of their power can also be found in Eutropius (8.9.2), who operated in a similar political atmosphere as Festus, but not in Victor (16.3), who emphasizes the superiority of Marcus. Festus concludes with a description of the shameful surrender of Persian territory under Jovian. The work thus serves Valens' purpose of explaining an upcoming war as necessary to avenge a major loss.

Though Festus' *Breviarium* is straightforward and factual, it is not without stylistic adornment (Wölfflin 1904; Baldwin 1978: 212–17). Festus shows a liking for pleonasm, such as "kings seven in number" (2) or "pirates and maritime bandit" (12), and for the poetic plural, found in the phrases "sub amicitiis" (7), and "regna Babyloniae" (26). Baldwin remarks, "It is noteworthy how much he has in common with the *Panegyrici Latini*," which can be seen in the combination of literary figures and allusions with occasional late and vulgar usage (1978: 217). Despite the great popularity of the work in the Middle Ages, the work is very much the product of a particular commission for a particular time, a document to be read or circulated at court to establish an official line on the history behind Valens' coming campaign.

Text and translation

Latin text edited by J.W. Eadie (1967). There is no English translation, but there is the French translation of M.-P. Arnaud-Lindet (1994), Budé.

5

EUNAPIUS

Life

Eunapius was the author of two works which have come down to us in part or entire. The *Nea Ekdosis* (New Edition) of the *History after Dexippus* of Eunapius of Sardis is fragmentary, but his other work, the *Lives of Philosophers and Sophists*, is extant. It is from this second work that we can retrieve some information about the historian's life.

Eunapius was a native of Sardis, a city in Asia Minor, and spent most of his life there. The sophist Chrysanthius, a relative by marriage (*Lives* 477), was one of his early teachers. At age 15 he sailed to the "university town" of Athens (*Lives* 485), suffering greatly from illness along the way, and he studied there for several years with the Christian sophist Prohaeresius. At Athens he was initiated into the Eleusinian mysteries (*Lives* 475). He considered a trip to Egypt after his stay in Athens, but his parents compelled him to return home (*Lives* 493). Returning at age 19 to Sardis (*Lives* 461), he taught rhetoric in the morning and studied philosophy with Chrysanthius in the afternoon. He witnessed the death of Festus in Smyrna in 380 (*Lives* 481) but there is otherwise no evidence of his leaving Sardis as an adult. He published part of his history before turning to the *Lives*, a collection of anecdotal biographies about sophists who were active primarily in the fourth century. After the publication of this biographical work in 399 (Banchich 1984), Eunapius returned to his historical work and published a second edition, with changes and additions.

Robert J. Penella (1990: 2–4) and Thomas Banchich (1987) have provided a reliable chronology of the major events of Eunapius' life, correcting the work of Goulet (1980) upon which Blockley (1981) depends. It is apparent that when Eunapius arrived at Athens, his teacher Prohaeresius was banned from teaching rhetoric under governmental sponsorship by the anti-Christian legislation of the emperor Julian (*Lives* 493). This ban went into effect on 17 June 362 (*Cod. Th.* 13.3.5), and Julian died on 26 June 363 (Penella 1990: 2). Thus Eunapius must have reached Athens in either 362 or 363, and was therefore born in 347 or 348. He left Athens just after his fourth year there, in either 366 or 367. Since his history covers the period up to the year 404, he must have lived at least until then.

Eunapius was an accomplished sophist and, like many sophists, his interests extended also into philosophy and medicine. Chrysanthius, his instructor in philosophy, was a student of Aedesius, who in turn had been a student of one of the greatest Neoplatonic philosophers of the age, Iamblichus. When Chrysanthius was an old man, he requested the presence of Eunapius when doctors were performing a bloodletting upon him (*Lives* 504–5). Eunapius boasted on this occasion of his skill in medicine, and felt confident enough to interfere when he felt that the doctors were bleeding his mentor excessively. The physician Oribasius, a confidant of the emperor Julian, wrote four books on medicine dedicated to his friend Eunapius, whom he calls "philiatros," an amateur doctor. This extant work, the *Libri ad Eunapium*, is designed for an amateur doctor like Eunapius, who was knowledgeable enough to be unsatisfied with guides for laymen but aware that certain medical tasks are suitable only for a professional (Penella 1990: 6–7; Baldwin 1975).

Work

The ninth-century Byzantine patriarch Photius describes the history of Eunapius in his *Bibliotheca* (*cod.* 77). Most of our fragments of the work are derived from two tenth-century collections of excerpts from historians prepared under the emperor Constantine Porphyrogenitus, the *Excerpta de Sententiis* and the *Excerpta de Legationibus*. Fragments have also been garnered from entries in the tenth-century Byzantine encyclopedia called the *Suda*. In addition, much of the central narrative of the historian Zosimus, who wrote at the turn of the sixth century, clearly derives from Eunapius (on this question see Paschoud 1985b: 244–53; Ridley 1969/70; Blockley 1980b, 1983: 97–8). Photius tells us (*cod.* 98) that Zosimus "did not write a history, but rather copied out Eunapius." A comparison of the fragments of Eunapius with the narrative of Zosimus suggests that Photius should be taken at his word, although differences between the two arise from Zosimus' compression of fourteen books of Eunapius into about four of his own. (Zosimus 1.47 or 1.48 to 5.25 covers the same ground as Eunapius' history.) When Zosimus ceases to use Eunapius as a source and begins to use Olympiodorus, he changes his method of dating and he shows a striking change in attitude toward Stilicho. Zosimus' ability to present such contradictory positions increases our confidence that he is faithfully recording his sources, rather than substituting his own judgements. Nevertheless, he does make errors in his use of Eunapius, and sometimes presents different opinions and emphases. Other historians who used or may have used Eunapius are surveyed by Blockley (1983: 97–100). None is a significant source of information for our knowledge of the historian.

Photius tells us that the history of Eunapius was published in two editions. He differentiates between the two by claiming that the first was filled with anti-Christian diatribes, which were partially removed from the second, and that the second was difficult to read because of the gaps left by the removal of passages from the text. The nature of the first edition of the *History* has generated considerable scholarly debate (Chalmers 1953; Blockley 1971, 1981: 2–5; Barnes 1978: 114–23; Paschoud 1980b, 1985b; Baldini 1984: 75–117). In the *Lives of the Sophists*, Eunapius refers often to his history (seventeen examples are collected in Paschoud 1985b: 254–6). Since the *Lives* was composed in 399, and the historical fragments we possess extend to 404, we must have the second edition of the history. The references in the *Lives*, however, must be to the first edition.

How far advanced was the first edition of the history when Eunapius wrote the *Lives*? *Lives* 480 makes it clear that Eunapius had discussed the death of Valens at Adrianople (in 378). Two passages suggest that the history stretched to a later date. At *Lives* 472, Eunapius discusses the contemptible behavior of the monks responsible for the destruction of the Serapeum in 391. He adds that he had given information "concerning these things" in his *History*. The natural interpretation of these words would be "concerning the destruction of the Serapeum," but Barnes suggests that the phrase could also be interpreted simply as "concerning bad behavior of this sort" (1978: 116). At *Lives* 476, Eunapius discusses the disasters that struck Greece, which had been prophesied by a priest at Eleusis. He claims that some of these disasters he has already treated in his *History*, while others he hopes to return to when he continues the work. This latter category includes the invasion of

Greece by Alaric in 395/6, and thus the *History* must not have advanced to that point by the time of the writing of the *Lives*. The earlier disasters, included in the first edition of the history, may have occurred in the 370s (Blockley 1981: 4; Barnes 1978: 116) or might include the anti-pagan measures of Theodosius after 392 (Paschoud 1980b: 150–2). No definite conclusion is possible, but the natural reading of Eunapius' words suggests that the first edition was complete before 396 but after 391, perhaps extending to the death of Theodosius in January 395. If this date is accepted, it would mean that Eunapius published his *History* in 395, spent four years at work on the *Lives*, which he published in 399, and then returned to the *History* to correct, extend, and publish it after 404. Some claim that Ammianus was dependent upon Eunapius for part of his narrative of the Persian war, which would require that Eunapius' work was available to Ammianus before the publication of his work in 391. But even if this dependence is accepted, it could be explained by assuming that Eunapius published his work in stages, allowing Ammianus access to the earlier parts of the history in time for his own (Blockley 1981: 4).

Fragment 41 is sometimes scrutinized as evidence for understanding the differences between the first and second editions of the history. It has been argued that Eunapius claims in this fragment that, in the first edition, he had only presented information about the origins of the Huns which he derived from ancient writers. In the second edition, however, he has added more accurate oral information which he has recently received. In fact, no reference to the different editions is implied in this fragment. Eunapius simply states that he will juxtapose the less accurate account derived from literature with the more accurate account he has received orally, and provides several verbose and tiresome explanations for the presence of this contradictory material. Eunapius intends only to contrast oral and written information (Blockley 1983: 140 n. 90). Zosimus 4.20.3–4 summarizes Eunapius' findings: Herodotus said that the Huns came from the Danube, but it also has been claimed, presumably more recently, that they came from Asia.

Photius (*cod.* 77) provides a few pieces of information of debatable reliability about the *New History*. He tells us that the work was divided into fourteen books, and that it began with the reign of the emperor Claudius II at the point where the history of Dexippus had ended. He adds that it concluded with the expulsion of the bishop John Chrysostom and the death of Eudoxia, the wife of the emperor Arcadius. These events correspond to the dates 270 and 404.

Photius adds that Eunapius was a pagan who filled his work with vituperation of Christian emperors, particularly Constantine, and with praise of Julian. He judges his style to be elegant, although a bit too rhetorical for history, and marred by occasionally excessive use of neologisms and figures of speech.

The history of Dexippus, which Eunapius continued, covered all of history from mythical times to Claudius II in twelve books (Millar 1969; Blockley 1971; Buck 1987). Eunapius begins his own history with a long reflection on his predecessor's work (*fr.* 1). He praises the beauty of Dexippus' preface, the detail he provides in the body of the work, and his use of many sources. Dexippus' intricate chronology, however, he rejects. It appears that Dexippus' history was organized in an annalistic (year-by-year) fashion, and that he attempted, with varying success, to reconcile several different chronological traditions. Eunapius quotes Dexippus himself as saying that his chronological method had resulted in a work full of errors and contradictions. Eunapius also criticizes the irrelevance of certain details which Dexippus had incorporated, such as the birth years of poets and playwrights. "What do dates contribute to the wisdom of Socrates?" he asks. He emphasizes that, although his work may pick up where Dexippus' left off, it will be a very different kind of work in its style and organization. Instead of dating by days or years, which he considers unimportant, he plans to date by the reigns of emperors. Other writers are free to worry about the trivialities of exact dating. The kind of arrangement Eunapius used in organizing his history by emperor can be seen in fragment 20.1, where he states that, having completed his description of events which took place in the early career of Julian, he will now turn to the acts which Constantius II undertook at the same time, despite the repetition that this will entail.

Eunapius declares that detailed chronology distracts the reader from the true goal of history, the portrayal of moral models for the reader to follow or to shun. Concern for dates is proper for accountants and astrologers, he suggests, but not for his audience of well-educated sophists (Breebaart 1979). Of course, other, less lofty reasons for this contempt for chronology can be suggested. Eunapius' lack of competence in dealing with dates is demonstrated by the following example. To support his contention that it is impossible and useless to determine chronology by the year and the day, he bizarrely refers in the first fragment to a specific dispute discussed by Thucydides (4.122). Thucydides writes that two days after the Athenians and Spartans had signed a peace treaty, the city of Scione had revolted against Athens, but that the Spartans had claimed falsely that this revolt had occurred before the treaty, not after. Eunapius asserts that Thucydides' uncertainty about the date of the revolt proves the futility of chronology, but in reality Thucydides is perfectly clear about the date and expresses no uncertainty at all (Paschoud 1989a: 205). Eunapius' disdain for chronology may further be attributed to his desire to manipulate the order of events in order to make polemical points. Paschoud lists three significant errors of chronology in the Eunapian section of Zosimus. Zosimus erroneously states that Constantine converted to Christianity after putting his wife and son to death, that Gratian refused the title of *pontifex maximus* at the start of his reign, and that Theodosius abolished pagan rites after his defeat of Eugenius (1989a: 210). All three of these "errors" further Eunapius' anti-Christian polemic, and all three would be revealed as false if they were dated by year rather than by reign.

The first fragment served as a preface to the entire work, not just to the first book, since it states that the work will reach its climax in its description of the reign of Julian. Fragment 15 provides something of a second preface, which allows us to understand better Eunapius' plan and purpose. He describes the earlier part of the history as a summary which concentrated only on important events, and states that he will now turn to a discussion of Julian, his main purpose from the beginning. The first book, then, was an epitome of events from 270 to 355, the year in which Julian became Caesar. Blockley offers a speculative outline of how the rest of the material of the history may have been organized: perhaps four books on Julian, three on Valentinian and Valens, and six more to the conclusion of the work in 404 (1981: 8).

The first books of Eunapius' *History* cover many of the same events discussed in Ammianus' *Res Gestae*, though with a stronger and more explicit anti-Christian bias. The *Suda* reports that Eunapius was very negative in his judgement of Constantine. His account of Julian is perhaps even more laudatory than that of Ammianus, and he claims that the emperor was worshipped as a divinity by all (*fr.* 1; cf. *frs.* 15, 17, 28). Eunapius' condemnation of Jovian's settlement with the Persians (*fr.* 29) lessens Julian's culpability for the failure of his campaign. He also accuses Jovian, a Christian, of burning a temple and library dedicated to the emperor Trajan.

Eunapius' judgements on other historical figures often correlate with their religious beliefs. The staunchly Christian Theodosius is harshly criticized (*fr.* 46), whereas the general Fravitta, who worshipped the old Greek divinities, is idealized (*frs.* 59, 69). He blames the destruction of the Serapeum and the cults of the gods at Alexandria on the swinish behavior of monks (*fr.* 56), and his description of barbarians who sneaked into Roman territory dressed as monks (*fr.* 48.2) may be seen as a comment on the dangers of Christianity. Eunapius' anti-Christian bias does not completely overwhelm his historical judgement, however. He did not blame Christians for the death of Julian (*fr.* 28.1), and his criticisms of tyrannical behavior and bureaucratic corruption are not solely aimed at Christians (Sacks 1986).

Blockley (1980b) suggests that the name Eudoxia should be substituted for the manuscript reading of Pulcheria in fragment 72, an emendation which makes sense out of the concluding fragments of Eunapius and supports Photius' claim that 404 was the last year of the history. The work probably concluded with broad criticism of the empress Eudoxia, the wife of Arcadius. Eudoxia was perhaps blamed for the political strife between east and west because of her patronage of the treasury official John, with whom she was reputed to have had a sexual affair. She would also have been held responsible for the turmoil at Constantinople which arose from her conflict with John Chrysostom, and would have been condemned for the general corruption associated with her court. Her early death from miscarriage on 6 October could have been portrayed as an appropriate expression of divine will (Blockley 1981: 5–6).

Eunapius writes his history with the traditional moral purpose of providing historical figures for emulation or rejection. He relies upon the classical view of character as a fixed quality which may be revealed in actions but does not change. He asks, rhetorically, in his rejection of careful chronology, if Socrates or Themistocles were more or less virtuous in the summer than in the winter (*fr.* 1). When he criticizes Gratian for incompetence, Eunapius adds that, if the young man had had true greatness of soul, this greatness would have allowed him to overcome the deleterious effects of a childhood spent in the palace (*fr.* 50). This view of character adds to the shrillness Eunapius displays when he describes his subjects, who tend to be portrayed as either wholly depraved or wholly virtuous.

Evidence of Eunapius' sophistic profession and interests is visible throughout his *History*. He was encouraged to write by his famous and learned friends, who offered their support (*fr.* 15). He suggests that he had to take up the task of writing about the deeds of Julian because they had been previously described by those without sufficient rhetorical skills (*fr.* 15). His faith in traditional education is apparent when he claims that a literary education is valuable in choosing appropriate tactics on the battlefield (*fr.* 44.1). Eunapius' sophistic approach to history reveals itself in his dismissal of chronology and apparent lack of concern for details, accurate numbers, and accurate geography (Blockley 1981: 15). Also typical of sophistic style are Eunapius' frequent use of quotations and citations of earlier authors, of *exempla*, and of speeches (Blockley 1981: 11–13). He quotes Plato (*fr.* 30), Homer (*fr.* 39.1), and Pindar (*fr.* 66.2), among other great Greeks of antiquity. He even quotes a (now unknown) comic writer, who wrote that "the possessions of an ex-magistrate are public property," and follows the quote with the threat that "the one who is ignorant of who this writer is, is unworthy to read this history"! (*fr.* 72). In keeping with the moralizing purpose of the history, Eunapius frequently speaks proverbially, as in his comment on Valens' punishment of the associates of the usurper Procopius: "it is godlike to spare even the guilty, but it is human to condemn even the innocent" (*fr.* 34.9; cf. 23.3, 23.4). Only one full-scale speech survives in the fragments, but we are dependent on summaries, and the work probably contained many more. This exchange between Julian and a leader of the barbarian Chamavi concludes with the barbarian prostrated before the emperor, "thinking he was some sort of god because of his words" (*fr.* 18.6).

The style of Eunapius' *History* appears to be similar to the style that he used in his *Lives* (Giangrande 1956; Baldwin 1990). He frequently uses rare, archaic, and poetic forms, and is fond of periphrasis and excessive use of the superlative. His use of neuter substantives is reminiscent of Thucydides and of late Greek philosophy. In general, his style does not appeal to modern tastes, and his writing appears contrived and hyperbolic. Blockley points to the most grotesque simile of the extant fragments (Blockley 1981: 14), where the winning over of the barbarian chief Charietto is likened to the movement of the Pythagorean monad toward the dyad (*fr.* 18).

Eunapius claims, unhelpfully, that the sources for his early books were unspecified writings and oral traditions (*fr.* 30). The historian's sophistic friends who encouraged him to write may also have provided him with material. Sophists appear in the historical fragments and some, such as Libanius, who were discussed in the *Lives*, are also discussed in the *History* (Penella 1990: 13–16). One such sophist, his friend Oribasius, presented him with written information about the career of Julian, whom Oribasius served as doctor and advisor (*fr.* 15). Eunapius was also familiar with the works of Julian himself. At one point he declines to narrate the details of a battle in deference to Julian's already existing account (*fr.* 17), and elsewhere he makes reference to the emperor's letters (*frs.* 23.2, 27.1, 28.5). Fragment 66.2 explains the difficulties involved in obtaining information during the struggles between Stilicho in the west and Eutropius in the east and provides a bit more insight into Eunapius' method, although it mostly consists of historiographical commonplaces. It appears that Eunapius is arguing that contemporary histories of the events he recounts were flawed, both by partisanship and by the difficulty of gathering information, but that his own account will be accurate, thanks to the passage of time and his own zeal for the truth. He explains that during the time of the eunuch Eutropius it was difficult to learn about events in the west, since information was often out of date because of the length of the sea voyage, soldiers and administrators were biased, and merchants were driven by profit, rather than truth.

Although the work of Eunapius was the only full-scale narrative source in Greek for the events of the fourth century, its anti-Christian tone and the fact that it was summarized by Zosimus probably contributed to its disappearance. Eunapius sought to create a work for his readers' moral edification and his own rhetorical display. His history was less valuable than others since he was removed from the centers of power where a historian could gain reliable and important information, a weakness which he occasionally admits (e.g. *fr.* 50). The loss of most of the history is thus regrettable less for its historical detail, although it would have provided a welcome check on the narrative of Ammianus, than for the insight it provides into the historical vision of a committed Hellene and supporter of Julian in an age when this vision was being suppressed.

Text and translation

Greek text and translation by R.C. Blockley (1983), *The Fragmentary Classicising Historians of the Later Roman Empire II*.

6

OLYMPIODORUS

Life

Details of the life of Olympiodorus must be drawn almost exclusively from the fragments of his work, but fortunately he spends considerable time digressing upon his own adventures. Although he writes in Greek, he is in some ways reminiscent of Ammianus, another Greek imperial official who provides a detailed narrative of near-contemporary political history. Olympiodorus was born around 380 in Egyptian Thebes. Our primary source of information about the historian is the summary written by the ninth-century Byzantine patriarch Photius, who describes him as a poet by profession. One verse of his, which he inserted into his history, survives (*fr.* 41.1). Because Olympiodorus had spent time with the people of upper Egypt known as the Blemmyes, he has been credited, probably incorrectly, with the authorship of the "Blemyomachia," an epic poem recently discovered on a papyrus fragment (Livrea 1978; Clover 1983: 153–6).

Olympiodorus was a Greek who knew Latin well. Although he writes for a Greek audience in the eastern Roman empire, he incorporates an unprecedented amount of transliterated Latin. Olympiodorus was also a pagan, as were many of the literary-minded administrators of late antiquity. Hierocles, a teacher and Neoplatonist, dedicated his (extant) philosophical work *On Providence* to the historian. Several fragments reveal Olympiodorus' belief in magic and in the traditional gods, such as *fr.* 36, which describes how the empress Galla Placidia foolishly rejected the help of the magician Libanius, although he had previously demonstrated his ability to defeat barbarian invaders with the occult arts (Blockley 1981: 38–40). Olympiodorus seems, however, to have refrained from the kind of anti-Christian rhetoric which we find in Eunapius, among others.

The friends and associates whom Olympiodorus mentions further situate him in the literary-administrative class. He received some information about magical statues from Valerius, the governor of Thrace (*fr.* 27). He was involved in the installation of the professor Leontius in a sophistic chair at Athens (*fr.* 28); the daughter of this Leontius would grow to become the empress Eudocia. Another friend, Philtatius, was a philologist whom the Athenians honored with a statue (*fr.* 31). His numerous digressions seem designed to parade his learning. For example, in a discussion of Egypt he makes reference not only to the famous historian Herodotus, but also to the obscure poet Herodorus (*fr.* 32).

Olympiodorus was well traveled and discussed a number of his journeys, including several accounts of the dangers he faced at sea (*frs.* 19, 35.1). Around 412, he went on an embassy to meet a certain Donatus, the leader of a group of Huns. In the course of the meeting Donatus was deceived and killed. This angered a more powerful Hunnic king, Charaton, but Olympiodorus managed to placate him with gifts (*fr.* 19). Although it has been suggested that Olympiodorus' mission was from the beginning one of assassination (Cameron 1965: 497; Matthews 1970: 80), it seems unlikely, if this were the case, that the historian would have described the murder as taking place "unlawfully" as the result of the breaking of an oath.

Olympiodorus' next attested journey was in 415 or 416, when he had the aforementioned Leontius appointed against his will to a sophistic chair at Athens. Olympiodorus may have undertaken this mission under imperial orders. His trip to Egypt was the source of a digression on the region called the "Oasis," which he claimed had been an island at one time. One of his pieces of evidence for this claim reveals that he had visited it personally, for he had seen sea shells in the area that now was desert but had once been sea (*fr.* 32). He also traveled "for the purpose of research (*historias*)" in remote parts of the Thebaid in Upper Egypt inhabited by the Blemmyes (*fr.* 35). Whether this research was undertaken for his history or as part of official business is unknowable. The Blemmyes allowed him access to their cities, but he regretted that he was unable to visit their emerald mines in the region. Photius says, simply, that the historian was invited by the Blemmyes because of his "reputation." This might refer to his poetic reputation or, more likely, to his governmental position and influence.

Perhaps it was on this trip to Egypt that Olympiodorus again ran into trouble at sea, and barely escaped death, when what he described as a "star" hit the mast of the ship (*fr.* 35). While

Olympiodorus survived, his parrot, a companion for twenty years, may not have. This parrot, he claims, was a gifted mimic, which would dance, sing, and call people by name.

Olympiodorus' discussion, at the end of the work, of the immensity of the buildings in the city of Rome and the enormous incomes of the Roman nobility suggests that he had traveled to the west (*fr.* 41). In conjunction with this western visit he may have inserted the digression on the wanderings of Odysseus, which he claims took place along the coast of Italy (*fr.* 42). The western bias of some of his sources is further evidence of this visit. If he traveled to Rome on official business, he may have been involved in suppressing the usurpation of John (Baldwin 1980a: 217–18), or he may have assisted with the restoration of the emperor Valentinian III under the auspices of the eastern emperor Theodosius II (Matthews 1970: 80). It is likely that he attended, and he may have been involved in, Valentinian's coronation, the dramatic event with which Olympiodorus concluded the history.

Work

Olympiodorus' work, though Greek, is almost entirely concerned with events in the western half of the empire. The *History* (or, more properly, the *hyle historias*, the *Material for History*) of Olympiodorus survives only in paraphrase and summary. Photius preserved in his *Bibliotheca* a description of the work in around forty paragraphs (*cod.* 80). Olympiodorus is also the source of the last part of the *New History* of Zosimus, which was written at the turn of the fifth century. The lack of innovation in Zosimus' work fortunately preserves for us a fairly close approximation of whatever source he is dependent upon. While Zosimus is following the work of Eunapius, which extended to 404, he describes eastern events, he is vague and imprecise, and he is hostile to the western warlord Stilicho. Zosimus turned to Olympiodorus for the years 407 to 410, which are covered in chapters 5.26 to 6.13 of the *New History*. Here he emphasizes western events, is precise and accurate, and becomes a partisan of Stilicho, all characteristics of the Photian summary of Olympiodorus (Matthews 1970: 81–2).

Olympiodorus is also the main source for the section of the *Church History* of Sozomen which runs from 9.4 until its conclusion. At this transition point, not only are western events suddenly emphasized to the exclusion of eastern events, but the subject matter itself largely shifts from ecclesiastical to secular history.

Whether the *Church History* of Philostorgius shows dependence upon Olympiodorus is less clear. Philostorgius, like Olympiodorus, is only extant in a paraphrase of Photius, and if he did use Olympiodorus' work, it was just one of several of his sources for the period (Baldwin 1980a: 228–9; Gillett 1992: 3–6).

Olympiodorus' work must have been published after 425, the date of the coronation of Valentinian III which concluded the work, and before the death in 450 of Theodosius II, to whom, Photius says, the work was dedicated. Sozomen, who must postdate Olympiodorus, published in the late 440s. The church historian Socrates, who published in 439, did not make use of Olympiodorus, and perhaps this suggests that the work was not yet available to him (Gillett 1992: 4–6). Thus we can conclude that the history was probably published sometime in the 440s.

Olympiodorus was connected to the empress Aelia Eudocia through her father Leontius. Eudocia, though not a pagan, was a patron of the kind of Hellenized literature which Olympiodorus produced, as was her protégé, Cyrus of Panopolis (Cameron 1982). Although Olympiodorus was in government service prior to the rise to power of Cyrus and Eudocia, the atmosphere they fostered until they were forced to leave Constantinople in 441 would have been particularly congenial to him. Gillett comments that the work seems to celebrate the growing closeness of the eastern and western empires under the guidance of Theodosius II. Following the installation of Valentinian III in 425, the east and west had continued to work together, both on the compilation of the Theodosian Code and with the dynastic marriage of Eudoxia, the daughter of Theodosius II, to Valentinian III. Olympiodorus' work, by tracing the evolution of the relationship between east and west from alienation to cooperation, may be in part understood as an argument in favor of the continuation of such cooperation in the face of new threats, such as the rise of Vandal power in Africa (Gillett 1992).

Photius states that Olympiodorus' history began in the year 407, although it seems that information on the earlier career of Stilicho was included, possibly as part of the preface which Photius says adorned the beginning of each book (Blockley 1981: 30). In fact, since the first consular date noted in Zosimus is 408, the year of Stilicho's death, rather than 407, the work may have officially begun in that year (Paschoud 1985a). In any case it is clear that Olympiodorus did not intend to formally continue the history of Eunapius, which concluded in 404.

Olympiodorus' history was divided into twenty-two books. Photius' comment that Olympiodorus' account of the embassy to the Huns was the conclusion of the first ten-book section implies that the work was further divided between the first ten books and the subsequent twelve. The first part may have been published separately from the second part, and some have noted differences in, for example, the length and ordering of the earlier fragments, but there is no firm evidence (Zuccali 1993; Blockley 1981: 33). If the history was divided into books equal in length to those in Ammianus, it would have been around 900 pages long, which emphasizes the severe compression of Photius' compilation, and even of Zosimus'.

The work was arranged in broadly chronological order, and used consular dating to help guide the reader, although Photius complains that it was "loosely organized." Italy was the central focus of the history, with events in Gaul and Spain treated in digressions (Matthews 1970: 87).

Olympiodorus begins the main narrative of his work with the death of Stilicho, the generalissimo and guardian of the emperor Honorius, and describes the series of tragedies which befell the west thereafter. The first ten books are accordingly filled with disasters. The failure of Rome to successfully negotiate with Alaric leads to three sieges of the city, to the reduction of the Romans to cannibalism, and finally to the sacking of the city in 410. Alaric is succeeded by his brother Ataulf after his sudden death, and chaos throughout the west leads to the rise of numerous usurpers in Gaul and in Spain. The tenth book ends with Olympiodorus' embassy to the Huns, perhaps with the message that negotiation is preferable to the use of force (Zuccali 1993: 254).

The second half of the work describes the gradual improvement, in fits and starts, of western affairs. It begins in 412, when Ataulf made an alliance with the emperor Honorius and suppressed the usurper Sebastian. The marriage of Ataulf to the princess Galla Placidia further cements the Roman–Gothic alliance. The work ends in 425 with an encomium of the city of Rome and a description of the extraordinary wealth of its inhabitants, which emphasizes how strongly the Romans had rebounded from the destruction fifteen years earlier. Valentinian III was installed as western emperor with military help from the east. It is a satisfying ending in literary terms, tracing the fall and then rise of the city of Rome, carrying with it a political message which emphasizes the necessity of eastern help and eastern supremacy to ensure order in the west.

Photius tells us that Olympiodorus considered his work a *hyle*, or "material," for history, rather than a history itself, and he criticizes its vulgarity and emptiness. Byzantine notions of high style, however, do not correspond with ours, and a charitable interpretation of Photius' comments might suggest that he recoils at exactly those features which moderns find so useful and admirable in Olympiodorus' work, such as his frequent use of numbers and his careful attention to geography. The level of style may have been elevated in the prefaces which Photius says began each of the twenty-two books. Whether the work contained speeches is not known, but the surviving fragments show no evidence of any.

Of the forty-six Photian fragments, twelve are digressions: linguistic, ethnographic, geographic, and others. This would suggest that roughly a fourth of the work was digressive, a percentage even higher than that of Ammianus' *Res Gestae*. This, perhaps, was another feature of the history which brought the stylistic criticism of Photius upon it. Since the digressions often deal with eastern events, Blockley suggests that they were not well integrated into the narrative. They were, rather, used to mark transitions between major events (Blockley 1981: 35–6).

The digressions contain much of interest. Olympiodorus explains that Alaric was unable to cross from Rhegium to Sicily due to a magic statue which warded him off. He claims that the statue was set up in antiquity in order to protect against the fires of Mount Etna and to prevent barbarians from crossing the sea. As predicted, its removal led to volcanic eruption and invasion (*fr.* 16). He describes the sophistic cloak, a garment which could be worn at Athens by would-be scholars only with the permission of the sophists and after the completion of the following ritual. The candidates were brought before the baths and shoved forward by their teachers. Another team of men tried to block the candidates, forcing them away from the baths and shouting, "Stop, stop, don't take the bath!" After this ritual, successful candidates entered the baths, washed, and then exited wearing their cloak, escorted by community leaders (*fr.* 28). Olympiodorus also describes the immensity of Rome and its buildings, particularly the public baths and the great private homes, which contained within their walls everything one might find in a medium-size city (*fr.* 41.1). Olympiodorus' description of Rome was probably presented at a higher stylistic level than other parts of the work, and the historian was even moved to include a piece of poetry in the digression. The description of his dangerous sea voyage (*fr.* 19) to the Huns may have aimed at pathos, as Photius claims that the historian *ektragoidei*, "declaimed tragically." The details Photius provides of the wedding of Ataulf and Galla Placidia suggests that it was an elaborate set-piece, with descriptions of the location, the clothes that each wore, the wedding gifts (among other things, Ataulf presented her with jewels and gold which had been looted during the sack of Rome), and the celebration of Romans and barbarians after the nuptials (*fr.* 24).

Olympiodorus showed a particular interest in geography (Thompson 1944: 45, 49–50). Insofar as he refers to earlier authors, it is usually to make a geographical point. For example, his digression on the Oasis (*fr.* 32) cites Herodotus and Herodorus, and in addition he claims that Homer had been born in the Thebaid. He presents a lengthy argument on the location of the wanderings of Odysseus (*fr.* 42), and on the founding of the city of Emona by the Argonauts (at Zos. 5.29.1–3), information which he derived from the obscure poet Pisander. He also quotes the third-century historian Asinius Quadratus on the founding of Ravenna (at Zos. 5.27.1–2) and the geographer Ammon on the length of the walls surrounding the city of Rome (*fr.* 41.1). A large amount of geographic information can be found among the fragments, but it is difficult to determine the degree of accuracy that Olympiodorus' account possessed before its severe compression by Photius, Zosimus, and Sozomen.

The geographical information often comes with exact figures (e.g. *frs.* 17, 26.1; Zos. 5.48.2), and Olympiodorus also provides numbers at other junctures. The size of armies, the number of seats in the Roman baths, and various sums of money are given in what appear to be fairly reliable figures. A famous fragment of his work provides numerical information on the finances of the Roman elite (*fr.* 41). For example, he reveals that Probus spent twelve hundred pounds of gold celebrating his praetorship, whereas Symmachus spent two thousand pounds of gold in celebration of his son's praetorship. The amount of quantification in Olympiodorus' history was probably greater than in any historian of antiquity. On the other hand, Olympiodorus' passion for numbers is great only in comparison to other ancient historians, and the accuracy of his figures should not be overestimated (Maenchen-Helfen 1973: 459).

Another oddity of Olympiodoran style is his frequent use of transliterated Latin (Matthews 1970: 85–7). This is most common in his use of the Latin names of political and bureaucratic offices, and he also often uses the Latin names for provinces of the empire. In addition, Olympiodorus provides weights and measurements in

Latin, as well as certain phrases, quotes, and inscriptions which he transliterates in their entirety. Sozomen and Zosimus generally translated Olympiodorus' Latinisms with the Greek equivalent, but Olympiodorus' intended audience must have been the "Latinized" administrators and courtiers who had no need of translation.

Even through the paraphrase one can glimpse some of Olympiodorus' deft characterizations. Consider his memorable sketch of the general Constantius III: "In public processions Constantius was downcast and sullen, a man with bulging eyes, a long neck and a broad head, who always slumped over the neck of the horse he was riding, darting glances here and there out of the corners of his eyes, so that all saw in him 'a mien worthy of a tyrant,' as the saying goes. But at banquets and parties he was so cheerful and affable that he even competed with the clowns who often played before his table" (trans. Blockley 1983: 187; *fr.* 23). Olympiodorus favors the general Boniface, whose love of justice he demonstrated through the following anecdote. A soldier complained to Boniface that his wife was having an affair with a barbarian ally. That very evening the commander rode almost ten miles to the site of the adultery, removed the barbarian's head from his body with his sword, and rode back, presenting the soldier with his rival's head on the following day. The soldier was understandably stunned into silence, but Olympiodorus assures us that later he was filled with thanks (*fr.* 40).

The historian spoke favorably of Stilicho, pointing to the many wars he won on behalf of the Romans (*fr.* 3) and defending him against the charge that he plotted against the eastern emperor (Soz. 9.4). He is, therefore, hostile toward Stilicho's enemy Olympius (*fr.* 5). Olympiodorus was also critical of the ineffectual emperor Honorius, and goes beyond faulting his poor policy decisions to complain that his frequent kissing on the mouth of his sister Galla Placidia gave rise to unsavory suspicions (*fr.* 38). Olympiodorus criticized Placidia further in blaming the turn of Constantius from virtue to avarice on her influence (*fr.* 37).

Olympiodorus' assessment of some of these figures is quite unusual for a fifth-century historian. Stilicho claimed guardianship over both the eastern and the western emperor, which ensured continuing hostility toward him from the eastern court. Placidia, on the other hand, was a more popular figure in the east than in the west. The marriage of Placidia to Ataulf, which Olympiodorus described in a positive manner, was not well received in the east. It appears that Olympiodorus' western biases must reflect western sources for much of his history (Sirago 1970; Matthews 1970: 90–1).

Since there is no evidence of any other narrative history of the period, Olympiodorus presumably gathered much of the evidence firsthand while in the west, or from westerners who had made their way east. His role as an imperial official would have allowed him to gain access to those close to the principal actors of the time. Blockley (1981: 34–5) suggests that the soldier Candidianus, who was in Placidia's retinue and who received favorable treatment from the historian, may have been one of those sources. Olympiodorus also had access to documentary material, as is evident from his use of a *relatio* of the city prefect Albinus which describes the resettlement of Rome (*fr.* 25).

Olympiodorus is rightly considered one of the great historians of late antiquity, despite the fact that his work only survives in fragments (Thompson 1996: 11–12). His information seems to have come from knowledgeable sources. He provided the sort of detail which ancient historians often omit, but which modern historians appreciate, and the fragments do not reveal major bias or partisanship. The loss of his work is thus particularly unfortunate, and the early fifth century would be far better understood if his history had survived as a guide.

Text and translation

Greek text and translation by R.C. Blockley (1983), *The Fragmentary Classicising Historians of the Later Roman Empire II.*

7

PRISCUS

Life

The historian Priscus was from Panium in Thrace, as his entry in the Byzantine encyclopedia *Suda* informs us. The *Suda* also states that he lived during the reign of Theodosius II. Many sources describe him as a sophist or rhetor, and in addition to a history in eight books he is credited with "Rhetorical Exercises" and with letters, none of which survives.

Other information about Priscus' life must be derived from the surviving fragments of his history (Bornmann 1979: xi–xv; Blockley 1981: 48; Baldwin 1980b: 18–25). He gives a lengthy description of his participation in the embassy to Attila of 448/9 in fragments 11–14. If he were roughly 30 years old at the time of this embassy, he would have been born around 420. He was apparently at Rome in 450 (*fr.* 20.3), Egyptian Thebes in 451 or 452 (*fr.* 27), and Alexandria in 453 (*fr.* 28). He last appears in the extant fragments of his history as an advisor to the *magister officiorum* Euphemius in negotiations with Gobazes, leader of the Lazi, inhabitants of western Georgia (*fr.* 33.2). He must have lived at least into the 470s, since his history covers up to that point.

Priscus accompanied a friend, an imperial official with the common name Maximinus, on many of his travels. The Maximinus described in the fragments of Priscus seems to have pursued a military career, and thus we should agree with Blockley in rejecting the association of this Maximinus with the lawyer of that name who was on the commission to create the Theodosian Code (Blockley 1981: 48). This association had prompted the suggestion that Priscus served as an imperial lawyer or bureaucrat (Baldwin 1980b: 21), but given the extant evidence it is impossible and perhaps unnecessary to attach an official role of any kind to Priscus' involvement. He accompanied Maximinus to the camp of Attila only after being cajoled (*fr.* 11.2), which suggests an unofficial role, and although he may have served in some official capacity under the functionary Euphemius (*fr.* 33.2), the wording could suggest that he was simply an advisor or friend.

The fragments in which Priscus discusses his participation in the embassy to Attila are quite lengthy and provide us with many memorable pictures of the Huns as well as of the historian himself. Fragment 11 begins with the arrival of the Hun Edeco at Constantinople bearing letters from Attila. Attila was demanding territorial concessions along the Danube, the return of Hun fugitives, and a Roman embassy composed of high-ranking officials. The eunuch Chrysaphius, at that time the most powerful advisor to emperor Theodosius II, met with Edeco, and the eunuch offered him fifty pounds of gold to assassinate Attila. The Roman translator Vigilas was informed of the plot and was ordered to accompany Edeco and his retinue to meet with Attila. Maximinus, who was apparently unaware of the plot, was selected to join the delegation to Attila, and Maximinus convinced Priscus to come along.

Thirteen days of travel brought Edeco, Vigilas, Maximinus, Priscus, and the rest of the embassy to Serdica (modern-day Sofia in Bulgaria), where the men feasted and toasted both Theodosius II and Attila. When Vigilas, who had perhaps overindulged in wine, suggested to the Huns that it was improper to equate a god such as Theodosius with a man like Attila, tempers flared. Only the presentation of silk and jewels to the Huns smoothed things over.

The party arrived at Naissus, which had become a ghost town after its complete destruction by the Huns. Bones littered the river bank. Several more days through rough territory brought them to the Danube, which they crossed with the help of barbarian ferrymen. After further travel, the attendants of Edeco went to announce the arrival of the embassy to Attila.

At this point, however, the ambassadors were rebuffed. Hun leaders, including Edeco, Orestes, Scottas, and others, demanded to know the purpose of the embassy. The Romans refused to talk to anyone but Attila. The Huns then revealed that they had read the secret correspondence of Theodosius, and ordered the surprised Romans, who continued to insist upon a meeting with Attila, to depart immediately. It appears that Edeco had informed Attila of the assassination plot, but Vigilas was unaware that his cover had been blown. Maximinus and Priscus were mystified at what they saw as the inexplicable hostility of the Huns. The Romans packed their baggage and were ordered to leave in the morning.

The ambassadors discussed how they ought to react to this turn of events. Vigilas argued that they should claim to have new information to provide to Attila, in the hope, presumably, that the assassination plan could continue, while Maximinus was dejected and silent. Then Priscus, with the help of an interpreter, put his persuasive rhetorical skills to work. He offered the Hun Scottas gifts for his help and claimed that a meeting with Attila would benefit both Romans and Huns. Then he slyly added that although he had heard that Scottas was a powerful Hun leader, he would find it difficult to believe if Scottas was not able to arrange a meeting with Attila. This last challenge caused Scottas to leap on his horse and head for Attila's tent. Priscus returned to an overjoyed Maximinus and Vigilas, who unpacked the baggage and began to decide on the proper gifts and protocol for their meeting with Attila.

Maximinus addressed Attila politely when the embassy came before him, but the Hun did not respond in kind, instead showering angry abuse upon Vigilas. Attila demanded that Vigilas leave immediately and that Hunnic fugitives be handed over, and then he dismissed the embassy. The Romans marveled at the harshness of Attila. Priscus suggested that perhaps Attila had been made aware of Vigilas' earlier claim that Theodosius was a god but Attila a man. In reality the Hun leader must have been aware that Vigilas was implicated in the plot to assassinate him. In the midst of this confusion, Edeco pulled Vigilas aside and instructed him to bring the gold which was to be distributed to those involved in the planned assassination. Shortly thereafter, some of Attila's men ordered the Romans not to purchase anything until the embassy had been completed. This was a cunning trick to trap Vigilas with the gold and without a convincing rationale for his possessing it.

The embassy then traveled with the court of Attila as he set out to marry the daughter of an ally. Priscus describes the inhabitants of the villages they pass through. At one village, the Romans were frightened by a storm but succored by the (female) ruler, who offered them food and attractive women. The first was accepted, the second declined. The party also encountered a second Roman embassy, this one from the western court.

The travelers came to a village where Attila maintained a particularly large palace. The elegant wooden structure was near another set of wooden buildings which had been built by Onegesius, Attila's second-in-command. Onegesius had also had baths of stone constructed. The builder, a prisoner from Sirmium, had hoped to win his freedom in return for his service, but instead had been pressed into service as a bath attendant for Onegesius and his friends. The Romans dined at the compound of Onegesius with Attila's son and daughter-in-law, while Onegesius met with Attila in private. The next morning Priscus waited with gifts outside shut doors hoping to meet with Onegesius. Here Priscus tells us that he encountered a Greek in Hunnic dress who told the historian that after being taken captive by the Huns, he had won his freedom, but married a Hunnic wife and was now an attendant to Onegesius himself. The historicity of their conversation, a philosophical set-piece about the relative superiority of the Roman or Hunnic systems, is rather doubtful.

Priscus intercepted Onegesius as he exited his palace and convinced him to meet with Maximinus. Maximinus' attempt to have Onegesius come to Constantinople was rebuffed, but Onegesius invited Priscus to return to confer with him. On the next day, Priscus brought gifts to one of Attila's wives, Hereka, and then went to wait for Onegesius. Outside of Onegesius' house Priscus met members of the western embassy. They discussed the possibility of the Huns invading the Persian empire, and while Priscus prayed that Attila would turn his forces away from the Romans, the western ambassador Constantiolus worried that success in destroying the Persians would strengthen the Huns even further.

Priscus acted as an intermediary after Onegesius appeared (*fr.* 13). When asked which high-ranking officials would serve as ambassadors to Attila, Priscus consulted with Maximinus and told Onegesius that the emperor would send whomever he wanted. Maximinus was then led in to consult with Attila, who provided a list of men of consular rank with whom he would deign to meet. With business concluded for the day, the Romans were invited to a banquet. After the ceremonial drinking of wine, dinner was served. Priscus notes that Attila used only wooden tableware, while the others had plates and cups of silver, and that his sword and boots were plain, not adorned with jewels like that of the other Hunnic nobility. Attila also ate only meat, while the others indulged in fancy prepared dishes. Postprandial entertainment included the chanting of songs celebrating Attila's victories, a deranged Hun shouting unintelligibly, and Zercon, a hunchbacked Moor who amused the crowd with his appearance and his mixture of Latin, Hunnic, and Gothic speech. Attila alone was able to resist the general hilarity, softening only at the arrival of his young son Ernach. The celebration and drinking continued throughout the night, but Priscus and the Romans left early.

Onegesius drew up several letters for the Romans to bring to Theodosius upon their return, and the Romans managed to ransom a few of their compatriots. Several more days of Hunnic hospitality followed. The Romans dined at the invitation of Attila's wife the following evening, and with Attila again on the next. They were allowed to leave three days later accompanied by Berichus, a Hun in search of gifts from Theodosius. Berichus, who had begun the journey in a friendly mood, grew unfriendly after the party crossed the Danube and accused the Romans of unfairness toward barbarians. Attempts to mollify him were unsuccessful. The Romans also crossed paths with Vigilas, who was returning to the court of Attila intending to carry out the assassination. He was, in fact, walking into a trap, and after he was caught with the fifty pounds of gold, he would confess in response to threats against his son (*fr.* 15). The son was sent to retrieve another fifty pounds to ransom his father, and Attila sent ambassadors to Constantinople to demand the surrender of the eunuch Chrysaphius, who first conceived of the plot. But Priscus' role in these events apparently ended with his return to Constantinople.

This narrative of the extraordinary events surrounding the embassy to Attila is the centerpiece of the surviving fragments, and was probably the centerpiece of the whole work. The historian presents himself as curious and careful in his descriptions, and sensible and confident in his dealings with others. It is not surprising that Maximinus thought his presence would be beneficial.

The other fragments in which Priscus himself was involved are much briefer. Priscus states that "we" saw the younger son of the recently deceased Frankish king while in Rome (*fr.* 20.3). This suggests that he was in Rome with someone else, perhaps Maximinus, who was probably the courier for a letter (*ep.* 75) of Pope Leo, dated 9 November 450 and addressed to the clergy of Constantinople. Priscus and Maximinus next appear in Damascus in 451 or 452, where they found the general Ardabur in peace negotiations with the Saracens (*fr.* 26). From Syria they traveled to Thebes in Upper Egypt, where Maximinus worked out a treaty between the Romans and the defeated Blemmyes and Nubades (*fr.* 27). Shortly thereafter Maximinus fell ill and died (Zuckerman 1994: 176–9).

Priscus went from Thebes to Alexandria and there witnessed the major rioting in protest at the selection of the bishop Proterius (*fr.* 28). Rioters put troops to flight and burned them alive. Within a week, two thousand more troops had arrived and proceeded to abuse the wives and daughters of the Alexandrians. The governor, acting on Priscus' advice, put an end to the rioting by allowing the shows to continue and by restoring the payment of the regular dole. Priscus appears no further in the extant fragments, but these surviving examples demonstrate that he was an active participant in the events of his time.

It is not certain whether Priscus was a Christian or a pagan (Baldwin 1980b: 43–7; Blockley 1981: 59–60). As with other classicizing historians, it is difficult to ascribe the avoidance of Christian terminology to animus against Christianity rather than to desire to follow traditional style. The religion of his patron Maximinus has been described as pagan, because of his toleration of the Blemmyes' worship of Isis (*fr.* 27), but also as Christian, because of his relationship with Pope Leo (*ep.* 75). Neither argument is compelling, nor would Maximinus and Priscus necessarily share a religion. Priscus praises both pagans, like Cyrus of Panopolis (*fr.* 8) and Apollonius (*fr.* 23.3), and Christians, like the emperor Majorian, and religious belief does not seem to play much of a role in his approach to history.

Work

Most of our fragments of Priscus survive in the compilations made under the supervision of the Byzantine emperor Constantine VII Porphyrogenitus (913–59), the *Excerpta de Legationibus Romanorum ad gentes* (Excerpts of Roman Embassies to Foreigners) and the *Excerpta de Legationibus Gentium ad Romanos* (Excerpts of Foreign Embassies to the Romans). Photius does not mention Priscus, nor does the *Suda* depend explicitly upon his work in more than a few places. Priscus' history was influential in the centuries following its publication, and a number of later historians drew upon it either directly or through intermediaries. The extent of this influence, however, is difficult to discern. The *Getica*, or *Gothic History*, of Jordanes, written in the sixth century, draws upon Priscus, perhaps secondhand from the lost Gothic history of Cassiodorus. The sixth-century ecclesiastical historian Evagrius Scholasticus names Priscus as a source, and some of the fragments of the seventh-century chronicler John of Antioch rely on Priscus. These two authors may have gotten their Priscan material indirectly via the (lost) sixth-century chronicler Eustathius of Epiphania. Procopius, writing in the sixth century, also used Priscus as a source for his *Wars*. Finally, the anonymous author of the seventh-century *Paschal Chronicle*, the ninth-century chronicler Theophanes, and the fourteenth-century *Ecclesiastical History* of Nicephorus Callistus, all derive material from Priscus, again perhaps through the intermediary Eustathius (Blockley 1981: 113–18).

The title of Priscus' work is unknown. The *Exc. de Leg. Gent.* gives simply *History*, the *Exc. de Leg. Rom.* gives *Gothic History*, and the *Suda* provides both *Byzantine History* and *Events in the Time of Attila*. The title *Byzantine History* is anachronistic, and the *Suda* frequently gives the subjects of works rather than their actual titles, so these suggestions are unhelpful (Bornmann 1979: xiii). The Huns are occasionally referred to as Goths by classicizing historians, which perhaps explains the title *Gothic History*. No definitive conclusion is possible, but perhaps the simple title *History*, that is, personal investigation, fits the work best (Blockley 1981: 49).

The period covered by the history is also unclear. The earliest datable fragment (*fr.* 2) describes the death of the Hunnic king Rua and the succession by his sons Attila and Bleda. This took place perhaps in 433 or 434. The first fragment, which describes the entrance of the Huns into Europe, may have been part of a flashback introducing the Huns. Since Attila is the focus of the early fragments, this would be a reasonable place to begin. The last datable fragment which is definitely of Priscan origin describes the murder of the general Aspar in 471 (*fr.* 61). The work may have concluded with the death of Leo in 474. Another possible ending point would be the death of Anthemius in 472, which is supported by the fact that according to Photius (*cod.* 78), the historian Malchus, who may have continued the work of Priscus, began in the year 473 (Blockley 1981: 51).

Since even the title and the scope of the history are uncertain, it is unsurprising to discover that the structure of the work cannot be reconstructed with any confidence. The *Suda* tells us that the history was divided into eight books. About forty years of history in eight books provides an average of five years per book, but the majority of the surviving fragments concern Attila and come from the years 447–50. Blockley suggests that perhaps the first four books concluded with the death of Theodosius II in 450, that the fifth covered the reign of Marcian, and that the sixth, seventh, and eighth treated events during the reign of Leo (Blockley 1981: 49–50).

Priscus' treatment of two military figures, Basiliscus and Onoulphus, is central to determining the date of publication of the

History. Basiliscus was commander of an expedition against the Vandals in 468. After the failure of the campaign, he was accused of accepting bribes from the enemy and his life was spared only through the agency of his sister, the empress Verina. He later forced the emperor Zeno to flee, in 475, and reigned as emperor for a year and a half, until Zeno's return in August 476. Zeno then exiled Basiliscus and his family to Cappadocia, where they were imprisoned and starved to death. Priscus' critical comments on Basiliscus thus suggest a publication date after 476. The Hun Onoulphus served in the Roman military in the 470s and rose to the position of *magister militum per Illyricum* from 477 to 479. He is criticized by John of Antioch (*fr.* 209.1), and if this fragment is derived from Priscus, it suggests that Priscus published his work after 479, when Onoulphus no longer held a powerful office in the east (Blockley 1981: 49–50).

The *History* covered a period of western instability and of frequent foreign wars. Under Valentinian III in the west, Aetius became *magister militum* and held real power until his death in 454, shortly after the death of Attila in 453. After the death of Valentinian in 455, a series of puppet emperors were dominated by the general Ricimer until his death in 472. In the east, Theodosius II contended successfully with the Persians and less successfully with the Huns until his death in 450. The soldier Marcian, who succeeded him, married Theodosius' sister Pulcheria. His successor, Leo, took power in 457 with the support of the *magister militum* Aspar, who was assassinated in 470.

The fragmentary state of Priscus' history makes it quite difficult to determine his views on some of the significant actors of the period. The negative judgements in John of Antioch and the *Suda* on Theodosius II have usually been attributed to Priscus (*fr.* 3). A few other passages suggest that Priscus may not have attacked Theodosius directly but was clearly opposed to his policy of subsidies to Attila, which Priscus saw as cowardice (*frs.* 9.3, 15.2). This may explain his apparent support for the eunuch Chrysaphius in his attempt to assassinate Attila (*fr.* 15.3). Here, however, the evidence is mixed: John of Antioch is extremely critical of the eunuch, and Priscus' apparent praise may be ironic (cf. Blockley 1981: 64; Baldwin 1980b: 35; Thompson 1996: 222). Priscus appears to have supported Marcian (*fr.* 19), who withdrew subsidies from Attila and avoided retribution by the timely death of the Hun. No explicit Priscan judgements of Leo survive. The available fragments provide a fuller account of events in the east than in the west, but one western figure whom Priscus clearly disliked was Ricimer (*frs.* 36.2, 64).

Priscus presents some reflections on the empire under Theodosius II in the unusual extended set-piece he creates in the form of a debate between himself and a Greek who has defected to the Huns (*fr.* 11, lines 407–510; Blockley 1981: 55–9). The paired speeches begin with an allusion to Plato (*Phaedo* 227a), which signals to the reader that the following dialogue ought not be judged by the usual historical criteria. The Greek says that he had settled on the Danube as a merchant and had been enslaved when his city was taken by the Huns, but that he had since won his freedom by military service and lived happily as a dependant of Onegesius. He then proceeds to extol the superiority of Hunnic life to Roman life. Because Romans are forbidden by their rulers to carry weapons, he says, they must depend upon others for safety, and those Roman soldiers who do bear arms are put at risk by cowardly generals. In peacetime, Romans face heavy taxes and corrupt courts. Legal matters stretch on indefinitely, and the rich are always successful while the poor always lose.

Priscus replies "gently" to the Greek, with a response based on Platonic ideas. The founders of the empire, he claims, established that one class of men would be made soldiers who specialized in guardianship and could fight without fear. Another class of men would support these guardians through specialization in agricultural work. Still other men would serve as judges or advocates. Legal specialists ensure that judgements are paid off in order to prevent further litigation. If cases take an excessive amount of time, it is simply because of the importance of getting a just result, and for the Romans the law applies equally to everyone, including the emperor. Finally, Priscus points out that Romans treat their slaves better than the Huns do. The Romans treat slaves like children, are forbidden to put them to death, and frequently manumit them. The Huns, on the other hand, had required dangerous military service of the Greek in return for his freedom. The dialogue concludes when the Greek bursts into tears, agreeing with Priscus that the constitution of the Roman state is excellent but lamenting its corruption by rulers with contempt for tradition.

Priscus' reply has been condemned as weak and unconvincing; Gibbon denounced it as a "feeble and prolix declamation" (quoted in Baldwin 1980b: 40). Priscus may respond to the Greek's specific complaints with abstract constitutional theory, but he does address each of the complaints seriously, albeit not in a manner likely to gain much sympathy from modern readers. To the argument that mercenary armies are dangerous for citizens and cowardly in battle, Priscus responds that specialized training creates more fearless soldiers. To the complaint that taxation is too high, Priscus reminds the Greek that citizens without the need for military service are able to devote themselves fully to working the land and can thereby support those fighting on their behalf. The dialogue concludes with the unremarkable suggestion that Priscus' arguments about the excellence of the Roman system are well founded, but that poor leadership prevents the proper working of the system. It is noteworthy that several of the accusations leveled by the Greek, particularly about the cowardice of Roman generals and the oppressiveness of taxation, reappear in the mouths of others in other fragments. Blockley describes these accusations as examples of the indirect method of criticism favored by Priscus (1981: 58–9).

The exchanges between the Greek and Priscus are reported indirectly in the fragments, but may have been in direct speech in the *History* itself. It is to be expected that a sophist would have included other speeches in his work, but only traces survive in the fragments. Evidence for his use of formal digressions is also difficult to evaluate, but it appears that Priscus has primarily digressed to introduce various foreign peoples with whom the Romans and the Huns came into contact (Blockley 1981: 61–2).

Priscus' style is similar to that of other classicizing historians, and is neither as ornate as that of Eunapius nor as clotted with technical terminology as that of Olympiodorus (Baldwin 1980b: 50–3; Blockley 1981: 52–4). He avoids most, though not all, Latinisms, and uses technical terms inconsistently. He is also inconsistent in his use of ethnic names, as, for example, in his use of the terms "Hun" and "Scythian" interchangeably. There is little evidence of the use of numbers or of serious attention to chronology in the extant fragments.

Priscus frequently alludes to Herodotus and Thucydides (Bornmann 1974; Blockley 1981: 54–5). For example, distance is measured by reference to so many "days' journey for a well-girt man" (several times in *fr.* 11), a Herodotean usage. More significantly, in several places Priscus explains events with stories from Herodotus, such as his explanation of the movements of the "tribes of the northern Ocean" who were driven south by attacks of gryphons (*fr.* 40.2). This tale, it seems, was derived from a similar explanation of the movement of the Arimaspians in Herodotus 4.13. These Herodotean explanations seem to be confined to stories of people far from the borders of the Roman empire, for whom Priscus could find no reliable information. Priscus' borrowing from Thucydides is particularly evident in his account of the Huns' siege of Naissus (*fr.* 6.2), which is modeled on the famous account of the siege of Plataea (Thucydides 2.75–8) as well as on Dexippus' own imitation of Thucydides (*fr.* 27) (Thompson 1947b; Blockley 1972b; Baldwin 1980b: 53–6). Priscus' imitation of Thucydides here is primarily at the level of diction. For example, both remark that the defenders were sheltered by a screen "covered with skins and hides (*derreis kai diphteras*)." These allusions need not have corrupted Priscus' historical accuracy, and the details of the siege do differ markedly from the Thucydidean model. The Herodotean borrowings likewise seem to be used only in circumstances where distance in time and space would have made any story suspect. Such borrowings and allusions suggest a sophisticated audience who would be expected to recognize and appreciate the references.

Priscus makes no mention of other historians as sources for his own work, and most of his information must have been drawn from autopsy or from interviews. He was clearly well traveled and well connected, and thus would have had access to participants in the events he discussed. He must also have had some access to documents and archival information such as treaties (e.g. *fr.* 2).

Priscus' skillful and careful narration of the events as an eyewitness is the most striking and rewarding part of the extant fragments of his history. His work was probably at its best when he concentrated on the diplomatic and foreign affairs which he knew first hand through his association with Maximinus, Euphemius, and possibly others. The loss of his *History* is, of course, greatly to be regretted. The extant fragments, however, probably preserve many of the highlights, in particular the account of the embassy to Attila.

Text and translation

Greek text and translation by R.C. Blockley (1983), *The Fragmentary Classicising Historians of the Later Roman Empire II*.

8

RUFINUS

Life

Tyrannius Rufinus was not only the author of a very influential
Ecclesiastical History, but also an important translator, polemicist,
and monastic founder. Consequentially, we are richly informed
about his life, to such an extent that he is the subject of a full-
length biography which remains the authoritative account of his life
(Murphy 1945; also see Kelly 1975; Fedalto 1992). Rufinus became
enmeshed in controversy with the ever-irascible church father
Jerome, which spawned three polemic *Apologies* from Jerome and
two from Rufinus (to Pope Anastasius as well as to Jerome) and
which provide us with much biographical detail. We also have near-
contemporary comments on his life and works from the pen of
Gennadius of Marseilles, references to Rufinus in the *Lausiac History*
of Palladius, and evidence for Rufinus' activities in the correspondence of many of the church fathers, including Augustine and
Paulinus of Nola.

Rufinus was born in Concordia, a small town in northwest Italy.
He attended school with Jerome, but appears to have completed his
studies a little before him. Thus he is usually considered to have
been a year or two older than Jerome, which places his birth around
345. Palladius tells us that he was well born, which we would have
assumed in any case because of his high level of formal education
(Murphy 1945: 1–9).

The presence of the exiled Athanasius in the west in the middle
of the fourth century aroused interest in monasticism and in the
new experiments in communal living under way in the east. As a
young man, Rufinus became interested in these more serious and
ascetic forms of Christianity, and after his schooling he lived in a
community of like-minded Christians, including the bishop
Chromatius and his friend Jerome. He was baptized in either 369 or

370. When the group broke up, it was, for some, the beginning of a more monastic way of life. Jerome left for the desert of Syria, and Rufinus went to Alexandria (Murphy 1945: 21–31).

In Egypt he studied under the Christian teacher Didymus the Blind, and met with the many monks who lived in the desert. He was jailed during the persecution of homoousian (Nicene) Christians which broke out in the east at the instigation of Valens after the death of the homoousian champion Athanasius. It was in Egypt around this time that Rufinus met Antonia Melania the Elder (Murphy 1945: 32–58). Melania, born of a wealthy Roman aristocratic family, had dedicated herself to an ascetic Christian life. After traveling to Egypt, she toured the desert, and traveled from there to Palestine, accompanied by monks who had been exiled during the persecutions of Valens. A few years later Rufinus followed her there, and together they became the first westerners to establish a monastery in Palestine.

The monastery, on the Mount of Olives, operated a hostel for pilgrims. Melania supervised fifty virgins, and Rufinus oversaw a number of monks engaged in the copying of manuscripts. Both Melania and Rufinus spent much time studying both Christian and secular texts. Rufinus had studied the writing of the third-century church father Origen under the tutelage of Didymus, and he encouraged Melania also to explore Origen's works. Rufinus was ordained as a priest during this time.

Jerome, while in Antioch around 374, heard rumors that his old schoolmate and friend Rufinus was exploring the desert of Egypt, and the two corresponded in a friendly fashion. After the establishment of the monastery by Rufinus and Melania, and Jerome's departure from Rome in 385, Jerome came to visit and then to establish his own monastery with his protégé Paula in nearby Bethlehem. The two became friends, and Jerome and Paula's monastic foundation was based largely on Rufinus' model.

This friendship was not to last. While the proximate cause of their disagreement was a theological dispute, it is fair to say that the severity and length of the conflict can be attributed to Jerome's extreme contentiousness. Rufinus was far from the only friend or acquaintance of Jerome to find himself enmeshed in conflict with the brilliant theologian, whose frequent moves from city to city were in part the result of his tendency to alienate those around him. Jerome's enmity toward Rufinus lasted for decades, and he even continued to criticize Rufinus in savage terms after his death.

The two men split as part of the struggle over the legacy of the third-century Alexandrian theologian Origen. The extremely prolific Origen was a pioneer in translation, in exegesis, and in the application of Greek philosophical thought to Christianity (Crouzel 1998; Trigg 1998; Barnes 1981: 81–105). He was eagerly studied by many in the late fourth century, including both Rufinus and Jerome, but certain of his positions had come to seem heretical after a century of theological disputes. Among the most important were his Trinitarian views (he held that the Son was inferior to the Father, and the Holy Spirit to both) and his doctrines on the body and the Resurrection (he argued that souls were inserted into bodies at birth and departed at death, and that the resurrected would not be in their physical bodies).

In the mid-390s the bishop Epiphanius of Salamis came into conflict with the bishop John of Jerusalem. Epiphanius had been fanatically anti-Origenist for decades (Clark 1992: 86–104). To further his goal of purging the monasteries of Palestine of Origenists, he had sent a band of monks to Jerome and to Rufinus, demanding their abjuration of Origen, and while Jerome had readily complied, Rufinus had shut his gates and threatened the monks with a beating. Rufinus was close to John and defended the bishop against the accusations of Epiphanius. Jerome, on the other hand, was friendly with Epiphanius. Conflict increased after Epiphanius ordained Jerome's brother, Paulinian, thereby trespassing on John's jurisdiction as bishop. A widely circulated letter of Epiphanius accused John of being a follower of Origen and included Rufinus among those infected by Origenism. Jerome translated this letter into Latin (*ep.* 51), with additions and alterations that made the letter even more harsh. This quarrel was finally mediated by Theophilus of Alexandria, and Jerome withdrew his virulent diatribe *Against John* from circulation and was reconciled with Rufinus in a church in Jerusalem on Easter 397 (Kelly 1975: 195–209; Murphy 1945: 59–81).

In the same year Rufinus returned to Italy, where he became close to Melania's niece, Avita, and Avita's husband Apronianus. He embarked upon a career of translation, particularly of the works of Origen which had recently created so much controversy in the east. Rufinus produced paraphrases rather than literal translations, taking the liberty to suppress material which he felt was heretical and to insert in place of these omissions other comments by Origen which were orthodox. He translated the *Apology* for Origen by the martyred Pamphilus of Caesarea, and added his own preface, which stressed the value of Origen's theology and hermeneutics. Rufinus appended to the translation his own short work, *The Falsification of the Books of Origen*, in which he explained his translation method. He argued that Origen himself had not held heretical views, but that such views had been inserted into the works by heretical enemies of the great man. He cites a letter of Origen in which the theologian complains to friends that his work has been adulterated, and he points to similar, more modern cases of interpolation to back up this theory, which he sincerely, if naively, held. Rufinus then traveled to the monastery of a friend, Ursacius, south of Rome, and there translated the monastic rule of St Basil (Murphy 1945: 82–91).

The translation of one of Origen's most important works, the *Peri archon* (*On First Principles*), renewed his struggle with Jerome. In a preface to the work explaining his method, Rufinus heaps praise upon Jerome's earlier translation of some of the biblical commentary of Origen which he had written at the behest of Pope Damasus. Because Jerome was now engaged in more impressive and complex work than mere translation, Rufinus continues, it has fallen to him to pick up where Jerome had left off and to continue the translation of Origen for the benefit of westerners. This preface, and then his second preface to the third and fourth books of his translation, reveal his familiarity with a circle of anti-Origenists at Rome who took offense at his efforts to bring the thought of Origen to the west. It seems likely that his fulsome references to Jerome were strategic attempts to blunt further criticism (Kelly 1975: 232–4).

Eusebius of Cremona, a friend of Jerome and an extreme anti-Origenist, managed to steal a copy of Rufinus' incomplete work. The work was immediately sent off to Jerome with a cover letter expressing concern that his name was perhaps being used as justification for Rufinus' heretical project (Jer. *ep.* 83). Anti-Origenists at Rome immediately began to vilify Rufinus, and so, after receiving letters of recommendation from Pope Siricius and writing a friendly letter of explanation to Jerome, he set off for the friendlier surroundings of Aquileia in 398. Jerome, who had used and translated Origen for years, may have attacked Rufinus in order to firmly separate himself from any imputation of heresy (Clark 1992: 121–51). Jerome then proceeded to translate the *Peri archon* himself in a highly literal manner for his friends, in an attempt to demonstrate the many heresies of the author which Rufinus had smoothed over or ignored. This translation was brought to Rome with two letters, one a more temperate letter to Rufinus (*ep.* 81), and one a sharp attack on Origen's writings and on the methods used by

Rufinus to interpret them (*ep.* 84). But anti-Origenists suppressed the first letter and widely publicized the second, increasing the enmity between the two men.

At Aquileia, Rufinus continued his translations, which included several homilies of the Cappadocian fathers Basil and Gregory Nazianzan and the *Ring of Sixtus*, a collection of aphorisms falsely attributed to Pope Sixtus II. He also translated the *Adamantius: Dialogue on True Faith in God*, an anti-heretical work which was falsely attributed to Origen. Rufinus' desire to prove Origen's orthodoxy seems to have overcome his critical sensibility and allowed him to overlook the many non-Origenist sentiments expressed in the work. It incorporates entire sections from the work of Methodius of Olympus, a major opponent of Origen (Murphy 1945: 125; cf. Buchheit 1958).

In late 399, Pope Siricius, Rufinus' protector, died, and was replaced by a more ambivalent pope, Anastasius I. Further bad news followed for Rufinus. Theophilus of Alexandria, who had earlier mediated Origenist strife between John and Epiphanius, had a change of heart and became strongly anti-Origenist in order to pacify the anti-Origenist monks of Egypt. Jerome signed on enthusiastically with Theophilus in this campaign. A council in Alexandria in 400 condemned Origen, and the council proceedings were forwarded to the new pope. In a conflict at Milan, Rufinus discovered that his nemesis, Eusebius of Cremona, had altered the Latin of his works in order to demonstrate that he was a heretic. Rufinus blamed the smear campaign against him on Jerome, and he wrote an *Apology* to the pope in order to explain his position. The pope, in a letter responding to John of Jerusalem, reiterated his condemnation of Origen, and expressed his hope that Rufinus would translate Origen only to refute his heretical doctrines (Murphy 1945: 111–37; Kelly 1975: 243–9). Rufinus may have written his *Commentary on the Apostles' Creed* at this time in an attempt to demonstrate his orthodoxy (Hammond 1977: 389). The work draws heavily upon the *Catechesis* of Cyril of Jerusalem but contains much original content as well.

Rufinus' anxiety and anger are on display in his *Apology against Jerome*, which he published in 401. The *Apology* begins with a lengthy defense of his own orthodoxy, and an explanation of the purpose for his translation of the *Peri archon*. He then shifts to the offensive, and outlines the many outrages Jerome and his followers had committed against him. He criticizes Jerome's study of the pagan classics and his study of Hebrew with a Jewish teacher. In particular, he points out that Jerome had shifted from being an early supporter of Origen to being a leading partisan against him, and he concludes that any condemnation of Rufinus or Origen would logically have to include Jerome himself. He supports this assertion with substantial quotes from works of Jerome which argue an Origenist line. Jerome began a reply to the rumored appearance of Rufinus' work even before its publication. His response, *Apology against Rufinus* in two books, is a masterpiece of polemic, viciously mocking his adversary's arguments, writing style, and personal appearance. In 402 he added a third book, further insulting his former friend. In the face of this assault, Rufinus refrained from open, personal criticism of Jerome for the remainder of his life, but Jerome continued to attack him as "scorpion" or "grunting pig," even after Rufinus' death (Murphy 1945: 138–55; Kelly 1975: 249–58). Perhaps Rufinus' omission of any mention of Jerome in his church history provided a bit of revenge.

Despite the distractions of the quarrel with Jerome, Rufinus continued his translation work. Not long after completing his *Apology*, at the request of his friend, the bishop Chromatius of Aquileia, he began his translation of the *Ecclesiastical History* written by Eusebius (Barnes 1981; Grant 1980; Chesnut 1986: 1–174). In the preface Rufinus says that Chromatius hoped that reading church history would help assuage the fears of his flock in the face of the Gothic invasion of Italy in 402. Eusebius was the inventor of church history and of some of the features which successor church histories would incorporate, such as the liberal use of quoted documents and avoidance of invented speeches. Eusebius proclaimed in his preface that his themes would include bishops, heretics, Jews, and pagans. These remained the central themes for the successor ecclesiastical historians such as Socrates, Sozomen, and Theodoret, and Rufinus' translation made this immensely influential genre accessible to the Latin west upon its publication in 402. Rufinus decided to add to Eusebius' work himself, abridging the tenth book, adding information in that book on Gregory Thaumaturgus, and then writing an eleventh and twelfth book which brought the history down to the death of Theodosius I in 395.

After completing the *Ecclesiastical History*, Rufinus may have returned to Rome. The Origenist controversy had been overshadowed in the early 400s by the controversies surrounding John Chrysostom, which began in the east but soon spread to the west, and the climate at Rome had become more hospitable to Rufinus (Hammond 1977: 372–9). Rufinus' friends were supporters of

John, and Rufinus' translation of the anonymous *History of the Monks in Egypt*, which details the lives and careers of thirty-four desert fathers of Upper Egypt, may have been done in support of John and his monastic supporters (Jer. *ep.* 133). Rufinus must have translated it after completing his *Ecclesiastical History*, since it refers the reader to book 11 of that work.

Rufinus continued to translate the works of Origen, focusing on the homilies which Origen had written on numerous books of the Bible. If he had indeed returned to Rome, the absence of prefaces for some of these translations may be attributed to his desire to lie low and not flaunt his presence and his topics (Hammond 1977: 397). Again Rufinus adapted, shortened, and altered his translations to make them accessible and orthodox. He followed these translations with a translation of the *Recognitions*, falsely attributed to Pope Clement.

Between 405 and 408, Jerome and Rufinus continued to snipe at each other in the prefaces to their works. Rufinus criticized Jerome's preference for the Hebrew over the Greek Bible and recalled his hypocrisy over his use of Origen, and Jerome accused Rufinus in scathing language of constant attacks on his own work and of mediocrity and illiteracy. Rufinus' next work, an original *Commentary on the Benediction of the Twelve Patriarchs*, contains a pair of letters from Paulinus of Nola which serve as prefaces. The tone of the letters suggest that the two had been friendly for some time and that Paulinus was an ally of Rufinus in his struggle against Jerome (Hammond 1977: 412–21; Murphy 1956). Rufinus fled Rome with Pinian and Melania to escape the Gothic invasion of Italy which culminated in the sack of the city in 410. In his preface to a translation of Origen's homilies on *Numbers*, he asks how one can write when he has seen "the destruction of cities and country, when he has had to flee from the dangers of the sea? … the barbarian was within our sight, he had burned the city of Rhegium," and the only protection was the strait between Italy and Sicily. Rufinus thanks the abbot of Pinetum, Ursacius, for his help in transcribing the works under such difficult conditions, and says that he will soon turn to a translation of Origen's homilies on *Deuteronomy*. But Rufinus died shortly after completing this translation. The news reached Jerome in the middle of 411, prompting his charming reflection that "the scorpion is buried and the many-headed hydra has ceased to hiss against us" (*comm. ad Ezech.*, *pref.*). Other contemporaries were more charitable in their judgements, and his works found enthusiastic audiences continuously for centuries thereafter.

Work

Before considering the *Ecclesiastical History* in depth, a preliminary controversy must be addressed. Is Rufinus the author of the two books which continue Eusebius' ten books, or are the last two books merely a translation from the Greek work of Gelasius of Caesarea? The relationship between the two works has dominated scholarship for much of the twentieth century (survey with bibliography in Amidon 1997: xiii–xvii), although there now seems to be a consensus that Rufinus' history is original.

The work of Gelasius of Caesarea is entirely lost, but it is clear that he was the first historian to continue the work of Eusebius. In 1914, Anton Glas studied the fifth-century work of Gelasius of Cyzicus and the ninth-century work of George the Monk. These works cite Rufinus, impossibly, as the source of some material which occurred prior to the period which he covered in his history, and also attribute some information to "Gelasius or Rufinus" (Glas 1914). To Glas, these incorrect citations suggested that the two works had become confused, and by comparing Greek material from these later writers, which he assumed to be from Gelasius of Caesarea, with the Latin material of Rufinus, he argued that Rufinus had translated Gelasius. Photius believed that Gelasius, whom he had read, was a translation of Rufinus (*cod.* 89), but we know that Rufinus wrote in 401 or 402 and that Gelasius was dead by 400 (Jer. *ep.* 92). Therefore, any similarities which Photius saw in the works must be proof of Rufinus' dependence upon Gelasius and not the other way around.

Many obstacles remained for those who claimed that Rufinus' two books were simple transcriptions of Gelasius. Rufinus firmly claims that he himself is responsible for the material from Constantine to the death of Theodosius in the prologue to the work. There would appear to be no good reason for him to write deceptively. Even more telling are the comments of the fifth-century historian Socrates, who describes his use of Rufinus and criticizes his chronology (Soc. 2.1). It would surely be unprecedented for a Greek writer to forgo the use of the Greek original in favor of a Latin translation. Furthermore, the content of Rufinus' work is not what we would expect from Gelasius. For example, Gelasius' uncle and patron, Cyril of Jerusalem, is not presented in a wholly admirable light (10.24; Bihain 1962b). A large part of Rufinus' second book concerns the monks of Egypt, whom Rufinus knew and had lived with. Gelasius, however, may never have even visited Egypt. Jacques Schamp administered the *coup de grâce* to the theories which argued for substantial dependence of Rufinus upon Gelasius by a close reading of the fragments preserved by Photius which demonstrated that Gelasius' history must have ended with the death of Arius in 335 and therefore could not have been Rufinus' source for much of his work (Schamp 1987a, 1987b). It is certain, then, that Rufinus wrote the two books from the death of Constantine to the death of Theodosius I by himself, although he may have used Gelasius sparingly, as one of his many sources.

The original books of Rufinus have received the majority of scholarly attention, but it is worthwhile to provide a glimpse at Rufinus' translation of Eusebius as well (Oulton 1928; Christensen 1989; Inglebert 1996: 334–9). Rufinus applies the same translation techniques to the work of Eusebius as he did for Origen. The translation is a paraphrase, with material altered for stylistic or doctrinal purposes. Rufinus' task was complicated by the frequent obscurity or infelicity of the original Eusebian text, and by Eusebius' penchant to wander into territory of questionable theological orthodoxy as judged by late-fourth-century standards. Rufinus, for example, translates Eusebius' description of the Son as "second after the Holy Father" (1.2.9) as "the Lord Himself with Himself" in order to avoid Arianism, and in many other cases Rufinus adds a clarifying or explanatory note to ensure that the reader does not fall into a suspect Christology (Oulton 1928: 153–6). Rufinus claims that to translate the panegyrics of bishops in book 10 of Eusebius would be "superfluous" and would "add nothing to our knowledge," but perhaps he truly sought to avoid presenting the Arian sentiments expressed in this section. He also suppresses doubts that Eusebius expressed about the canonicity of certain books of the New Testament (Oulton 1928: 156–8). Rufinus sometimes ignores or summarizes the documents which Eusebius reproduced, in keeping with the greater emphasis on narration which he will adopt for his two original books.

Rufinus' alterations of Eusebius' original text are so numerous that his translation has been described as "an independent piece of work" (Christensen 1989: 333). He frequently breaks up Eusebius' long sentences into several smaller ones, avoids translating parts of Eusebius which he finds unclear or superfluous, and adds explanatory notes to clarify difficult material. At times, of course, such revision has the effect of substituting Rufinus' own ideas about the progress of Christianity for those of Eusebius. In particular, Rufinus' changes tend to emphasize the fourth-century concerns of church hierarchy and the importance of heresy, and to de-emphasize the importance of martyrdoms (Inglebert 1996: 336).

Rufinus has also added some new information to Eusebius' history (Oulton 1928: 158–74). In addition to the material in the tenth book on Gregory Thaumaturgus, Rufinus provides the original Latin of Tertullian in two places. Western pride perhaps inspires his additional comment that Tertullian was "the most noble of writers" (6.43). It is not surprising to learn that he expands upon Eusebius' account of Origen, drawing from his own wide knowledge of the theologian. Personal knowledge allowed Rufinus to augment Eusebius by the addition of certain topographical and historical details. Rufinus also added details to Eusebius' accounts of martyrdoms. Comparison between Rufinus' account of the martyrdoms of Phileas and Philoromus and the extant *Acts* of the martyrs demonstrates that Rufinus had used these *Acts* as a source (8.9). Rufinus' addition of significant details to other martyrdoms from Eusebius' work may likewise depend on martyr *Acts* no longer extant.

Rufinus provides a brief preface to his translation. He addresses his remarks to Chromatius, bishop of Aquileia, who had asked him to provide a distraction for the Aquileians, who are disturbed by the incursions of the Goths into Italy. Despite the dedication, the work does not seem to be particularly designed for the community at Aquileia, nor does Rufinus say that Chromatius had requested specifically an *Ecclesiastical History*. Rufinus may have already begun work on this historical translation and addendum before the request, which merely served as the proximate cause for its publication (Ventura 1992: 8–20). Rufinus expresses concern that his Latin skills may not be up to the task of the translation, but this should be understood as a conventional rather than a serious worry. Equally conventional is Rufinus' claim that the material for his new books was drawn partly from the writings of others, and partly from his own memory. He concludes with a comparison of his work to the five loaves and two small fishes with which Jesus fed the multitude (John 6: 1–14): the ten books of Eusebius correspond to the loaves, and his two additional books correspond to the fish. Rufinus suggests that his work will nourish the faith of his readers as the loaves and fishes nourished their recipients.

The tenth book of the *Ecclesiastical History*, the first of Rufinus' two books, is dominated by the struggles between those holding homoousian and homoiousian understandings of the Trinity. The other themes of Rufinus' work are interspersed throughout the main narrative of book 10. Among the topics treated are sketches of noteworthy holy men, struggles against paganism and Judaism, the expansion of Christianity into foreign territories, and a few mentions of secular events. All of these themes can also be found in book 11, although in different proportions. In this second book, the struggle against paganism provides the main theme. The tenth book culminates in the death of Julian and the failure of the plan he inspired to rebuild the Jewish Temple in Jerusalem. With the accession of Jovian which begins the eleventh book, Rufinus celebrates the return of the army and the state to Christianity. The history concludes with a series of decisive blows against paganism: the destruction of the temple of Serapis in Egypt, the destruction of other pagan shrines in Alexandria, and the defeat of the usurper Eugenius by the emperor Theodosius, which is portrayed as the victory of Christianity over paganism.

Françoise Thélamon, the premier modern interpreter of Rufinus' historical work, has described the *Historia Ecclesiastica* as a "sacred history" (Thélamon 1979, 1981, 1992). Rufinus has carefully selected and framed his topics to demonstrate his belief that history provides evidence of the working of God in time, and that history has a progressive, if fitful, movement toward the fulfillment of a divine plan. Eusebius had described the divinely inspired spread of Christianity and the transformation of Christianity from persecuted religion to imperial power with the conversion of Constantine; Rufinus traces the spread of Christianity outside of the boundaries of the empire, and the conquest of its twin enemies, heresy and paganism, under the guidance of Theodosius.

Rufinus' strong ideological purpose seems to have encouraged him to alter the chronology of some of the events in his history in order to fit his presuppositions. For example, Rufinus portrays the reign of Constantine as an especially holy period, as symbolized by the prominent space given the discovery of the True Cross by the emperor's mother Helena (10.8). Discreditable details of his career, such as the execution of his son Crispus, are effaced, as they had been by Eusebius. By contrast, the reign of the Arian emperor Constantius II, Constantine's son and successor, is connected with strife and decline. It appears that Rufinus has placed the mission to the kingdom of Aksum, which took place under Constantius, in the reign of Constantine, in order to credit the orthodox emperor with the glory of evangelizing (10.10; Thélamon 1981: 60–2). For similar reasons Rufinus distorted the timing of events in the careers of Athanasius and Arius. Although Constantine, toward the end of his life, had allowed Arius to reconcile with the church, and had sent Athanasius into exile, Rufinus moves these events into the time of Constantius II. Arius' death, which should be dated to 336, is likewise necessarily pushed forward in time into the reign of Constantius. It is presumably these misstatements which the historian Socrates complains about (2.1), and which he had to correct in his own work by reference to works of Athanasius and others.

Athanasius is the hero of the first book of Rufinus' history. As a child he was observed baptizing as a pretend-bishop, and as an adult he struggled against "nations, kingdoms, and armies" in his fight for orthodoxy (10.15). While in hiding, he managed to evade capture through miraculous means, and God granted him the perfect words during an audience before the emperor (10.20). His virtue was enhanced by his persecution by both Arian emperors and by the pagan Julian, who had been originally conciliatory (10.33–5). The emperor Valens, later a persecutor of homoousians, was divinely restrained while Athanasius lived (11.2), and at Athanasius' death, the bishop was succeeded by Lucius, a bloodthirsty monster (11.3).

One way that God continued to work in history, according to Rufinus' vision, was through the performance of miracles by holy men. Paphnutius had been mutilated during the persecution of the emperor Maximian, but miracles "arose through him no less than through the apostles long ago" (10.4). He was renowned for his healings and exorcisms, and the emperor Constantine demonstrated his respect by frequent kisses on the bishop's empty eye socket. The words Rufinus chooses to describe the miracles of Paphnutius are carefully chosen to echo scriptural passages describing the acts of the apostles and of Jesus himself. Rufinus similarly uses biblical phraseology to describe the miracles of the monks of Egypt (11.4; Thélamon 1981: 376–402).

Rufinus is our major and sometimes only source about several cases of the spread of Christianity outside of the borders of the empire, including Ethiopia (10.9–10), Georgia (10.11), and Arabia (11.6). The historical veracity of his details is not always possible to ascertain, but he clearly reveals his belief in the progressive and inevitable spread of Christianity throughout the world. He also provides a new paradigm for the barbarian, for in his work the apparently uncivilized and dangerous outsider may turn out to be the most pure and devout Christian.

Eusebius' ecclesiastical history had been innovative in its frequent presentation of original documents, such as creeds and imperial letters. Rufinus very rarely indulges in this innovation. He reproduces the Nicene Creed (10.6), but otherwise Rufinus stands apart from Eusebius and from successors like Socrates and Sozomen, who also frequently reproduce documents of all sorts. Such documents allow the reader to engage in the kind of scrupulous exegesis typical of contemporary theological dispute, and Rufinus' rejection of documents may be seen as a reflection of the anti-intellectual message he presents in his history. He often contrasts the excessive cleverness of heretics and pagans with the pure and simple faith of monks or ordinary Christians. Perhaps Rufinus' experiences in the Origenist controversies had strengthened his distaste for theological argument, although the triumph of simplicity would be a major theme in the successor church histories as well. In the beginning of his history Rufinus points to the importance of "simplicity of faith" for the orthodox resisters to the Arians, who were "cunning in debates" (10.2). When a pagan philosopher debated bishops at Nicaea, his rhetorical skill left the Christians embarrassed and unable to respond. But the recitation of foundational Christian beliefs by a "simple" man was enough to convert the philosopher, who is convinced not by words, but by the irresistible power which came out of the speaker's mouth (10.3). Heretics trick simple western Christians by demanding whether they prefer "homoousios or Christ"; in their ignorance of Greek philosophical terms, they naturally prefer Christ (10.22). The pagan priests of Egypt, whose power is destroyed at the end of Rufinus' work, also manipulate by means of their mystification. The priest of Saturn, Tyrannus, used deception to convince well-born women that they were serving the god when he was raping them. The exposure of his fraud led many pagans to destroy idols and shrines (11.25).

The continuing struggle against paganism is a major theme of the *Ecclesiastical History*. Just as the reign of Constantine was presented by Rufinus as especially holy, so too was the reign of Theodosius. Although Theodosius' anti-pagan initiatives included legislation and temple destruction around the empire, Rufinus chooses to focus narrowly upon events in Alexandria, which culminate in the destruction of the great temple to Serapis and its reconsecration to Christ. Thélamon speculates that Egypt's renown for paganism in both biblical and Greco-Roman tradition, and perhaps the familiarity with Isiac religion among Rufinus' immediate audience in Aquileia, may have made Egypt an appropriate symbol for paganism as a whole. Although Rufinus does not mention his sources for the events, Sophronius, a student of Jerome, is known to have written about Alexandria, and Rufinus may have found his work a ready source of information (Thélamon 1981: 160–2, 260–3).

Rufinus begins with a description of a pitched battle in Alexandria, during which pagans fortified a temple and forced Christians to sacrifice. After numerous woundings and killings, the Roman government suppressed the violence and the pagans fled (11.22). Rufinus then describes the magnificence of the temple and cult statue of Serapis, carefully describing the tricks using light and magnets designed to impress worshippers. Despite a pagan rumor that the sky would fall if the cult statue were damaged, a pious soldier dramatically struck it with an axe, and then with a cry many joined in to chop and burn the statue to pieces. That ended "the vain superstition and ancient error of Serapis" (11.23). Although Rufinus has been selective in the details of Serapis worship which he relates, comparison with other ancient sources and with archaeology suggests that he has provided many reliable details on the cult (Thélamon 1981: 165–205). Further destruction of temples and looting of their shrines uncovered evidence of horrible pagan crimes, such as the murder of children, which Rufinus claims led many pagans to embrace Christianity (11.24–6). These temples were then leveled and the areas dedicated to the Christian god, and all traces of Serapis on buildings were removed and replaced with crosses (11.27–9). Rufinus' account of the events in Egypt concludes with the triumphant proof of the superiority of Christianity over paganism. The tools to measure the extent of the Nile's flood had customarily been brought to the Serapeum, since the god was the guarantor of the seasonal flow. Though pagans feared that the destruction of Serapis would lead to a disruption in the river's rise, divine beneficence assured that the flood was more abundant than it had been in many years (11.30).

The momentum of the chapters of the history which dramatically detail the destruction of temples prepares the reader for the conclusion of the work, the victory of Theodosius over paganism at the Battle of the Frigidus River. The victory over the pagan gods in their historic Egyptian heartland is paralleled by this victory on the battlefield. Rufinus portrays the battle entirely as a contest of Christian against pagan, although Eugenius, the emperor installed in the west, was himself a Christian. Thus, in place of Eugenius, he presents the arch-pagan Nicomachus Flavianus as Theodosius' primary opposition. The emperor is portrayed as a Christian champion, who is credited with handing control of churches over to homoousians and offering copious resources for building and refurbishing churches (11.19). Even his ordering of a massacre at Thessalonica (attributed to demons) was the occasion for his new and "amazing" law requiring a thirty-day "cooling-off period" before commands of emperors are carried out (11.18). When Theodosius prepared for battle, Rufinus tells us that he first sought God's will through the monk John, who prophesied victory (11.32). Then the two sides underwent spiritual preparations: Theodosius' men prayed and sought help from martyrs and saints, while the pagans performed constant animal sacrifices. Rufinus claims that Nicomachus Flavianus committed suicide not from despair over the military failure, but because of his realization that his religion was false, and others of the usurping force defected to Theodosius. The final battle went poorly at first for Theodosius, who was observing from high on a rock, until he prostrated himself and prayed to God for help. His prayer evokes both biblical models, such as Judas Maccabee, and classical models, such as Aeneas (Courcelle 1969; Thélamon 1981: 318–20). A fierce and divinely inspired wind arose with such force that the enemy's weapons were blown back into their lines, and they were defeated. The pagans who survived, says Rufinus, were chagrined and ashamed at the failure of their gods (11.33).

The repeated use made of Rufinus' *History* by later writers is proof of its popularity and success. While Rufinus drew upon Eusebius for the genre and its primary themes, his exploration of those themes in the post-Constantinian world created a new model for church history in a Christian state. The twin battles against heresy and paganism, the power of simplicity and monasticism in the face of sophistry and traditional hierarchy, and the expansion of Christianity among the barbarians are themes that successor church historians would take for granted. His translation of Eusebius brought the history of the early church and the progressive view of world history to those without Greek. The barbarian invasions had the potential to raise questions about the idealized Eusebian view of historical progress, and Rufinus' work was designed to refute these concerns by its emphasis on Christian victory. His idealized portraits of numerous figures of the fourth century, such as Constantine, Athanasius, and Theodosius, became standard in later writers. The work became one of the very few in Latin to both be a source for later Greek writers and to be translated into Greek itself.

Text and translation

Latin text edited by T. Mommsen (1908), *Eusebius Werke* 2.2. English translation by P. Amidon (1997), Oxford University Press.

9

SOCRATES

Life

We have no information about the life of Socrates outside of what can be inferred from his history, and thus any account of his life must be both brief and speculative. The historian's name is often given as Socrates "Scholasticus," a surname which suggests its bearer might be a lawyer. However, Urbainczyk, in her full study of the historian, points out that the title seems to have been a late addition to the manuscripts. The scribes may have confused the historian with another church historian, Evagrius Scholasticus, who was a lawyer, or the title may have been added to distinguish the historian from the philosopher. Socrates shows no particular knowledge of the law and, as Urbainczyk points out, his reference to "the worthless and unjust lives of those in the courts" (6.3.2) would reflect a rather unusual attitude toward his own profession (Urbainczyk 1997b: 13–14; Errington 1997: 403–6).

Socrates was born in Constantinople around 380. The date can be estimated by three pieces of information. In his preface to the sixth book of his history, which begins with the accession of Arcadius in 395, he claims to be turning to events from his own time (6.pref.6; Urbainczyk 1997b: 19). Also, he says that when he was a boy he studied under the grammarians Helladius and Ammonius (5.16.9). These men probably fled Alexandria for Constantinople around 390, and if Socrates were 10 when he studied with them he must have been born by 380. Finally, the priest Auxanon, who died during the reign of Theodosius I (and thus before 395), told stories about the monk Eutychian to Socrates "when he was very young" (1.13.3).

Socrates says he was born, educated, and lived at Constantinople (5.24.9, 5.16.9). He provides us with a bit of information about his teachers, the aforementioned Helladius and Ammonius. The former was a priest of Zeus, the latter of the ape god Pithekos, in Alexandria. After the destruction of the temple of Serapis at the urging of the bishop Theophilus, religious objects taken from the interior of the temple were paraded through the streets, leading to civil unrest in which many Christians and a few pagans were killed. Socrates recalls the complaints of Ammonius, who was offended at the prominent place given to display of an ape statue in the Christian attempt to mock paganism, and the boasts of Helladius, who had successfully killed nine Christians during the rioting (5.16.13–14).

The education of Socrates by non-Christians provides no certain information about his childhood religion, but may help to explain his generally sympathetic attitude toward the study of the Greek classics (Allen 1987: 371–3). While his citations of non-Christians are limited, there are more than were found in the works of his predecessor, Eusebius. He often praises or denigrates figures in his history based on the extent of their traditional schooling. Most striking is the digression (3.16) on Greek learning, where Socrates explicitly argues for the study of the Greek classics. He supports traditional education both because the ancients have wisdom which is true and which supports Christianity, and because training in ancient literature prepares the student to successfully refute the arguments of non-Christians.

A central concern expressed in Socrates' work is the necessity for order and harmony in the church, which perhaps explains why he is more tolerant of doctrinal difference than other church historians. It is in this context that his sympathy for the Novatian sect should be examined. The Novatians were not "heretical," which is to say that their understanding of Christian doctrine was in line with the proto-Orthodox or "homoousian" position. They were, instead, "rigorist," insisting that Christians who had apostatized in the face of the persecutions of the third century could not be forgiven and that forgiveness for any serious sin after baptism was generally impossible. They were also more ascetic in their practices and were more likely to reject classical culture and learning (Gregory 1975: 1–18; Urbainczyk 1997b: 26–8). Socrates mentions numerous contacts with Novatians, who served as sources for his history, and he sometimes defends their views, stressing their opposition to the Arian heresy. In 1.10.4, for example, he criticizes Eusebius for overlooking Constantine's support of the Novatian Acesius. His omission of six imperial laws hostile to the Novatians, and inclusion of the one which was favorable, only underlines his partisanship (Allen 1990).

It is possible that Socrates himself was a Novatian, but his references to the Novatians as separate from "the church" (2.38.5) suggest otherwise. His sympathies with the sect are clear in any case.

Socrates lived at least until 439, when his history concluded. We know of no other works by him.

Work

Socrates' *Ecclesiastical History* was intended as a continuation of the pioneering work of Eusebius of Caesarea, and indeed "Eusebius" is the first word of the first book. In the preface to the work, Socrates announces his intention to write in a plain style, to treat the heresy of Arius, which Eusebius had not fully discussed, and to "give an account of the events concerning the churches from that time until today."

The date of publication cannot be exactly pinpointed. Sozomen's *Ecclesiastical History* depended heavily upon Socrates' work, and Sozomen's work must have been published before 450, as he invites the emperor Theodosius II, who died in 450, to suggest possible corrections or improvements. Socrates' history finishes in 439. The last chapters refer favorably to Eudocia, the emperor's sister. She was charged with adultery and exiled to Jerusalem, perhaps in 443 (Holum 1982: 193–4), after which such favorable mention would be unlikely. The year 439 also marks the publication of the Theodosian Code, the empire-wide compilation of laws which had been in preparation for years. The last section of the *History*, with its fulsome praise of the reign of Theodosius, might be expected to make some reference to its publication if time had allowed, and this provides some slender evidence that the work was published closer to 439 than to 443 (Urbainczyk 1997b: 19–20).

Socrates writes in a clear and uncomplicated style. He asserts his desire to write without affectation for the benefit of both learned and unlearned men (6.*pref.*). In his first edition he did not include documents, in an attempt to avoid boring the reader by excess (2.1.5–7). This concern to avoid prolixity is also apparent in his harsh critique of the *Christian History* of Philip of Side (7.27). Socrates charges that this (lost) work, in a thousand books, was written in a style too lofty for the unlearned, yet was too tedious and detailed for the learned. Socrates also suggests that his own simple style is evidence of his accuracy and concern for truth, while ancient (classical) historians, who exaggerated and invented, were at liberty to write more ornately (6.*pref.*).

The history is divided into the rather unsymmetrical number of seven books. In contrast to many classical works and to Eusebius' *Ecclesiastical History*, the successor church histories of Socrates, Sozomen, and Theodoret are all divided into odd numbers of books. It has nevertheless been suggested that the original plan of the work was limited to the first five books (discussed in Urbainczyk 1997b: 61–2). Socrates claims, however, in the preface to the first book, that he will treat the history of the church all the way up to his own day. Also, the end of the fifth book would make a particularly unsatisfying end to a work so concerned with the unity of the church, as the last books discuss the disagreements in the church concerning the date of Easter, the further factionalization of Arian and Eunomian heretics, the assassination of the emperor Valentinian III, and the death of Theodosius.

Although the work was conceived as a whole, the preface to the sixth book does attempt to differentiate the last two books from those that came before. Here Socrates writes that he has worked to fulfill the expectations of his dedicatee, the otherwise unknown Theodore, and that he now turns to events of his own time. As was common for historians preparing to treat contemporary events, he comments on the dangers of arousing anger from those whom he criticizes or toward whom he is insufficiently respectful. These traditional themes are similar to those in the preface to book 26 of Ammianus' *Res Gestae* and elsewhere.

In addition to the sixth book, Socrates' first, second, and fifth books also contain prefaces. The preface to the second book reveals that at least some books were circulated separately and then revised in later editions. Socrates says that he had completed the first and second books of his history relying heavily on the church history of Rufinus. Later, however, he had discovered some works of Athanasius and some other unspecified letters which revealed Rufinus to be an inaccurate guide to certain events, a discovery which necessitated the rewriting of several sections. Socrates' attempts to repair the chronology of Rufinus' account were only partly successful, although the self-contained episodes are generally accurate (Barnes 1993b: 200–4). In addition to altering the chronology, Socrates decided upon a stylistic change. While previously the work contained only a narrative history, he decided to include letters and documents in emulation of the work of Eusebius. While it has been suggested that the documents were added at the insistence of Theodore, Socrates does not explicitly say so, claiming only that the documents will be beneficial to his patron.

Socrates' work depends on a wide variety of sources, both written and oral (Geppert 1898; Barnes 1993b: 205–6; Urbainczyk 1997b: 48–64). In the first category, he is particularly dependent upon Eusebius (especially the *Life of Constantine*), Rufinus, Athanasius, and the *Synagoge* of Sabinus, a collection of church documents with the author's commentary which is no longer extant. In addition to these major sources, Socrates mentions many other works which he has used, including orations of Libanius (3.22–3) and Themistius (3.26, 4.32) and an epic poem by one Eusebius Scholasticus on the war with Gainas (6.6.36). He also comments upon the works and the style of a variety of heretical writers, including Nestorius (7.32.8), Eunomius (4.7.4–9), Origen (whom he defended, 6.13, 7.45.5–7; cf. Chesnut 1986: 177–81) and the aforementioned Sabinus, whom he accuses of supporting the Macedonian heresy (2.15.8–11, 2.17.10–11) and of being "half Arian" (4.22). For a chronological framework, Socrates was apparently dependent upon a chronicle of events at Constantinople and a list of bishops. A glance at the section-by-section breakdown of sources for the *History* in the work of Franz Geppert (1898: 112–32) will reveal how intricately Socrates has woven together the various written sources for his work.

Socrates also relied on numerous oral sources, particularly for the last two books of his work. The preface to book 6 emphasizes his reliance on oral sources and his methods used to evaluate them. He will write what he has seen and what he has learned from eyewitnesses, and he will carefully compare stories to ensure their accuracy. Socrates makes much use of oral sources, particularly in the later books of the history, not only for information but also to create atmosphere and to allow Socrates to describe contemporary rumors and opinions. Consider Socrates' use of oral sources in chapter 19 of book 6, for example. Cyrinus, bishop of Chalcedon, had both of his feet amputated due to gangrene, and Socrates reports that "many" claimed this was a form of divine punishment for the bishop's opposition to John Chrysostom. A powerful hailstorm and the death of the empress were put forth as further evidence of divine anger at the treatment of John, although Socrates adds that "others" found the deposition of John to be just due to his violent behavior.

The elderly priest Auxanon, who was an important source for Socrates, was present at the Council of Nicaea. Auxanon also provided information about the monk Eutychian (1.13) and about the cruelty and tortures which Macedonius inflicted upon the Novatian church and the homoousian church (2.38). The historian says that he is undeterred by the risk of incurring the enmity of his readership for his use of a Novatian-like Auxanon as a source (1.13.2). Socrates' ecumenical approach to oral sources is also revealed in his citation of an Arian priest, Timothy (7.6.6), and the priest Eudaemon (5.19.10), a homoousian (Urbainczyk 1997b: 18).

Church history centers upon conflict, and Socrates portrays both religious and secular controversy. The principal Christian protagonist of the work is Athanasius, the homoousian bishop of Alexandria, whose struggles with church and state authorities dominate the first four books. Almost as important is John Chrysostom, the homoousian bishop of Constantinople, whose struggles dominate book 6 and whose corpse makes an appearance in book 7. Socrates' interest in the unity of the church under a single, strong emperor is demonstrated in the overall structure of the work, which begins with the conversion of Constantine, laments the disunity which embroiled the church after that period, and finally concludes on a positive note with praise of Theodosius II and the restoration of church unity. The return of the body of John to Constantinople under the sponsorship of the bishop Proclus signifies the unity of the church, and the visit of the empress Eudocia to Jerusalem recalls the pilgrimage of Helena, the mother of Constantine, in the first book.

Socrates has some success in avoiding monotony by varying his subject matter, as a quick outline of the first book may illustrate. Of course, doctrinal disputes predominate. Early in the first book, for example, Arius is introduced in the context of his Christological conflict with the bishop of Alexandria, Alexander (1.5). A failed attempt by Constantine to reconcile the two (1.7) is followed by the synod at Nicaea (1.8–10). After the death of Alexander, Athanasius takes up the anti-Arius cause, while Arius is supported by Eusebius of Nicomedia. Arius and Athanasius fall in and out of favor with the emperor and the bishops, and a synod at Tyre and then one at Jerusalem attempt to settle their differences. Partisans of Eusebius and Arius bring charges, which Socrates views as spurious, against Athanasius, most memorably accusing the bishop of the murder of one Arsenius. The production of Arsenius' severed hand provides evidence for the accusation. Athanasius, however, manages to locate Arsenius, who is both alive and in possession of all of his limbs, and to produce him at a crucial moment. "Arsenius has been found to have two hands, as you see. Let the accusers point to the place where the third was cut off" (1.29.9). This first book, which featured the rise of Arius in its early chapters, portrays the ignominious death of Arius (in a public restroom) in one of its last chapters (1.38.7–9).

Socrates illustrates these doctrinal disputes, according to the model of Eusebius, with lengthy quotations of documents. In the first book, these include a letter of Alexander to other bishops, explaining his excommunication of Arius (1.6.4–30), imperial letters, such as that of Constantine to Arius and Alexander (1.7.3–21), and creeds accepted by synods of bishops, such as the one set forth at Nicaea in 325 (1.8.4–11). These are the documents which Socrates had inserted in his second edition, having omitted them in the interest of avoiding tedium in his first edition (2.11). The documents were culled from the collection of Sabinus (1.8) and other historians, or had been discovered by Socrates in his research.

Interspersed within this central narrative of doctrinal dissension are several other sorts of stories. Bishops or monks of outstanding sanctity are brought forth for the reader's edification. In book 1, for example, we hear of the bishop Paphnutius, who, although unmarried himself, argues in favor of married clergy (1.11), and of the miracles performed by the bishop Spyridon (1.12), the monk Eutychian (1.13), and the monk Antony (1.21). These digressions provide more enlightened examples of Christian behavior which contrast with the often discreditable actions of the doctrinal disputants in the main narrative. Socrates also digresses in the first book upon the spread of Christianity beyond the boundaries of the empire in sections on the conversion of the Indians (1.19) and the Iberians (1.20). Similar information on Christianizing abroad can be found in later books, including the conversion of the Goths (4.33), the Saracens (4.36), and some Persians (7.8). Socrates also occasionally digresses on other topics. These digressions include the value of the pagan classics (3.16), the divisions in the church over the date of Easter and other ritual issues (5.22), and the origins of the singing of responsorial hymns in church (6.8.10–12).

Along with the religious material, Socrates presents many accounts of secular events. When Christianity became the state religion, it was certain that chroniclers of church history would have to devote more attention to imperial affairs than Eusebius had. The historian points out that it was necessary to include information about emperors because of their great influence on church affairs (5.*pref.*9–10). Socrates, however, includes even more secular material than might be deemed strictly necessary, in keeping with his philosophical approach to history which held that secular events are inextricably mixed with church events (Chesnut 1975, 1986: 190–200; Urbainczyk 1997b: 69–79). He discusses this theory in the preface to the fifth book, by way of apologizing for what some might see as excessive attention to secular affairs. "When state matters were disturbed, as if by some sympathy also the matters of the church were disturbed. For if someone looks closely, he will find that evils of church and state flourish at the same time. ... Sometimes events of the church came first, and then secular events followed, and sometimes the reverse happened" (5.*pref.*).

This idea of "cosmic sympathy," a mystical link between seemingly unconnected human events, and between human events and natural events, is an old one in ancient thought. It was particularly prominent in Stoic philosophy and in earlier Christian writings. Political and military events thus play an important role in Socrates' history because he believes that they "sympathetically" affect church events and because they reflect disturbances in church events. Socrates often makes or implies these connections. In book 4, for example, Socrates connects the persecution of homoousians by the emperor Valens (4.2) to the rise of the usurper Procopius (4.3). This union of disturbances in church and state is echoed in natural events as well by an earthquake and the shifting of the sea level (4.3).

Socrates' concern with disunity and disturbance outweighs any doctrinal concerns he has. He frequently portrays religious controversies as the product of quarrelsome clerics rather than as principled struggles for doctrinal correctness. His portrayal of John Chrysostom, for example, is notably cooler than other extant portrayals of the bishop, and he reports several criticisms of his actions and temperament (Urbainczyk 1997b: 133–7). Socrates' desire for religious harmony and distaste for persecution are exemplified in his praise of the bishop Proclus. "He was gentle to all heretics, thinking that by this rather than by violence they would best be won over" (7.41.5).

In his praise of Proclus, Socrates adds that the bishop, in avoiding persecution, imitated the emperor Theodosius II. Socrates' scorn for bishops who foment dissension is accompanied by praise for emperors, particularly sole emperors, who ensure unity. He claims that Constantine was aggrieved by the divisions which the dispute between Arius and Alexander had created, and works admirably to heal the split (1.7.1–2). By the end of the work, peace has returned to the empire under the protection of the devout emperor Theodosius II (7.42). Piety is the most remarkable quality of Theodosius II in Socrates' panegyric (7.22); as Urbainczyk points out, the emperor is portrayed more like a holy man than like an emperor (Urbainczyk 1998). Ironically, perhaps, the emperors are more "Christian" than the bishops in Socrates' history.

The work of Socrates, like other products of the mid-fifth century by Olympiodorus and Sozomen, is a celebration of the peace in both church and state in his time, and an exploration of the causes of disunity in the past. He concludes with a prayer that the churches, cities, and nations be at peace, and he remarks that the work could only come to an end because the "lovers of trouble" had grown silent (7.48.7). Socrates modernized the genre of ecclesiastical history by integrating secular history into his framework. His work is valuable because of his judicious use of a wide variety of sources, his lack of sharp partisanship, and his generally humane attitude toward the people and events he describes. His plain style may have encouraged successors to attempt a more elegant treatment of the period and events he covered, but no successor was more accurate or reliable.

Text and translation

Greek text edited by G.C. Hansen and M. Sirinjan (1995), *Griechischen Christlichen Schriftsteller*. English translation by A.C. Zenos (1890), *Nicene and Post-Nicene Fathers*. Available on-line at http://www.ccel.org/fathers2/NPNF2-02/Npnf-02-05.htm.

10

SOZOMEN

Life

The full name of the ecclesiastical historian Sozomen was Salamanes Hermeias Sozomenos, according to Photius (*cod.* 30). Our knowledge of the life of Sozomen is derived almost entirely from comments in his own work, which Grillet and Sabbah have conveniently collected (1983: 9–25).

Three sixth-century writers, Cassiodorus, Theodore Lector, and Gregory the Great, use Sozomen's work, and refer to the historian simply as "Sozomen." He was born in Bethelia, a town near Gaza in Palestine (5.15.14). According to Sozomen, Bethelia was noteworthy for its large population and for a number of highly regarded ancient temples. In Sozomen's time, the most remarkable and celebrated temple was called by its Greek name "Pantheon," or "temple of all gods," and gave its name to the town as well, since Bethelia means "temple of all gods" in Syriac.

Sozomen's grandfather, who had been born a pagan, was one of the first in the town to convert to Christianity. When a certain townsman Alaphion was possessed by a demon, neither pagans nor Jews were able to cure him, but by speaking the name of Christ the monk Hilarion expelled the demon (5.15.15). Sozomen (3.14.21–8) describes some other exploits of Hilarion, who lived from 291 to 371, and still more can be found in Jerome's *Life of Hilarion*. Because Jerome's *Life* does not include the exorcism of Alaphion with the other miracles which first brought the monk fame in 329, it probably occurred after that date. Alaphion and his family immediately embraced Christianity, as did Sozomen's grandfather. Sozomen adds that his grandfather was a learned man, knew mathematics, and became famous in the surrounding area for his great skill in interpreting the Bible. The grandfather and other relatives of Sozomen were forced to flee the town for a time during the reign

117

of Julian, perhaps in 362, when the emperor suggested to locals that Christians were agents of sedition. The family of Alaphion was responsible for the creation and support of the first monasteries and churches in the region. Sozomen says that he knew some members of this family when he was very young and they were very old, and adds that he will have further reason to discuss these men later in his history (5.15.13–17).

Sozomen refers to four monks who had been taught by Hilarion and who lived in Bethelia during the reign of Valens (6.32, 8.15). If these men were the members of Alaphion's family to whom he promised to return, it is possible to speculate a bit on Sozomen's date of birth. If the monks were around 40 years old at the high point of their fame in the 360s, then they were born around the 320s. For Sozomen to know them when he was 10 and they were 70 would suggest a birth date around 380 (Grillet *et al.* 1983: 12).

One of the clear differences between Sozomen's and Socrates' church histories is the much greater emphasis Sozomen places on monks and monastic activity. The historian's knowledge of monasticism and his claim to have spent time with monks in his youth suggest that he may have received his earliest education in a monastery. This form of education was still rather uncommon in the fourth century. His later schooling must have been more traditional, as he frequently reveals his knowledge of the classics in his history. It is possible that Sozomen studied rhetoric at the famous schools of Gaza. Sozomen's title *scholasticus* implies that he went to law school, probably at Beirut, where he would have studied law and Latin. That he knew Aramaic as well is evident from his comments on the Greek translations of the Syrian writer Ephrem (3.16).

Sozomen asserts that he himself can vouch for the regular attendance at church services of the bishop Zeno of Maiuma in Gaza, when Zeno was almost a hundred years old (7.28.6). Since Zeno is included in a collection of those bishops who flourished at the end of the time of Theodosius, this trip must have been around 395 or 400, shortly before the end of his schooling. This is one of a number of places in the history where Sozomen demonstrates familiarity with people and places in Gaza, which he may have frequented as a boy or as an adult.

Sozomen appears to have been well traveled, to judge from his frequent references to places around the empire. Unfortunately, he provides us with no certain itinerary, but his survey of the customs and traditions of churches around the world (7.19) provides several suggestive details. In Scythia, Sozomen claims, there is only one bishop for all the cities of the region, but in other places bishops serve even individual villages, "as I have seen in Arabia, Cyprus, and among the Novatians and Montanists in Phrygia" (7.19.2). Sozomen states that monks in Palestine greatly revere the non-canonical *Apocalypse of Paul*, which they claim was discovered in a marble box under the house of Paul at Tarsus in Cilicia. An elderly priest of the church in Tarsus denied to Sozomen that this story was true, although whether the conversation took place at Tarsus or Constantinople is not clear. Sozomen mentions the common habit among the Romans of swearing by an annual hymn, and gives further evidence that he may have visited Italy by his knowledge of Sicilian topography (2.24.2) and of specific details of the rite of penance in the Roman church (7.16.4–7).

Sozomen may have been familiar with the contemporary appearance of the Church of the Holy Sepulchre in Jerusalem (2.1) and he appears to have spoken with those who participated in the election of Maximus to the bishopric of that city (2.20). He provides detailed information about the geography of the area around Hebron (2.4). The historian also visited Bithynia near Mount Olympus, where he saw many of the Huns who had been settled there after the defeat of Uldis in 409 (9.5.7). Other references could suggest still other journeys, perhaps to Alexandria or to Antioch.

Sozomen was a resident of Constantinople when he wrote his *Ecclesiastical History*, as he reveals in a couple of anecdotes. A church outside of the city dedicated to the Archangel Michael was the scene of many healing miracles. Aquilinus, "a man now dwelling among us and practicing law in the same courtrooms" (2.3.10), was the recipient of one of these miracles, when a divine power instructed him to dip his foot in a mixture of honey, wine, and pepper to cure a digestive disease. From this it is evident both that Sozomen was living in Constantinople and that he was practicing law while he composed his work. Another miraculous event took place when Proclus was bishop of Constantinople, between 434 and 446. The empress Pulcheria dreamed of forty soldier martyrs who had been killed during the Great Persecution of Licinius. The site of the burial was discovered, and the sweet smell of myrrh which arose from the grave inspired confidence in the workmen and the bystanders that they were digging in the right place. The relics were honored with a procession and reburial in an expensive casket at a ceremony which Sozomen claims to have attended (9.2.17).

It appears that Sozomen was not yet in Constantinople in 403–4, when John Chrysostom was active, since he never mentions his own participation in any of the events he recounts about him. He also says that his information about Atticus, the bishop of the city who died in 426, is derived from other people who knew him (8.28.7; Gillett 1992: 20–2). This is the extent of our information about the date of his arrival.

The description of the martyr ceremony in the ninth book of the history leads the reader to believe that Sozomen is writing not long after the death of Proclus in 446, as he describes the event as occurring "when Proclus was bishop" and mentions that many are still alive who remember it (9.2.18). Since the work is dedicated to the emperor Theodosius II, the dedication at least must have been written before his death in 450 (Rouché 1986). Because the last book is incomplete, it is reasonable to believe that Sozomen died perhaps in 448 or 449.

Work

Sozomen tells us that he had originally planned to write an ecclesiastical history "from the beginning," but upon reflection he realized that the task had already been completed by many wise men, including Clemens, Hegesippus, Africanus, and Eusebius. He therefore wrote a summary in two books tracing events from the Resurrection to the defeat of Licinius in 324 (1.1.12). This work does not survive, but perhaps served as practice to prepare him for the more ambitious project which we have before us.

Sozomen lays out the plan of his work in the dedication. His history will begin with the third consulship of Crispus and Constantine (323) and continue to the seventeenth consulship of Theodosius II (439). The work is subdivided as follows: events under Constantine, books 1 and 2; events under his sons, books 3 and 4; events under Julian, Jovian, Valentinian, and Valens, books 5 and 6; events from Gratian to Theodosius and his sons, books 7 and 8; the rule of Theodosius II, book 9. The division of books according to the reigns of the emperors demonstrates Sozomen's adherence to the standard chronological arrangement of church historians, as seen in Eusebius and Socrates before him.

Sozomen follows the outline he proposed in his history with the exception of the incomplete ninth book. There are several reasons to believe that the last book is unfinished. It contains no events after 425 except for the narrative of the discovery of the forty martyrs. While praising the empress Pulcheria, Sozomen promises to describe later how she prevented heresies from spreading (9.1.9).

This must be a reference to her conflict with the heretical bishop of Constantinople, Nestorius, who does not appear in the book (Holum 1982: 152–4). In the penultimate chapter of the work, he promises to narrate the discovery of the relics of Zechariah and of Stephen (9.16.4). Although in the last chapter of the work Sozomen claims that he will "begin" with the relics of Zechariah, no mention of Stephen follows (9.17.1). Instead, the work ends abruptly. Finally, in contrast to the first eight books, the ninth book is largely concerned with secular rather than ecclesiastical events.

The unfinished ninth book may reveal something of the method Sozomen used to write his history. He seems to have first constructed a framework of secular material (derived in this book from Olympiodorus of Thebes) and must have planned to fill out and to complete the book by inserting religious information into this framework. The existence of an incomplete book further suggests the possibility that the history was published in sections, like that of Socrates, with the dedication attached to the first installment.

The dedication, to the emperor Theodosius II, is written in a fulsome manner, thick with classical and biblical references and with panegyrical praise of the emperor. The encomium is largely traditional, emphasizing the wisdom, the virtue, and, especially, the piety of the emperor. Two features deserve special attention. One is the lengthy praise of the generosity of the emperor. Sozomen states that Theodosius regularly judges poets and writers and favors them not only with applause but also with gifts, statues, and gold. The fabled benefactions of the ancients, such as the gift of a gold piece for each line of poetry given by the emperor Septimius Severus to the poet Oppian, fall far short, he claims, of the beneficence of Theodosius (*pref.*5–7). Rarely is an ancient writer so open in his celebration of the possibility of financial reward from a patron. The second is the presentation of the work to the emperor. "Knowing all things, and having every virtue, particularly piety, which the Holy Word says is the beginning of wisdom, take this writing from me and examine it, and by adding or removing things with your accurate knowledge, cleanse it by your labors" (*pref.*18). This request to the emperor to serve as editor of the work has often been taken at face value, implying that Sozomen moved in the highest circles and was comfortable asking Theodosius for favors. It could equally well demonstrate simply a prudent statement of submission, without any serious expectation that the emperor would become involved.

The first chapter of the first book is a lengthy and stylized introduction. The first phrase, "It has often crossed my mind," seems to deliberately evoke the beginning of the *Cyropaedia* of Xenophon (1.1.1). Sozomen's choice of introductory topic is rather surprising. He asks at some length why it is that so many of the Jews, despite their familiarity with the biblical prophecies which identified Jesus as the Messiah, refused to convert to Christianity. His tone is not hostile, but is one of puzzled surprise, and it has been suggested that Sozomen writes in part for an audience of Jews or Christians attracted to Judaism (Urbainczyk 1997a: 364–6). While Eusebius had stated that one aim of his ecclesiastical history was to describe the misfortunes which the Jews suffered (Eus. *HE* 1.1), Sozomen's concern here is more what he sees as a failure of the intellect than the punishment which resulted from that failure.

Another purpose of Sozomen's rumination on the Jews becomes clearer as the introduction continues. The historian turns to reflect upon those who espoused Christianity, who were unskilled in rhetoric or science, but who convinced others to convert by their brave endurance of torture and martyrdom. The superiority of deeds to reason is an important theme of Sozomen's history, which elevates the unstudied asceticism of monks and scorns the divisive hair-splitting arguments of heretical bishops and priests. The failure of the Jews to recognize the truth is merely one example of the general failure of reason when confronted with simple faith.

Sozomen proceeds to discuss the methods of investigation he employed to gather the information in his history (1.1.13–16). His statement on oral sources is wholly conventional (compare Soc. 6. *pref.*9–10): he will record the actions which he himself witnessed, and those which he learned from others who had participated in them. For earlier events, he says that he will rely upon documents including laws which pertain to Christianity, proceedings of synods, and letters of emperors and religious figures. He provides us with a welcome insight into his working methods when he says that he has discovered these documents preserved in palaces, churches, and in the individual holdings of private citizens.

The source he does not mention, however, is by far the most important one. A very large percentage of Sozomen's ecclesiastical history is lifted directly from that of Socrates, without attribution (Schoo 1911: 19–25; Grillet *et al.* 1983: 59–87; Urbainczyk 1997a). There is no precedent in ancient literature for two works written at nearly the same time which share so much detail. Since neither historian mentions the other, it is only through one passage that the priority of Socrates can be made certain. Socrates records a witty comment of the emperor Constantine to Acesius, a Novatian bishop, and he adds that neither Eusebius nor any other historian had recorded this conversation, but that he had heard it himself from a trustworthy source (1.10.4). When Sozomen provides the story (1.22.1), it is introduced by a simple, "it is said."

It has been suggested that Sozomen followed the narrative of Socrates' history in order to correct his errors (Downey 1965: 64). Sozomen did clearly introduce new oral and documentary evidence to his work, and he returned again for a first-hand inspection to the sources used by Socrates, such as Sabinus, Athanasius, Rufinus, and Eusebius. For example, in Socrates' account of the Council of Nicaea (1.8.31), he names five bishops who did not sign the Nicene Creed and who did not support the deposition of Arius. In Sozomen's retelling (1.21.2), he correctly states that although the bishops did support Arius, they also signed the Creed. Independent research must have made Socrates' error apparent.

The correction of a few factual mistakes in Socrates could not, however, have provided a justification for Sozomen's work. Rather, he aims to correct broader stylistic and thematic flaws that he sees in Socrates' work. Although the historians cover the same events, the differences are clear to the reader. Sozomen's style is more literary and complex than that of Socrates, and Photius praises its richness (cod. 30). There is nothing in Sozomen to compare with the apologies for stylistic simplicity in Socrates, or with Socrates' suggestion that the classical historians could write in a loftier style because their concern for the truth was less than his (Soc. 6. pref.3). The use of a more elevated style is one way in which Sozomen writes a church history closer to the models of classical historiography (Grillet et al. 1983: 63–70). Although Sozomen presents some unaltered documents (seventeen in all), he generally abides by his intention (1.1.15) to paraphrase the contents of documents referred to, including many offered verbatim by Socrates. This provides the narrative with a smoother flow, and also allows the author to shape and control his message more effectively. Ecclesiastical struggles often revolved around a few disputed words, so the exact quotation of documents might have considerable importance for understanding the conflict. Sozomen's paraphrasing, however, underlines his general contempt for what he understood as needlessly complex theological arguments (cf. Mazza 1980: 382–5).

Sozomen's interest in artful structure differentiates his work from the less sophisticated work of Socrates, who allows natural chronology to dominate the arrangement of information in his narrative. Sabbah shows, in his comparison of the first book of Socrates with the first two of Sozomen, how Sozomen has arranged his material to provide regular alternations between progress and retrogression (Grillet *et al.* 1983: 60–3). The first fourteen chapters of the first book narrate the conversion of Constantine, his defeat of Licinius, his promotion of Christianity, and accounts of some great monastic figures. The triumphant progress of Christianity is disturbed by two central chapters (1.15–16) which detail the origin of the Arian heresy, but the book concludes with the successful council at Nicaea presided over by the emperor which restores order to the church. In the second book Sozomen similarly engineers an alternation between positive and negative events, most notably inserting the account of the conversion of the Indians to Christianity (2.24) in a place designed to break up the narration of the spread of heresy in this period.

In addition to making an ecclesiastical history more classical with an emphasis on style and structure, Sozomen also expands the scope of ecclesiastical history in two significant ways. Again the key passage is from the first chapter of the first book, where he states that he decided not to limit his work to events connected with the church in the Roman empire, but to include also events of religious interest that transpired among the Persians and barbarians. The historian adds that he also believes that ecclesiastical history ought to include accounts of the originators of monasticism, and those who succeeded them (1.1.18). He provides more information about the spread of Christianity into foreign lands, particularly into Persia, than does Socrates. The best of his many biographical digressions on notable ascetics derive from his own experiences in Palestine and Syria. Sozomen includes far more information on individual Christians than Socrates had, often with graphic details of martyrdoms and miracles which Socrates had eschewed. We learn of the Egyptian monk Apelles, a smith, who used a hot iron to drive off the devil when he appeared in the form of a woman to tempt him (6.28.7), and of a pagan mob of Gaza, who attacked the Christians Eusebius, Nestabus, and Zeno with boiling water, with pieces from a loom, and with spits until "they crushed their skulls and the martyrs' brains poured onto the ground" (5.9.5).

While Sozomen shares Socrates' concern over church disunity and perhaps surpasses him in his rejection of quibbling theological disputation, he does not share Socrates' glorification of the emperor as the solution to strife. He alters Socrates' narrative in several places to emphasize that bishops are superior to emperors, as when Valentinian is quoted as saying that, as a layman, it is not proper for him to decide church affairs (Soz. 6.7.2, cf. Soc. 4.2.2–3; Urbainczyk 1997a: 359–62). There is no ambivalence in Sozomen's portrait, in the eighth book, of the heroic bishop John Chrysostom struggling against unjust secular power. Sozomen is, of course, properly reverential toward Theodosius II, in his preface, and toward Pulcheria and the other women of the Theodosian house in the last book of the history (9.1–3). Their power, however, lies in their piety and closeness to God, and the success of their rule is attributed to prayer and to their generosity toward the church. The supremacy of religious over secular views is most clear in Sozomen's reflections upon the sack of Rome. The sack and the rise of western usurpers occupies several chapters, but in the end the usurpers were defeated and the rightful emperor Honorius remained in power. Sozomen states that he has mentioned the deaths of the usurpers only to present the moral that imperial stability depends solely upon the emperor's continuing devotion to God. Honorius' piety ensured his continuing rule, and the success of the eastern empire, despite the youth of Theodosius II, was equally ensured thanks to the favor of God. Despite some recent disturbances in the west, Sozomen rejoices that the empire now enjoys peace in both religious and secular affairs. We see in Sozomen's conclusions the standard position of eastern historians in the middle of the fifth century, whether sincerely held or the product of Theodosian propaganda.

Text and translation

Greek text edited by J. Bidez and G.C. Hansen (1995), *Griechischen Christlichen Schriftsteller*. English translation by C.D. Hartranft (1890), *Nicene and Post-Nicene Fathers*. Available on-line at http://www.ccel.org/fathers2/NPNF2–02/Npnf2–02–13.htm.

11

THEODORET

Life

Theodoret of Cyrrhus was an accomplished dogmatist, apologist, exegete, and hagiographer, in addition to being the author of an *Ecclesiastical History*. He brings his history only up to 428, thus avoiding direct treatment of the Christological controversies to which he devoted much of his intellectual energy in the 430s and 440s.

Theodoret's family was from Antioch (Theod. *hist. relig.* 9, 13; Leroy-Molinghen 1980; Young 1983: 266–71). They were well off but not aristocrats, and Christians. His mother was converted to a more ascetic form of Christianity at age 23 in 386 as the result of an encounter with Peter the Galatian, a monk in the Syrian desert. After she climbed into the abandoned tomb in which the monk lived, Peter cured her of an eye disease, and instructed her to stop using cosmetics and jewelry. Peter also performed curative miracles for Theodoret's family cook and for his grandmother, and as a boy Theodoret visited him once a week for spiritual instruction. He would sit on the monk's lap and be fed grapes and bread (*hist. relig.* 9.4).

Theodoret's parents were childless until his mother was 30, to his father's distress. His mother had been regularly supplying the monk Macedonius with the barley which was his only food and which gave him his epithet, "the Barley Eater." Macedonius guaranteed the woman that she would have a boy, but added that the child would have to be "given back to the one who gave him." Seven years later, when the boy was born in 393, he was given the name Theodoret, "gift of God," as a sign of this pledge. The young Theodoret spent much time with Macedonius as well. The monk continually reminded the boy that he was a gift from God and must dedicate his life to virtue in return (*hist. relig.* 13).

Theodoret tells us that he once was addressed by a demon, who spoke to him in Syriac, which suggests that Syriac was his first language (*hist. relig.* 21; Brock 1994: 154). His Greek, however, is polished and elegant. In addition to a monastic education, it is evident that Theodoret received a classical education of the kind customary for one of his class, since his works are filled with classical references and allusions. In his work the *Cure for Hellenic Maladies*, for example, over one hundred classical authors are cited, and he has been referred to as the "last great torchbearer of Christian rhetoric in Asia" (Halton 1988: 4). Theologically, Theodoret was influenced by the teachings of the bishops Theodore of Mopsuestia and Diodorus of Tarsus, and his fellow students included Nestorius and John of Antioch.

When he was 23 years old, Theodoret's parents died. He distributed his inheritance among the poor, and entered a monastery at Nicerte near Apamea, about seventy-five miles from Antioch. Despite his desire to remain a monk, he was raised to the bishopric in 423 at the age of 30 in the village of Cyrrhus. Nothing is known of the circumstances of this consecration. Cyrrhus itself was a small town, but the diocese was huge and included nine hundred churches. Theodoret's letters reveal that he was a conscientious bishop, who commissioned numerous public works and pressed for reductions in imperial taxation. He was also diligent in championing orthodox Christianity against pagans, Jews, and the many types of heretics who dwelled in his remote and mountainous see. Both before and after his ordination he produced a wide range of writings, which include about thirty-five works.

Theodoret is perhaps best known today for his role in the controversy over the nature of Christ known as the Nestorian controversy (Kelly 1959: 310–43; Young 1983: 178–289). In this conflict between the Alexandrian and Antiochene schools of theology, Theodoret sided with Nestorius, patriarch of Constantinople, on the Antiochene side. Both sides sought to clarify the relationship between Christ and the Logos or Word, and the eventual settlement drew from each position, but the provocative and quarrelsome style of Nestorius and his antagonist, Cyril of Alexandria, seems to have increased the level of acrimony of the debate.

In 428 and 429, Nestorius was attacked for his preaching against the use of the term "Theotokos," or "God-bearer," as an epithet for Mary. God, he argued, could not have a mother. Cyril saw in this refusal an attempt to split Christ too sharply into human and divine natures, or a potential revival of the "adoptionist" heresy which downplayed the divine nature of the Son. Cyril and Nestorius both wrote to Pope Celestine, who held a synod at Rome in August 430 and defended the use of "Theotokos" against Nestorius. Cyril followed the pope's threat of excommunication to Nestorius with a provocative series of Christological claims, the "Twelve Anathemas," which he ordered Nestorius to accept. The bluntness of the anathemas brought moderate followers of the Antiochene theology into the fight, including Theodoret, who exchanged angry broadsides with Cyril over the nature of Christ.

Theodosius II held a synod at Ephesus on Pentecost in 431, but after the faction of Cyril passed a condemnation of Nestorius, a rival eastern synod voted to depose Cyril and repudiate the Anathemas. The Cyrillian side won the day, and Nestorius was never reinstated, but nevertheless compromise followed within a couple of years after the death of Celestine in July 432. A formula which blended Antiochene and Alexandrian language to describe Christ was signed by all parties in 433. Theodoret refused, however, to endorse the deposition of Nestorius, and wrote to Nestorius that he would prefer to cut off his own hands than to sign such a condemnation (*ep.* 172). The Christological dispute subsided for a time, though not Theodoret's strong feelings about the matter. When Cyril died in 444 Theodoret rejoiced in a letter to a friend, and he suggested that the undertaker had better place a large stone in front of Cyril's tomb, to prevent him from being driven back among the living by the angry ghosts of outraged theologians he might preach to in Hell (*ep.* 180).

Theodoret was friendly with the bishop of Antioch, Domnus, and frequently traveled to Antioch and preached there. In an attempt to weaken the power of Antioch, Dioscorus, the new bishop of Alexandria and a devoted partisan of Cyril's theology, complained to the emperor about Theodoret and his preaching, and an imperial decree of 448 ordered him confined to his own see to prevent him from "disturbing the orthodox" (*ep.* 79). Theodoret's troubles mounted when Theodosius II, under Dioscorus' influence, summoned the Second Council of Ephesus in 449. At this synod, called the *latrocinium* or "Robber Synod" by Pope Leo, Theodoret was removed from his see along with others accused of being "Nestorians" such as Flavian of Constantinople, and Cyril's "Twelve Anathemas" were resurrected and approved as doctrine. Dioscorus had soldiers brought in to enforce the Alexandrian line; riots broke out and Flavian was badly beaten and died soon afterwards (Frend 1984: 766–70).

THEODORET

After the death of Theodosius in July 450, however, the balance of power shifted as the emperor's sister Pulcheria, sympathetic to Leo and the Antiochenes, was able to intervene more forcefully. The Council of Chalcedon was called to review the actions of the "Robber Synod," and a doctrinal compromise was reached. The ban on Theodoret's movement was reversed and he was able to attend the synod. There he was reinstated, but only after a grudging condemnation of his old friend Nestorius had been wrung from him.

We are poorly informed of the activities of Theodoret during the period from Chalcedon to his death because none of the letters which he wrote after 451 survive except for a few fragments (Azema 1984). He continued to write exegetical works, either from Cyrrhus or perhaps back in Nicerte at the monastery where he began his career. The date of his death is the subject of much controversy. The absence of Theodoret from a list of addressees of the emperor Leo I concerning Chalcedon in 457 has led some to suggest that he must have been dead by that time, but his successor in the bishopric of Cyrrhus is equally absent from the list. On the other hand, a remark by the chronicler Marcellinus seems to imply that the second edition of Theodoret's work *Eranistes* was published in 466. The biographer Gennadius says that Theodoret died during the reign of the emperor Leo, that is, between 457 and 474 (*vir. ill.* 89). It may also be the case that Theodoret himself revised his life of Simeon Stylites after the monk's death in 459 (*hist. relig.* 26). Finally, the Syrian historian John Diacrinomenus mentions a letter of Theodoret to "Sura," who may have been the bishop of Germanicia in northern Syria starting in 460. Azema, having weighed this evidence, admits to a lack of certainty, but suggests 460 as the most likely date (Azema 1984: 151).

Theodoret's collection of works is too extensive to receive more than superficial attention here (a full list may be found in Bardy 1946). Most numerous are his exegetical works, which include commentaries on most of the books of the Old Testament, and on the letters of Paul (Guinot 1995, 1984). Early in his career Theodoret wrote one of the last great works of Christian apologetics, the *Cure for Hellenic Maladies*, a demonstration of the bishop's wide reading in pagan authors and evidence of the continuing vitality of paganism in Syria (Canivet 1958). Among Theodoret's most popular theological works is his treatise *On Divine Providence*, a collection of ten discourses which may have been delivered at Antioch around 437 (Halton 1988). Theodoret argues that the

129

natural order of the world is not random and uncertain but rather is in fulfillment of a divine plan, in spite of the existence of poverty and injustice. The treatment is not rigorously philosophical, but is clear and well argued. More original is Theodoret's *Eranistes*, a series of three dialogues on Trinitarian issues between the characters Eranistes, that is, "Beggar" or "Collector," and Orthodoxus (Ettlinger 1975). Theodoret saw the heretic as a "collector" of ideas which did not form a coherent whole. The dialogues are nevertheless fair to Eranistes, who holds Alexandrian views on the nature of Christ, but who is allowed to make reasonable and realistic points. Each dialogue ends with a series of quotations from patristic authors which support the claims of Orthodoxus. The work, written in 447 or 448, has been called "perhaps the most original work to stem from Syria in the fifth century" (Ettlinger 1975: 3). Also of interest is the *Collection of Heretical Myths*, a work Theodoret wrote late in his life (Young 1983: 287–8). He arranges this encyclopedic work by the nature of the heresy, rather than in chronological order, as earlier compilers such as Epiphanius had done, and he concludes with a fifth book which offers an explanation of correct Christian doctrine. Surprisingly, Theodoret includes a chapter on Nestorius, which perhaps he felt he had to do for political reasons after Chalcedon.

Closer in form and content to his historical work is Theodoret's hagiographical *Religious History*, written in 440, which the author had called *History of the Monks* or the *Ascetic Life* (Price 1985; Canivet and Leroy-Molinghen 1977). This collection of about thirty lives of monks of the eastern desert reveals Theodoret's deep attraction to and knowledge of the ascetic, individualized monasticism of Syria. He knew many of his subjects as a child or as an adult, and was familiar as well with the oral tradition of the monks of the recent past. The monastic history makes use of vivid narrative and classical style, which Theodoret would bring to his *Ecclesiastical History* as well. Theodoret's monks are "athletes" or "gladiators" for God, who perform miracles and amazing acts of self-denial. The most famous, perhaps, was Simeon Stylites, who lived on top of a high pillar for decades. The *Religious History* is frequently referred to in Theodoret's *Ecclesiastical History*.

Work

Like the works of Socrates and Sozomen, Theodoret's *Ecclesiastical History* is written as a continuation of the work of Eusebius. From its beginning in 324, the history spans 105 years to 429. The work must have been published before 28 July 450, since it refers at one point to the emperor Theodosius II as "now" ruling (5.36.1). The *Ecclesiastical History* contains references to the *Religious History*, and therefore must have been written after 440 when that work was published. References to his *Religious History*, published in 440, provide a *terminus post quem* for the work. The fifth book seems to contain a reference to his struggles over Christology, which would most likely have been written after 447 (5.3.8). It seems likely that Theodoret drew upon Socrates, but he probably wrote before Sozomen's work was available, although this is still debated (Güldenpenning 1889; Barnes 1993b: 209–11).

Theodoret's very brief prologue opens with an analogy between painters of historical scenes and writers of history (1.1). While both provide delight and preserve the past, writers provide a more permanent as well as a more vivid record. In a comment familiar to classical historiography, he says that his purpose is to ensure that important events ignored by earlier ecclesiastical historians are not forgotten. He claims to have been often urged by friends to write a church history, and concludes with the similarly classical concern that his talent might not be sufficient for the task. Trust in God, however, will allow him to proceed. Unlike other church historians, Theodoret does not provide other prefaces or notices which address methodological concerns.

Theodoret's information is often derived from the earlier church histories as well as from Athanasius (Güldenpenning 1889). He relies, however, on some independent sources, and offers some letters and other primary documents which are found only in his work, most notably a letter written by Arius (1.5.1–4), and other letters or creeds which may derive from the collection of Sabinus but which are not reproduced by Socrates or Sozomen, such as the lengthy letter of Alexander of Alexandria to Alexander of Constantinople (1.4.1–61) and the letter of the synod at Constantinople to George, the bishop of Alexandria, concerning the heresy of Aetius (2.28). He also makes use of lost works which provide local Antiochene material, such as the *Against Eunomius* of Theodore of Mopsuestia (Bihain 1962a).

The *Ecclesiastical History* is divided into five books, with the divisions arranged around the lives of the emperors. The first book ends with the death of Constantine, the second with the death of Constantius II, the third with the death of Julian, and the fourth with the death of Valens at Adrianople. The fifth concludes with praise of the reign of Theodosius II, a notice of Theodotus' rise to bishop of Antioch, an account of martyrdoms in Persia, and finally a notice of the death of Theodore of Mopsuestia.

Theodoret's *Ecclesiastical History* is a stripped-down version of the genre, lacking many of the digressions and secular details which Socrates and Sozomen had experimented with in different ways. It may be that his history was a purposeful reaction against those earlier works (Harries 1991: 276). The work also shows little interest in chronological detail or order, and it has been said that it might be "better described as dogmatic and polemical, rather than apologetic or historical" (Allen 1987: 377). Even when Theodoret uses information from Socrates or Sozomen, he often freely alters it in order to highlight the moral or doctrinal point he wishes to make.

While all late antique church histories after Eusebius devoted considerable amounts of attention to Arianism, the progress of the heresy in the fourth century is more central to Theodoret's work than to any other. Rufinus, Socrates, and Sozomen had begun their histories with the conversion of Constantine to Christianity, for example, but Theodoret plunges almost immediately into the actions of Arius in Alexandria (1.2). In his conclusion, he describes his work as beginning "from the commencement of the Arian madness" (5.40). One might also compare the treatment of Ulfila and the Goths in Socrates and in Theodoret. While Socrates admits that the Goths had become "infected" with Arianism, he points out the political circumstances surrounding their conversion and ends by pointing out that many had been admirably martyred owing to their faith in Christ (4.33). Theodoret emphasizes only theological issues, focusing on how the Goths were tricked into Arianism by the wicked bishop Eudoxius (4.37).

Theodoret has, purposely it seems, avoided bringing his history up to the times of his own doctrinal struggles, and few specific references to those disputes can be found in the work. One of them appears in a discussion of the rise of the Apollinarist heresy. Apollinaris the Younger was a staunch supporter of the Nicene Creed who was held to have too severely downplayed the human nature of Christ, teaching that the Logos substituted for his human soul. The conclusions which followed from this interpretation, according to Theodoret, show that Apollinarianism was "the root from which has sprung up the evil doctrine now prevalent in the church" and such people have excited "great controversy" in the present day (5.3.8). In a broader sense, however, Theodoret's anti-

Arian work served the purpose of championing his own orthodoxy and of allowing him to demonstrate that, despite the dualistic nature of his Christology, he had not fallen into Arianism himself. When Theodoret wrote to Pope Leo to vindicate his orthodoxy after the Robber Synod, he cited his previous writings to demonstrate his good faith, and while he did not refer to the *Ecclesiastical History* by name, it could easily fit under the category of works written "against the Arians" (*ep.* 113).

Theodoret's history does show evidence of an Antiochene bias, and in a study of Theodoret's treatment of several bishops of Antioch in the fourth century, Allen has demonstrated that the historian has presented the bishops' rule in a considerably more favorable light than had Socrates (Allen 1990). Theodoret undoubtedly had access to local traditions concerning these bishops, and would have had both patriotic and doctrinal reasons to overlook the flaws and exaggerate the talents of the anti-Arian holders of the bishopric. Theodoret presents a scene where Theodosius I dreams of being crowned by an unfamiliar bishop, Meletius, whom the emperor later recognizes and greets in a crowd (5.6). This Meletius is praised in Theodoret's letters and was close to important Antiochenes such as John Chrysostom. Socrates, by contrast, writing from Constantinople, preserves many unflattering details about Meletius, whom he blames for the schism in the anti-Arian forces at Antioch. Theodoret is similarly favorable toward the bishop Flavian, who was an associate of Diodorus and of the monks with whom Theodoret would later be associated. Socrates and Sozomen, on the other hand, portray Flavian as a perjurer and schismatic (Allen 1990: 275–80).

Although Theodoret's classical learning is clear from some of his other works, in keeping with the genre, his ecclesiastical history contains few allusions or citations. Exceptions are of the most banal sort, such as the comment that "it would require the magniloquence of Aeschylus and Sophocles" to describe the sufferings of a bishop during the reign of Julian (3.7.6). Theodoret, like Sozomen, includes some discussion of monks and monastic communities in his work, although the two writers have almost no overlap in the monks they discuss. In a list of twenty-three outstanding hermits of the fourth century presented by Theodoret, for example, only two can be found in a similar list in Sozomen (Theod. 4.28; Soz. 6.32–4; Price 1985: xvii–xviii).

Theodoret's *Ecclesiastical History* is largely a success if judged on its own terms. The bishop has excised much of the extensive material on political and military events which earlier church historians had included. Emperors and warfare are presented not for their own sake, but to further the historian's moralizing purposes, and his accuracy concerning secular events is correspondingly low. Theodoret includes the letters and church documents which Eusebius had made an essential part of the genre, but he focuses more narrowly on the Arian heresy and related doctrinal matters, rather than attempting to encompass all of the controversies of the church during the period. Stylistically, he may have been trying to cleanse the genre of what he saw as material extraneous to his definition of church history. Theodoret also wrote for personal reasons, both to demonstrate his own orthodoxy and to correct the record offered by two writers from Constantinople with an Antiochene perspective.

Text and translation

Greek text edited by L. Parmentier (1954), *Griechischen Christlichen Schriftsteller*. English translation (1843) in *Greek ecclesiastical historians of the First Six Centuries. Nicene and Post-Nicene Fathers*, translation available on-line at:
http://www.ccel.org/fathers2/NPNF2–03/Npnf2–03–04.htm#P112 _4318.

12

OROSIUS

Life

Our information about the life of Orosius is almost entirely limited to the period between 414 and 418. Since Augustine describes Orosius during these years as a "young priest" (*ep.* 169) and as a "son by age" (*ep.* 166), Orosius was then presumably around 30 years old, and was therefore born around 375. After his departure from Africa for Spain at the beginning of 418, Orosius disappeared from history.

Contemporaries of Orosius referred to him by the single name, and it is not until the mid-sixth-century history of Jordanes that the historian is referred to as "Paulus Orosius." This name may, however, be a mistaken expansion of a "P" for "presybter" (priest) (Arnaud-Lindet 1990: xiii). Augustine says that Orosius had come to him "from the shore of the Ocean." Avitus, a priest of Bracara (modern-day Braga) on the Portuguese coast, wrote a letter in which he called Orosius his fellow priest. Avitus also entrusted Orosius with certain relics of St Stephen to bring to Palchonius, the bishop of Bracara. It can therefore be assumed that Orosius was ordained as a priest in that town. His work suggests that in addition to theological training, he also had at least the rudiments of a classical education.

The only information we have from Orosius about his life prior to 414 is a cryptic passage lamenting misfortunes he suffered at an unspecified time in the past. " … how I first saw the unfamiliar barbarians previously unknown to me, how I evaded enemies, how I flattered the powerful, how I guarded against heathens, how I fled from those who would ambush me, and, finally, how hidden in a sudden mist I evaded those pursuing me on sea and seeking me with rocks and javelins, even almost seizing me once" (3.20.6–7). Past interpretations of these lines have often suggested that Orosius is recounting his forced flight from Spain during barbarian invasions. Elsewhere, however, Orosius downplays the problem of barbarian–Roman rapprochement. Arnaud-Lindet suggests that the passage would apply more easily to an escape from captivity than to flight from an invasion. Noting that in his geography Orosius mentions twice, with praise, the relatively insignificant coastal town of Brigantia (1.2.71, 1.2.81), he speculates that Orosius had been captured by Scottish pirates during the invasion of 405 and found refuge in Brigantia after his escape (Arnaud-Lindet 1990: xi–xii). Elsewhere Orosius alludes to disturbances which forced his departure to Africa, which might have been theological controversies rather than military invasions (5.2).

Orosius arrived in Hippo in 414 and presented Augustine with the first of the three works he is known to have written. The *Commonitorium de Errore Priscillianistarum et Origenistarum* is a short "memorandum" to the bishop on heretical ideas which were prominent at the time. In it he claims that neither his will nor accident had brought him to Africa, but the will of God. It seems clear from the introduction that the two had already discussed some of the heretical ideas which Orosius addresses in his pamphlet. Priscillian was a Spaniard born around 340 who preached ascetic renunciation (Burrus 1995; Chadwick 1976). After being condemned, restored, and condemned again after 380, Priscillian and several of his followers were executed in 385 or 386. While Priscillian was revered as a martyr for a time after his death, councils in 400 and afterward condemned his doctrines, which were considered excessively dualistic and "Manichaean." Orosius' criticisms of Priscillian in his *Commonitorium* are sharp but may rely on material falsely attributed to him (Chadwick 1976: 202). Orosius also criticizes Origenist ideas which he claims had been brought to Spain from Jerusalem, and begs Augustine for his thoughts on these errors. Augustine, responding with "as much brevity and clarity as possible" (Aug. *Retractiones* 2.44), criticizes the Origenist principles as described by Orosius, but refrains from dismissing Origen altogether.

It is during this time that Orosius was first enjoined by Augustine to compile a list of the misfortunes which the Romans had endured in the past. Augustine desired such a collection to supplement his work in the *City of God*, which sought to refute pagan charges that the Gothic sack of Rome in 410 had resulted from the abandonment of the traditional gods. This collection was to serve as the seed from which Orosius' full history would grow.

Orosius remained with Augustine for about a year. In the spring of 415, he set off to Palestine and to Jerome bearing letters from Augustine. In a letter to Jerome introducing Orosius, Augustine says that he has taught the young priest all that he could and was now handing him over to Jerome for further instruction. Augustine sent along with Orosius information about the dangers of the thought of Pelagius. The theologian Pelagius had rejected interpretations of original sin which deprecated the power and responsibility of Christians to use their free will to act justly, and he demanded that all Christians, not just priests and monks, should perfect themselves (Rees 1988; Evans 1968; Brown 1972: 183–226). Having left Rome, perhaps because of the invasion of 410, Pelagius had gone to Carthage and then to Palestine. Pelagius' more radical follower Caelestius had been condemned for rejecting infant baptism by a Carthaginian synod, perhaps in 411, and Augustine had been preaching and writing against Pelagianism since that time. Orosius probably brought some of these anti-Pelagian writings with him to strengthen Jerome's position against Pelagius, at a time when Pelagius' position was strengthened by the politically powerful patronage of Bishop John of Jerusalem.

In Palestine Orosius confronted Pelagius directly in an informal meeting before Bishop John in July, and in December a synod formally took up the question of Pelagianism. In both cases Orosius and Jerome were defeated (Hunt 1982: 202–20; Kelly 1975: 317–21). Orosius' *Liber Apologeticus*, written at the end of 415, is a pamphlet which tries to explain his loss, in part by claiming that Pelagius' work, written in Latin, could not be properly understood in the Greek-speaking east. His failures likely made him unwelcome in Jerusalem, and he returned to Africa in 416.

On his departure from the east, Orosius carried relics of St Stephen, along with an account of their recent discovery by Lucian, which were to be brought to Bishop Palchonius of his native Bracara. After delivering a letter (*ep.* 134) from Jerome to Augustine, he set out for Africa by way of Minorca. Unable to continue on to Spain, presumably because of barbarian incursions, he was forced to return to Africa and to abandon the relics on the island, where they were responsible for numerous miracles (Hunt 1982). In Africa he wrote his major work, *Seven Books of History Against the Pagans*, and is not heard from again after its completion in 418. Perhaps he died in a shipwreck on his return to Spain.

Work

Orosius' *History* was tremendously successful and became one of the primary sources of information about antiquity in the Middle Ages. Its reception among moderns has been substantially cooler. The sources Orosius drew upon have generally survived, and his sloppiness and constant rhetorical asides have not won him favor. But while his recounting of the facts is often unimpressive, his complex systematizing reveals his bold and original mind. *The History against the Pagans* sought to encompass a large part of world history with a geographical and chronological scope which exceeded most of the other narrative historians of later antiquity.

The sources upon which Orosius depended are well known. For his treatment of the Roman republic, he drew heavily upon Livy, garnering information from all but eight books of the 142 of the *Ab Urbe Condita*. Orosius also used Caesar's *Gallic Wars*, the republican material of Eutropius, and the second-century epitomator Florus. For the history of the east, of Greece, and of Carthage, Orosius looked particularly to the epitome of Pompeius Trogus prepared by Justin. He also used the *Chronicle* of Eusebius, as translated and supplemented by Jerome, and found a bit of information about Babylon in Herodotus. For the imperial period, Orosius continued to depend upon the *Chronicle*, Florus, and Eutropius, with added material from Tacitus and Suetonius. Further information was derived from Rufinus' translation of Eusebius' *Ecclesiastical History* and, for the fourth century, Rufinus' continuation of the work. For the last twenty years of the work, Orosius depended upon oral sources and his own recollections.

Orosius' style is typical of late Latin rhetorical writers (Bartalucci 1976; Fabbrini 1979: 110–25). Both Augustine (*ep.* 166) and Gennadius (*vir. ill.* 39) describe him as "eloquent," and he displays the expected features of late Latin eloquence: frequent use of chiasmus, alliteration, and personification, elaborate metaphors, and the use of poetic language and allusions to Vergil to evoke pathos or excitement.

Orosius dedicates his work to Augustine and reveals that he wrote it in response to a request from the bishop for details to support his position against the pagans. Pagans disturbed by the recent sack of Rome had been claiming that disasters had multiplied as the worship of idols ceased and Christianity spread. It seems that Augustine asked Orosius to research the "histories and annals" and compile a list of all sorts of misfortunes – war, disease, famine, natural disasters – with the goal of demonstrating that misfortunes had not increased with the spread of Christianity, but were constant throughout history. Orosius was asked to list these misfortunes "systematically and briefly." Orosius' excessively servile tone in the preface, including a lengthy comparison of himself with a dog, has sometimes blinded readers to the fact that he substantially exceeded Augustine's mandate both in the length and in the complexity of his work. A hint of what is to come appears in Orosius' musings toward the end of the prologue. "I discovered that past times were not only equally as grave as those of today, but that they were even more terrible in accordance with how much more distant they were from the assistance of the true religion" (1.*pref.*14). In Augustine's *City of God*, the bishop would make the case that suffering is found at all times and is a fundamental part of earthly human existence. For Orosius, however, suffering had been endemic in pre-Christian times, but with the coming of Christ and the spread of Christianity, suffering had been substantially reduced and would continue to diminish with the further spread of the gospel.

Orosius was extremely ambitious, and he set out to write a true universal history which would cover the history of all peoples and of all time. He first postulated a division of time into three great parts: from Adam to Romulus, from Romulus to Christ, and from Christ to the present day (1.1.5–6). The seven books of the history are arranged in accordance with this division: the first division is covered in book 1, the second in books 2 through 6, and the last in book 7. The books vary greatly in length, and in particular the last book is more than two-thirds the length of the second through the sixth books combined.

The scope of the seven books can be briefly summarized. Book 1 covered 1,307 years, from the reign of the Assyrian king Ninus to the founding of Rome (2060–753). Book 2 brings the story up to the Gallic invasion of 390 (363 years), with the inclusion of events in Persia and Greece. Book 3 covers 109 years up to 281 and describes, in addition to Roman affairs, the wars of Philip, Alexander, and his successors. Book 4 treats the three Punic Wars and ends in 146 (136 years). Like book 4, book 5 is entirely Roman and brings the story up to the uprising of Spartacus in AD 73 (73 years). Book 6 covers 73 years and ends with the triumph of Augustus and the coming of Christ, two events closely linked in Orosius' view of history. The last book, book 7, treats the history of the empire from Augustus to the advent of pacific Gothic leaders such as Ataulf and Wallia in 417.

Orosius begins with Adam in order to emphasize the importance of original sin to his concept of history. This may reflect his concerns with the issues which Pelagianism had raised. Certain preoccupations which will color the entire history are adumbrated in the first chapter of the first book. The evils enumerated throughout his history, he says, have their roots in the sin of Adam. Evils which existed in the past, and which continue to exist "to some extent" today, "are undoubtedly either obvious sins or the hidden punishments of sins" (1.1.12–13). In particular, war is always to be considered an evil, since what are wars but "evils befalling one side or the other"?

After Orosius' discussion of Adam demonstrates that his work will be universal in time, he provides a lengthy chapter on the geography of the world which reveals that his work will also be universal in space (Corsini 1968: 73–83; Janvier 1982). Orosius' geography is in general accord with the state of geographical knowledge in his time and depends ultimately, through an intermediate source or sources, on the map of the world made by Agrippa for his father-in-law, the emperor Augustus. The inclusion of geographical information is quite common in classical historiography, and thus Orosius seeks to emphasize the historical element of his work over the apologetic element. But his presentation of the geography of the entire world at the beginning of the work differs from the traditional geographic digression in a more typical history, which covers only the specific portion of the world which has come into the ambit of the historical narrative. Instead, Orosius reveals the importance of the entire world to his history. "Among Romans, as I have said, I am a Roman; among Christians, a Christian; among men, a man. … I enjoy every land temporarily as my homeland, because what is truly my homeland and what I love, is not entirely on this earth" (5.2.6).

Christians attacked by pagans after the sack of Rome sought to refute the criticism by demonstrating that Rome had endured similar hardships in the past, even before the spread of Christianity. Although Orosius may have begun his research at the behest of Augustine with this modest aim, he ended up formulating a far more radical thesis in his work, a veritable "counter-history" to the histories of the preceding centuries (Inglebert 1996: 511). Orosius' belief that a universal Christian God acted in history demanded that the period before the coming of Christ be not only comparable in misfortunes to his own time, but substantially worse. To the pagan charge that modern times had been corrupted by neglect of the traditional gods and the embrace of Christ, Orosius rebuts that the worship of the Roman gods and the ignorance of Christ had corrupted earlier times. Orosius thus stands against the historical vision of classical historians such as Sallust and Livy, which was adopted even by Christians such as Jerome and Augustine. These thinkers had portrayed the Romans of the early republic as glorious and virtuous, and had seen the following years as marked by a drastic decline in morals and virtue which led to the disastrous civil wars of the late republic.

Orosius portrays the period of the kings in a negative light. He judges Romulus guilty of kidnapping and rape in the affair of the Sabine Women, and he adds that Romulus was the murderer of his grandfather, his brother, and the kindly and honorable Titus Tatius, and that he populated the Roman state with criminals who were promised immunity. The other kings are described as equally ignoble; Orosius notably omits mention of the saintly Numa Pompilius, who would not fit his argument well (2.4). But Orosius' republic does not represent progress from the earlier period. Brutus, the tyrannicide and first consul, merely rivals and surpasses Romulus in the murder of members of his family (2.5.1). The parricide of Romulus serves, in fact, as a kind of original sin of the Roman state, and the Romans "sprung from Romulus" are not surprised when Publicius Malleolus (in 101) kills his mother (5.16.23–4).

Orosius' case against the Roman republic is not limited to the cruelty and evil of particular Romans, but includes natural disasters as well. Plague devastated Rome in 463, killing both consuls (2.12.3), and again in 267 (4.5.8), leading Orosius to comment that plagues do not take place "without the will of all-powerful God." Likewise the devastation of constant war was occasionally exacerbated by fires and floods (4.11.6–9) or by swarms of locusts, such as the one which Orosius claims killed almost a million people in Africa in 125 (5.11).

Orosius' polemic against the republic centers, however, upon the prevalence of war. Most striking is the pathos he arouses by his rhetorically excessive description of the Gallic invasion of 390, which stresses how much more a catastrophe that sack of the city was compared to the more recent sack in 410. Many other examples may be found in the first six books of the *History*. Orosius' focus on the blessings of peace distinguishes him sharply from other classical thinkers. His comments on the bellicose Philip and Alexander demonstrate his ideology. About Philip, he concludes, "the fraud, savagery, and domination of a single king resulted in the burning of cities, the devastations of wars, the subjugation of provinces, the slaughter of men, the theft of property, the plundering of flocks, robbery of the dead and the enslavement of men" (3.14.10). Of Alexander, he scorns the idea that his conquests "are judged to be praiseworthy more on account of the courage by which the whole world was conquered than to be despised on account of the vision by which the whole world was overturned" (3.20.10). It is this last point, the recognition that every conquest, Roman or otherwise, is a defeat for the vanquished, that Orosius makes so effectively. In contradistinction even to other late antique Christians, he rejects the idea of just war that served to elevate the wars of the republican period over the decadent imperial era. He knows that some will look at the victorious republican period as a fortunate one, but points out that "Rome conquers happily, to the extent that whatever is outside Rome is unhappily conquered" (5.1.3). Orosius' perspective as a Spanish provincial perhaps encouraged this critical approach. He presents two hundred years of slaughter in Spain, and equivalent disasters in Carthage and Italy, as examples of the price of Roman republican expansionism (5.1.5–9, and cf. 5.5).

In the republican period, Orosius claims, before the coming of Christ, original sin ensured disaster for men, but in the Christian era, the possibility of Christ's intercession allowed for gradual improvement. The key moment in Christian history, the birth of Jesus, coincided with a key moment in Roman history, the rule of the first emperor Augustus, and this coincidence served as the basis for the political theology of Eusebius and then Orosius. In the beginning of his sixth book, Orosius credits God with conferring "by his arrangement all things upon one and the same emperor who was most powerful and merciful." This was done to provide a peaceful and free area in which the followers of Jesus, from many nations, might spread the Christian faith (6.1). God chose to come to earth in heavenly form at the very time that a census was under way, in order to be counted as a Roman citizen (6.22.6). Orosius claims that Octavian entered the city of Rome on 6 January 27 BC, to celebrate a triumph and to close the doors of the temple Janus, signifying peace throughout the world. On this day, too, the emperor was first saluted as Augustus. This very same day is also the feast of the Epiphany, the appearance of the Magi before the baby Jesus, a coincidence which reveals the divine plan. Orosius, however, makes these claims only with the help of several chronological errors, since the gates of Janus were actually closed on the eleventh of January, and Octavian's triumph did not take place until August (Arnaud-Lindet 1990 vol. 2: 269). Orosius adds that other signs proclaimed the connection of Augustus and Jesus, as when a spring of oil, a symbol of Christ "the anointed one," flowed for an entire day after a victory of the emperor (6.20.6–7). Further evidence of the link between the emperor and the Savior is found in Augustus' adamant refusal to be addressed as *dominus*, "lord," a title to be reserved for Jesus alone (6.22.5).

Even if Augustus did not take the title of lord from Jesus, the two figures are nevertheless presented as parallel, with Augustus the temporal ruler of the universe just as Jesus is its ultimate ruler. Orosius then naturally prefers monarchy to other forms of government, not only because he sees the rule of a single man as necessary to impose peace on the world, but because this form of terrestrial government parallels monotheistic spiritual rule (3.8.5–8). Orosius' thought may be distinguished from that of Eusebius by his emphasis on a different messianic sign. While Eusebius portrayed the military victory of Octavian at Actium over his rivals as comparable to the victory of God over demons, Orosius saw the peace prompting the closing of the gates of the temple of Janus as a sign of Christ's arrival (Inglebert 1996: 574). Orosius, as always, stresses the peacefulness of the victory of Christianity.

Orosius' insistence on the supremacy of Christian times over ancient times sometimes reaches absurd heights (Corsini 1968: 115). He mentions, for example, a serious earthquake in Greece in 376 BC which destroyed two cities, and adds that, although earthquakes continue to threaten the world, the prayers of the emperor Arcadius and his Christian subjects prevented a recent earthquake from causing serious harm (3.3.2–3). Similarly, the devastation of the plague of locusts which ravaged Africa in 125 BC has never been repeated in the locust swarms of the Christian era, thanks to God (5.11.6). The success of the emperor Claudius in conquering Britain without bloodshed is contrasted with the failure of Julius Caesar, and the success of Claudius is attributed to the divine favor of Christian times (7.6.9–10).

While evil acts continue to be perpetrated in Christian times, Orosius says that they are now to be interpreted as just punishment for wrongs committed. His unusual interpretation of the reign of Tiberius exemplifies this view. Tiberius began as a peaceful and popular emperor, who, Orosius claims, proposed to the senate after Christ's crucifixion that Jesus be officially recognized as a god. This breach of senatorial protocol poisoned relations between emperor and legislature, and Tiberius' ensuing desire to punish the senators gradually corrupted him. In his new and wicked mode, he killed numerous senators and relatives. In the twelfth year of his reign, the collapse of an amphitheater which killed twenty thousand people revealed divine displeasure with his rule. Though chronologically, in fact, the collapse preceded the crucifixion, Orosius placed it after a recounting of Tiberius' sins to forge a link between crime and divine punishment (7.4). Orosius likewise places the civil war in which Septimius Severus defeated Pescennius Niger out of place chronologically to characterize it as punishment for Severus' persecution of Christians (7.17). Consider as well Orosius' interpretation of the reign of the next emperor, Gaius Caligula (7.5). On the one hand, Caligula's depravity served well the need of God to punish sinful Romans and Jews. On the other hand, Caligula's instincts toward evil were suppressed thanks to the mercy of God. Evidence of just how much worse he might have been arose after his death, when a large supply of poison and a long list of senators marked for murder were found in his private quarters.

Orosius judges Constantine favorably, but not blindly (7.28). The emperor successfully conquered his rivals, who were persecutors of Christians, and restored peace to the church. He was militarily successful in his defeat of the Sarmatians, and he peacefully suppressed pagan worship. He is also praised for his creation of Constantinople, a city without idols. Orosius is more positive toward the emperor than is Jerome, who in his *Chronicle* accused Constantine of Arian sympathies and condemned his creation of Constantinople. On the other hand, Orosius does mention and condemn the emperor's execution of his son, Crispus, and he refrains from the kind of panegyric found in Eusebius and Rufinus. Orosius portrays Theodosius I very favorably. While Rufinus had been content to portray Theodosius as a replica or reflection of Constantine, Orosius' historical theology requires ever-increasing virtue in Christian times, and thus his Constantine must be inferior to his Theodosius (Inglebert 1996: 560–1). Theodosius and his sons, Honorius and Arcadius, are depicted as perfect and orthodox Christians, militarily successful through faith in God (7.34, 36, 42).

Orosius' vision of history is more complex than the simple distinction between bad, pre-Christian times and good, Christian times. The historian attempted to form an explanation for the succession of empires throughout all of world history through the identification of parallels between biblical passages and historical events. Although discovering such patterns in the historical record sometimes led to distortions in his account of the past, Orosius' innovative attempt to place all of history into a coherent framework was immensely appealing to later ages.

Orosius' attention to chronology results from his desire to explain world history through a particular understanding of the succession of empires (Arnaud-Lindet 1990: xlv–lviii; Fabbrini 1979: 348–65; Corsini 1968: 158–68). The idea of a succession of empires is found in pagan works, notably in Justin's epitome of Pompeius Trogus, which Orosius drew upon (41; and cf. Vell. Pat. 1.6), but the biblical book of Daniel provides a more immediate influence upon our author (2: 31–45). Daniel gives an allegorical interpretation of Nebuchadnezzar's dream of four beasts, which are to be associated with the four successive kingdoms which ruled over the Jews: the Babylonian, the Median, the Persian, and the Macedonian. Interpretations of this vision several centuries later, in apocalyptic Jewish texts and in the New Testament book of Revelation (Rev. 13), saw the last beast as symbolizing not the Macedonian empire, but the Roman empire. Closer to the time of Orosius, the identity of the four empires had been given by Eusebius (*dem. evang.* 15.*fr.* 1) as the Assyrians, the Persians, the Macedonians, and the Romans, and in Jerome's commentary on the book of Daniel (at 2:38–40), which Orosius may have read in Palestine, as the Babylonians, the Medo-Persians, the Macedonians, and the Romans. In book 20 of the *City of God*, published in 425 or 426, Augustine had directed readers curious about the identity of the kingdoms to Jerome's work, overlooking or deliberately avoiding the solution offered by Orosius in the meantime.

Orosius identifies the four empires as the Babylonian, the Carthaginian, the Macedonian, and the Roman (2.1.4–6). The introduction of the Carthaginian empire is perhaps the most noticeable change in Orosius' schema. Orosius identifies the four empires with the four cardinal directions, with Carthage serving as the "southern" empire. Its inclusion demonstrates Orosius' western orientation and focus on the Mediterranean, as opposed to the near eastern orientation of other exegetes. The system also entails the neglect of Persia and of the Jews, neither of which occupies a prominent place in his historical philosophy. Orosius also innovates in portraying Babylon and Rome as the predominant empires, "father and son," and stating that the intervening empires of Carthage and Macedonia are not linked by "inheritance" but served as "guardians" during the transition between the two more important empires.

In the beginning of his second and his seventh book Orosius describes the extensive numerical correspondences he has discovered between the empires, sometimes at the expense of accurate chronology (2.3.1–4, 7.2.8–15). Orosius claims that "all ancient histories" begin with the reign of Ninus, and "all" histories of Rome with the reign of Procas. Each of these rulers served as "seeds" of their future kingdoms, for sixty-four years after each came the rule of Semiramis, the restorer of Babylon, and Romulus, the founder of Rome. The reign of Procas and the rise of Rome occurred simultaneously with the fall of Babylon, and the overthrow of Babylon by King Cyrus occurred simultaneously with the ejection of the Tarquins by the Romans and the establishment of the republic. Thus "the power of the East fell, and that of the West rose." The numerology is linked to Christianity by Orosius' observation that Abraham was born in the forty-third year of the reign of Ninus, and Christ was born forty-two years after the accession of Augustus. The transitional empires of Carthage and Macedon each lasted approximately seven hundred years, and Rome, although destined to last in order to provide a platform for the coming of Christ, suffered a serious fire in its seven hundredth year. Babylon existed for 1,164 years before it was conquered by the Medes, and it was likewise around 1,164 years after the founding of Rome that the city was sacked by Alaric and the Goths. More apocalyptically minded thinkers might have taken this last correspondence as evidence of the imminent destruction of the fourth kingdom and the end of the world, but Orosius draws the opposite conclusion. While irreligious Babylon was destroyed, Rome survived the fateful year through the mercy of God. Orosius has therefore removed the apocalyptic purpose from the biblical passage. While Daniel's four kingdoms progressively declined and were then followed by a messianic fifth kingdom, Orosius' kingdoms culminate in the divinely inspired fourth kingdom, the Roman empire.

The system as a whole is judged by Inglebert as "more ingenious than coherent" (1996: 521). It sits uneasily with his division of history into time before and after Christ as well as his tripartite division of history into creation to Romulus, Romulus to Christ, and Christ to the present day, although some scholars have heroically attempted to reconcile the systems (Paschoud 1980a; Corsini 1968: 144–50). These attempts to explain history and the succession of empires in such elaborate detail are the most innovative part of Orosius' work.

Orosius' love of peace and his belief in Rome's divinely favored status leads him to a strikingly original view of the sack of Rome and the question of the barbarian. Barbarian invasions are portrayed, on the one hand, as the just punishment for the sins of the Romans and their leaders. The homoiousian Valens, for example, attempted to press monks into military service, and to destroy orthodox churches, and these sins led to the movement of Huns and Goths and the Roman defeat at Adrianople (7.33). Following this reasoning, Orosius suggests that when the Goths threatened Rome, and the inhabitants blasphemed Christ and returned to the celebration of pagan rituals, the city was justly sacked (7.37). On the other hand, God's mercy may be seen in the comparatively mild effects of these invasions. Rome was sacked, not by the pagan Radagaisus, but by the Christian Alaric, who respected the sanctity of the churches and acted mildly toward the city as a whole. In any event, Orosius hastens to add, the destruction was nothing compared to the fire during the reign of Nero, or the complete destruction by Goths in the fourth century BC. At the time of writing, a few years after the event, Orosius claims that the city is like new again (7.39).

In addition to the minimizing of the destructiveness of the barbarians, Orosius argues that Roman encounters with the barbarians are leading to a fulfillment of the divine plan. Matthew 24: 14 commanded the spreading of the gospel to all the nations. The arrival of barbarians on Roman soil, although traumatic at first, had in Orosius' telling quickly led to comity and peace. "Barbarians, hating their swords, turned to their plows, and they treat the resident Romans as allies and friends, with the result that some Romans may be found who prefer to dwell among the barbarians, poor but free, rather than among the Romans, burdened by worrisome taxes" (7.41.7). The invasions had provided the opportunity to spread Christianity: "throughout the east and west the churches of Christ were replete with Huns, Suebi, Vandals, and Burgundians" (7.41.8). The marriage of the Gothic king Ataulf and the emperor's daughter Galla Placidia provided the perfect symbol of this union. Orosius had heard Narbo, a Roman general close to Ataulf, claim that the Goth had once been eager to replace "Romania," the Roman empire, with "Gothia," but had learned from his devout wife Galla Placidia that he should instead be restorer and increaser of the Roman state (7.43.4–7; Marchetta 1987).

Orosius writes that his research has been done at Augustine's request, and concludes his history with an assertion of his obedience, but the size of the work and its philosophy seem to exceed and contradict Augustine's mandate. The relationship between Orosius' history and Augustine's *City of God* has thus engendered much critical speculation and argument (La Croix 1965: 199–207; Frend 1989; Corsini 1968: 193–215; Mommsen 1959). After completing the first ten books of the *City of God*, Augustine had, according to Orosius' account, asked the Spanish priest to prepare simply a list of calamities which had befallen the Romans during pagan times, with the aim of refuting pagan arguments which had gathered in strength after the sack of Rome in 410. Orosius mentions that he read Augustine's work and used it as a source, and there are several places where his borrowing is evident (Corsini 1968: 197–8). On the other hand, the second half of *City of God* contains no mention at all of Orosius or his work. Closer inspection reveals that Augustine has not simply ignored the work of his protégé, but has undermined his conclusions with an attitude of what Corsini calls "irritated disapproval" (Corsini 1968: 200). For example, Orosius had interpreted the ten plagues of Egypt as foreshadowing the ten persecutions of the Christian church, each plague a prophecy of the type of calamity the empire suffered under each persecuting emperor (7.27). But Augustine argues that despite what "some" have argued, and "however nicely and ingeniously" they have compared the two, the plagues are not in fact to be interpreted as signs of persecutions (18.52). Likewise, Augustine points out that although "some" say that Semiramis was the founder of Babylon (18.2), in reality the city was founded by the giant Nimrod (16.4). These statements may be understood not just as Augustine's correction of a minor chronological detail, but as an undermining of the entire series of chronological coincidences which drive Orosius' numerological theology. Orosius' determinism and materialism were at odds with Augustine's political thought, which continued to move in the direction of spirituality and grace under the influence of his reflections on Pelagianism. Thus Orosius' completed history was not useful to Augustine, since his focus had moved away from the paganism which had absorbed him in the early books of the *City of God*. The crudeness of Orosius' philosophy seems rather to have been contradictory and even embarrassing in the light of Augustine's more complex and sophisticated reflections on human history.

While the historical philosophy of Augustine's *City of God* may be more sophisticated, Orosian analysis proved more popular throughout the Middle Ages. Many hundreds of manuscripts survive. As a world history with a Christian viewpoint, it had great value for Latin-speaking westerners, and in the early Middle Ages was read by Isidore, Bede, and Gregory of Tours. In the ninth century, King Alfred made an adapted translation of the work into Anglo-Saxon, and in the tenth century it was translated into Arabic after being offered as a gift from the Byzantine emperor Romanus II to the Caliph of Cordoba. Orosius was of great importance for the epochal twelfth-century historical works of Orderic Vitalis and Otto of Freising, and Dante drew heavily upon Orosius' work (Fabbrini 1979: 21–9). While Orosius has won praise from some modern theorists of history, including Benedetto Croce and Karl Löwith, his sloppiness and the extravagance of his vision of history has resulted most often in modern reactions which range from lukewarm to extremely cold. Nevertheless, modern scholarly interest in Orosius is likely to continue, if only because he has so often erred in such new and unusual ways.

Text and translation

Latin text edited by C. Zangemeister (1882), *Corpus Scriptorum Ecclesiasticorum Latinorum*. English translation by R.J. Deferrari (1964), *Fathers of the Church*.

13

HISTORIOGRAPHY

Self-presentation

History writing was a form of rhetoric, or persuasive speech. The ancient historian had to convince the reader that his history was worth reading, and that he had both the ability and the integrity to write a trustworthy history. In a recent book, *Authority and Tradition in Ancient Historiography*, John Marincola explores the way Greek and Roman historians of the classical period had sought to convince readers of the merits of their works through their self-presentation (Marincola 1997). Late antique historians continued to share the needs of their predecessors to demonstrate to readers the value and reliability of their works. They employed new methods of authentication, however, in response to changing ideas of political and religious authority in late antiquity.

The most traditional method of convincing the reader of the importance of a history is the simple assertion of the greatness of the deeds which the history will treat. We lack the preface to Ammianus Marcellinus, and the surviving books contain no explicit discussion of his reasons for writing history. Nevertheless, because Ammianus gives such disproportionate attention and praise to the emperor Julian, it is very likely that he used his introduction to claim that his history was necessary in order to ensure that the outstanding deeds of the emperor are not forgotten. Eunapius explicitly states that the greatness of the deeds of Julian made a historian of his times necessary (*fr.* 15). One might, more tentatively, suggest that Olympiodorus and Priscus, whose prefaces also did not survive, had likewise referred to the commemoration of outstanding deeds as the reason for their histories.

Pagan, classicizing historians were not alone in claiming the desire to preserve the memory of significant deeds. Theodoret's *Ecclesiastical History* begins with remarks on the need to ensure that events deserving of fame will not fall into oblivion. He compares the words in a history, which endure, with the colors of a painting, which fade (1.1.1–2). Socrates too considers it important that "the deeds of the churches" are not forgotten (1.18.15). In his preface, Eutropius also makes reference to the significance of the events he will discuss. The deeds in his history, Eutropius claims, will be of significance to one reader in particular, the emperor Valens to whom the history is dedicated. For Valens, at least, the deeds are worthy of remembrance since they will reveal that the emperor's own great deeds have been anticipated by the great deeds of earlier Romans (Eut. *pref.*).

History may also have a moral purpose. Victor's constant moralizing interpretations of historical events make it clear that he presented his history as an aid to reflection upon morality, although he does not explicitly claim such a purpose. Eunapius reveals that moral education is the primary goal of his history in his first fragment, where he suggests that knowledge of the many facts of history allows a younger man to have the experience of an older man, and thereby to learn what ought to be sought and what ought to be avoided (*fr.* 1). Theodoret apologizes for the inclusion of a particularly unpleasant incident, the massacre of thousands of civilians in Thessalonica, by explaining that it is essential to teach a moral lesson. The various passions of lust, greed, envy, and anger, Theodoret says, are constantly threatening to overcome reasonable behavior. The reader will better understand this important lesson, thanks to Theodoret's presentation of this story (5.16.7). When Socrates apologizes for the inclusion of material on heresies, he explains his aim, as Theodoret had, as moral education. Knowledge of these heresies, he claims, renders the reader better able to resist error, and to see through the seductive but empty arguments of heretics (1.18.16).

Other historians provide different reasons why a reader should want to read their histories. Rufinus portrays his work as a cure or remedy for those afflicted by fear and worry over recent barbarian violence (*pref.*). Simple diversion, rather than instruction, is the stated purpose for Rufinus' work. Sozomen also claims that the pleasure of the reader is his object. After musing that Greek writers in the past had demonstrated their eloquence by descriptions of mythological events, Sozomen wonders why he should not do the same with a history of the church (1.1.11). Sozomen is heavily dependent upon Socrates for the events he describes, and it seems fitting that in the preface to a history which is largely a rewriting of another's work, he should put particular emphasis on style rather than content.

Orosius' history is more rhetorical than the others treated here, insofar as he is more devoted to winning over the audience to a specific point of view. The historian frequently pauses to directly address the reader, with the aim of persuading him to accept that times prior to the Christianization of the Roman empire were worse than Christian times. While the actual audience for the work was probably Christian, Orosius maintains the conceit that he is addressing unbelievers, who, he hopes, may someday be convinced by his evidence (7.1).

Once a historian has explained why the subject matter he will treat is worthy of the reader's attention, he must next convince the reader that he is capable of writing the history and can be trusted to do so fairly. Some late antique historians credit friends or authority figures who encouraged or commissioned the work, which allows the historian to show that others vouch for his abilities. Theodoret, for example, states that his friends had been encouraging him frequently to write a history (1.1.3). For Eunapius, it was not just friends but those who were "preeminent in learning" who urged him to write (*fr.* 1). Eunapius' claim is repeated as he embarks on his description of the career of Julian. The most learned men had encouraged him and even assisted him in describing the emperor and his reign (*fr.* 15). Rufinus' preface directly addresses his patron, the bishop Chromatius of Aquileia, who has requested the work at hand (*pref.*). Socrates also addresses a patron or friend, Theodore, in prologues to his second and sixth books. Theodore not only commissioned the work (6.*pref.*1), but also, it seems, may have requested changes when Socrates' first book did not meet his expectations (2.1.6).

Historians hoping to give the appearance of independence might acknowledge friends or patrons, but would avoid admitting that a superior had commanded them to write. Both Eutropius (*pref.*) and Festus (1.1) acknowledge that their *breviaria* have been composed at the direction of their imperial sponsor, Valens. To the ancient reader, their works thus hover uneasily between history and panegyric. Because Orosius' work is less traditionally historical, the revelation of its origin in an express request from Augustine is less damaging to his reliability (1.*pref.*). Instead, as a work of religious orthodoxy, its value may be enhanced by the approval of a religious thinker as respected as Augustine. At the conclusion of his work, Orosius calls upon Augustine to destroy his work if it is displeasing.

This cleverly allows Orosius to suggest that the entire work carries the imprimatur of the bishop (7.43.20).

Some historians attempt to assert their reliability by the bald claim that they are dedicated to the truth. This seems to be more characteristic of the classicizing style of history. Thus, Ammianus concludes his history with the claim that he has never knowingly strayed from the truth (31.16.9). His assertion of his truthfulness prior to his satirical digression on the morals of the inhabitants of Rome is, perhaps, itself a satire of this traditional historical stance (14.6.2). Eunapius claims that the purpose and highest goal of history is to describe events without bias (*fr.* 1), and he later adds that despite the bitterness and horror of the events he is about to recount, the reader will appreciate them nevertheless because of their truthfulness (*fr.* 66.2).

Historians may also demonstrate their truthfulness through descriptions of their sources. Many historians support particular details in their works by reference to their personal involvement. The simple claim by the historian that he has witnessed the events himself, or has heard them from eyewitnesses, is common. The "seen or heard" formula may be found in its pure form in Ammianus (15.1.1), Eunapius (*fr.* 30), Socrates (6.*pref.*9–10), and Sozomen (1.113). Ammianus also reveals his participation in large parts of his history by his use of first-person pronouns. In the preface to his continuation of Eusebius' history, Rufinus says that he will include events that he personally has remembered (10.*pref.*), including his familiarity with the life and works of Didymus the Blind (11.7) and with the activities of various monks of Egypt (11.4, 11.8). Eutropius points out that he had been a member of Julian's expedition to Persia (10.16.1), and Sozomen vouches for the healing power of the church called the Michaelion, because he himself has been a beneficiary (2.3.9). Sozomen relates several other first-hand accounts. When a sinful woman ate bread during a religious ceremony, for example, the bread miraculously turned into stone in her mouth. Sozomen has seen the stone, complete with tooth marks, in a church (8.5.6). He has also witnessed the barbarian Sciri, who were turned into farmers and settled in different parts of the empire, during a visit to Bithynia (9.5.7). Olympiodorus' argument that the Oasis was once an island is supported by his personal observation of fossil seashells in the desert (*fr.* 32), and is reminiscent of Orosius' proof of Noah's flood based on seashells found on mountaintops (1.3.4).

The oral sources from whom the late antique historians claim to have gained information range from specific individuals with special knowledge of events to more vague reports from the inhabitants of a particular area or simply from "people" in general. Church historians seem more likely to directly cite their sources. Rufinus credits Aedesius and Bacurius for accounts of the foreign missions in which they participated (10.10, 10.11), and his account of the torture of Theodore during the time of Julian comes straight from the victim (10.37). Socrates claims to have always sought out eyewitnesses and carefully weighed their stories, to ensure that his account is truthful (5.19.10; 6.*pref.*9–10). He apparently judges that he will win more respect from his readers by revealing his sources among the Novatians, such as the priest Auxanon, than he will lose for his association with schismatics (1.10, 1.13.2, 4.28). Other church historians also reveal their sources for oral information. Sozomen, for example, has spoken with people who witnessed miracles performed by Arsacius (4.16.13), and Orosius cites a man from Narbo for his claims about the Gothic leader Ataulf (7.43.4).

Historians also refer to oral sources with less specific detail. Socrates says that the events surrounding the discovery of the True Cross by the empress Helena are known to be true by most of the people of Constantinople (1.17.10). Similarly, the miraculous deeds of Spyridion are known to be true, Sozomen says, by the inhabitants of Cyprus (1.11.1). Orosius recognizes that the destruction of Gildo and his barbarians would seem unbelievable if it were not for the testimony of eyewitnesses (7.36.12). Eunapius says that he has drawn upon oral sources for his description of the Huns, but offers no evidence of their identity (*fr.* 41).

Historians refer to the written works which they have consulted to prove their reliability and to give evidence of the arduous task of gathering and weighing evidence. The bald citation of sources is relatively rare in classicizing histories that treat contemporary events. Ammianus cites Timagenes as his source for a geographical digression on the original inhabitants of Gaul (15.9.2), and Cicero and Sallust on the habits and history of the Gauls (15.12.4, 6). The massive cliffs called the Symplegades, Ammianus says, seem motionless, and it would be difficult to believe that they had once magically crushed any ships passing between them, were it not for the evidence of all of the songs of the poets (22.8.14–15). Ammianus also claims to have combed the records to discover evidence of any eunuch in the past who could be compared to the excellent Eutherius (16.7.8). To demonstrate his extensive knowledge of the subject, Ammianus anticipates the reader's possible suggestion, the eunuch Menophilus, and explains why this eunuch does not reach the level of excellence attained by Eutherius (16.7.9–10).

Orosius will often cite non-Christian writers to support Christian contentions. Tacitus' *Histories*, for example, is cited in order to demonstrate that pagan authors, too, know something of the destruction of Sodom and Gomorrah (1.5). Orosius similarly uses the pagan historian Justin to provide evidence for Joseph's sojourn in Egypt (1.8). After making reference to many sources in his first book, however, Orosius follows single sources almost exclusively in the later books.

The Greek church historians, following in the footsteps of Eusebius, contain not only verbatim documents but also large direct excerpts from writers such as Athanasius and Rufinus. Rather than pointing the reader toward the source for a section of church history, the historian reproduces the source directly. Occasionally a historian will simply direct the reader to another work for further information on a subject. Rufinus, for example, refuses to repeat information about the life of the monk Antony, since the reader may more easily turn to available translations of Athanasius' work on the saint (10.8). Similarly, Socrates encourages his readers to peruse the sermons of John Chrysostom themselves (6.4.9). If readers wish to learn more about the philosophy of the heretic Eunomius, Sozomen suggests that they go to his works or those of others which explain them, for Sozomen himself finds them rather difficult to understand (6.27.7).

Late antique historians are particularly prone to mention their sources in order to refute or attack them. Classical historiography was born in polemic, with Herodotus criticizing Homer and Thucydides criticizing Herodotus in turn. Criticism of predecessors allows the historian to boast of his own strengths and reveal his own historiographical ideals in attacking their opposites. Socrates' work, in particular, contains a continual series of criticisms of his sources and of other historians. Socrates draws often, for example, upon the collection of church documents made by a certain Sabinus and known as the *Synagoge*. Sabinus was a bishop of the Macedonian heresy, whose perspective on the documents in his collection was hostile to Socrates' Nicene orthodoxy. Socrates complains that Sabinus has called those promulgating the Nicene Creed "fools and simpletons," and that he has ignored some evidence and twisted other evidence to fit his views (1.8.24–7). Socrates also accuses

Sabinus of inconsistency for using Eusebius as a trustworthy source even though Eusebius, unlike Sabinus, was a supporter of the Nicene Creed (1.8.26, 1.9.28). Sabinus criticized the flaws of Athanasius, and Socrates defends Athanasius by accusing Sabinus of overlooking similar or worse flaws in the activities of Athanasius' enemies (2.15.8–11). Socrates further accuses Sabinus of purposefully omitting from his collection the letters of Pope Julius on behalf of Athanasius, in the interest of sullying Athanasius' character (2.17.10–11).

When Socrates criticizes his predecessor Eusebius, he points more gently to omissions or errors, without attributing to him the willful dishonesty he attributes to Sabinus. Socrates says that his history is necessary to supplement the work of Eusebius because Eusebius failed to treat Arianism thoroughly, and because his praise of Constantine was excessive (1.1). By disassociating himself from Eusebius in this way, Socrates proclaims that he sees doctrinal disputes as central to his successor history, and that his work will be history rather than panegyric. Later Socrates says that Eusebius had not treated the history of Manichaeism with enough detail, and that he himself will supplement Eusebius' account with more information drawn from the work of a certain Archelaus (1.22.2–3). The aim is less to criticize his predecessor than to highlight Socrates' resourcefulness and value independent of Eusebius. Socrates' criticism of Rufinus has a similar tone (2.1). Although Rufinus' chronology has proven to be incorrect, Socrates still plans to use his work where it has been verified, and no hint of purposeful fraud on Rufinus' part is insinuated. Instead, Socrates emphasizes his own thoroughness and accuracy.

Socrates is sharply contentious when he discusses pagan writers. Upon the death of Julian, for example, he quotes a section of the funeral oration performed over the emperor by the pagan Libanius, in order to refute it (3.23). He later differentiates his history from pagan history by suggesting that authors of the latter felt free to deviate from the truth (6.*pref.*3). In addition to criticizing secular historiography, Socrates attacks the work of Philip of Side, who had written not an ecclesiastical history but rather a Christian history. This sort of history, Socrates complains, is stylistically uneven, excessively long, and confused in chronology (7.27).

Neither Sozomen nor Theodoret provides many targeted criticisms in the style of Socrates, perhaps because their histories are more derivative than his and are thus less concerned with source criticism. When Sozomen warns readers against the dangers involved in consulting document collections, since these collections were made by partisans, he may be echoing in more general terms the specific criticisms Socrates made against Sabinus (1.1.15–16). Sozomen is also critical of unnamed pagan sources. For example, he rejects the suggestion attributed only to "pagans" (probably Eunapius) that Constantine's conversion to Christianity was motivated by a desire for absolution after his execution of his son, Crispus (1.5). Sozomen demonstrates that the chronology does not support such a charge, and that this form of absolution would in any case have been obtainable through the traditional Greek cult. He concludes that this accusation, then, must be the result of purposeful slander of the Christian religion.

Orosius begins his narrative with an accusation, claiming that other historians, both Greek and Latin, by starting their histories with the Assyrian king Ninus, had suggested that the world did not have a beginning (1.1.1–5). Orosius will, instead, begin with Adam, the first human being. Throughout his work, Orosius suggests that the dishonesty of earlier historians stems from their patriotic desire to vaunt the successes of their homelands (4.20.6–9, 5.3.4). The historian twice suggests that, given this motivation, the historical record contains a bias toward success and prosperity (4.5.12–13, 5.19.22). Each instance of failure or disaster should then, Orosius argues, be magnified, which further emphasizes his thesis of the misery of pre-Christian times.

Eunapius also begins his history with an accusation, criticizing Dexippus for what he characterizes as his slavish devotion to chronology at the expense of morally instructive narrative (*fr.* 1). This criticism, however, comes only in the midst of other reflections on Dexippus and his historical abilities. Later Eunapius is careful to draw a distinction between historians who are purposely deceitful and those whom necessity or haste led into error (*fr.* 66.1). Eunapius is forgiving to those who wrote during politically dangerous times and therefore were overly favorable to those in power, although he says that he himself has chosen, instead, the path of truth. Eunapius is also indulgent toward those whose histories are inadequate simply for lack of care and attention. He directs his outrage toward those historians who have altered their histories to flatter the powerful with irrelevant details. His criticism recalls Ammianus' concern that the writing of contemporary history may require the historian to include trivial material, which is beneath the dignity of history, in order to please an audience desirous of recognition and fame (26.1.1–2).

It was commonly understood in antiquity that skill at rhetoric was dependent upon the good character of the speaker. If the reader approved of the character of the writer of history, he would be more trusting toward its contents. Some of the methods already described, such as professions of truth-seeking, the support of the powerful, and the demonstration of skill in handling sources, contribute to the portrayal of the historian as a man to be trusted. Other methods of self-portrayal are also deployed to incline the reader to feel more confident about the historian's character.

The inclusion of the historian himself as a character in his history not only increases the trustworthiness of the events he narrates as an eyewitness, but also may encourage the reader to see the historian as a more trustworthy man, owing to the competence and cleverness he reveals. Ammianus, Priscus, and probably Olympiodorus narrate their own participation in events to highlight their good judgement and success. Ammianus' boldness and ingenuity in his escape from Amida, and Priscus' diplomatic skill and good sense during the embassy to Attila, are evidence of their commendable character. Olympiodorus may have demonstrated his fortitude during the many near-disasters at sea he seems to have described (*frs.* 19, 28, 35.1). Perhaps Orosius' lamentations over the tribulations he had endured can also be seen in this light (3.20.6–7). Orosius claims to better understand the turmoil he describes because of his own sufferings, and the description of his own sufferings may also serve as a defense against charges that he is insensitive to the horrors of the sack of Rome which he seeks to minimize.

Ammianus not only portrays himself in the role of a soldier in history, but adopts the title of soldier as a qualification for his role as historian in the last line of his history (31.16.9). In this same line he also states that he is a Greek as a further qualification. Elsewhere, too, he makes his Greekness known (e.g. 20.3.4, 23.6.20, 25.2.5), often in digressions, where he exploits the superior reputation of the Greeks in antiquarian knowledge. Ammianus also makes a pointed reference to his high social standing (19.8.6), a traditional guarantor of character and historical ability, especially among Latin historians.

Aurelius Victor provides an atypical self-portrait during his discussion of Septimius Severus (20.5). Victor describes himself as the son of a poor man who has gained success through education. This suggests that the historian saw his audience as composed of other imperial functionaries who similarly valued education and social mobility over noble birth.

Sozomen discusses his family in order to provide a Christianized version of noble birth (5.15.14). He boasts of his Christian grandfather, who was learned in Scripture and was forced to flee Bethelia during the persecutions under Julian. Sozomen's claim that he does not fully understand the reasoning of heretics like Eunomius and Apollinaris may also be understood as an attempt to improve the perception of his character in the eyes of his Christian audience. His intellectual credentials may be weakened, but he suggests that his personal piety is so strong that he is unable to even comprehend the works of the heterodox.

Speeches, letters, and documents

From the beginning, classical historians had included speeches delivered by their subjects. Speeches in ancient history are presented directly, as if they represent a verbatim transcript of the words spoken. In reality, of course, without recording technology, such speeches could be only approximations of what was actually said. In addition, it is clear that some historians allowed themselves some latitude in their presentation of speeches, and understood their responsibility to be the presentation of the sort of speech a historical figure might have been expected to deliver rather than the closest approximation to words that were actually spoken.

Lengthy speeches were an ornament to a history in the high style in a culture where attending an oratorical performance was a common form of entertainment. The summary works of Victor, Eutropius, and Festus, therefore, omit speeches altogether. Because the histories of Eunapius, Olympiodorus, and Priscus have come down to us in similarly reduced forms, the full extent of these historians' uses of speeches cannot be known. Eunapius' love of rhetoric and the preservation of one pair of speeches suggest that the historian had made frequent use of the device. In these surviving speeches, a barbarian king speaks and then hears the response of Julian (*fr.* 18.6). The surely ahistorical words of the king of the Chamavi amount to a reflection on the nature of fatherhood and kingship. Eunapius uses Julian's response to characterize him as noble and just. The enthusiastic response of the barbarians to Julian's words further emphasizes the power of his speech. Priscus, too, who is referred to as a "rhetor" by several ancient sources, probably included many more speeches in his history than survive in our excerpts. We have a speech which Priscus claims to have delivered himself in defense of the Roman system against a Greco-Hunnic critic (*fr.* 11). Like the speech provided by Eunapius, Priscus' speech also has a philosophical tone. The practice of Olympiodorus, however, is not as clear. As the writer of "material for history" rather than a full, formal history, he may have eschewed ornaments like speeches. On the other hand, other ancient works which present themselves as merely material to be used for a more elaborated form of history, such as Caesar's *Gallic Wars*, do contain formal speeches.

Although Ammianus is in many ways the most self-consciously classicizing of the late antique historians, he does not use speeches as often or in as varied a manner as did many of his classical predecessors. Of the dozen or so speeches which Ammianus presents, almost every one is spoken by a general to his troops, either to encourage them before battle or to introduce to them a newly appointed holder of imperial power. Imperial speeches almost always result in approval from the soldiers. In Julian's case, the soldiers show their enthusiasm after his speech before the Battle of Strasbourg (16.12.9–12), upon his acceptance of the title of Augustus (20.5.3–7), before crossing into Persian territory (23.5.16–23), and after mollifying mutinous soldiers by assuring them that they would soon possess the wealth of the Persians (24.3.3–7). The exception to these cases is the hostile reaction of the soldiers to Julian's brief attempt to refuse the title of Augustus (20.4.16), which serves to bolster Ammianus' contention that Julian was compelled to accept the promotion.

Despite the criticism which Ammianus generally expresses of Constantius, the emperor's speeches are as elegant and as well received as those of Julian. Even Constantius' denunciation of Julian's usurpation results in uniform support in Ammianus' telling (21.13.10–15), and before Constantius' speech celebrating his conquest of the Sarmatians, Ammianus notes that he was received favorably "as usual" (17.13.26–33). Only after a speech by Constantius in which he explains to the men his decision to make peace with the enemy does Ammianus provide the unflattering observation that Constantius' general lack of success in foreign wars influenced the opinion of the army (14.10.11–16). Nevertheless, the army is still described as unanimous and full of praise for the emperor.

The only extended speech in Ammianus which is not given by a general before his troops is the speech of Julian on his deathbed (25.3.15–20). The scene, which is purposely composed to suggest parallels between the emperor and Socrates, reveals Julian's nobility in his high-minded reflections on the state and on his own career.

This speech is received by Julian's tearful associates, whom the emperor rebukes as did Socrates to his similarly weeping companions at the conclusion of the *Phaedo*.

Church history as a rule avoids speeches. Instead, the narrative flow of a church history is broken up by the insertion of original documents, particularly letters from church councils or emperors. Original documents appeared very rarely in classical historiography. While Ammianus does present a pair of letters exchanged by Constantius and the Persian king Shapur, these are not given as original documents, but are rather reworked by the historian and function as speeches in the narrative (17.5). Ecclesiastical historians, however, take their cue from Eusebius' history, which seems to have begun as a collection of documents with commentary, and was only later fleshed out with the kind of narrative we consider integral to history.

Rufinus deviates from the Eusebian tradition and provides only one document, the Nicene Creed (10.6). Rufinus' work is far more rhetorical than that of the Greek church historians. In his illustration of the victory of orthodoxy over paganism and heresy, the details of doctrine are less important than the evidence that God's presence continues to favor the church. With the triumph of Theodosius at the end of the work, heresy has ceased to be a problem, and thus the study of doctrinal disputes is no longer necessary for the reader.

Although Socrates and Sozomen both praise the peace within the church brought by Theodosius II in their own day, neither suggests that Christian factionalism has been put to rest. Thus Socrates, for example, provides information on heresy, because it will help the reader avoid error in the future (1.18.16). The preface to Socrates' second book suggests that he had originally only summarized documents, following the style of Rufinus, but that in his second edition he had inserted the original documents into the work. Socrates' work is particularly thick with documents in the first two books, during which he is especially dependent on the collection made by Sabinus. Later books of Socrates, by contrast, contain very few documents. Sozomen claims to have collected documentary evidence from palaces, churches, and private collections (1.1.13). Some of his documents are taken from Socrates, but many are not. Like Socrates, he provides hardly any contemporary documents, perhaps because these would have been more readily available elsewhere to those who wished to see them. At one point Sozomen explains that the reproduction of documents was generally welcome because of their usefulness for future generations, but that wise men had counselled him to refrain from including certain documents for fear that the unbaptized might read them (1.20.3). This concern does not recur in Sozomen nor in the other church historians, and what Sozomen and his advisors feared to reveal remains a mystery.

Theodoret's work was perhaps inspired by the doctrinal disputes in which he himself was embroiled in the 430s and 440s. The historian's work is both more didactically focused on the "Arian" heresy and its successors than are the more variegated works of Socrates and Sozomen. Theodoret also provides less of the contemporary history which had yielded fewer documents in the works of Socrates and Sozomen. Perhaps for these reasons there is a greater density of documentary material in Theodoret's history. His first two books, in particular, are little more than lists of documents with occasional narration to link them together. In this way Theodoret manages to blur the line between history and antiquarian collection, and to turn the genre back to its roots in the first editions of Eusebius' *Ecclesiastical History*.

14

GOVERNMENT

The emperor

The power of the emperor was theoretically supreme in late antiquity. At the end of the third century, the emperor Diocletian had attempted to set up a system in which two senior emperors, or "Augusti," would rule, one in the east and one in the west. The two Augusti would then nominate two junior emperors, "Caesars," who would eventually succeed them. This system sought to solve two problems that plagued the empire in the third century. First, the empire was too large to be effectively governed by one man, and second, the lack of a fixed rule of succession led to frequent turmoil and civil war. Diocletian's system failed to prevent the civil wars which erupted even during his lifetime. Multiple emperors needed multiple armies to meet threats throughout the empire, but the existence of multiple armies often led to conflict.

A more enduring innovation of Diocletian was what has been called the "sacralization" of the emperor. The elevation of the late antique emperor to divine status represented, perhaps, yet another attempt to discourage civil war. The emperor was garbed in silk and jewels, and was kept apart from his subjects by a large body of court officials and by elaborate court ceremonial. As Christopher Kelly has noted, however, despite this newer imperial image there remained the older ideologies which demanded that an emperor be merely the "first citizen," or that he eschew ostentatious display as a "philosopher king" (Kelly 1998: 138–50). The tension between these competing theories of kingship is frequently palpable in the historians of the fourth and fifth centuries.

The *breviaria*, in comparing earlier emperors with contemporary ones, confront these competing images of the ideal emperor explicitly. Victor's history and values are generally traditional, and his formula for the good emperor combines good morals with a liberal education (8.7–8; Bird 1984: 24–9). The historian does not deny or challenge the supremacy of the emperor, but he claims that men require civilian values and education to properly exercise power. As an example of the "excessive arrogance" of Domitian, he points out that the emperor had demanded that the senate address him as "lord and god" (11.2). Although the title was abandoned by his immediate successors, Victor complains that this title "was revived more forcefully" by emperors much later. He is openly critical of Diocletian's assumption of autocratic dress and presentation. The emperor's use of silk, gems, and purple demonstrated that he was "vain" and "tasteless." Even worse, Diocletian allowed himself to be "worshipped and addressed as a god" (39.4–5). Victor attributes these innovations to the emperor's humble background, for, in the historian's experience, when the humble receive great power they become excessively proud. It is easy to see why Victor would have eagerly served Julian, the late antique emperor who most closely approximated his ideal of the educated and civil emperor who eschews the trappings of power.

Many other writers continued to reject the autocratic image of the emperor and to champion a more civilian style of rule. Although Eutropius was an imperial bureaucrat writing at the command of the emperor himself, he produced a work as civilian in ideology as is that of Victor. When Eutropius discusses the creation of the office of *dictator* during the early republic, he suggests that nothing is more similar to the power which Valens now holds (1.12.2). This appears to be an attempt by the historian to sanction and to limit imperial power by grounding it in past precedent. Eutropius states that Julius Caesar acted tyrannically and "contrary to the custom of Roman liberty" by not respecting the privileges of senators and the people (6.25). He complains that Diocletian first introduced the foreign custom of commanding that he be revered by prostration, "more associated with royal custom than with Roman liberty" (9.26). By way of contrast, a good emperor like Marcus Aurelius "acted as an equal to all at Rome" (8.12.1).

Ammianus' consideration of the self-presentation of the emperor is more nuanced and perhaps more conflicted (Matthews 1989: 231–52). The historian may generally be considered a traditionalist, and thus in his praise of Julian, for example, he naturally compares him to emperors of the past such as Titus, Trajan, and Marcus Aurelius (16.1.4). In terms similar to those found in Victor and Eutropius, and perhaps drawn from them or their common source, Ammianus criticizes Diocletian's introduction of prostration, "this foreign and royal form custom" (15.5.18). Ammianus also shares with Victor and Eutropius the desire for an emperor who was properly educated and even philosophical.

Nevertheless, Ammianus does not approve of an emperor who is excessively familiar or civil. Instead, he favors an emperor with the military virtues of discipline and authority. Ammianus praises Julian's ability to abstain from food, sex, and sleep, which sets him apart from the ordinary man (25.4.2–6). According to the historian, one of Julian's virtues was his "citizenly behavior," which he explains by commenting that Julian only demanded honors "which he thought necessary to keep him from contempt and insolence" (25.4.7). Julian did not, however, always successfully avoid slipping inappropriately into familiarity. A desire for popularity, Ammianus says, led him to talk with unworthy persons (25.4.18). His dismissal of most of the palace staff was not wholly admirable, perhaps because the imperial majesty would not remain sufficiently exalted without a contingent of courtiers (22.4.1–2). When the emperor went on foot in the procession with the consuls for the year 362, Ammianus notes that some thought this creditable, but others thought it "affected and cheap" (22.7.1). And it was extremely undignified for the emperor to leap up from the judge's chair and embrace Maximus in public (22.7.3–4). Ammianus' nostalgic or reactionary view of imperial power harkens back to Hellenistic models of the philosopher king, rather than to Roman models of the republican citizen.

Ammianus' portrait of Constantius II serves as a useful contrast to his portrait of Julian. His description of the emperor's entrance into Rome in 357 is one of the most famous and most analyzed passages in the *Res Gestae* (16.10). The emperor's chariot gleamed with gold and gems, while the banners and flags and the shining armor of his attendants added to the splendor of the procession. Despite the frenzy of motion and the echoing cheers around him, Constantius himself remained completely passive and motionless, and he "was never seen to spit or to wipe or rub his face or nose or to move his hand" (16.10.10). Ammianus is critical of this performance because he believes that Constantius is unworthy of the honor, but not because he disapproves of the style, which to the historian demonstrates that Constantius has "an unusual degree of self-control." In Constantius' obituary notice Ammianus recalls this event as an illustration of one of the emperor's virtues, along with his general chastity and moderation in eating and drinking (21.16.5–7).

Eunapius' ideal emperor, Julian, was a philosopher king, a divine being who had condescended to rule on earth. This sort of emperor played the role of an ordinary citizen, but possessed more exalted motives. Julian had, through his philosophical studies, raised himself far above the material world. He became emperor not from any grasping desire for power, but on behalf of mankind, and he was a friend to the soldiers not from the base desire for popularity, but for love of the state (*fr.* 28.1). Although Eunapius divinized Julian, he also praised him for the friendliness and accessibility which made him a more effective judge (*fr.* 25.1).

Olympiodorus, an imperial diplomat, shares a concern for imperial dignity with Ammianus and Eunapius. His description of Constantius III, who briefly shared power with Honorius in 421, contrasts with Ammianus' picture of Constantius II. In public processions Constantius was "downcast and sullen," he slouched forward over his horse's neck, and his eyes darted from side to side (*fr.* 23). All this added up to "an image worthy of a tyrant." Olympiodorus reveals that subjects were constantly evaluating the self-presentation of their emperors to determine their fitness for power.

Socrates speaks for the entire genre of ecclesiastical history when he states that he should only relate the deeds of the emperor that relate to Christianity, not his other accomplishments, which belong in a separate treatise (1.18.14). The proper deportment of an emperor remained an important issue in church history, however. When church historians present idealized portraits of Christian emperors, they reveal a desire for the same combination of civility and sublimity expressed by the pagan historians.

The Christian emperor demonstrated his civility by his behavior not only before his subjects but also before God and the church. Church historians suggest that the good emperor, like Constantine, does not exaggerate his majesty, is humble before Christ, and civil with bishops, whom he treats as equals. The most extreme example of such humility was the submission of Theodosius before Ambrose, for he knew that it was Ambrose's job to point out the fault and provide the remedy, and his own responsibility to obey (Theod. 5.18.15). Another example of imperial humility, less extreme but more unsanitary, is Socrates' praise of Theodosius II for wearing the filthy sackcloth of hair belonging to a recently deceased bishop (7.22.14).

Sozomen presents the education of the young Theodosius II by his sister, Pulcheria, as the ideal training for Christian kingship.

The emperor is taught to be "orderly and princely" in his manners, and how to walk, sit, and wear his robes in proper regal fashion. The most important element of Pulcheria's instruction, however, is training in piety. Theodosius is taught to pray continually and to have constant reverence for members of the church (9.1.8). In Theodosius II's adoption of the practices of a monastic life, we see elements of the aloofness or exaltedness demanded of the emperor expressed in Christian terms (Soc. 7.22; Soz. *pref.*). This emperor, like Julian, has a tremendous ability to resist heat, cold, thirst, and hunger. In Julian's case, his moderate diet demonstrates his closeness to a common soldier, while for Theodosius, fasting demonstrates his resemblance to a monk. Theodosius' palace is like a monastery (Soc. 7.22.4), and although he wears a crown and purple robe, it is his piety which truly distinguishes him (Soz. *pref.*3). The portrayals of Theodosius and of Julian express an essential paradox of late antique leadership. Historians yearn for an emperor who is both far superior to his subjects, yet simultaneously meek and humble.

The bureaucracy

With the exception of the army, the Roman empire had always operated with a surprisingly small number of government employees by modern standards. Tax collection and the erection and maintenance of public works were performed almost entirely at the local level. In comparison with the negligible size of the early imperial administration, however, the later empire saw an explosion in the number of imperial functionaries. This expansion was in part a product of the large increase in the number of provinces and other geographical subdivisions of the empire, which was in turn a product of the increasing demand for tax revenue. This increase in the imperial reach did not, however, necessarily lead to the diminishment of the power of the individual subject. Several layers of government, and in some cases ecclesiastical government as well, created opportunities for some Romans to manipulate the system to their own ends.

Posts in the bureaucracy were filled through a vast network of patronage. Emperors repeatedly promulgated laws which sought to prevent those who would normally have served in local government from receiving exemptions through imperial appointment. This suggests that service in the imperial administration had become increasingly more appealing in the later empire. The highest ranking officials of the bureaucracy, both civilian and military, formed the *consistorium*, the emperor's group of advisors, who discussed policy, heard legal cases, received embassies, and participated in ceremonial activities.

Historians held emperors responsible for the quality of their appointments and the activities of their subordinates. For Eutropius, a mark of Antoninus Pius' honor is that he "gave office to good men" and "detested evil ones" (8.8.2). Eutropius, who himself held several high offices, alternately considers the issue from the perspective of a subject and of an official. He strongly praises Augustus for his great loyalty to his friends, whom he raised to positions of great dignity (7.8.4), while criticizing both Constantius and Julian for being too trusting and generous toward friends (10.15.2, 10.16.3). For Victor, the reigns of Constantine, Constans, and Constantius II were all marred by the poor behavior of some of their subordinates, although this sort of criticism may simply serve as a way for the historian to criticize near-contemporary administrations without insulting the emperors themselves (41.21, 41.23, 42.25). Victor elsewhere considers the roles of subordinates in shaping an emperor's reign. The emperor Claudius, for example, made outstanding decisions early in his reign, despite his incompetence, because of his good advisors (4.1). Unfortunately, by the end of his reign Claudius was making worse decisions under the influence of his wife and freedmen (4.5). Commodus was such a bad emperor that his dissolute advisors tried to poison him, as he was even more depraved than they were (17.7).

In his account of the reign of Constantius, Ammianus stresses the influence of the eunuchs. The centralization of power and the isolation of the emperor had resulted in the rise of numerous unofficial channels of influence, and for Ammianus, as for many of his contemporaries, the power of eunuchs was thought to be particularly disgraceful (Hopwood 1978; Guyot 1980; Matthews 1989: 274–7; Tougher 1999). It had been illegal to create a eunuch within the empire since the time of Domitian. In the absence of such a law, Ammianus claims, the empire would be teeming with them (18.4.5). Eunuchs were widely believed to be devious and greedy, and the historian attributes these characteristics to the whole of Constantius' reign by the constant portrayal of an emperor under the thumb of eunuchs. Ammianus ironically describes the Grand Chamberlain Eusebius, a eunuch, as an official "with whom, to tell the truth, Constantius had much influence" (18.4.3).

While Ammianus depicts Constantius as dominated by his eunuchs and advisors, he describes Valentinian as more successful in staffing the bureaucracy. He checked the excesses of the imperial court and never showed favor to his relatives (30.9.2). He was also careful to ensure that offices were not sold and that governors of provinces did not have improper financial connections (30.9.3). Ammianus does describe one exception to this generally admirable record. Sextus Petronius Probus was a corrupt aristocrat whose death shortly before the publication of the *Res Gestae* perhaps encouraged the historian to reflect upon his career in full (27.11; McCoy 1985; Cameron 1985; Barnes 1998: 117–19). Probus had immense wealth and property, "whether justly or otherwise," Ammianus remarks, "is beyond my humble ability to judge." Probus used his imperial positions to operate a massive web of patronage, and Ammianus says that, while he never himself broke the law, he turned a blind eye to the activities of his clients and friends.

Just as Ammianus depicted his patron Ursicinus under constant attack from the eunuchs of Constantius, so too did Eunapius portray the incorruptible general Sebastian elbowed aside by the imperial eunuchs (*fr.* 44.3). The rise to power of the eunuch Eutropius in the east provided contemporaries with endless opportunities to vent their hatred and, in the case of Eunapius, to revel in grotesque imagery. The historian claimed, for example, that the success of Eutropius encouraged even men with beards to castrate themselves, in the hope of imperial favor: "they lost their minds along with their testicles" (*fr.* 65.7). Eunapius also expresses disgust at the subordinates of Eutropius' successor, the corrupt Rufinus. His administrators, who had formerly been "runaway tavern-servants and bench-cleaners and floor-sweepers," now appeared garbed in gold and purple (*fr.* 62.2).

Eunapius also laments corruption in the governing of provinces, which he says were offered at auction during the supremacy of Eudoxia (*fr.* 72.1). He suggests that officials who became involved in this corruption were liable to be defrauded themselves by corrupt superiors. Eunapius most likely exaggerates the extent of the corruption to increase the contrast with the exalted time of Julian, when he boasted that incorruptible subordinates like Salutius Secundus admirably served the state (*fr.* 25.5). In fact, the historian deplores the normal operation of the late Roman state, whereby governors would purchase their offices and then attempt to recoup their costs through extortion and judicial corruption. The legal codes, which were unable to eradicate this practice, merely set limits on the sums charged in the sale of various offices. Priscus complains that the greed of the eunuchs who dominated Theodosius II corrupted the state, since able administrators could not afford to purchase their offices, which were held instead by the incompetent (*fr.* 3.2).

When Eunapius sought to describe the character of the emperor Gratian, he found that because of the secrecy surrounding the palace and the emperor's circle he was unable to gather reliable information (*fr.* 50). The late antique emperor is often depicted making policy in secret and doing the bidding of eunuchs or other unsavory counselors. The difficulty of obtaining trustworthy information about imperial decision-making often led historians to rely on rumor and speculation to explain decisions which seemed mistaken or evil. Socrates, for example, explains Constantius' rejection of Athanasius and the homoousian creed by evoking a backroom plot (2.2). He claims that the priest who had delivered Constantine's will to Constantius upon his accession was rewarded by the emperor with gifts and access to the court. This priest became close to Eusebius, the eunuch chamberlain, and persuaded him "to adopt Arius' views." Eusebius in turn converted the other eunuchs of the palace, as well as the empress, and the doctrine spread throughout the other palace officials and from there to the citizenry. Sozomen adapts Socrates' version of events in his own history (3.1), while Theodoret, the church historian least interested in governmental affairs, condenses the conspiracy into the arguments of a single priest directly convincing the weak-minded emperor himself (2.3).

Justice

One of the enduring accomplishments of the Roman empire was its system of law. The fifth century saw the monumental compilation of the Theodosian Code, a collection and arrangement of laws dating back to the age of Constantine. Yet the legal corruption of the later empire is an equally prominent theme in the modern imagination (Harries 1999; Matthews 2000; Honoré 1998). Late antique histories rarely provide details of the technicalities of ancient laws or legal practices, but they reveal more generally the attitudes and expectations of their writers toward law and justice.

For Ammianus, the administration of justice was equal only to leading the troops in war as a primary task of the emperor. Matthews shows the serious moral weight that the law held for

Ammianus (Matthews 1992). Ammianus considered Roman law essential to the maintenance of a just empire and suggests that the law is the means by which the vagaries of fate might be avoided. Just rule exists, according to Ammianus, for the safety and benefit of imperial subjects (30.8.14), and regularized legal procedure is necessary to prevent justice from being driven out of the law courts, as happened under the rule of Gallus (14.7.21).

A good emperor must uphold the law fairly, and Ammianus praises Julian, for example, for never failing to distinguish between right and wrong (18.1.2). Ammianus, like other late antique historians, feels that greater danger lies in the risk of an emperor being too harsh in judgement, rather than too gentle. Clemency is therefore an essential virtue for the emperor. Thus Constantius, though he was in fact the object of various plots, is criticized for his merciless and inhumane pursuit of suspects and his excessive use of torture (21.16.8–11). Valentinian, too, is condemned because he was pleased by cruel judges and encouraged them to act with severity (30.8.13). While Valens wished to seem to allow judges independence, in reality no judgement was made against his will (31.14.6). Julian's clemency is praised by Ammianus even when he commutes the sentence of a rapist (16.5.12).

Treason trials are a regular part of Ammianus' narrative and are the object of highly rhetorical criticism from the historian. The trials under Gallus lacked even the form of law, which Ammianus claims previous cruel emperors had used to cloak their tyranny (14.1.5). The criticisms Ammianus levels about legal procedure in his account of these trials seem stereotypical, as they recur in his portrayal of corrupt legal proceedings under later emperors as well. Men are executed without the opportunity to speak in their own defense (14.1.3); men of low social standing spy on citizens and give maliciously elaborated reports of their actions to the emperor (14.1.6); and dubious evidence is brought forth to condemn the innocent (14.7.20). In his discussion of the treason trials at Rome at the time of Valentinian (28.1) and in the east at the time of Valens (29.1–2), Ammianus contrasts the triviality of the infractions with the savagery of the punishments inflicted (Matthews 1989: 209–26; Zawadski 1989; Elliott 1983: 148–58; Blockley 1975: 104–22; Funke 1967). Ammianus does recognize the legitimacy of trials held in defense of the imperial majesty, and he supports the illegality of "black magic" directed toward the emperor (19.12.17; 29.1.15–18). The historian demonstrates that some were punished in these trials for benign forms of magic, as when Bassianus was nearly executed for simply attempting to foretell the sex of his unborn child (29.2.5). Ammianus does not comment on the guilt or innocence of many of the defendants, however. His focus remains on the need for fair legal procedure and imperial clemency.

Legal proceedings also figure in the *Res Gestae* as an arena in which the courage of those unjustly accused might be tested. Torture was used in late imperial trials in order to gain evidence, and was not meant to be a punishment in itself. Ammianus shows that information gained from torture was, not surprisingly, often inaccurate. When Pergamius was suspected of illegal divination and was tortured, he named many thousands of accomplices from the furthest corners of the earth (29.1.15). Diogenes, a man of lowly origins, implicated Ammianus' friend Alypius under severe torture to please the emperor (29.1.44). Endurance under torture was a particularly prized virtue, and Ammianus often highlights this heroism. The philosopher Pasiphilus was brutally tortured in an attempt to get him to implicate Eutropius in a plot, but his will did not break (29.1.36; Angliviel de la Beaumelle 1992).

While the emperor was in theory the final judge of all disputes in the empire, in practice it was of course impossible for him to hear more than a fraction of cases. Ammianus criticizes Valens for following the advice of his praetorian prefect, Modestus, to refuse to hear private cases at all. He claims that this left complainants at the mercy of an alliance between their powerful opponents and the lawyers, since the prospect of appeal to the emperor had been removed (30.4.1–2). This inspires Ammianus to digress upon the faults of various types of lawyers (30.4.3–22; Matthews 1992: 48–50). The historian claims to have personally experienced the corruption of the four separate types of lawyers he will discuss, but the muddled digression swiftly degenerates into a traditional, satirical denunciation of outrageous legal behavior. Ammianus decries lawyers who stir up trouble between family members (30.4.9), those who use obscure parts of the law to secure acquittals for guilty clients (30.4.12), those who manipulate the law to cause confusions and delay (30.4.13), and those who milk clients by extending cases indefinitely (30.4.18). His complaints are so stereotyped, however, that they cannot be taken seriously as evidence of legal corruption specific to late antiquity.

Victor and Eutropius follow Ammianus in holding clemency to be the most important imperial virtue in legal proceedings. Victor accuses Tiberius of cruelty in punishing the innocent and guilty alike (2.1), and Eutropius likewise condemns Domitian for executing senators (7.23.2). Carinus, according to Eutropius, executed many innocent men, and upon becoming emperor even avenged himself upon some of his schoolmates who had called him names when he was a child (9.19.1). By contrast, the good emperor is clement even toward the guilty. Eutropius says that Titus was so clement toward conspirators against him that he not only pardoned them but treated them as friends (7.21.2). Victor portrays Vespasian as clement even toward supporters of his opponents in the civil wars which had brought him to power, although he adds that Vespasian did execute a few who "perhaps had acted far too atrociously" (9.2). In his defense of Septimius Severus, Victor apologizes for the emperor's lack of clemency. Severus had been accused of cruelty for the many executions which he ordered, both against his opponents in civil wars and against potential conspirators during his reign. Victor explains that these executions were performed so that the emperor might act more gently in the future, and in order that the example of harsh punishment might prevent further uprisings. He concludes by explaining that the necessity of executions was imposed upon Severus by the general "corruption of the times" (20.13).

Eunapius praised Julian as a judge, noting particularly his accessibility and his refusal to postpone trials (*fr.* 25.1). The suppression of imperial anger was also an important element in Julian's fair administration of justice (*fr.* 28.2). In reflecting upon Valens' harshness, Eunapius draws a distinction between erring on the side of harsher penalties, which he condemns, and erring on the side of pardon or clemency, which he praises. The former he sees as a symptom of a theory of power based on fear, while he argues that the appearance of clemency magnifies the perception of imperial power (*fr.* 34.9).

Church historians echo some of the same concerns about law and punishment found in secular historians. The admirable resistence of the innocent man in the face of torture, for example, is recast as the Christian courageously undergoing torture and even martyrdom at the hands of pagans or heretics. The torture of Theodore by agents of the emperor Julian, related by Rufinus and then picked up by the three Greek church historians, provides an example. Through ten hours of agony, with torturers on each side, Theodore sang hymns with a beatific look on his face (Ruf. 10.37; Soc. 3.19; Soz. 5.20; Theod. 3.11). Afterwards, he told Rufinus that he felt no pain thanks to an angelic youth who wiped his brow. Theodore even stated that he had enjoyed the experience so much that he was unhappy when he was removed from the rack.

As the church gained power over the course of the fourth century, it adopted various roles which had previously been the domain of secular government, in particular the judicial role. In his praise of the bishop Silvanus, Socrates reveals the risks which were incurred from the involvement of clergy in judicial decision-making. Silvanus collected the documents in legal cases entrusted to his judgement and had them judged by a pious layman, since he had witnessed how the power of judging had often corrupted members of the clergy (7.37.14–15). The importance of imperial clemency is another theme which the church historians preserve and imbue with Christian meaning. In his panegyric of Theodosius II, Socrates compares the Christian emperor with Julian (7.22.7). Julian had claimed to be a philosopher, but had been consumed by rage against the people of Antioch and had ordered the torture of poor Theodore. Theodosius, however, had mastered his emotions, and never sought revenge upon enemies. He never practiced capital punishment, since it denied the criminal the opportunity to repent, and he refused the request of the people to have criminals thrown to the wild beasts of the arena.

The treason trials under Valens are briefly described in some of the church historians. Socrates notes that Valens had sought to kill all men whose name began with the letters "theo" as the result of a prophecy which predicted the accession of such a man as his successor (4.19). This resulted in the unfortunate execution of Theodotus, Theodulus, and others, and prompted still others to quickly change their names. Sozomen provides an elaboration of Socrates' account, which harshly condemns Valens for allowing himself to be so influenced by the un-Christian belief that the stars could predict his successor (6.35).

Socrates says that John Chrysostom had considered a career in the law, but reflection upon the unjust nature of those who practice law dissuaded him (6.3.2). Sozomen, by contrast, omits negative judgement on lawyers, undoubtedly because he was one himself (8.2.5). Sozomen's greater knowledge and interest in legal matters set his work apart from the other church historians. Errington has demonstrated some of these differences in the specific case of Theodosius' religious legislation (Errington 1997). For example, Sozomen presents in some detail the law of Theodosius which made homoousian doctrine the only legal form of Christianity (7.4.5–6). Socrates does not mention this immensely important legislation, and says only that Theodosius favored those who shared his faith (5.14.7). Sozomen has clearly read the original law of Theodosius in the

Theodosian Code, since he understands that the law was limited in its original application to the city of Constantinople (Errington 1997: 414–15). Sozomen's interest in law and use of the Code is equally evident in his treatment of Constantine's religious legislation (1.8, 9), his discussion of some of Julian's legislation (5.1), and the legislation of Jovian (6.3). Other historians, however, made no use of the compilation.

Economics

Ancient historians are notoriously uninterested in economic history, and the historians of late antiquity are no different in their general disregard for the subject and their ignorance of economic tenets. Nevertheless, historians reveal their beliefs and concerns about some economic topics in passing. At the intersection of state policy and the economy are two such topics, taxation and price regulation. Church historians also touch upon Christian attitudes toward money in their discussion of church finance and charity.

The late Roman state maintained a complex system of taxation in both coinage and in kind, which historians rarely describe in much detail (Jones 1964: 411–69; Frank 1972). Instead, the charge of excessive taxation is generally used without much supporting detail to condemn emperors whom the historian dislikes. Historians generally attribute high taxation to the personal avarice of the emperor, as Ammianus does in his characterization of Valentinian, whom he accuses of excessive "greed of possessing more" (30.8.8). Ammianus is aware that some try to explain Valentinian's need for additional revenue by saying that the failure of Julian's Persian campaign had left the empire with serious financial problems, but he dismisses this suggestion with the statement that some things ought not to be done even if one has the power to do so. Ammianus strangely contradicts his claim of Valentinian's rapacity only a chapter later, when he praises the emperor for lowering taxes everywhere (30.9.1; Matthews 1989: 239–41). Ammianus' praise of Valens for his prevention of tax increases is also personalized. Valens, he says, protected the provinces from financial injury as he would his own household. Eunapius' view is different in substance but similar in style when he claims that Valens was an insatiable taxer owing to his "love for money" (*fr.* 39.9). Lowering taxes was, for Ammianus, a significant part of Julian's great triumph in Gaul. When the Caesar succesfully resisted a tax increase, the Gauls were so relieved that they paid their taxes in advance (17.3.6). Likewise, when Julian reduced taxes from twenty-five gold coins per person to seven, the Gauls rejoiced with dances (16.5.14).

Victor and Eutropius generally agree that "good" emperors lowered taxes and "bad" ones raised them. Trajan, for example, did nothing unjust in collecting taxes (Eut. 8.4), and Constantius I, an "outstanding" man, cared more for the wealth of the provinces and of individuals than of the treasury (Eut. 10.1.2). On the other hand, Maxentius, "an inhuman beast," invented an entirely new tax for senators and farmers (Vic. 40.24). The good emperor is also frugal with imperial resources, as Marcus Aurelius demonstrated when to avoid instituting new taxes he held a "garage sale" of various luxurious items from the palace (Eut. 8.13.2). Vespasian receives mixed evaluations from both historians. He was too strict in collecting taxes, Eutropius says, but he was not unfair, and he distributed the proceeds freely, especially to those in need (7.19.2). Victor says that the emperor placed new and temporary taxes on the provinces only to pay for the devastation of civil war, but admits that many faulted him for this (9.6).

In Priscus' conversation with the Greek who defected to the Huns, he allows the Greek to complain about the high taxes of the empire. In response, he explains that taxes are more readily paid by farmers who can concentrate on their fields without facing conscription themselves (fr. 11.2). Priscus is, however, a strong critic of using tax revenue for payments to the Huns and other barbarians (fr. 9.3). This, he claims, required the institution of such high taxes that many of the wealthy were required to sell jewelry and furniture, and some even committed suicide.

Ancient governments, both imperial and local, were major players in commodity markets, both by providing goods such as grain and oil at low costs or for free to favored clients, and by ordering higher or lower prices in cases of food shortages. As an example, Victor describes the institution by Aurelian of a system of free pork distribution to the people of the city of Rome (35.7). Shortages of grain at Antioch under both Gallus and Julian drew the attention of both Ammianus and Socrates (de Jonge 1948; Downey 1951; Liebeschuetz 1972: 126–32; Matthews 1989: 406–9). In each case it seems that the presence in Antioch of the imperial court and of an army preparing for the Persian war sparked temporary food shortages. The intervention of the emperor was unsuccessful and resulted in criticism from the historians in each case as well. Ammianus says that when the city council of Antioch told Gallus that his policy of price ceilings would fail, he threatened them with death. When more common citizens begged Gallus for help, he blamed the crisis on the hapless governor of Syria, who in consequence was beaten and ripped to pieces by the mob (14.7). Ammianus suggests that the emperor could have alleviated the crisis by ordering the importation of grain from neighboring provinces (14.7.5).

In discussing a recurrence of crisis eight years later, Ammianus attributes Julian's attempt to fix a maximum price for grain to his "love of popularity" and points out that "sometimes" this policy causes scarcity and famine (22.14.1). Ammianus seems to deny that any crisis existed, siding with the council of Antioch who again warned the emperor against any attempt to fix prices (22.14.2). In Julian's own work, the *Misopogon*, he blames merchants and speculators who hoarded cheap grain. This excuse plays on the general distrust of trade in antiquity, as revealed, for example, in Eunapius' characterization of merchants as liars who seek only profit (*fr.* 66.2). Socrates, however, provides the most reasonable account of the crisis (3.17.2–4). Like Ammianus, Socrates blames the crisis on Julian's desire for popularity. He adds, however, that the presence of an army must necessarily lead to price hikes, and he even understands that merchants cease selling grain when prices are artificially low since they are unable to sustain the losses they suffer.

Church historians champion ecclesiastical generosity toward the poor. The preaching of Basil of Caesarea, according to Rufinus, urged the distribution of money to the poor and for the establishment of monasteries and nunneries (11.9). Socrates relates an affecting story about a bishop melting down the church's holdings of gold and silver sacred objects in order to raise money to allow the return of Persian prisoners of war (7.21), and in praising Atticus, the bishop of Constantinople, Socrates lauds his distribution of gold not only to the poor of his own city but also to the poor of other cities (7.25.1–9). Theodoret praises John Chrysostom for sending a troop of zealous monks to Palestine in order to destroy some pagan temples (5.29). The money for this operation came not from the public treasury but from John's fundraising among wealthy noblewomen of Constantinople. The imperial opposition to John was probably strengthened by his access to large sums of money independent of imperial control. Access to wealth brought with it the possibility of corruption for clergy, as Socrates shows in his account of the bishop Theodosius of Synada. Theodosius was a fervent persecutor of the Macedonian heretics, but he was impelled not out of orthodox zeal but rather from lust for the seizure of wealth from the dispossessed sectarians (7.3).

Conclusion

Ancient historians are not an ideal source for information about the administration and economy of the late antique state, but they do often reveal the opinions and attitudes held by the educated elite about these institutions. In general, late antique historians attempt to combine, sometimes uneasily, ancient and traditional beliefs about society with more contemporary ideas. Thus, the civil and republican ideals of imperial presentation collide with more elevated visions of imperial dominance. The idealized vision of the relationship between emperor and subject often harkens back to a bygone era no longer commensurate with the reality of the larger and more intrusive late antique administration. While ideals of justice remained unchanged, the reality of punishment became harsher. Economic issues were personalized, and complaints about taxation, for example, generally reveal more about the historian's view on the emperor and the times than on the historian's grasp of imperial fiscal policy.

15

THE ROMAN PAST

For historians writing in the fourth and fifth centuries, the period of the late republic stood at roughly the same distance as does the age of Columbus for modern historians. The earlier republic was as ancient then as the Norman conquest is today. Nevertheless, given the Roman respect for the past, it is not surprising that many historians reflect upon the earliest history of Rome. A few late antique historians directly treat the regal and republican periods, but even those who are only chroniclers of their own time often find opportunities to refer to people and events of the distant past. Such reflections shed light, both explicitly and implicitly, on the historian's understanding of the meaning and purpose of the broad sweep of human history. The omission of republican material by some late antique historians is itself a reflection of the historian's attitude toward his work and the expectations of his audience.

Of late antique histories, Ammianus' *Res Gestae* most deliberately adapted the style of the classical historians, and so not surprisingly it contains numerous allusions to Rome's distant past. Ammianus provides us with an elaborate schema of Roman history, which recognizes the changes in government from antiquity to his day but at the same time expresses a belief in the unity and progression of the Roman state (Matthews 1986). In a familiar ancient image, Rome is depicted as a man passing through the stages of life. From "cradle" to "childhood," the Romans fought around their walls, and in "adulthood" waged war across the seas. In Ammianus' time, the city, having retired, had wisely entrusted its patrimony to the emperors, who skillfully manage this inheritance (14.6.3–6). The image creates a direct link between the earliest history of Rome and the fourth-century empire. Roman history has come full circle with the return of the tranquillity of the time of King Numa. While Tacitus had worried about the prospects for liberty in an imperial world, Ammianus suggests that the fourth-century empire, the product of a pact of eternal peace between Virtue and Fortune, had transcended the conflicts of the earlier empire.

The *Res Gestae* makes frequent reference to figures from the republic. In the surviving books, famous figures of the republic appear more often than the emperors who ruled in the first, second, or third centuries. In this respect, Ammianus is similar to other fourth-century Latin writers, such as Claudian or the panegyricists, who depend almost entirely on republican *exempla*, to the exclusion of imperial ones (Stertz 1980: 491). For example, Ammianus supports his contention that the earlier inhabitants of Rome were superior in modesty to their decadent successors with a quote from Cato the Elder (14.6.8), and he demonstrates the fickleness of Fortune by references to Pompey, Regulus, and other republican military leaders (14.11.32). Ammianus' frequent recourse to such references is less a reflection of his opinion of the republic than an assertion of his belief in the continuity and centrality of *Romanitas* over so many centuries. His traditionally educated audience would have appreciated his references, which establish Ammianus' link with the classical historiography of the past.

Ammianus often reaches for republican *exempla* when passing judgement upon military events. The ability of Rome to recover after Cannae (31.13.19) and the Gallic invasions (31.5.12) suggests that Rome has the potential to recover from the massacre at Adrianople, if only Roman moral standards can return to those of their republican antecedents. Ammianus treats with scorn the cession of Nisibis to the Persians by Jovian in 363, adding a reminder that earlier peace treaties signed under duress, such as the one following Rome's ignominious defeat at the Caudine Forks, were readily abandoned (25.9.11).

Ammianus often compares Julian to the glorious heroes of the republic. The emperor's battle exhortation recalls the example of Sulla (16.12.41), his habit of writing while on campaign recalls Caesar (25.2.3), the unfair attacks upon him are like those directed against Scipio Aemilianus and Pompey (17.11.3), and his victory at Strasbourg surpasses the Punic Wars in excellence (17.1.14). The exhortation to the troops which Ammianus attributes to Julian before the invasion of Persia (23.5.16–23) contains several instances of Ammianus' use of republican history. First is the utility of the republic as a source for providing historical lessons which still resonate in the present day. To demonstrate that his proposed expedition is in no way a novelty, Julian points out that, contrary to the muttering of some critics, the Romans had often been successful in past campaigns against Persia under such figures as Lucullus, Pompey, and Ventidius. Ammianus has Julian claim that the expedition seeks the complete destruction of the Persian empire, and he draws upon the examples of cities such as Carthage and Fidenae to prove that Romans have eradicated their rivals in the past. Second, the history of the republic offers moral *exempla* for the behavior of a Roman general. Julian is willing to follow the example of the Curtii, the Mucii, and the Decii, and give his life in return for Roman victory. Both the magnitude of Julian's expedition and the greatness of his character are emphasized through his references to republican precedents. Ammianus thus frames Julian's achievements as evidence of the continuing power of the classical republican spirit.

Aurelius Victor aimed to take the pedestrian *Kaisergeschichte* and present a rhetorically and morally improved version. This rewriting entailed the addition of both republican *exempla* and of a broader meditation on historical change. The meaning of the transition from republic to empire for Victor is evident in his first sentence, where he states that under Octavian the Romans began to "obey one man alone." The assassination of Caligula provided an opportunity for the restoration of the republic, but the Romans had been corrupted by the transfer of their historical duty of military service to foreign mercenaries (3.14–15). For Victor, the republic was dependent upon Romans who remained virtuous through continued military service. Victor's derogatory attitude toward the army throughout his history makes it clear that he felt the shift to a professional army was a mistake (Bird 1984: 41–52). (The third-century historian Dio Cassius, too, had seen a professional soldiery as a key to the shift from republic to empire, although he supported the change (52.14).)

Republican figures are ubiquitous in Victor's work. He often demonstrates the wisdom or goodness of an imperial figure through a comparison with an ancient one. Hadrian's attention to religion, for example, is praised through comparison to the similar attention paid by Numa (14.2). Because of his learning, morality, and frugality, Pertinax is likened to the Curii and Fabricii (18.1). The military valor of Claudius II, culminating in the sacrifice of his life for the state, is hailed as a return of the long-lost tradition of the similarly selfless Decii (34.2). Constantius' installation of a king on the Sarmatian throne is praised as an action unmatched since the eastern conquests of Pompey (42.22). Such comparisons imply not only that Victor believes in the excellence of the republican period, but also that he believed it possible for later figures to rival the accomplishments of the ancients.

When Victor presents observations or theories, as he is wont to do, he sometimes includes republican *exempla* which help universalize his points. His contention that Rome has often been aided by the contributions of foreigners receives confirmation both in his depiction of the Cretan emperor Nerva and in a reference to the Etruscan Tarquinius Priscus (11.12). He supports his assertion that Probus was a good general by explaining his similarity to Hannibal: both emphasized rigorous training and prevented the soldiers from becoming idle by engaging them in the planting of trees (37.2–3). Victor's theory that men of low birth are more likely to act tyrannically when they receive power is demonstrated by the example of the republican Marius as well as that of the late imperial Diocletian (39.6).

Eutropius, who unlike Victor begins his history from the founding of Rome, presents a view of early history designed to emphasize the continuity of one institution in particular, the Roman senate. Eclipsed in the third century by the rise of military rule, the senate began to regain its importance and power in the post-Constantinian empire (Arnheim 1972). Senatorial prestige received a temporary boost under Julian, but the rise to power of the Pannonian generals Valentinian and Valens produced strained relations between the court and the senate (Matthews 1975: 32–56). Eutropius, himself a senator as well as an administrator for Valens, is particularly concerned with emphasizing the importance of the ancient senate. Of sixteen mentions of the senate in his account of republican history, only one is negative (Bird 1992: xxvii–xxx).

Eutropius' pro-senatorial bias is particularly clear in his account of the conflict between Marius and Sulla. Marius is directly blamed for the war (5.4), which Eutropius attributes to his spurned desire to lead the campaign against Mithridates. Sulla's campaigns in the east are described as a stunning success (5.6), and his return to Rome is portrayed as the result of a senatorial delegation begging him to restore order after the massacre of nobles perpetrated by Marius (5.7.4). Sulla's own proscriptions are passed over with the phrase "the restoration of order to the state" (6.1). This pro-senatorial stance is presumably also the explanation for Eutropius' complete omission of the revolutionary Gracchi (Bird 1986).

Eutropius condemns Julius Caesar for his refusal to lawfully run for senatorial office (6.25), and also omits mention of Caesar's posthumous apotheosis (den Boer 1972: 156). Eutropius' negative treatment of Caesar based on his poor relations with the senate is echoed in the imperial section of the history, where the historian judges emperors largely on their behavior toward the senate. Nero's evil is demonstrated by the fact that he executed a vast number of senators and was "an enemy of all good men" (7.14.1), while Vespasian, on the other hand, was "friendly to the senate, the people, and, finally, to everyone" (7.20.2).

While Eutropius' emphasis on the senate provides continuity from republic to empire in his account of Roman history, Festus focuses on the continuity of the Roman military. Festus' introduction presents the traditional separation of Roman history into regal, republican, and imperial periods (2), but he frequently elides these distinctions in the early sections of the work, which are arranged geographically rather than in strict temporal order. In describing Roman foreign policy in the east, Festus provides a story of expansion which moves smoothly from Sulla and Pompey to Augustus and Trajan without reference to the political discontinuity between republic and empire.

Unlike Eutropius, Festus does not refrain from dwelling upon failure. A disproportionately large amount of the history is devoted to the gruesome demise of Crassus (17). While Eutropius had blamed the disaster on Crassus' failure to heed certain omens (6.18), Festus blames the failure of Crassus on his refusal to accept a proffered peace and on his reliance on a treacherous deserter. These historians' views of the defeat of Crassus may have been influenced by their attitudes toward the more recent failure of Roman armies under Julian. Festus' account of Julian is, like his account of Crassus, more critical than that of Eutropius (10.16). Festus' Julian rejected a chance for peace (28) and foolishly continued the Persian invasion until he was killed, while Eutropius' Julian, victorious, died merely by chance on his triumphant return to Roman territory (10.16.2). Both historians also have kind words for Lucius Cassius, the quaestor of Crassus. Cassius' success in preserving the defeated army and even in gaining some victories over the Parthians after the death of Crassus is perhaps meant to contrast with the failure of Jovian (Fest. 29; Eut. 10.17) after the death of Julian.

The nature of our evidence makes impossible a definitive judgement on the treatment of the republic in the fragmentary historians Eunapius, Olympiodorus, and Priscus. It seems likely that comparisons of contemporary historical events and figures with those of the classical period would generally have been extraneous to the main thread of the narrative, and would thus be particularly likely to have been suppressed in the summaries by Photius, Zosimus, or the Byzantine excerptors.

Eunapius is a more devoted traditionalist than is Olympiodorus or Priscus, and perhaps for this reason he seems to have been more drawn to *exempla*. His *exempla*, however, are derived largely from the Greek rather than the Roman past. As a successor to Dexippus and Dio, his historical pedigree ultimately stems from Herodotus, Thucydides, and classical Athens. In his extant *Lives of the Sophists*, there are no references to early Roman history, but there are several passing references to Greek figures like Nicias (479), Pericles (498), and Peisistratus (488). The *History* suggests a similar interest in the Greek past. In his preface, he uses "the wisdom of Socrates" and "the acuity of Themistocles" as examples of virtues which histories describe (*fr.* 1). Alexander the Great receives several mentions (*frs.* 28.5, 34.10), and Zosimus' comparison of Julian's victory in Gaul with that of Alexander over Darius (3.3.3) may derive ultimately from Eunapius.

Despite his Hellenic bias, Eunapius occasionally made reference to figures of the Roman republic. The *Excerpta de Sententiis* preserves two such references. Marius (whom he calls "the Roman Marius") used to say of Sulla that he was two beasts, a fox and a lion, and that he feared the fox more. Eunapius comments that Constantius was surrounded by no lions, but by many foxes (*fr.* 20.4). Another preserved quip concerns the Carthaginian general Phameas and his respect for Scipio Aemilianus (*fr.* 69.5). Blockley suggests that Eunapius had likened Fravitta to Scipio and Gainas to Phameas (1983: 148 n. 167). These mentions of republican figures were presumably derived from collections of *sententiae* rather than original research, but given the narrow, Greek-oriented world of sophistic *exempla*, they are still worthy of note (on sophistic historical *exempla* cf. Anderson 1993: 101–32).

Two passages in Zosimus which survey early Roman history could conceivably be derived from Eunapius. In his critical account of Jovian's surrender of Roman territory to the Persians after the disastrous defeat of Julian, Zosimus provides a quick survey of Roman–Persian relations, with reference to Lucullus, Pompey, Crassus, and Augustus (3.32). The comparison with republican figures who had never lost Roman territory ensures that particular opprobrium falls upon Jovian. Second, Gratian's refusal to take up the ancient pagan title of *pontifex maximus* prompts Zosimus to sketch the history of the office, pointing to Numa as its originator and Augustus as the first emperor to hold the title (4.36.3). If these passages originated with Eunapius they would provide evidence for an attempt to systematically compare fourth-century Rome with an earlier period, but they could easily be additions by Zosimus, written to support his comprehensive theory of Roman decline.

It is even more difficult to determine Olympiodorus' use of the Roman past. His extant fragments contain no references to the republic or early empire. Olympiodorus was familiar with Latin and with contemporary Rome, and the digressive nature of his history might have provided opportunity to reflect upon the ancient past. But as a writer of "material for history" rather than proper, formal history, he probably omitted the lengthy, rhetorical comparisons of ancient and modern times which characterized the more traditionalist works of historians like Ammianus or Eunapius.

Priscus' fragments contain no references to early Roman history. Priscus' work, like Olympiodorus', focuses heavily on contemporary events. His emphasis on eastern rather than western events would have limited his opportunities to discuss the republic. The historian's treatment of Rome in his debate with the Greek who became a Hun further suggests a lack of interest in the ancient history of Rome. His defense of Rome centers primarily upon the value of Roman law and the Roman constitution. The institutions which Priscus defends are those of the late Roman state. He gives no attention to the virtuous heroes of early Rome or to the republican constitution which earlier historians had seen as integral to the success of the Roman state.

Orosius provides a vision of the Roman republic strikingly at odds with that of the pagan and classicizing historians. Under the influence of the Eusebian vision, he depicts a corrupt and bellicose republic which gave way, at the time of the coming of Christ, to a more benevolent and progressive empire. The Roman state, according to Orosius, was born in bloodshed and violence, as Romulus murdered his grandfather and brother, abducted the Sabine Women, and gathered together a band of criminals as the first citizens (2.4). But the regal period did not lead to a liberated republic. Instead, Orosius describes the regicide Brutus as the murderer of his sons and thus as even worse than Romulus. The horrors of the republic only ceased with the coming of Augustus. Augustus' opening of the doors of the temple of Janus, which signifies the peace of the empire, is purposefully misdated by Orosius in order to link it directly with the Epiphany (6.20.3; Inglebert 1996: 543).

Orosius aims to show that the disasters of the early fifth century, which some had blamed on the abandonment of traditional Roman religion, paled in comparison with the disasters of the Roman state prior to the coming of Christ and the establishment of Christianity. The Eusebian framework he adopts to explain Roman history suggested that the sole rule of Augustus over a world empire was the secular counterpart to the rule of one God over the world, and that the two threads, secular and divine, became united with the coming of Constantine, at once the worldly emperor and the head of the Christian church. Orosius does not clearly suggest that the troubles of the republic rested upon a flawed political system; in fact, he only occasionally recognizes any systemic difference between republic and empire. Instead, every kind of disturbance, whether in warfare, in domestic affairs, or in natural events such as pestilence and earthquake, is set forth as evidence of the corruption of the early Roman state.

Orosius' approach to warfare is of particular interest. Ammianus had adduced the military disasters of the republic to soften the impact of contemporary disasters in Persia and Adrianople. The Roman state had weathered such storms before, he reminds despairing contemporaries, and would doubtless do so again. Orosius' emphasis on republican military disasters, such as the destruction of Rome by the Gauls (2.19), is aimed at similarly pessimistic contemporary critics. But Orosius' conclusion reaches further. He suggests that the relative mildness of contemporary troubles proves that the Roman state has evolved from a depraved past to a superior present. When Orosius reflects on the proscriptions of Sulla (5.22.5–15), for example, he points out that civil wars have been much milder in his own time due to Christianity. Similarly, the civil wars of the late republic, which culminated in the death of Caesar, were the result of the competition between arrogant nobles. This competition has now been suppressed thanks to the coming of Christ and his teachings of humility (6.17.9–10).

Orosius presents the empire as a period of peace. Tiberius' resistance to military expansion is praised (7.4.2–4), and in Christian times even the depravity of Caligula cannot prevent peace (7.5.4). What warfare did persist into imperial times was the result of the just chastisement of God. The civil wars after Nero, for example, resulted from Nero's persecutions of Christians (7.8.2), and the Flavian suppression of the Judaean revolt reflected divine displeasure with the Jews (7.9.2).

In general, historians writing in Greek devote less attention to the republic than do historians writing in Latin, and historians writing later in the fifth century devote less attention to the republic than do those who write earlier. The importance of the republic recedes as the later empire emerges in its new Greek and Christian form. This would appear to be true even for a historian like Olympiodorus, who was deeply involved in western affairs and eager to promote western and eastern unification. For the ecclesiastical historians, however, the republic is no longer useful as a source of lessons or models. The biblical past became more accessible than the classical past for some late antique Christians.

In western circles at the turn of the fifth century, the republic was considered an integral part of Roman history and could be appropriated for moral (Victor), institutional (Eutropius), or military (Festus) ends with regard to contemporary affairs. The more elaborate apparatus of Ammianus presents a republican spirit handed down to the emperors and embodied in particular by Julian. Continuity with the distant past serves to legitimate the present order for these fourth-century authors. Orosius, too, in a quite different way, legitimates the present through his treatment of the past. In contrast with the corruption and violence of the republican past, the late empire represents, for Orosius, a new and higher level of history marked by peace and unity.

Orosius' view was more sustainable than Ammianus' for many historians. With the exceptions of Eunapius, who seems to have drawn equally, if tenuously, upon both Greek and Roman antiquity, and Rufinus, whose history may have been mostly complete before the writing of his pessimistic preface, the other historians described here have optimistic and progressive views of their own time. Socrates, Sozomen, and Theodoret write in the shadow of the pious and long-lived Theodosius II, while Olympiodorus and Priscus celebrate their own successful diplomatic missions. Rather than attempting to link their histories to an increasingly alien past, they have jettisoned the distant past altogether, deeming it irrelevant to the new concerns of court and church at Constantinople.

16

RELIGION

Christianity versus paganism

"Pagan" was an insulting term, carrying an implication of rustic "backwardness," which was invented by Christians to disparage practitioners of traditional religions (Chuvin 1990; Bowersock 1990a; MacMullen 1981; Lane Fox 1987). Those who used the word sought to lump into a single category the near-infinite constellation of practices and beliefs regarding man's relationship to the divine that had evolved over millennia of Mediterranean life. The definition of pagan, therefore, was in flux throughout late antiquity. At the time of Constantine, the erection of temples and the sacrifice of animals were considered part of pagan cult, but many gray areas remained. The emperor continued to receive divine honors. Both pagans and Christians used magic and divination to tell the future. Classical literature and art were deeply imbued with the pagan gods, and were therefore suspect to some Christians. Late antique historians open a window onto the diversity of pagan thought and the continuing prominence in the Christian empire of certain practices now considered pagan.

Eutropius and Victor were pagans writing presumably for a mixed audience of Christians and pagans. They provide, as a result, useful insight into what ordinary members of the elite, without intense feelings about religion, would consider non-objectionable material. Eutropius, whose quasi-official work was written at the command of a Christian emperor, mentions the apotheosis of each emperor awarded divine status by the senate after his death. The offering of worship to an emperor was clearly considered an act of respect without anti-Christian overtones. Half a century later, the Christian Sozomen would refer to citizens naturally offering obeisance to painted pictures of the emperor (5.17.3–5). Even Constantine, according to Eutropius, was "enrolled among the gods" (10.8.3).

Victor provides a bit more commentary on religion in his work than had Eutropius (Rike 1987: 114–17). He praises Diocletian and Maximian for the respect they showed for the most ancient religious cults (39.45), and Caracalla for his piety in bringing the cults of Egypt to Rome (21.4). Victor assimilates Constantine's imposition of Christianity as a state religion into this model when he praises the emperor for "regulating religious practices" (41.12). Victor also makes several references to traditional methods used to predict the future. The death of some particularly white chickens kept in Rome for divinatory purposes, for example, marked the end of the Julio-Claudian dynasty (5.17). Victor adds that these chickens were so useful for divination that they continued to be used for divinatory rituals in his own day. The validity of divination is further empha-sized by the emperor Gordian's successful prediction of his fate from his skillful analysis of an unusual sacrifice (26.4). Victor provides several interpretations of the prodigy which appeared during the reign of Philip the Arab, when female genitalia were discovered on the belly of a hog (28.3–9). While Philip understood this sign as a threat to the virtue of the young, and therefore outlawed male pros-titution, other soothsayers claimed that it meant the triumph of the effeminate over the good. Victor rejects these interpretations, instead drawing the moral lesson that those without shame cannot be happy.

Divination and magic were not necessarily considered pagan if they were performed without animal sacrifice, and Constantine's legislation banned divination by animal entrails only if it was performed in secret. Thus, Christians would not have recoiled in disbelief or horror when told about the ancient magical statues which Olympiodorus discusses (*frs.* 16, 27). Olympiodorus reveals that Christians rejected the Etruscan soothsayers who promised to protect Rome from Alaric with thunder and lightning, due to opposition from the pope (*fr.* 7.5; Zos. 5.21). The rites of the Asian Libanius, a magician who likewise claimed to be able to ward off barbarians, seem to have required secrecy, and when they came to the attention of the devout Christian empress Galla Placidia, he was put to death (*fr.* 36).

The paganism of intellectuals often included complex Neoplatonic explanations of the gods. Late antique religious Neoplatonism was henotheistic, directed toward the One (Greek *hen*) supreme power, from which emanated multiple levels of increasingly less powerful planes of existence. The skilled practi-tioner of this religion might, through study or magic, elevate himself beyond the low, shadowy, material plane on which we live to a higher and more substantial level of reality. Eunapius refers to this process in his eulogy of Julian, who, the historian claims, was able to transcend his flesh through force of character and raise himself up to the heavens, where he mingled with divine spirits (*frs.* 28.1, 28.5). The secret rites which Julian and Oribasius performed in order to prepare for the civil war with Constantius may have been "theurgic" in nature, aimed at questioning and perhaps controlling the gods (*fr.* 21.1). Eunapius does not, however, scorn more traditional pagan rites, and expresses general disgust at the destruction of temples (*frs.* 64.2, 64.3) while praising Fravitta's dedication to the traditional worship of the gods (*fr.* 69.4). But his form of paganism saw temples and rituals as superficial manifestations of more profound religious truths, and thus he can mock those who destroy and sack temples for merely "waging war on stones" (*fr.* 56).

Ammianus' religious position has long been contested. While he is a pagan, historians have differed in their interpretations of his comments about Christianity and about Julian's paganism. It has been argued that Ammianus is quite hostile to Christianity, omitting information which would be to the credit of Christians and Christianity and slanting other information to discredit Christians (Barnes 1998; Elliott 1983). While acknowledging some hostility and inaccuracy in Ammianus' treatment of Christianity, others cite his disparagement of some of the pagan policies of Julian in order to argue that the historian is evenhanded in his religious criticism (Hunt 1985, 1993; Matthews 1989: 435–51). The key to understanding Ammianus' religious opinions lies in recognizing the multiple systems of belief which we lump under the term "paganism." The historian is a partisan pagan who nevertheless rejects aspects of Julian's pagan practices (Rike 1987).

Ammianus is particularly critical of Julian's excessive sacrificing and indiscriminate divination. By his continual sacrifices, the emperor overemphasized the gross, physical aspects of paganism, wasting money and filling the streets with drunken and gluttonous soldiers (22.12.6). Julian also indiscriminately allowed anyone to read omens and portents, despite their lack of qualifications (22.12.7). For these reasons, Ammianus characterizes the emperor as "superstitious rather than truly religious" (25.4.17).

For Ammianus, paganism is a system of thought as rigorous as a science. His digressions on Nemesis and on the guardian spirit, for example, cite ancient authorities who have investigated these divine phenomena (14.11.25–6; 21.14.3–5). Ammianus is never critical of the religious wisdom of ancient cultures. He praises the depth of knowledge of the Druids (15.9.8), whom Victor had criticized as "notorious" (4.2). He refers to the "ancient wisdom" of hiero-glyphics, and encourages the reader to investigate the primeval religious knowledge of the Egyptians (17.4.8, 22.16.19–22). He also cites the ancient Etruscan religious writings of Tages and Vegoe, and the "most incorruptible" form of worship performed by the Persian Magi (17.10.2, 23.6.32–6).

In Ammianus' account, in the background of Julian's march toward Persia and subsequent defeat, death is a competition between two rival schools of paganism. Julian's philosophers are shown continually misinterpreting the divine signs which urge against the invasion. They repeatedly disregard the superior wisdom of the Etruscan soothsayers (23.5.10–11). By the end of the invasion, Ammianus can say that Julian struggled against "the entire science of divination" (25.2.7–8). Ammianus thus locates Julian's tragic flaw in his failure to be properly pious. Christian emperors, of course, are even less pious, in Ammianus' view.

Christian historians concentrate on the physical evidence of pagan cult. Socrates, Sozomen, and Theodoret refer to temples, sacrifices, and festivals in various permutations to characterize paganism as a whole (Soc. 3.1.39; Soz. 2.3.7, 9.9.1; Theod. 3.6.1). Because of the varieties of practices and beliefs traveling under the name of pagan, church historians are able to describe the most repugnant practices of pagans as if they represented all non-Christians. Paganism in the church historians therefore rests on frauds and evils, and can be effectively challenged through the dramatic demonstration of its errors. Rufinus reports that magnets and tricks of the light were responsible for the miracles of the Egyptian divinity Serapis, and that a priest of Saturn speaking through the cult statue was able to have his way with numerous married women (11.23, 25). Sozomen likewise claims that machinery was in use in temples to create the appearance of demonic visitations (5.2.5).

The church historians frequently equate paganism with human sacrifice, although there is generally no convincing evidence for the charge. For Rufinus, paganism in Alexandria is exemplified by corpses and by the decapitated heads of babies discovered in jars (11.24). Socrates reports on the discovery of the skulls of those who, he claims, had been sacrificed in order to tell the future by the inspection of their entrails (3.2). Theodoret likewise claims that, after the death of Julian, a woman was found who had been cut open for divinatory purposes, and other body parts were discovered in the palace (3.26, 27).

Orosius makes occasional jibes at temple corruption (3.16.12–13), sacrifice (4.21.5–9), and divination by the inspection of entrails (5.4.8). In one lengthy aside, he asks how powerful the Roman gods could be, if they were unable to resist the coming and the triumph of Christianity (6.*pref.*). But despite the fact that Orosius' history is written "Against the Pagans," he shies away from detailed criticism of pagan practices. To prove the superiority of Christianity to all other forms of religion, he cannot be distracted by fine-grained distinctions between "paganisms."

Christianity versus Christianity

The doctrinal disputes which wracked the church in the fourth and fifth centuries dominate the work of the ecclesiastical historians. In the first centuries of Christianity, Christians had shared common enemies in an unfriendly Roman state and a powerful pagan establishment. But the rise of a Christian state with a Christian emperor who distributed wealth and patronage to "orthodox" bishops and churches made the issue of orthodoxy worth fighting over. The application of more sophisticated methods to scriptural interpretation and theological discussion produced endless sources of disputation.

The activities of Athanasius of Alexandria dominate the early books of the Greek church historians (Barnes 1993b; Hanson 1988: 239–73). Athanasius was a major figure in the struggles over the definition of orthodoxy in the middle decades of the fourth century, and his career demonstrates the mixture of theological, personal, political, and financial motives which drove these conflicts. He presented himself as an indefatigable champion of Nicene orthodoxy. The historians, quoting Athanasius directly or paraphrasing his voluminous writings, highlight his willingness to undergo repeated exiles and to suffer numerous condemnations at the hands of church councils and emperors alike. While Athanasius is an unalloyed hero in the works of the church historians, modern scholars have tended to be rather critical of the bishop for his continual attempts to claim that legitimate complaints about his improper conduct as bishop were motivated by ideological opposition to Nicene Christianity. In particular, the discovery of certain papyrus documents at the beginning of the twentieth century made it clear that Athanasius and his supporters had indeed been guilty of the violent behavior which was imputed to them by their enemies and which the church historians had dismissed as outrageous lies (Bell 1924). The case of Athanasius, then, serves to remind us of the dangers and challenges of reconstructing church history through the use of the church historians. The historians often depend on unreliable sources, such as the polemical works of Athanasius himself. In addition, the church historians seek to recreate the past with the aim of comforting, edifying, and inspiring their readers. They met these goals most effectively by presenting a morally uncomplicated Athanasius, and by framing his conflicts as battles over doctrinal disputes which had been settled by their own times.

A closer look at another important and controversial Christian leader of late antiquity will reveal important differences in the perspectives of the Greek church historians. The bishop John Chrysostom was active a generation after Athanasius, and thus the testimony of the historians on the dramatic events of his life is likely to be more reliable. The conflicts in which John was entangled touched only slightly upon doctrine; instead, they reveal the conflicts engendered by the new power of the bishop in a major city of the east (Kelly 1995; Liebeschuetz 1990: 166–227; Mayer and Allen 2000; for background, Bowersock 1986). The rapid rise to power of the bishop through the fourth century upset long-established relations of power in the ancient city. Chrysostom's oratorical skills and moral sway enabled him to mobilize the mass of citizens, and his administrative and financial skills set him in charge of an army of clergy and a network of charitable organizations funded by the wealthy of the city. His location in Constantinople placed him in constant contact with the imperial family and in an uneasy relationship with other major bishoprics, such as Alexandria, and with less powerful sees in Asia Minor and the Levant.

John was born around 349 in Antioch and was raised by his mother alone after his father died shortly after his birth. He prepared briefly for a career in law, and studied rhetoric with the famous sophist Libanius, before turning to a more ascetic, Christian way of life in a community of monks in the Syrian desert for several years. The rigors of monastic life damaged his health and he returned to the city, where he served the bishop Flavian in various capacities and was ordained as a priest in 386. For a decade he worked as an priest at Antioch, where he was involved in charitable work and became popular and well known for his powerful sermons. When Nectarius, bishop of Constantinople, died in October 397,

John was selected to replace him either by the emperor Arcadius, or by the eunuch Eutropius, who was extremely influential at court at the time. From the start, the bishop made enemies. Theophilus, the bishop of Alexandria, supported a different candidate, and rumor suggested that Eutropius had to blackmail him into acquiescence. John's firmness with clerical discipline angered many of his subordinates, and his habit of speaking his mind may have caused friction with members of the imperial family and court.

John is a heroic figure in the works of all three church historians, who all condemn his eventual deposition as an injustice. Nevertheless, Socrates is markedly cooler toward John than the other historians, and in many cases we can see Sozomen at work rejecting the criticisms of Socrates and providing refutations to other charges. Socrates, for example, describes John as upright, yet somewhat haughty, and suggests that John was a little too arrogant in his relations with his clergy, who were therefore cold toward him (6.3–4). Sozomen rejects any hint of blame in John's conduct, seeing his regulation of the life of clergy as evidence of his goodness and character (8.3.1–2). The descriptions of another incident during John's tenure bring out the differences between the two historians. The eunuch Eutropius fell out of favor with Arcadius and fled for his life to John's church, seeking sanctuary. With Eutropius present, John delivered a sermon which used the eunuch's situation as an example of the malleability of human fortune. Socrates calls this speech an "interrogation," and says that it made some unhappy, as it seemed to lack compassion toward one so wretched (6.5.1–7). Sozomen, on the other hand, begins with an elaboration of Eutropius' sins to emphasize his wickedness, and describes John's speech as simply an "oration." He adds that "the enemies of John" reproached him for cruelty, and then moves swiftly to a description of Eutropius' decapitation, the just result of the wrath of God (8.7).

The conflict which arose between John and the bishop Severian is also worth examining as an example of varying treatments of the same material by Socrates and then Sozomen. The manuscripts of Socrates' history preserve two different versions of the conflict, apparently representing the two separate editions of the work (6.11). The first version is considerably more favorable toward John. Severian was a substitute preacher for John, and his success, reported regularly to John by his trusted advisor Serapion, evoked feelings of envy in John. Serapion and Severian grew to dislike one another, and Serapion one day did not stand as the bishop walked past. Socrates, in this first version, denies being able to ascertain whether Serapion's behavior was disrespectful or inadvertent. Severian became incensed, and despite John's urgings and the condemnation of a council, Severian refused to forgive Serapion and became estranged from John. The other version of the story preserved in Socrates' manuscripts presumably represents the second edition, since Sozomen seems dependent upon it. In this version, Severian's snub was unquestionably an insult. Severian, exasperated, swore, "If Serapion should die a Christian, then Christ did not become a man!" Serapion went to John and reported that Severian had claimed that "Christ did not become a man!," and rather than the repeated conferences and councils of the first account, here John immediately reacted to the apparent blasphemy and sent the bishop into exile. Sozomen, faced with a story suggesting that John had unfairly overreacted, attempted to restore John's honor in his account (8.10). In Sozomen's version, Serapion reports Severian's entire statement to the bishop, who considers it blasphemous even without emendation, since it would imply that Christ might possibly not have become man should Serapion abjure Christianity. This clumsy attempt to excuse John's unreasonable behavior reveals the lengths to which Sozomen will go to ensure that his John is free from fault.

The church historians also narrate the conflict which arose between John and Bishop Theophilus of Alexandria. Theophilus is portrayed as an opportunist, willing to use vague charges of hetero-doxy against opponents for nefarious purposes. Socrates claims that Theophilus had at first been a supporter of Origen's theory of the incorporeal nature of God, but that he had switched to the opposite, anti-Origenist theory for crass, political reasons (6.9). Out of disgust toward Theophilus' position, Socrates includes a long digression supporting Origen and praising the brilliance of his ideas (6.13). Socrates also draws a sharp distinction between Proclus, the excellent contemporary bishop of Constantinople, and the perse-cutor Theophilus (7.45). Sozomen is less tolerant of doctrinal deviation than Socrates, and he omits any defense of the question-ably orthodox Origen and plays down the role of ideology in Theophilus' behavior. Neither Socrates nor Sozomen had empha-sized the role of Theophilus in an earlier exploit, the destruction of the temple in Alexandria called the Serapeum, which might, perhaps, have interfered with their later portrayal of his villainous behavior (Soc. 5.16; Soz. 7.15). By contrast, Theodoret lauds Theophilus as "intelligent and courageous" in his description of the destruction of the temple (5.22.1). Perhaps for this reason

Theodoret's abbreviated account of the trials of John begins with a hesitant note that, owing to his respect for the virtues of John's enemies, he will refrain from even mentioning their names (5.34).

The empress Eudoxia, who clashed several times with John, is another one of the bishop's persecutors whose name Theodoret passes over. Socrates reports that John gave a sermon directed against the evils of women, which was understood by the empress to be directed toward her personally (6.15.1–4). Socrates implies that the empress was not paranoid, but that John did in fact mean for her to be the object of his diatribe. Sozomen, on the other hand, says that he cannot know whether the empress' anger was justified (8.16.2). John's congregants, he claims, attached "riddling" meanings to his words. Sozomen is also more favorable to John in his treatment of the affair of the statue. The empress was being honored by a silver statue and raised to the rank of "Augusta," a controversial idea which had been rejected by the western emperor Honorius. The erection of the statue south of the church was celebrated "with dances and mimes," says Sozomen, and John charged that this sort of behavior reflected poorly on the church, thus angering Eudoxia (8.20). This is a softening of the account of Socrates, who points out that while the bishop would have been acting properly if he had politely asked the officials to desist, John instead railed against the empress with abusive language (6.18.1–5). This is one of several occasions where Socrates makes it clear that, despite his admiration for John, at times he finds the bishop to blame for his difficulties.

John's various conflicts eventually resulted in a trial *in absentia* conducted by his enemies at the Constantinople suburb known as "The Oak" in 402. The bishop was exiled, recalled by the empress, but then exiled once again in 403. John was sent to a distant town in western Armenia, where he remained for three years, and then died in 407 while undertaking a forced march to an even more distant place of exile. In Constantinople, supporters of the exiled bishop stayed in contact with him and agitated for his return, refusing to take communion with the new bishop and instead meeting outside the city walls. The three church historians treat events after John's exile and death with sharp differences in emphasis. At John's departure, riots had resulted in the burning of the church and the senate house. Socrates briefly reports the fire and then declines to provide details of the tortures suffered by the followers of John who had been responsible (6.18.19). Sozomen, however, claims that it was unclear who was responsible for the blaze (8.22.5). He then provides the details, which Socrates had thought it best to omit, on the tortures suffered by various partisans of John after the fire (8.23–4).

Contemporaries disagreed whether the disasters which struck John's enemies and the city of Constantinople were the result of divine displeasure at the bishop's maltreatment. While Socrates is neutral on the question, Sozomen and Theodoret see these disasters as sure signs of the retributive justice of God. Not long after his participation in the deposition of John, Cyrinus was compelled to have his legs amputated because of gangrene. The death of Eudoxia and a major hailstorm were also, says Socrates, attributed by "some" to John's exile. But others, Socrates reveals, felt that the bishop deserved his fate because of his high-handed behavior, which included the removal of churches from the Novatians, the sect from which Socrates drew many of his informants (6.19). Sozomen provides no balancing statement, but merely a list of the disasters which befell the opponents of John (8.27.1–2). He also attributes a Hunnic invasion and Alaric's invasion of Illyricum to the disordered state of the church (8.25). Theodoret, too, while continuing his policy of refusing to provide specific names, claims that most of the guilty were indeed punished (5.34.10).

Sozomen provides in full, and Theodoret in abbreviated form, the strife between the eastern and western churches which resulted from John's deposition, while Socrates omits it (Soz. 8.26, 8.28; Theod. 5.34.10–11). If Sozomen's work were complete, it would surely contain the account of the return of John's remains to Constantinople in 438, which plays a significant role in the conclusion of both Socrates' and Theodoret's histories. For Theodoret it serves as an opportunity to praise the piety of the reigning emperor Theodosius II, whom his history otherwise would not reach. Socrates' account of the return of John's remains gives more credit to the bishop Proclus than to Theodosius II, and he includes a lament that Origen is still not respected after two hundred years, while John is after only thirty-five (7.45). More important for Socrates, the return of John's remains and their installation in the church are one of a constellation of events with which he ends his history, all of which signal an end to conflict of some sort: the conversion of Jews, the accession of Proclus, the pious reign of Theodosius, the destruction of the barbarians, the marriage of Valentinian and Eudoxia, and finally a pilgrimage by the empress Eudocia to Jerusalem. Thus for Socrates the restoration of the partisans of John into the church represents an end to the entire range of disputes and problems which he has chronicled in his history.

Monasticism

The deserts of the Levant and of Egypt in antiquity had long been home to religious dissidents as well as to those fleeing economic, social, or legal problems in more settled areas (Chitty 1966; Rousseau 1985; Brown 1988: 213–58; Markus 1990: 157–97). In the first century AD, for example, Philo of Alexandria described Jews who had withdrawn from city life to live contemplative lives of labor in the country. Other pagan, gnostic, and Manichaean precedents existed for similar rejections of urban life. The taxation reforms of Diocletian, which encouraged communal responsibility for land, probably further sparked new experiments in communal living arrangements.

The first major movement of Christians to the desert came in the third century, as a response to the persecutions of Decius, Valerian, and Diocletian. Antony, perhaps the most famous monk, heard his priest read from the book of Matthew (Matt. 19: 21) one Sunday around the year 270: "Go, sell what you possess and give to the poor." Taking the message literally, Antony distributed his family's inheritance to the poor and moved to the outskirts of the village, and in years to come retreated deeper and deeper into the desert. The monastic movement grew quickly through the fourth century, and a proliferation of monastic rules and communities allowed for many different models of monastic life. With increasing numbers came increasing political clout, and the organized power of monks began to be felt in the church and in the wider world of the empire.

The growth of monasticism challenged the established power of the church hierarchy and of the civil authorities. The late antique church historians are, as a group, generally very favorable toward the position of the monks. Rufinus and Theodoret wrote separate works celebrating the deeds of the monks, and Sozomen was close to the monks of his native land of Gaza. Only Socrates, with his more favorable attitude toward imperial power, hesitates to lavish unstinting praise on monastic communities.

Historians had several different models by which to explain monastic behavior. Sozomen and Theodoret commonly refer to the monastic life as the true "philosophy." Sozomen considered the philosophy of the monks to be "the most useful thing given to men by God" (1.12.1). He further explains that monastic philosophy ignores some elements of learning, such as mathematics and oratory, in favor of studying virtue, and that the monk demonstrates his virtue not by argument but by action (1.12.1). He says that he has included monastic founders and their successors in his history to provide models for emulation by his readers (1.1.19). Some pagan as well as Christian philosophers in antiquity had long been associated with ascetic behavior. Sozomen demonstrates a peculiarly late antique use of the concept of philosophy, however, which considers only the body and soul of the monk. The intellect is so tangential to Sozomen's use of the term "philosophy" that some of his philosophers were illiterate, such as John of Egypt (6.28.1–2). Another monk whom Sozomen describes, Theonas, had a deep understanding of Roman, Greek, and Egyptian learning, but in an act of self-abasement did not speak for thirty years (6.28.3).

Monasticism was often portrayed as an attempt to return to the original condition of man prior to the Fall. While sexual continence was one aspect of this return to Eden, late antique historians are more likely to emphasize the tremendous abilities of monks to abstain from food, following a literal interpretation of Genesis which saw Adam's consumption of the apple as the cause of his separation from God (Brown 1988: 220). Socrates writes that one of the founders of Egyptian monasticism, Ammoun, abstained from wine and oil and ate only rarely (4.23.11). More radically, Sozomen says that John of Egypt ate nothing but herbs, roots, and water (6.28.2) and that the monks of Nisibis eschewed bread, meat, and wine, and ate only grass (6.33.1–2). The monk Ammonius of Scetis ate nothing treated by fire except for bread throughout his entire life (6.30.3). Historians also demonstrate the return to Edenic simplicity by describing the ability of monks to mingle with wild animals. Rufinus' brief comments on Antony mention that he mingled with the beasts (10.8), and he adds an anecdote from the life of Macarius, who once healed a baby hyena and was rewarded with gifts by the hyena's mother (11.4). Despite Zeugmatos' blindness, Theodoret says, he was a successful herder with no difficulty keeping wolves from his flocks (4.28.2).

The ability of monks to perform miracles also demonstrated that they possessed the powers of the Christians of the apostolic age. For Rufinus, the monks perform "signs and wonders" like those of the apostles (11.8), including the curing of blindness and of shriveled limbs (11.4; Thélamon 1992). Sozomen says that Macarius had raised a man from the dead to prove the possibility of resurrection to a skeptic (3.14.2). He also tells of the healings and exorcisms of the monk Julian, who lived near Edessa (3.14.29), and of the activities of Martin of Gaul, who performed miracles like the apostles (3.14.41).

Basil of Caesarea divided monks into two classes. Some lived in close-knit communities under a rule like that devised by Pachomius in Egypt. Other monks were more devoted to individual excellence, like the "athletes of God" whom Theodoret described in his *Religious History*. The former type of monk was more common in Egypt and the west, while the latter was particularly prominent in Syria and the east. In practice, of course, these distinctions did not always hold for individual monks, and the late antique historians do not often stress these differences in living arrangements in their surveys of monastic "superstars." Sozomen discusses Pachomius and the thousands of monks who lived in his community (3.14.4–17). Pachomius' monastic rule was presented to him by an angel on a tablet, which Sozomen claims still existed in his own time. This rule closely regulated the activities and duties of the monks. These monks wore distinctive garments: their tunics, for example, lacked sleeves, to remind them to be slow to allow their hands to do evil, and they wore a hood like that of a nursing infant, to remind them to be pure as a baby (3.14.7–8). Monks not bound by a formalized rule performed more radical forms of self-denial, such as Hilarion of Palestine, who lived in a cell too small to stand in or lie down in fully (Soz. 3.14.21–8) or Theodoret's Acepsemas, who spent sixty years in his cell without speaking to or seeing another person (Theod. 4.28.1).

The glorification of monasticism and of monastic deeds over words brought those who spoke neither Greek nor Latin into historiography in a new way. Many of the monks of Egypt spoke only Coptic. Both Sozomen and Theodoret give special prominence to the monk Ephrem and to the fact that he spoke and wrote only in Syriac (Soz. 3.16; Theod. 4.29.1–3). Sozomen claims that the works of the Greek fathers translated into Syriac would lose their force, but that translations of Ephrem into Greek had been quite successful. Theodoret adds that Ephrem was able to refute the falsehoods of the Greeks in his writing despite his ignorance of the language.

When the emperor Valens asked the monk Aphrahat what he was doing on the road, he said that he was praying for the safety of the empire, according to an anecdote told by Theodoret (4.26). Valens suggested that he should return to his monastery and pray there, but Aphrahat said that his presence was necessary, likening the empire under the persecution of Valens to a neighbor's house which was on fire. One of the emperor's attendants who spoke insultingly to the monk paid the price shortly thereafter when he was scalded to death while preparing a bath. Theodoret approves of the involvement of monks in political and ecclesiastical disputes, saying that the best monks knew when to remain in the desert and when to head to the city (4.27.5).

One way in which the historians demonstrate the piety of an emperor is by noting his favorable attitude toward monks. Socrates describes the exploits of the monk Eutychian, who miraculously freed from chains an imperial official who had been unjustly imprisoned (1.13.1–10). Eutychian then journeyed to Constantinople to plead for the man's pardon, and Constantine granted his request. The monk Telemachus, according to Theodoret, attended a gladiatorial game while visiting Rome and descended into the arena to separate the combatants (5.26). While the audience was enraged, the emperor Honorius took the lesson to heart, and he abolished the games shortly thereafter.

Sozomen credits the monks with leading the resistance to Arianism (6.27.8–10). In his view, their simplicity and steadfastness ensured the survival of correct doctrine. His praise of their simplicity was in accordance with a predominant theme of the church histories, which held that the complexities of overly sophisticated heretics threatened the purity of true belief. Sozomen also champions the boldness of Ephrem, who preached against the rich men of Edessa during a famine (3.16.12–15). The city leaders were sufficiently chagrined to present him with money to distribute for the feeding of the poor.

Boldness and simplicity could yield less ideal result, as well. Sozomen describes how the followers of Eustathius of Armenia went too far in their teachings about poverty and virginity (3.14.31–7). Some refused even to meet with married people and denounced the rich excessively, and some women acolytes went so far as to cut their hair and dress in men's clothing. Sozomen also says that while John Chrysostom was favorable toward monasticism and a friend to the monks who lived in the desert, he was hostile toward the monks who lived in the city and meddled in urban affairs (8.9.4–6).

Socrates is particularly critical of the monks of Egypt who insisted on an anthropomorphic view of God, claiming that he possessed eyes, ears, feet, and hands (6.7). Exploiting their belief, Theophilus of Alexandria led a crusade against Origen, who had held, correctly in Socrates' view, that God was incorporeal. The monks' views were the result, says Socrates, of their ignorance, illiteracy, and simplicity. Socrates is also critical of the behavior of these same monks during a riot in Alexandria, when they assaulted the prefect Orestes (7.14). Socrates connects this riot to the murder of the philosopher Hypatia, the daughter of Theron (7.15). He reflects that "nothing is further from the spirit of Christ than allowing killings, fights, and occurrences of that sort" (7.15.6).

Ammianus' history was composed prior to the great wave of monastic violence at the turn of the fifth century, and so contains no specific mention of monks. Eunapius, however, reveals the attitude of a partisan pagan to the growing influence of monks (Bartelink 1969). Eunapius claims that barbarians entered the empire disguised as monks, a disguise which was not at all difficult, in his view, since merely wearing a gray cloak and tunic marked one out as a monastic "scoundrel" (*fr.* 48.2). Whoever wore this cloak, Eunapius complains, had tyrannical power to destroy religious monuments and temples (*fr.* 56). Those who were called monks, he adds, were men in appearance, but pigs in their way of life. The Christian piety, simplicity, and rejection of urban life at the heart of monastic life which Christian historians celebrated were the very traits which sophisticated pagans found so unfathomable and disgraceful.

Judaism

Late antiquity was a period of rapid change for Judaism as well as for Christianity (Simon 1964/86; Feldman 1993). The destruction of the Jewish Temple in AD 70, and the exclusion of Jews from Jerusalem after the failure of the Bar Kochba revolt in 135, paradoxically invigorated Judaism by strengthening the universal aspects of the religion over the national or ethnic aspects. In the second and third centuries, Judaism was a proselytizing religion which was attractive to many pagans and which competed directly with Christianity for converts. Roman imperial policy had been protective of the Jews, but the legal codes show a gradual shift throughout the fourth century after the conversion of Constantine. The fourth-century emperors alternated between the protection of Jews and the imposition of legal burdens upon them. By the turn of the fifth century, Judaism was in increasing disfavor with Roman authorities; for example, laws were passed in 404 and 418 prohibiting Jews from holding imperial positions. The compilations of the Jerusalem Talmud at the end of the fourth century and of the Babylonian Talmud a few decades later were symbolic of the triumph of a more inward-looking and self-protective form of Judaism in the face of the imperial onslaught. The center of gravity of Judaism itself migrated over the border into Persia, and the fate of the Jews in the Byzantine east and post-Roman west became increasingly grim as the governments became increasingly theocratic.

Pagan historians had long been contemptuous of the Jews, who were generally characterized as quarrelsome "haters of mankind," and whose ritual practices, particularly circumcision, were alternately mocked and abhorred (Stertz 1998). Ammianus has very little to say about the Jews, and his account of Julian's attempt to rebuild the Jewish Temple is curiously lacking in information on the importance of the Temple to either Jews or to Christians (23.1). In a confused passage, Ammianus does quote Marcus Aurelius condemning the Jews as "filthy and rebellious"; while the numerous uprisings of the Jews against Roman rule explain the latter epithet, his criticism of the Jews as "filthy" seems to lack any parallel and still demands scholarly explanation (22.5.5).

Victor's only substantive mention of the Jews is in connection with the poorly documented revolt in Palestine in 351 or 352, which he attributes to the criminal leadership of a self-styled king, "Patricius" (42.11). This has been alternatively considered a Messianic uprising or a simple attempt at imperial usurpation (Geiger 1979/80). The revolt was quickly crushed by Gallus, according to the short passages on the subject by Socrates (2.33) and Sozomen (4.7.5–6). It has been suggested that Ammianus' neglect of Gallus' role in suppressing these disturbances is an example of his bias against the Caesar. Talmudic sources, however, reveal that Ammianus' patron, Ursicinus, was the commander of the forces which defeated the Jews. It is therefore certain that Ammianus was not motivated by bias in this case, and probable that he related Ursicinus' success in the lost book 13 (Geiger 1979).

Rufinus treats the Jews only in the context of the attempted rebuilding of the Temple in Jerusalem under Julian's sponsorship (10.38–40; Thélamon 1981: 294–309). This carefully crafted section requires, for the sake of narrative suspense, a display of supreme arrogance by the Jews, who are pitted against the wisdom of the bishop Cyril and his interpretation of the Book of Daniel. This portrayal recapitulates an original Christian complaint against the Jews, their inability to properly interpret Scripture so as to identify Jesus as the Messiah. Sozomen begins his history in amazement at this failure: all of the signs were there, yet the Jews stubbornly and inexplicably refused to understand them (1.1.1–8). In reality, the absence of the attempted rebuilding of the Temple from Jewish sources suggests that the Jews were considerably less enthralled by the plan than Christian sources suggest, perhaps because existing power relationships would be upset by a restoration of the Temple priesthood (Levenson 1990a).

Marcel Simon points out that one of the attractions Judaism had for non-Jews was its festival days, which were publicly celebrated ,particularly in the cities of the east (Simon 1964/86: 312–13). The church sought, therefore, to firmly distinguish Easter from Passover in purpose and in date. Socrates reproduces letters from Constantine which rejoice in a synod's decision to celebrate Easter by the Roman and not the Jewish calendar. But Socrates' inclusion of a lengthy digression on the controversies arising over the proper date for the celebration of Easter suggests that the coordination of the holiday with Passover remained attractive in later centuries (5.22.1–29). Some Christians even celebrated the Passover seder, arguing, according to Socrates, that they were following in the footsteps of Jesus himself. The historian insists that Jesus' actions are to be understood only symbolically. His charge that the Jews are too literal-minded and do not understand allegorical readings of history and the Bible is a frequent one in early Christian thought. The danger of "Judaizing" is further revealed by the case of Sabbatius, who according to Socrates led a group of schismatics to celebrate Passover. It appears that God did not approve of their innovation, for a sudden panic arose and seventy people were trampled to death (7.5).

Another attraction of Judaism for the Christians was the reputed skills of Jews in magic and healing. Amulets and charms belonging to non-Jews which contain sometimes garbled versions of "Yahweh" or Jewish prayers have been found throughout the empire. In a story perhaps designed to counteract the popular belief in these Jewish skills, Socrates presented the success of the bishop Atticus, who healed a paralytic Jew by baptism after the prayers of his fellow Jews had failed (7.4).

In cases of strife between Jews and Christians, Socrates tends to favor peace and the secular authorities, despite the fact that imperial authorities were more likely to protect the Jews from Christian mob violence. After repeated conflicts between Jews and Christians in Alexandria, Bishop Cyril led a mob to drive the Jews out of the city and to plunder their belongings (7.13). Socrates' remark that Jews had inhabited the city since the time of Alexander the Great does not seem triumphant but rather poignant. Orestes, the prefect of the city, was angered by Cyril's lawless act and complained to the emperor. Five hundred monks from the desert showed up to support Cyril, and one bloodied Orestes with a thrown rock. After this monk was tortured to death by the secular authorities, Cyril gathered his remains and installed him in a church as a martyr. At this point Socrates says that even good Christians will reject this sort of honor for someone who in no way was killed for refusing to renounce Christ. Socrates reveals his idea of the proper way to deal with violent outbreaks in his description of an incident which took place in Syria (7.16). A group of drunken Jews, he claims, beat and then crucified a young boy. Conflict arose between the Jews and Christians of the area, but as soon as matters were handled through proper channels and the emperor was informed, the malefactors were dealt with promptly.

Socrates includes several more interesting anecdotes about the Jews in his last book, where most of his Jewish material is concentrated. He describes a Jew who repeatedly underwent baptism with different Christian groups, collecting a payment from each one (7.17). This story is designed to boost the reputation of the Novatians, Socrates' favored sect, since it was a Novatian bishop who discovered the fraud when the baptismal font refused to fill with water. The story suggests that the conversion of a Jew could win a Christian leader considerable renown, since Socrates describes a large crowd gathered around to witness the miracle. Socrates is also the only writer to describe the activities of a certain pseudo-Moses in Crete (7.38). This false messiah convinced many Jews of the island that he would lead them to the promised land, and after abandoning their property they followed him to a cliff and began to hurl themselves into the sea. Socrates concludes by claiming that many of the Jews who survived, disgusted by their own credulousness, converted to Christianity. The story seems to repeat in an allegorical form the traditional charges of literal-mindedness and stubbornness pressed against the Jews.

Sozomen shows his knowledge of the law regarding the Jews in a passage on religious legislation under the sons of Constantine. Jews were forbidden from purchasing a non-Jewish slave, and the punishment for a Jew circumcising his slave was death (3.17.4–5). Sozomen explains that this legislation was designed to prevent Jewish proselytizing and to thereby ensure that pagans were converted to Christianity rather than to Judaism, which was clearly seen as an attractive rival to the church. Elsewhere Sozomen provides a typical piece of anti-Jewish polemic when he claims that Jews are rather close to paganism, and are in danger of backsliding into sacrifice because of their insufficiently allegorical understanding of the Bible (5.22.3).

It is perhaps symptomatic of Orosius' western origins that in his complex, biblically based system of history the Jews play so small a role. By tying Christianity so tightly to Rome, it seems that he has loosened the connection between Christianity and Judaism which preoccupied Greek thinkers. Unlike the eastern Greek church historians, for whom Jews were a constant presence and possible threat, for Orosius the Jews remain a national group and not an ideological challenge. Orosius does, of course, see the defeat of the Jews by Titus and the destruction of the Temple in providential terms, as just punishment for the Jewish role in the crucifixion (7.9.2). In Orosius' history, however, all disasters are considered just punishment for some sin or other. The sins of the Jews were in no way as interesting to the historian as the sins of the pagans and the Christians, and the disasters these sins brought upon the west.

17

BARBARIANS

To modern observers, one of the most striking features of late antiquity was the prevalence and power of barbarians both inside and outside the Roman empire. The term "barbarian," which had originally been a Greek term to denote non-Greeks, in late antiquity embraced all those who were not citizens of the Roman state (Dauge 1981; Balsdon 1979; Cizek 1989). Because many barbarian nations were either nonliterate or have handed down little of their writings to posterity, we are often dependent on Roman sources if we are to reconstruct the culture and history of their societies. The Roman sources, unfortunately, frequently provide derivative or inaccurate portrayals of non-Romans. The exploration of treatment of barbarians by historians is therefore as much an investigation of the views and biases of the Roman writers as an attempt to understand the actions and opinions of the barbarians themselves (Heather 1999b; Chauvot 1998; Luiselli 1984/5; Ladner 1976).

The Roman empire was ringed by neighbors who were important players in the history and historiography of the fourth and fifth centuries. Always of great importance was the vast Persian empire to the east, Rome's only rival in size, power, and administrative complexity. Late antiquity was the setting for the considerable involvement of Germanic peoples in Roman political and military affairs, in particular the Goths. Behind the eruption of the Goths into the empire was the movement of a barbarian people hitherto unknown in the west, the Huns.

Persia

The Persian empire was the one state of comparable antiquity and sophistication to the Roman empire (Blockley 1992; Chauvot 1992; Rubin 1986). A revolution beginning in the third century in the far east of the then-Parthian empire replaced the Parthians with the more aggressive Sasanian Persian dynasty. The half century of war which followed threatened the continuing existence of the Roman state. In 260, the Persian king, Shapur I, captured the emperor Valerian in battle, but by 283 the emperor Carus had recaptured Mesopotamia. Nerseh, the son of Shapur, successfully invaded Armenia and Mesopotamia in 296 and defeated Galerius in 297. Later in the same year, Galerius returned with a new army, captured the family and harem of Nerseh, and took the Persian capital of Ctesiphon. The peace which the Romans imposed in 299 granted them land east of the Tigris and represented the greatest extension of Roman sovereignty over eastern territory in history. The Romans also were granted control of Armenia as a client state. The status of Armenia would remain a constant source of tension throughout the next century.

The Roman victory was destabilizing and led to a constant state of tension on the border throughout the first half of the fourth century. Frequent battles culminated in the invasion by Shapur II in 359 during which he captured Amida and other Roman cities in Mesopotamia. The failure of Julian's invasion of Persia led to the peace treaty signed under duress by Jovian, which resulted in the cession of the territory over the Tigris to Persia, as well as several forts and cities. The public was particularly dismayed by the loss of Nisibis and the expulsion of its civilian population to the west (Turcan 1966). Despite fears that the adjustment of the borders threatened the safety of the Roman east, the settlement proved remarkably durable. Outside of minor skirmishes and continued struggle over the control of Armenia, the two powers did not fight a major war again for more than a century.

In several set pieces Ammianus reveals his vision of Persian culture and of the aims of contemporary Persian leaders. A lengthy digression (23.6), the longest in the work, is devoted largely to the geography of the empire. The digression emphasizes the magnitude of the task his hero Julian faces in invading Persia (den Boeft *et al.* 1998: 129–233; Teitler 1999). Ammianus' treatment of Persian history is sketchy and omits the rise of the Sasanians altogether (23.6.2–9; Drijvers 1999). Although the historian elsewhere demonstrates his knowledge of the difference between Persian and Parthian, here it seems that he wishes to emphasize the great antiquity of the state which Julian will invade. Ammianus has a positive view of the Magi or Zoroastrian priests, and distinguishes them from practitioners of corrupt or dangerous forms of magic. His description of their activities does not appear to be contaminated by any actual knowledge of their religion. Rather, Ammianus has created magi who practice his ideal form of religion, a ritualized and virtuous system of worshipping the divine (23.6.32–6; den Boeft 1999).

Ammianus' comments on the customs and habits of the Persians conform to the stereotyped picture of the easterner in several regards (23.6.75–84). They are sex-crazed, and multiple wives and concubines do not suffice to fill their appetites. They talk loudly and often, and are boastful and threatening. They appear sloppy and effeminate because of their lack of discipline. Not all of Ammianus' comments are negative. His description of Persian military skills and discipline helps to explain the danger that Julian's army will face. With other comments, Ammianus follows in a long tradition of classical ethnographers by using virtues attributed to other nations to critique their own society. He claims, for example, that Persians do not eat luxuriously, but only as much as necessary. They are modest, and so one hardly ever sees a Persian standing and urinating. The Persians also select men of great experience and honesty as judges, and they laugh at Roman failings in this regard.

Ammianus provides a pair of letters which purport to roughly reproduce an exchange between Shapur and Constantius in 358 (17.5). The letters reveal what Ammianus thought Persian attitudes and objectives might be. Shapur describes himself as "partner of the sun and moon," while Constantius is content to style himself more modestly as "victor on land and sea." Shapur first claims the right to occupy all of the territory which was once ruled by the Achaemenid dynasty at the time of Alexander the Great. He then narrows his present claim to the land lost by his grandfather in the treaty of 299. Ammianus makes reference both to Shapur's "native arrogance" and to his "unbridled greed." Although Ammianus may have believed that the Persians hoped to restore their long-lost empire, history has shown that the more limited objective of the overturning of the treaty of 299 sufficed to end Persian territorial claims.

It was not only the Persians who expressed their territorial desires hyperbolically, as Ammianus' portrayal of Julian's speech to his troops before the invasion reveals (23.5.16–23). The emperor gives a summary history of the Romans who have previously invaded Persia, and at first expresses the reasonable hope that this invasion will be revenge for Roman losses in the past and will strengthen the eastern part of the empire. He moves from there, however, to the more extravagant hope that Persia will be utterly annihilated, as Romans had wiped Carthage, Numantia, and other cities completely off the map.

With the establishment of peace after the death of Julian, Ammianus carefully emphasizes that, despite appearances, the Romans were relatively strong and the Persians were under pressure (25.7.2). Nevertheless, the "timid" Jovian surrendered territory for which "it would have been better to fight ten times" than to lose. He emphasizes the terrible hunger of the army in retreat (25.8.15), and with considerable pathos describes the anger and despair at the loss of Nisibis and the train of refugees forced from the city (25.9.5–6). Ammianus concludes with the suggestion that the peace treaty should be disregarded, pointing out when territory had been lost under duress in Roman history before, Romans had felt free to ignore their oaths and retake the territory (25.9.11). In general, Ammianus seems to reject any possibility of Roman inferiority to Persia or of excessiveness in Roman demands.

Eunapius, who like Ammianus was a partisan of Julian, also attempted to pin the blame for Julian's failed invasion on the emperors who reigned before and after him. He seems to have downplayed Constantius' role in the Persian wars of the 340s, attributing their successful outcomes to subordinates and suggesting that Constantius' eastern victory was possible only because of Julian's successful campaigning in the west (Zos. 3.8). Eunapius was likewise blindly laudatory of Julian's invasion of Persia, and critical of Jovian's settlement (*fr.* 29.1).

Aurelius Victor was a decidedly civilian historian, critical of the military and more likely to emphasize an emperor's cultural achievements and building projects than his successful campaigns. Although he mentions the successes of early emperors in Parthia, he devotes more attention to military failure in the east, such as the death of Valerian, cruelly mutilated by the Persian king (32.5) and the death of Carus, who captured Ctesiphon but then, spurred on by an excessive desire for glory, continued forward and was killed by a bolt of lightning (38.3). While Victor praises Galerius' great success in Persia, he recognizes it as the cause for the "very serious war" which is going on "now" in 359 (39.35–7). Victor concludes his work with extended praise of Constantius, the emperor under whom he wrote, but only spares a part of a sentence to describe his Persian wars: "he repelled an attack by the Persians" (42.21). Overall, Persia and the Persians are not of great importance to Victor's understanding of Roman imperial history.

Eutropius and Festus, who write to prepare their readers for a coming Persian war, made quite different use of the *KG* than had Victor. A primary focus of Eutropius' work is the glory an emperor wins in war, particularly war against the Persians. Shapur had ejected the Roman-backed Arsaces from Armenia in 368, and perhaps Eutropius' praise of the emperor Augustus for recapturing Armenia in 20 BC is meant to remind the reader of these contemporary events (Bird 1992: xx–xxi). Eutropius' comments about the emperor Hadrian may likewise carry a contemporary lesson (8.6.2). Hadrian, who abandoned Trajan's conquests in the east out of envy of his predecessor, reminds the reader of Jovian's recent ignominious treaty. Eutropius claims that Jovian's loss of land fifteen years earlier was "necessary, but ignoble" and feels that he should have quickly repudiated the treaty as soon as he was able (10.17). It seems likely that Ammianus later took the examples Eutropius provides of Roman treaty abrogation for his own work (25.9.11). Festus follows the belligerent attitude of Eutropius. The second half of his work is almost entirely devoted to Roman wars against Persia. Festus' work is structured to emphasize the importance of conquest and to suggest that all previous Roman conquests have led naturally to the coming invasion of Persia by Valens.

Orosius places less emphasis upon Persia than one might expect, perhaps because the early fifth century was marked by conflict with Germans and peace with the Persians. Orosius does not include the Persian empire in his list of the biblical "four kingdoms" which are central to world history. Persia is, instead, merely the force that caused the transfer of world power from the major kingdom of Babylon to that of Rome (2.2). In Orosius' account of Romano-Persian relations, Roman persecution of Christians or apostasy explains Roman imperial failure. For example, Valerian ordered Christians to worship idols, and shortly thereafter was captured by Shapur. He then spent the rest of his life getting on his knees, to be used as a footstool whenever the Persian king needed to mount his horse (7.22.3–4). Julian's defeat by the Persians is naturally attributed to his rejection of Christianity and his threats of persecution upon his return (7.30.4–6). On the other hand, Orosius suggests that Severus Alexander successfully overcame the Persian king, because his mother was supposedly a Christian taught by Origen (7.18.6–8).

When Constantine I was preparing the invasion of Persia which was aborted because of his death, he planned to bring along a bishop (Barnes 1985; Brock 1982; Asmussen 1983). He had earlier written a letter to Shapur II, in which he explained that his Roman predecessors had been defeated in battle because of their persecution of Christianity, and he encouraged the Persian king to tolerate the Christians in his own empire, lest he suffer a similar fate (Eus. *Life of Constantine* 4.11). According to the Book of Acts (2: 9), Parthian Jews were present for the miracle of Pentecost, and by the early second century there is firm evidence for the existence of Parthian Christian communities. The Sasanian state, officially Zoroastrian, alternated between tolerance and persecution of its Christian minority. As Rome became Christian, Christianity represented potential political as well as religious subversion, and the practice of Christianity became increasingly suspect in Persia. Shapur II (309–79) persecuted Christians and suppressed the church. A successor, Yezdegerd I (399–421), however, was tolerant at first toward Christians, whom he used as a counterweight to the power of the Zoroastrian nobles, and he allowed the first synod in Sasanian Persia to take place in 410. Persecution of Christians returned, however, at the end of Yezdegerd's reign and into the reign of his son Vahram V (421–39). This wave of persecution coincided with the ascendancy of the extremely pious Pulcheria over her brother, the emperor Theodosius II, and led to conflict between the two powers (Holum 1982: 102–11).

Sozomen provides numerous anecdotes drawn from martyr stories of the persecution of Christians during Shapur's reign. Sozomen blames the Zoroastrian Magi and the Jews for inciting the trouble, claiming that they accused Persian bishop Symeon of complicity with the Romans (2.9). He portrays Shapur attempting to reason with Christians rounded up in the persecution, but after they refused to worship the sun, he ordered them to be decapitated. Sozomen's account suggests that Christians were to be found even among the highest ranks of the Persian courtiers. For example, the execution of the eunuch Azades, a favorite of the king, is said to have led Shapur to limit his persecution only to Christians who proselytize (2.11). After a horrifying account of the tortures which various Persian Christians suffered, Sozomen presents an excerpt from the letter of Constantine to Shapur derived from Eusebius calling for toleration (2.15.2–4). Sozomen misdates the letter to place it during the persecution, not before, so he can claim that "the emperor exercised the greatest protectiveness over Christians everywhere, Roman as well as foreign" (2.15.1).

While the historicity of Constantine's letter cannot be proven, its protective attitude toward Persian Christians was to become official

Roman policy during the reign of Theodosius II. Socrates describes the reign of Yezdegerd as wholly benevolent. He attributes the persecution of Christians which took place at the end of Yezdegerd's reign to his son's reign, and even claims that Yezdegerd was planning to embrace Christianity and was prevented from doing so only by his death (7.8). Socrates attributes the emperor's near conversion to the activities of the bishop of Mesopotamia, Maruthas, who was sent to Persia as part of an official embassy. He reports that Maruthas gained the trust of the emperor when he cured his painful headaches by prayer. This tale follows in the pattern of numerous stories of conversion which are inspired by healings. Maruthas also triumphantly exposes the deceptions of the Magi, who were in the habit of hiding under fire altars and speaking for the deity, as well as emitting unpleasant odors near the king and blaming the smells on the Christians.

The accession of Vahram V to the throne after the death of his father led to the persecution of Christians and a Roman military response in 421 (7.18). Socrates provides fully detailed accounts of this war, in which the appearance of angels predicting a Roman victory demonstrates the justice of the Roman cause. In an epilogue to the victory, Socrates tells the story of the bishop Acacius. Seven thousand Persian prisoners of war were starving and stranded in Roman Azazane, and the bishop organized his parishioners to melt the church vessels and to use the money raised to feed the Persians and return them home. This benevolence proved that the Romans "were accustomed to conquer by generosity as well as by war" (7.21.5).

Theodoret provides anecdotes from a war against Persia which he does not clearly date. It thus may be the same war of 421 which Socrates discusses, or the historian may be referring to the later conflict of 441 (Croke 1983: 300 n. 11; Blockley 1992: 203 n. 17). He emphasizes that the war is a holy war, fought on behalf of Christianity, which in one case featured a bishop as a combatant (5.37.5–9). Disgusted by the curses of the enemy, Bishop Eunomius himself commanded that the ballista which had been given the nickname "Apostle Thomas" be erected. When the ballista's stone crushed the skull of the Persian blasphemer, Theodoret tells us, the siege came quickly to an end. Theodoret reveals that the persecution of Christians which led to war was at least in part incited by the excessive zeal of some Christians who destroyed Zoroastrian fire temples (5.39). "I say that the destruction of the fire temple was not timely," Theodoret judges. The historian provides many details of the terrible tortures the Persian Christians endured. This section, the penultimate chapter of the work, concludes with a celebration of the survival and rejuvenation of true Christianity in the face of persecution, a message which would have resonated with the author himself as he wrote in the midst of heated theological controversy.

For the remainder of the fifth century, the two large empires remained usually at peace with each other while they fended off threats on their other flanks. Priscus reveals the importance of diplomacy during this period and displays an interest in the political and military situation in Persia which had been less prevalent in earlier historians. He reports the demands, for example, of a Persian embassy, which included the return of Persian refugees, an end to the persecution of fire worshippers in the empire, and subsidies for the defense of the Caspian Gates against the Kidarite Huns (*frs.* 41.1, 47). The Roman reply simply denied the existence of any refugees or persecution, and denied responsibility for the subsidies. When Priscus and the east Romans, while participating in an embassy to Attila, heard from western ambassadors that the Huns might turn away from the empire and launch an attack on the Persians, their first reaction was to pray that it might be true (*fr.* 11.2). But the parties are sobered by consideration of the possibility that Attila could return west after a conquest of Persia even stronger and more dangerous. This recognition, and the repeated requests by the Persians for Roman help in the defense of the Caspian Gates, were perhaps signs of a growing understanding of the interdependent relationship necessary among the two ancient civilized powers in the face of more barbarous threats.

The Roman state groped toward the establishment of a suitable relationship with Persia throughout late antiquity. After enduring the incessant warfare of the beginning of the fourth century, the two powers managed to avoid major conflict for more than a century. As violence increased in the other frontier areas, peace on the eastern border became particularly important to the Romans. Late antique historians recognized that the ancient civilization of the Persians set them apart from other, and in their eyes more contemptible, non-Roman peoples. Occasional remarks, such as those found in Ammianus' ethnographic digression, suggested that the Romans could even learn from them. It was more common, however, for fourth-century historians to urge military conflict with the Persians, and even to propose wildly unrealistic plans such as the complete annihilation of the Persian state. Christianity played conflicting roles in this process. The presence of a large Christian community in Persia probably helped at times to foster communication between the empires, and the ecclesiastical historians wrote favorably about Persian Christians. But the mistreatment of Christians also triggered support among Christian intellectuals like Socrates and Theodoret for military intervention and encouraged the outbreak of war (Blockley 1992).

The Goths

The Goths were an agricultural Germanic people who inhabited the territory northwest of the Black Sea, between the Danube and the Don rivers in modern-day Romania (Heather 1991, 1996; Wolfram 1988; Todd 1975). The third century had seen numerous Gothic raids into the empire. At the beginning of the fourth century, conflicts with the emperor Constantine ended in Gothic capitulation and the signing of a peace treaty in 332, which remained in effect for three decades. During this period, Goths were occasionally recruited as auxiliary soldiers by Roman generals, such as Constantius in 360 and the usurper Procopius in 365. Increasing Gothic hostility led to the outbreak of warfare with Valens from 367 to 369, but after three years of inconclusive battles, the parties made peace.

The *breviaria* record third-century conflicts with the Goths, including invasions under Decius (Vic. 29.2) and Gallienus (Vic. 33.3; Eut. 9.8.2), and the defeat of the Goths by Claudius II (Eut. 9.11.2). The accounts in Eutropius and Festus of Constantine's conflict with the Goths are colored by contemporary events, since they write during or immediately after Valens' Gothic campaign. Eutropius states that after Constantine's defeat of the Goths in several skirmishes "he left enormous gratitude in the memory of the barbarian tribes" (10.7.1). Eutropius here refers to the Goths' allegiance to the usurper Procopius, whom they claimed to support as the last surviving member of the line of Constantine. Perhaps we are additionally to understand Eutropius' remark as expressing the hope that the Goths will be equally loyal to Valens now that he has subdued them. Festus also draws a parallel between Constantine's victories and those of Valens. Buoyed by the glory that he had won from his Gothic victory, Festus claims, Constantine went to Persia, where ambassadors of the Persian king immediately submitted to him (26.1). Festus' instructions to the emperor in his last sentence call upon him to emulate Constantine's feats: add victory over the Persians to your great victory over the Goths (30.2).

Ammianus portrays Valens complaining to the Goths in 367 about their support of Procopius in the previous year (27.5). The Goths claimed that they had merely been supporting the legitimate heir to the throne, since Procopius was a relative of Julian. Rejecting this explanation, Valens invaded Gothic territory for three successive years. In the first year, the Goths hid in the mountains, and in the second year, floods bogged down the imperial army, but in the third year Valens defeated the Gothic king Athanaric in battle. Although Valens' victory was not decisive, Ammianus is favorable toward his decision to settle. He reports that Athanaric had sworn an oath at his father's demand never to set foot on Roman soil, and notes that "it would have been shameful and degrading" for the emperor to sign on Gothic territory. The two leaders met, therefore, in the middle of the Danube, on boats, to sign the peace treaty.

A fragment of Eunapius describes the war in slightly different terms (*fr.* 37). He suggests that the Gothic king had sent reinforcements to Procopius which arrived only after the defeat of the usurper. Eunapius believes that the war began when Valens seized these Goths and disarmed them, and that Valens' foresight allowed him to bring the war to a successful end. Eunapius is not generally an admirer of Valens (*fr.* 39.9; Zos. 4.4.1), but as a civilian and a traditionalist, he was a great hater of barbarians. He denounces the Goths as arrogant and contemptuous, and states that they acted particularly outrageously since no one restrained them. After the emperor disarmed them, they shook their long hair insolently (*fr.* 37). He adds that the Goths were mocked by the Romans because they were excessively tall, seemed too heavy to stand, and were narrow at the waist like insects.

Gothic raids into the empire in the third century had brought back many slaves, including some who were Christian. Ulfila, a second- or third-generation descendant of such Christian captives, was consecrated in Antioch in 341 as bishop of the Goths. Gothic persecution of Christians in the 340s forced Ulfila and his followers to flee to Roman territory, where he was active as a writer and evangelist until his death in 383. Trilingual in Gothic, Latin, and Greek, Ulfila invented a Gothic script in order to translate the Bible into his native tongue. Ulfila and his followers adhered to the predominant homoiousian ("Arian") Christianity of his time, with fateful results for the future, for when the Goths and other Germans converted to Christianity, their beliefs were heretical in the eyes of the Roman state after Theodosius I. The extent to which Christianity had penetrated Gothic society prior to the major crossing of the Goths into Roman territory in 376 is unclear (Thompson 1963; Heather 1986; Lenski 1995). It was considered enough of a threat that, following the peace treaty signed by Valens and Athanaric, Athanaric launched a second persecution of Gothic Christians, who were seen as supporters of Rome and whose faith undermined tribal authority.

Constantine's Gothic victory is portrayed in Socrates as resulting in the conversion of many Goths to Christianity (1.18.4), and Sozomen even more extravagantly claims that the Goths had long been Christianized by the age of Constantine, attributing their conversion to the presence of priests among the Gothic captives of the third century (2.6). When Sozomen returns to the subject, however, he appears to contradict his earlier statement, suggesting that most Goths were pagan before they entered the empire (6.37). Socrates pinpoints a crucial moment in the conversion of the Goths in the 370s, when a faction of Goths under Fritigern received help from Valens in a Gothic civil war and embraced Christianity in gratitude (4.33). Sozomen's less coherent account of these events locates them on Roman territory and therefore after 376 (6.37.7).

All three Greek church historians discuss Ulfila and provide explanations for Gothic Arianism. For Socrates, the conversion under Valens suffices to explain why the Goths were not orthodox, and he hastens to point out that many Goths, although Arian, acquitted themselves nobly under persecution in Gothic territory and were martyred. Socrates therefore does not attribute Gothic Arianism to Ulfila's personal beliefs (4.33.5). Although Sozomen also blames the original Arianism of the Goths on Valens, he adds that he does not find this sufficient explanation for the continuing lack of Gothic orthodoxy up to his own day (6.37.8–14). Ulfila's example was very strong among the Goths, Sozomen suggests, and he was personally converted to Arian beliefs at Constantinople, either from conviction or because he was told that it would help his position at the imperial court. Theodoret's account is shorter, but dramatizes the same themes which Sozomen had raised (4.37). His Ulfila was originally orthodox, but was convinced by Eudoxius of Antioch to convert and to lead his people to Arianism. Eudoxius convinces Ulfila by the force of his eloquence, which Theodoret suggests a simple Goth could not withstand, as well as with bribes.

Sozomen relates several martyr stories from the persecution of Athanaric, including the killing of women and children in the burning down of a Gothic church, which was inside a tent

(6.37.14). Orosius too remarks on the persecution, noting that there were many barbarian martyrdoms (7.32.9). His claim that many came as refugees to Roman soil, where they lived in peace with Romans as brothers, supports his argument that the distinction between barbarian and Roman has become less important than the distinction between Christian and pagan.

Peace between Romans and Goths did not last long. In the 370s a band of Huns from the east conquered the Alans of the Caucasus Mountains and subjected the eastern Goths to their rule. In 376, the Gothic leader Fritigern requested of Valens that he and his followers be permitted to settle on Roman territory. The reception of large numbers of barbarians into the empire was not new. Such peoples had been accepted under various conditions of submission as tenant farmers or freeholders, who owed taxes or military service to the empire. The Goths under Fritigern appear to have been granted the right to settle as free people, but were obligated to provide some military service, and perhaps were encouraged to convert to Christianity as a guarantee of their loyalty (Heather 1986).

Trouble broke out as the Goths crossed the river. Food supplies were inadequate because of Roman incompetence and corruption. With the emperor and his army in the east, Roman forces rapidly lost control of the migration, and Gothic warbands began devastating Thrace. Although Roman forces tried to prevent the onslaught, more Goths came across the river. In August 378, Valens met the Goths in battle and was killed at Adrianople in a tremendous Roman defeat which left the Balkans at the mercy of the Goths. Because Ammianus' history comes to an end with this battle, the depth of our knowledge of events declines precipitously. It is clear that the eastern parts of the empire suffered through several difficult years, until Gratian and the new emperor Theodosius managed to sign a peace treaty with the Goths in October 382.

Ammianus fully narrates the events leading up to the Battle of Adrianople in book 31 of the *Res Gestae* (Lenski 1997). He writes that omens of the coming death of Valens were visible everywhere, and that the ghosts of those whom the emperor had unjustly executed were particularly unquiet (31.1). Ammianus describes the Hunnic conquest of the Alans and their attacks upon the Goths, and he sees the Huns as the ultimate cause of the invasion (31.3). The historian further suggests that Valens agreed to the settlement because he was eager for army recruits and for the gold that the treasury would receive from the provinces in lieu of the regular draft (31.4.1–4). The crossing itself is described hyperbolically, with countless Goths crossing day and night on every sort of boat and raft (31.4.5–6). Ammianus singles out the generals in Thrace who oversaw the operation, Lupicinus and Maximus, for their greed and incompetence (31.4.9–11). These accusations, including the charge that the generals traded dogs to be used as food to starving Goths in return for the slavery of their children, may derive from an official report of an inquiry into the disaster. It is, in any case, very much in keeping with Ammianus' view of history for personal immorality to have led to disaster for the state.

As the generals supervised the crossing of the Danube, another group of Goths secretly crossed at a distance and made contact with those who had preceded them. At this point Ammianus tells us that Lupicinus invited Fritigern and Alavivus, the Gothic leaders, to dinner, and then had their guards treacherously put to death. These events outraged the Goths, and in a quick battle they defeated Roman forces. The size of the Gothic warband was augmented by the addition of Gothic slaves and others from the region who directed them to the richest parts of Thrace. "Without distinction between age or sex, everything was aflame with massacres and burnings" (31.6). The significance of the defeat is magnified by Ammianus' pause to compare it with events from the fourth century BC and the third century AD which had been even greater disasters for the state (31.5.10–14). Yet Ammianus seems to suggest that, just as those tragedies had been overcome, so too could this one.

Ammianus criticizes the generals sent by Valens, men of "high ambition but unfit for battle," for failing to realize that guerrilla warfare, not open battle, was necessary in the mountainous terrain of Thrace (31.7.1–3). Near the town of Salices the two forces met in a violent but inconclusive struggle. The continuing devastation of Thrace is described by Ammianus in pathetic tones (31.8.6–8). Frigiderius defeated a group of Goths, sending the survivors to Italy to work the land (31.9), but he was replaced by the less trustworthy general Maurus (3.10.21). In the meantime Gratian, coming east to bring reinforcements, was delayed by the need to fight Germans along the Rhine (31.10).

Valens departed from Constantinople determined to fight the Goths near Adrianople. Ammianus attributes the decision to meet in battle primarily to Valens' jealousy of the successes of Gratian and his subordinates, as well as to a mistake in scouting which suggested that the Gothic force was much smaller than it actually was (31.12). In a grim and bloody battle on 9 August 378, the Romans were defeated, and Valens' body was never found; the emperor may have burned to death in a house in which he sought refuge. Scarcely a third of the Roman army escaped.

In the morning after the battle, the Goths laid siege to the city of Adrianople, but were unsuccessful at taking it (31.15). Joining with a contingent of Huns and Alans, they marched on Constantinople, but were frightened away by a bizarre sight. Ammianus claims that one of the Arab defenders of the city, long-haired and in a loin cloth, cut the throat of a Goth and proceeded to drink the blood from the open wound (31.16.6). Another disturbing event concludes the narrative of the *Res Gestae*. The count Julius, Ammianus says, "distinguished himself by a swift and beneficial deed" (31.16.8). He sent secret directions to those who were supervising the Goths who had been dispersed throughout Asia Minor, ordering them to summon the Goths to congregate to receive military stipends and then to quickly put them to death *en masse*. "When this prudent plan," Ammianus remarks, "had been completed without outcry or delay, the eastern provinces were saved from great danger" (31.16.8).

A lengthy fragment from Eunapius covers this period in Romano-Gothic relations (*fr.* 42; Paschoud 1989c). Eunapius describes with pathos the slaughter of the Goths by the Huns and the gathering of weeping and supplicant Goths on the far side of the Danube. The historian attributes the blame for allowing the crossing of the Danube to Valens' desire for recruits, as Ammianus had. Eunapius claims that the greed and lust of the officers in charge led to large numbers of young Goths being admitted to the empire to serve as domestic slaves or field workers. In a chronologically confused and bizarre passage, Eunapius claims that these Gothic children matured with tremendous speed and were old enough to rise in revolt as their older relatives looted Thrace.

Just as Ammianus had been critical of the Romans' decision to meet the enemy in direct battle, so Eunapius seems to suggest that guerrilla warfare and supply disruption would have been superior methods of operation. Eunapius adds that this advice, which would certainly seem obvious enough after the proven failure of the direct method, is evidence for the value of an education in literature and history to the would-be general (*fr.* 44). This should be considered a gibe at the unlettered Valens, who is implicitly compared to the learned Julian.

A fragment of Eunapius once thought to refer to the period after Adrianople may rather be better associated with the Gothic crossing of the Danube (Heather 1986: 305–10). Regardless of date, the fragment neatly combines two of Eunapius' dislikes, barbarians and Christians, into one monitory tale. In an apparent reference to the agreement of the Goths to convert to Christianity in return for settlement over the Danube, he claims that barbarians swore false oaths which the emperors foolishly trusted. He adds that barbarians easily infiltrated the empire by disguising themselves as bishops or monks (*fr.* 48.2). The historian asserts that despite the disguise, the Goths in reality spurned Christianity and revered their own sacred objects in secret. So low had the Romans fallen that even ordinary people were deceived by this trick. Although Eunapius blames Roman degradation in the form of Christianization for Gothic success, he does not therefore absolve the Goths. On the contrary, he claims that the majority of Goths had sworn eternal enmity to Rome, to the effect that no matter how friendly the Romans were, they would always attempt to seize territory from them (*fr.* 59).

For Rufinus and the other church historians, the disaster at Adrianople can be largely understood as divine revenge for the Arian Valens' persecution of orthodoxy. Rufinus omits any details of the crossing but simply states that Valens, too late, turned his military forces from the churches to the barbarians (11.13). The emperor was burned to death "for his impiety," and Rufinus concludes with the comment that the battle was "the beginning of evil times for the Roman empire from then on."

Socrates' account is much more detailed than that of Rufinus. He comments that the emperor's decision to admit the Goths into the empire was the "one time alone that he showed compassion," although he quickly adds that there were more material benefits for Valens of Gothic settlement, such as the availability of recruits and the ability to commute the regular Roman draft to gold (4.34.2). Once Valens had arranged for Goths to be settled on Roman territory, he neglected to raise troops from among the Romans. Socrates pointedly alters the emphasis of Rufinus, claiming that "this change" in recruitment "was the beginning of evil times for the Roman empire for a short time after" (4.34.6). When disturbances broke out during the crossing of the Danube, Socrates says that a sluggish Valens had to be reprimanded by chants in the Hippodrome in Constantinople in order to encourage him to fight the Goths. Valens left Constantinople cursing and promising to take his revenge on the impudent residents upon his return. Despite his slow start, however, Socrates says that the emperor had great success against the enemy up until the Battle of Adrianople itself (4.38).

Sozomen's information about the Goths comes almost entirely from Socrates, although it is extended and elaborated rhetorically. In particular, Sozomen emphasizes that Valens' death was the result of his persecutions by having the monk Isaac boldly tell the emperor as he leaves for battle that he would not return to the East unless he returned the churches to those following the Nicene Creed (6.40.1; cf. Lenski 1997: 153–5). He also expands the simple sentence of Socrates which suggested the possibility that Valens had died in a fire into a vivid and dramatic version of the emperor's last moments (6.40.3–5).

Theodoret's treatment of events is predictably didactic and fuzzy in the details. He repeatedly emphasizes through anecdotes that Valens' heterodoxy was responsible for his downfall. After "the Lord roused the Goths to war," Theodoret says that Valens realized his weakness for the first time, and wrote to his brother seeking his help. Valentinian rejected his brother's entreaty, thinking it improper to help a heretic (4.31). Since Valentinian had in fact died a year before the crossing of the Goths, this story is particularly unlikely. Theodoret adds that when Valens criticized his general Trajan after his failure to defeat the Goths, Trajan boldly responded that Valens' heresy, not Trajan's cowardice, was responsible for the loss. Other generals concurred with Trajan's diagnosis of the problem (4.33). Because Valens rejected these warnings and the advice of the monk Isaac (4.34), his army turned and fled at Adrianople. "Thus in this present life he paid the price of his offenses" (4.36.2).

Orosius' account, like that of Theodoret, is heavily didactic, although less fanciful (7.33). The Huns provide the ultimate cause, and the avarice of the Roman officials the proximate cause, of the invasion. Valens' persecution of the orthodox, however, explains his failure and death. The emperor's death leads Orosius to a predictably dramatic lament. He is struck by the fact that an Arian emperor was killed by the Arian Goths, "and so, by the just judgement of God, those men who burned him alive will also burn when they are dead, for the vice of the error which he taught them" (7.33.19).

The treaty agreed upon by the Goths and the Romans in 382 remained in force until the death of Theodosius in 395. The Gothic revolt which followed took place under the leadership of Alaric, and may have been the result of dissatisfaction at the heavy losses suffered by Gothic troops fighting in Roman civil wars. Alaric and his troops exploited the hostility between the eastern and western courts which persisted for the next fifteen years. At times Alaric was allied with Stilicho, the guardian of Honorius in the west, and at other times he did the bidding of the successive guardians of Arcadius in the east (Liebeschuetz 1990; O'Flynn 1983: 14–62). After the assassination of Stilicho in 408 Honorius rejected Alaric's demands, and the Goths sacked the city of Rome in frustration on 24 August 410. Alaric died from illness a year later, and his brother-in-law Ataulf succeeded him. Ataulf married the sister of Honorius, Galla Placidia, who had been seized during the sack of Rome, and they had a son, Theodosius. Ataulf and his son were killed in a coup shortly after, however, and under the leadership of Theodoeric I, the Goths were settled in southern Gaul in 418. There they established the Kingdom of Toulouse, which would last until its destruction by Clovis and the Franks in 507. Throughout the fifth century, these Goths would fight often as allies of the Romans against newer groups of barbarians who threatened the empire.

The full account of the careers of Alaric and Ataulf was a major part of the history of Olympiodorus, which unfortunately does not survive intact. This part of Olympiodorus was a source not only for Zosimus, but also for Sozomen's ninth, unfinished book. Olympiodorus was a defender of Stilicho, as is clear, for example, in his apparent acceptance of Stilicho's claim of regency over both Honorius and Arcadius (*fr.* 1) and his statement that Stilicho "fought many successful wars for the Romans" (*fr.* 3). It appears, then, that Olympiodorus blamed the sack of Rome at least in part on Stilicho's assassination (*fr.* 7.5).

The Greek church historians do not describe the sack of Rome itself in detail. Sozomen emphasizes that because of Alaric's respect for St Peter, the large church around his tomb served as an asylum which provided safety to many Romans (9.9.4–5). Socrates states that after plundering the city, Alaric and his men left quickly when they heard that an eastern army was on its way (7.10.6–7). This appears to be a piece of eastern propaganda which attempts to explain the lack of interest in western suffering shown by the administration of Theodosius II.

In contrast to the Greek ecclesiastical historians with their eastern focus, Rome's sack was central to the very purpose of Orosius' work. Orosius draws a careful contrast between Alaric, a Goth and a Christian, and the pagan Gothic leader Radagaisus

BARBARIANS

(7.37.8–12; Teillet 1984: 113–60). He claims that the Romans, threatened by Alaric, turned to paganism, and he is thereby able to portray Alaric's sack as a Christian victory over a pagan city. Romans should be glad, according to Orosius' interpretation, that they were spared the horrific results which the victory of the pagan Radagaisus would have brought about. Although Alaric's invasion was temporarily frightening, by allowing the basilica of Peter and Paul to remain as an asylum he demonstrated, Orosius claims, that his Goths were eager for plunder but not for massacre (7.39.1). At one point during the sack, according to Orosius, gold and silver church vessels were transferred through the city without danger, with barbarian and Roman alike singing hymns. The occupation lasted a mere three days, he writes, and Rome has already regained its former strength (7.40.1).

Orosius depicts the capture of the princess Galla Placidia by the Goths during the siege and her betrothal to Ataulf as part of a divine plan, since the Goths and Romans were thereby united in marriage and friendship (7.40.2; Marchetta 1987). Orosius favors the union, which led Ataulf to support the Romans militarily and brought him under the influence of a Christian Roman wife. If Ataulf's son, provocatively named Theodosius, had survived, as a grandson of Theodosius the Great he would have been the obvious heir to the throne. Olympiodorus also supported this Romano-Gothic union. He describes their marriage, which took place in the home of a powerful Roman citizen and featured bride and groom in Roman dress (*fr.* 24). Ataulf presented his bride with fifty young men in silk, each somewhat tastelessly bearing a platter of gold and a platter of jewels looted from Rome. There are songs and revelry "by both the Romans and the barbarians among them" (*fr.* 24).

Despite the death of the child and then of Ataulf not long after, the optimistic histories of Orosius and Olympiodorus, different in so many ways, both envisioned a more peaceful future with Gothic forces allied with yet subservient to Roman power. Both are eager, therefore, to minimize the sufferings of the sack of Rome. Olympiodorus celebrated the wealth and splendor of Rome only a few years after the sack history for this reason (*fr.* 41). By the time that Olympiodorus wrote, of course, the Goths were no longer a major threat to the empire. Instead, both Goths and Romans worked together against both other Germanic groups and against the people who had brought them into conflict in the first place, the Huns.

224

The Huns

The sudden appearance of the Huns in the west in the last years of the fourth century struck contemporaries with fear and amazement (Thompson 1996; Maenchen-Helfen 1973; Zuckerman 1994; Gordon 1960). They were responsible for the movement of the Goths into the empire after 376 and probably for the movement of several Germanic peoples across the Rhine in 405. They can thus be fairly held ultimately responsible for the collapse of Roman political authority in the west (Heather 1995). The Huns managed to wreak such enormous havoc in a remarkably small amount of time. After several decades when the Huns only occasionally appeared on Roman territory, a Hunnic empire quickly coalesced in the 420s under the leadership of Rua. Rua's heirs were his nephews, Bleda and Attila, and Attila ruled alone after murdering his brother in 445 (Thompson 1996: 97). The Hunnic empire won several major and destructive battles against the Romans, but then, upon the death of Attila in 453, faded quickly from history.

Despite the importance of the Huns to the history of late antiquity, we are woefully deficient in contemporary sources for their activities. Only some unadorned chronicles and the fragments of Priscus allow us to reconstruct Hunnic history in any substantial way. Priscus, who dealt directly with the Huns on his embassy to Attila, is by far the most trustworthy source on their culture. Other historians tend to use the Huns simply as examples of unparalleled ferocity, and attempt to fit them into the historiographic tradition in ways which fatally distort the reliability of their accounts.

Sozomen's account of the first appearance of the Huns, which may derive ultimately from that of Eunapius, reveals both the ignorance of westerners of Hunnic origins and the willingness of historians to rely on mythical tales to supplement their knowledge (Thompson 1996: 19–24). The Huns, according to Sozomen, dwelled on the other side of an enormous marsh from the Goths, a body of water so huge that each people thought it marked the end of the earth. When one day the Huns pursued an ox, stung by insects, across the lake, they discovered the beauty of the other side and decided to conquer it (6.37.3–5). Orosius has a different version which nevertheless equally reveals the ignorance of the Romans. He claims that the Huns were for a long time separated from the west by a mountain range, but that a "sudden madness" drove them against the Goths. This rage was clearly connected, for Orosius, with Valens' persecution of the orthodox and closing of their churches (7.33.10).

Eunapius' Hunnic digression does not survive, but the manner in which he treated the subject is revealing (*fr.* 41). He explains that he has collected accounts from ancient authors and juxtaposed this material with material drawn from oral reports. This oral information he has sifted in accordance with the perceived accuracy of the report. The methodology of classicizing historiography and Eunapius' historical practices both likely stood in the way of the creation of an accurate account. Probably Eunapius' oral informants provided him with the "bull crossing the marsh" tale, to which he added stories taken from ancient histories of unknown peoples whom he identified as the ancestors of the Huns.

Ammianus' digression on Hunnic culture and customs has long been praised by scholars, albeit in a guarded fashion, for the details he provides of such an unknown people. Unfortunately, his information is far from first hand, and almost none of what he says can be trusted (31.2; King 1987). The historian has taken ideas and passages from ancient ethnographers and combined them in such a way as to make the Huns seem as uncivilized as possible. Ammianus claims that the Huns do not use fire or seasonings on their food, but eat raw meat which they warm under their saddles. They have no buildings, and actually fear roofs and cities. They never dismount from their horses, eating, drinking, urinating, and sleeping on horseback. "No one among them plows or ever touches a plow handle. They are without fixed habitation, without home or law or stable way of life." These Huns also completely lack morality and religion. In fact, they are barely human, more like beasts or like gargoyles than like men.

Some of Ammianus' descriptions of Hunnic society are drawn nearly verbatim from Pompeius Trogus and Livy. Many of the details are anthropologically impossible. In many cases, the details are clearly selected or invented to emphasize the extreme primitivism of the Huns, who are described as being as different as possible from the civilized Romans. While it should not be doubted, of course, that the nomadic Huns lived lives considerably unlike that of the Romans, Ammianus' account is too stereotyped and too derivative to reliably illuminate those differences.

The Huns in the time of Priscus lived in settled villages, with buildings and agriculture. Almost three-quarters of a century separate the description of Ammianus from that of Priscus, and it has often been claimed that Hun society underwent tremendous change owing to its proximity to and involvement with the empire. Due to the unreliability of Ammianus' account, however, the rate of change in Hun society, like so much else about them, must remain unknown (King 1987: 88).

In the 440s Huns devastated the Balkans, destroying major cities such as Sirmium and Naissus. In 447 a Hunnic army under the leadership of Attila stood before the gates of Constantinople. The Huns regularly demanded from the east Romans money and the return of fugitives who had fled from Hun territory. The Romans, distracted by military operations in the west, adopted a policy of payments which Priscus scorned as tribute. Priscus' embassy reveals that the Romans considered assassination, as well but, when the attempt to kill Attila failed, the empire was compelled to make even larger payments to the Huns.

Priscus describes his visit to the territory ruled by the Huns in detail. He portrays Attila as an autocratic leader, with full authority in administering justice and waging war (*fr.* 11.2). There were palaces and a bath built by Roman artisans. Money was in use (*fr.* 11.2). Priscus attended a lavish banquet with ceremonial wine-drinking (*fr.* 13). While most of the guests ate from silver, and wore clothes encrusted with gold and jewels, Attila ate from wooden plates and drank from wooden cups. While Attila's lieutenant Onegesius was illiterate, he had secretaries and a man captured in war who wrote letters for him (*fr.* 14). Priscus depicts the multinational nature of the Hun empire, with Germans and other peoples serving in important roles. Hunnic women were not secluded, and Priscus and his company even stayed in a village which was run by a woman.

On the death of Theodosius II in 450, his successor Marcian refused to continue to pay subsidies to the Huns. Attila turned west toward Gaul, where he announced his intention to attack the Goths as an ally of the western emperor Valentinian III. Honoria, the sister of Valentinian III, had been forced into an unhappy marriage, and in a rather desperate attempt to escape, had her ring smuggled to Attila along with a marriage proposal. Honoria's mother Galla Placidia had, one recalls, married a somewhat more tractable barbarian, the Goth Ataulf. Attila marched through Gaul on his way to claim his bride in Italy, but was rebuffed by the combination of an imperial army commanded by Aetius and a Gothic army under Theodoric I at Orleans, and then defeated a few days later. The next year, the Huns crossed the Alps and besieged and destroyed the northern Italian city of Aquileia. Perhaps for lack of supplies, however, Attila refrained from taking Rome and signed a peace treaty with a delegation led by Pope Leo I. Checked in

Europe, the Hunnic army returned to the east in 452 to fight Marcian over the cessation of payments, but in 453 Attila died in his sleep. After Attila's death, quarreling among his sons and revolts by his subjects broke the empire apart. The fleeting and destructive empire of the Huns left much fear and sensationalism in the late antique historians, but little reliable evidence outside of the first-person account of Priscus.

Missions

In the first two centuries of Christianity, Christians had not aggressively proselytized, and the anti-Christian pagan Celsus could gibe that "if all men wanted to be Christians, the Christians would no longer want them." By the middle of the third century, however, the Christian apologist Origen could respond to Celsus by stating that everyone could now see the eager missionary activities of Christians throughout the world (Frend 1970). The sphere of such activity soon came to include the non-Roman world, and ecclesiastical histories feature the conversions of numerous barbarian peoples. This recognition of barbarians as potential Christians is an innovation of late antique historiography.

Eusebius had presented a traditional Constantine as warrior king, a conqueror of foreign people. Rufinus was to alter this vision in his descriptions of the conversion of barbarians that form a major part of his work. He is followed very closely by Socrates, Sozomen, and Theodoret in his details of two representative stories, the conversions of the Ethiopians and of the Iberians.

Rufinus' account of the conversion of the Ethiopian kingdom of Aksum or "inner India" is the earliest we have (Ruf. 10.9–10; Soc. 1.19; Soz. 2.24; Theod. 1.23; Thélamon 1981: 31–83; Munro-Hay 1988: 196–213). "In the times of Constantine," Rufinus says that a philosopher, Meropius, with two young students, Frumentius and Edesius, went to explore Ethiopia. Meropius was killed and the boys were brought before the king, who made Edesius his cupbearer and the bright Frumentius the royal archivist. After the death of the king, the queen asked the young men to serve as regents for the prince, who was only an infant. Frumentius encouraged Roman Christian merchants who visited Ethiopia to establish churches, and instructed some of the native Ethiopians in the faith. Frumentius and Edesius returned to Rome when the prince reached maturity, and Frumentius told the Alexandrian bishop Athanasius about his adventures. Athanasius then appointed Frumentius bishop of Aksum and he returned there. Rufinus claims to have learned of these things from Edesius himself in Tyre, where he had become a priest.

Despite elements of fable in Rufinus' account, the broad outline of the story seems to be true. Rufinus specifies a particular source for his knowledge, which he rarely does elsewhere in his history and which enhances our estimate of his accuracy. Frumentius, bishop of Aksum, is also the recipient of a letter from Constantius preserved in Athanasius' works (*Apol.* 31), and Ethiopian Christians still to this day revere Frumentius, under the name "Feremnatos," as the founder of their church. Rufinus frames his account to emphasize certain points. By beginning the story with a reference to the work of the apostles from book 3 of Eusebius' church history, Rufinus demonstrates that the work of evangelization continues in his own day. The historian attributes Frumentius' decision to promote Christianity simply to God's will. Although the Christian Roman emperors may have seen the Christianization of foreign powers as a political goal, Rufinus avoids any such implication, presenting the Ethiopians as the objects of conversion rather than as either Roman allies or enemies.

Rufinus' account of the conversion of the Iberians follows similar lines (Ruf. 10.11; Soc. 1.20; Soz. 2.7; Theod. 1.24; Thélamon 1981: 85–122; Braund 1994: 246–58). The Iberians, a people dwelling on the shore of the Black Sea in modern-day Georgia, took captive a devout Christian, whose ascetic practices impressed them greatly. She became well known throughout the kingdom by curing the son of the king with an invocation of the name of Christ. The woman later cured the queen as well, and then persuaded the king, who was rescued when lost in the woods by prayer to the Christian God, to accept Christianity. Even more Iberians were converted when a miracle occurred during the construction of a church. After the conversion, the Iberians wrote to the emperor Constantine requesting clergy and an alliance with the Romans. Rufinus tells us that he learned of these events from Bacurius, a noble Iberian who fought in the Roman army.

Bacurius is certainly a historical figure, a correspondent of Libanius and a soldier at Adrianople according to Ammianus (31.12.16), and so this story should not be dismissed, although certain folktale motifs may be detected. The performance of healing miracles demonstrates again that the apostolic mission of the New Testament continues in Rufinus' own day. The figures of the pious queen and the king converted after receiving a divine sign may evoke Helena and Constantine, the prototypical Christian ruling family (Thélamon 1970). Rufinus mentions the political consequences of the conversion, which resulted in an Iberian alliance with Rome rather than with Persia, but in his formulation it is the religious choice which leads to the political one, rather than political calculation leading to the religious choice.

Rufinus' work was prompted by concerns over Gothic invaders, and contains a preface which refers to Goths as a "pestiferous disease." The historian nevertheless provides other paradigms of Roman and barbarian relations beyond that of invader and victim. While the Greek ecclesiastical successors of Rufinus reproduce his conversion accounts, they continue to maintain a more traditional view of barbarians as peoples to be subdued by the Roman emperor. Orosius, however, providing a western view later than that of Rufinus, takes his idea to its logical conclusion. Not only does Orosius believe that the conversion of barbarians in other nations is praiseworthy, but he even praises the arrival of barbarians on the territory of the empire, insofar as this leads to their conversion and, perhaps, pacification. At the end of his work, Orosius claims that the churches are packed with Huns and Vandals, and that the mercy of God has resulted in the entrance of so many barbarians into the empire, for "even with our own weakening, so many peoples are receiving a knowledge of the truth which they would certainly not have been able to find except with this opportunity" (7.41.8).

Barbarians and Romans

The Roman empire had always faced non-Roman neighbors and had always had to face non-Romans as allies, subjects, adversaries, or even models to be emulated. In the fourth and fifth centuries Romans often found themselves dealing with non-Romans, whether Persian, German, or Hun, on more equal terms than they had in the past. Traditional Greco-Roman thought, which tended to hold other cultures in contempt, was challenged by the power of Sasanian Persia and by the increasing presence and prominence of non-Romans in the empire itself. The writing of history was one way in which late antique intellectuals sought to answer some of the new questions which the change in Romano-barbarian relations had posed. Why had Roman armies begun to lose to non-Romans? What could restore Roman military preeminence? What sort of relationship should or could Romans have with barbarians?

It is useful to begin with Aurelius Victor, who expresses fairly standard and traditional ideas about the proper relationship between Romans and barbarians at a time when Roman preeminence was relatively unquestioned. Victor, a provincial, several times praises the contribution made to the Roman state by non-Romans (11.12, 39.16). On the other hand, his conventional views are clear when he explains that the German Magnentius revolted from the empire because of the "fierce and savage mind of the barbarian" (41.25). To Victor, the real tragedy of the civil wars which erupted after the death of Severus Alexander was that the energy of the emperors was diverted away from the subjugation of barbarians abroad (24.9). On the other hand, when Victor decries the surrender by the senate of its prerogatives, which resulted in rule by "soldiers and even barbarians," his criticism is directed more toward soldiers than barbarians (37.7). The barbarian threat remained an abstract idea in comparison with Victor's concern over the overthrow of traditional republican governance.

When reading Eutropius and Festus, it is important to remember that they speak not on their own behalf but as the official voice of the imperial government. Their works can therefore be read as expressions of the opinions toward the barbarians which the emperors would find acceptable for the average Roman official in the period immediately before Adrianople. Both works are straightforward celebrations of military conquest. The desirability of defeating barbarians in war is taken as self-evident, and the focus remains entirely on the Roman state. The need for aggressive warfare is not expressed but rather implied by the prominent and detailed descriptions of past warfare.

Ammianus has a more complicated conception of the barbarian (Wiedemann 1986; Bonanni 1981; Chauvot 1998: 383–406). His descriptions of the barbarians living across the Rhine or the Danube, on the one hand, are monotonously similar and negative. These barbarians typically display a combination of madness and rage, acting more like wild animals than like men. For example, when the once-arrogant Chnodomar is defeated by Julian, he behaves like a beaten puppy: "like all barbarians, he was humble in defeat and haughty in success" (16.12.61). Similarly bestial are the Sarmatians, "since with barbarians might makes right" (17.12.18). While Ammianus' contempt for barbarians is manifest, he does not simply put forth a dichotomy of virtuous Romans and animalistic barbarians, for he quite often directs imputations of madness and animality at Romans of all sorts as well (Barnes 1998: 107–11).

In sharp contrast to Ammianus' refusal to grant humanity to the barbarians he describes on the battlefield is his description of barbarians who served in the Roman army or administration. It is difficult to find a negative racial characterization applied to these Romanized barbarians (Chauvot 1998: 400–4). While he is critical of some German officials (14.10.8, 21.10.8), he praises others (17.10.5, 26.8.5, 31.9.2). He frequently praises the courage of the German troops fighting for the empire. Several passages reveal more clearly Ammianus' favorable attitude toward barbarians in official positions. When courtiers attacked Silvanus in Gaul, Malarichus, his fellow Frank, complained to other Franks "who were prominent at court at that time" (15.5.11), that this was an outrage to Franks who were so "devoted to the empire" (15.5.6). Ammianus places the claim of loyalty in Malarichus' mouth without comment, and he seems unconcerned by the prominence of Franks at court. When Julian sought the support of the Roman senate for his usurpation, he wrote letters attacking the reputation of Constantine, and he "openly reproached him for being the first to promote barbarians" to the consulship (21.10.8). Ammianus considered this "tasteless and thoughtless," pointing out that Julian himself would soon name Nevitta consul, a barbarian far inferior in reputation and experience to any that Constantine had appointed.

Ammianus describes the barbarians across the frontier as bestial while judging barbarians in Roman service, with whom he had lived and worked for many years, by the full range of criteria which he applies to Romans. Ammianus' support of very harsh policies toward barbarians, therefore, even including extermination, cannot be considered racially motivated. Rather, it reveals the historian's soldierly belief in the legitimacy of the use of any means to accomplish a given end. When the Romans ambushed and massacred the Saxons in Gaul, Ammianus recognizes that some might find the measure too strong, but states that it was nevertheless necessary (28.5.7). The massacre of Goths after Adrianople is considered by Ammianus a "wise" plan and the general Julius is praised for his "swift and beneficial" action (31.16.8).

Eunapius, unlike Ammianus, can fairly be charged with a general dislike of all barbarians, Romanized or otherwise. Goths are both arrogant and ugly (*fr.* 37). Eunapius particularly faults the barbarians' lack of Greco-Roman literary culture, as his depiction of the causes of the Battle of the Frigidus reveals. The barbarity of the Frank Arbogast is emphasized. He obtained his imperial position by murder, and when Valentinian III attempted to dismiss him from his office with a rescript, Arbogast howled and ripped the order to pieces (*fr.* 58). Eunapius further states that Arbogast loved war and slaughter, and upon his defeat "showed his native barbarian madness" by falling upon his sword (*fr.* 60). It was therefore Arbogast who compelled Eugenius, a professor "with a high reputation for eloquence," into a failed revolt, which was destined to end in his conquest at the Frigidus river (*fr.* 58). In Eunapius' account, barbarian madness has forced a peaceful scholar to a suicidal war (*fr.* 60).

Eunapius saw the Goths in particular as eternally hostile to the Roman state. Even before their entrance onto Roman territory the Goths had sworn an oath which he describes as "an unholy one that went beyond the normal savagery of barbarians" (*fr.* 59). The historian implausibly claims that the Goths pledged that even if the Romans were unceasingly benevolent toward them, they would nevertheless plot against them with the aim of conquering the entire empire. Eunapius' fragments do provide one honorable and heroic Goth, the Roman general Fravitta. One reason Eunapius supported Fravitta was presumably his successful campaign against the Goth Gainas, who attempted a coup in Constantinople in 400. More important for Eunapius, however, was undoubtedly the fact that Fravitta shared his traditional religious beliefs. The Goth is described as a "Hellene" (*fr.* 69.2) and an "initiate" of pagan mystery cults (*fr.* 69.4), who demanded from the emperor in return for his service the right "to worship God in the ancestral manner" (*fr.* 69.4).

Eunapius thus deplored the very existence of barbarians both on the frontiers and in Roman service, and he was not especially averse to extreme measures, such as massacres, if necessary (Zos. 4.26). In Eunapius' view, however, the empire's religious and cultural crisis was to blame for its military difficulties. He says that the invasion of Greece by Alaric, for example, fulfilled a prophecy which indicated that destruction would result as a consequence of the closing of the ancient cult site at Eleusis, and in general he links the destruction of temples with the invasion of barbarians (*frs.* 64.2, 64.3). In Eunapius' vision, the empire required a figure like Julian to fight both barbarism and Christianity on behalf of traditional Greek thought.

Olympiodorus may also suggest that pagan revival would aid the state against invasion. The removal of sacred apotropaic statues from Thrace occurred just days before a Gothic invasion (*fr.* 27). The historian also suggested the potential efficacy of pagan rites in defending Rome against Alaric, although Sozomen uses this section of Olympiodorus to argue for the opposite view (*fr.* 7.5; Soz. 9.6.3–4; Zos. 5.41.1–3). Nevertheless, Olympiodorus' work is a pragmatic diplomat's account of recent successes in restoring international order, not an expression of longing for cultural reaction. His work in its fragmentary form provides no evidence of anti-barbarian polemic or stereotyping. In fact, his support of Stilicho and apparent support of the marriage of Ataulf and Galla Placidia suggest a Roman both comfortable with Goths and other barbarians (such as the African Blemmyes, *fr.* 35.2) and interested in incorporating them into the Roman world.

From the evidence of the surviving fragments, Priscus, like Olympiodorus, refrained from gratuitous anti-barbarian language and approached barbarian conflict in a pragmatic spirit. Priscus appears fair-minded in his description of Hunnic customs and culture, despite the difficulties he encountered on his journey, and his other comments on foreign people are antiquarian rather than critical in nature (*frs.* 41.3, 66). Although diplomacy is central to his work, Priscus favors a hard line, particularly toward the Huns, and he condemns the payments made by Theodosius II to Attila as nothing better than tribute (*frs.* 3, 9.3). It is unclear whether Priscus was critical of the Roman reliance upon foreign troops and generals in particular, if he simply criticized the cowardice he saw in many generals regardless of ethnicity (Blockley 1981: 64–7).

Rufinus introduced an innovative approach to thinking about barbarians in history. The old model of conquest in war by the emperor had been replaced by a form of conquest by conversion, with the emperor present only in the capacity of a suitably pious sovereign. In a work written to comfort those afflicted by barbarian invasion, Rufinus had completely inverted the concerns of the sufferers. The real danger for the state, he revealed, was not the threat of invasion from outside of the empire, but internal subversion in the form of Arianism and paganism, which Theodosius had triumphantly suppressed. The study of the world beyond the borders of the empire revealed that the apostolic project was continuing in the present day and held forth the prospect of an entirely Christian world in the future.

While Socrates, Sozomen, and Theodoret reproduce the accounts of foreign conversions found in Rufinus, they draw back from complete espousal of his interpretations. The Greek church historians continue to be influenced by the Eusebian model of the triumphant Christian king who will protect his state and flock from foreign powers. Both Socrates and Theodoret preserve an anecdote, whose exact historicity is uncertain, set in the reign of Theodosius II (Soc. 7.43.1–4; Theod. 5.37.4). In the more full account of Socrates, careful and fervent prayer by the emperor caused a lightning bolt to strike the Hun leader, Ruga, and caused many of his followers to be killed by plague and by fire from heaven. The emperor's traditional power to destroy barbarians remained more important to these historians than the church's ability to convert them.

Orosius, on the other hand, carries even further Rufinus' suggestion that the division of the world into Christian and pagan supersedes the old division of Roman and barbarian. Orosius' account is often inconsistent, however, for he claims on different occasions that barbarian invasions were punishments for Roman sinfulness (e.g. 7.37), that good pious emperors will crush the barbarians (7.28, 7.34), and that the death of thousands of Goths in Theodosius' army at the Battle of the Frigidus was cause for rejoicing (7.35). Yet Orosius' optimistic vision is in the peroration of his work when he praises the felicity of the times, when "the most savage nations have been suppressed, restrained, incorporated, and destroyed with very little blood, with no struggle, and almost without any killing" (7.43.17).

Conclusion

Late antique historians reveal a wide spectrum of possible depictions of barbarians. More traditionalist historians such as Eutropius, Festus, Ammianus, and Eunapius all share a belief in the desirability of constant aggressive warfare against Persia and the northern barbarians. In the fifth century, historians like Olympiodorus and Priscus reproduce apparently accurate accounts of their own firsthand encounters with non-Romans. Olympiodorus boldly recommended Roman and Gothic cooperation, while Priscus, faced with the more intransigent Huns, favored a military solution over the payment of subsidies.

Rufinus was a great innovator in his recognition of barbarians as potential Christian partners rather than solely as the objects of conquest. Orosius extends Rufinus' idea to include barbarians entering the empire as well as those beyond the borders. The Greek church historians also show an interest in Christian barbarians, and recount persecutions in Gothic and Persian territory. For them, however, because of the relative stability of the eastern throne, and the increasingly flaunted Christian piety of the eastern emperor, no sharp distinction between Christian and Roman needed to be drawn. Instead, the fourth-century sense of Roman superiority over the barbarians could simply be enhanced by the Christian sense of superiority over the pagan. The Christian, Roman emperor was ideally placed to defeat the pagan barbarian, whether Goth or Persian, on behalf of the Christians abroad whom the emperor claimed as his own.

18

THE EMPEROR JULIAN
(THE APOSTATE)

Few figures from late antiquity have inspired more interest, both in their own day and in the present day, than the emperor Julian (Bowersock 1978; Athanassiadi 1981/92; Smith 1995; Browning 1975; Bouffartigue 1992; Braun and Richer 1978). The emperor was reviled by Christians, yet often treated with the respect due a worthy opponent, and although pagans praised him, they did not fail to mention his flaws. His bold attempt to restore paganism to the empire aroused tremendous passion among contemporaries, but his innovations in military, judicial, and fiscal policies were also controversial.

Our knowledge of Julian's life and reign comes not only from historians but also from orations, both in favor of and opposed to the emperor, and from numerous speeches, letters, and other works written by the emperor himself. The richness of our information allows us to know Julian as well as almost any other figure from antiquity, and serves as a useful check on the claims of partisan historians. Julian was the focus of the works of several late antique historians and occupied a substantial part of several others. A historian's treatment of the emperor can serve as a particularly effective guide to understanding his interests and biases.

Youth and education

Modern studies of Julian tend to place considerable weight on the emperor's childhood and education in an attempt to understand this psychologically complex man (Bowersock 1978: 21–32; Athanassiadi 1981/92: 13–51; Smith 1995: 23–48; Browning 1975: 31–66). Julian's father, Julius Constantius, was a half-brother of Constantine the Great. Julian was born in 331 at Constantinople; his mother died within months of his birth. At the death of Constantine in May 337, further tragedy struck. Soldiers, after announcing that they would obey only legitimate sons of Constantine, killed Julian's father and eight others, sparing only the 6-year-old Julian and his half-brother Gallus (DiMaio and Arnold 1992). Many years later Julian would point to this massacre as justification for his revolt against his cousin, Constantius II, who was widely believed to have had a role in the killings.

The orphaned Julian was brought to Bithynia, where he was raised by his maternal grandmother. At age 7 his schooling began at the hands of Eusebius, the Arian bishop of Nicomedia, and Mardonius, a Gothic eunuch who had long been associated with Julian's family. Julian would later remember Mardonius fondly as the man who had introduced him to Homer and other classics. In 342, however, Julian and his brother were sent into exile at an estate in Cappadocia, where they were isolated from their former teachers and friends. During this period it seems that Julian was guarded by eunuchs and taught by, among others, the Christian bishop George.

In 348, when Julian was 18, the sentence of exile was lifted, and while Gallus was taken to the court of Constantius, Julian was allowed to continue his education. He remained briefly in Constantinople, and then studied at Nicomedia. When Constantius elevated Gallus to the rank of Caesar in 351, Julian traveled to Asia Minor, where he studied Neoplatonism with Aedesius. Two traditions of late Platonism, descending from the philosophers Porphyry and Iamblichus respectively, were current at the time. The Porphyrean strain, which Aedesius professed, concentrated on the power of reason to know the soul. Julian was warned by Aedesius' circle against the practitioners of the more ritualistic "Iamblichan" sort of Platonism, which sought enlightenment through the use of magic and miracle-working. This type of philosophy proved, however, to be exactly what Julian preferred, and he left Aedesius and his school to study with Maximus of Ephesus, who was a master of "theurgy," the art of manipulating the gods through ritual. Julian later considered his education under Maximus to be responsible for his conversion to paganism, and Maximus would become an important advisor to Julian when he had gained imperial power. Julian's survival was momentarily in doubt when Gallus was recalled and executed by Constantius in 354, but he was spared by the intercession of the empress Eusebia. With the empress's support he then traveled to Athens, where he pursued further studies in theurgy with the philosopher Priscus, and where he was initiated into the

Eleusinian Mysteries. For years to come, however, he hid his apostasy from all but his closest intimates, and publicly continued to profess Christianity.

Ammianus' history is dominated by Julian, both in the percentage of the work allotted to him, despite his short reign, and in his role as the ideal emperor to whom all others are compared. In light of the importance of Julian to the *Res Gestae* as a whole, it is perhaps surprising to see how little information Ammianus gives us about Julian's youth. Julian first appears in the extant books as the object of slander at court after the execution of Gallus in 354, where it is stated that he was eventually allowed to go to Greece to further his education (15.2.7–8). Evidence for the presence of information about Julian in the lost books is very thin. Ammianus probably mentioned the massacre of Julian's family, since he later presents it as an example of Constantius' cruelty (21.16.8). But when Julian traveled to Nicomedia as emperor, Ammianus mentions, as if for the first time, that Julian had spent time there as a youth (22.9.4). When Ammianus discusses the murder of Bishop George of Alexandria and Julian's reaction to it, he surprisingly neglects to mention George's role as tutor of the young Julian (22.11.3–11). At the beginning of book 16, Ammianus provides a formal introduction of his hero as he prepares to lead an army in Gaul as Caesar. The only references to Julian's childhood in this passage are the passing remarks that Julian's success was all the more remarkable since he was brought up in seclusion and had come "from the quiet shadows of the Academy, not from a soldier's tent" (16.1.5).

Julian was raised a Christian and did not convert to paganism until his teens, as all of our other sources and Julian's own writings make clear. Ammianus' comment on Julian's religion comes, then, as a surprise: "Although Julian from the first beginnings of boyhood was rather attracted toward the worship of the gods, and as he grew older was gradually more aflame with desire for it, out of fear he was performing certain acts pertaining to divine worship, insofar as he was able, in the most extreme secrecy" (22.5.1). Ammianus seems determined to portray Julian's paganism as a gradually evolving tendency, rather than as something acquired in a sudden moment of conversion. Ammianus' later criticisms directed at Julian for his "superstition" and for his excessive reliance on theurgic wonder-workers such as Maximus and Priscus suggest that the historian did not approve of the "Iamblichan," theurgic paganism which the emperor professed (Matthews 1989: 128–9). The erasure of Julian's formative years allowed the historian to avoid extensive discussion of either his Christianity or his theurgic Neoplatonism, both of which Ammianus found distasteful.

Eunapius, like Ammianus, wrote his history in order to praise the deeds of Julian, as he explicitly claims. He and his companions felt that the history of the age had reached its apogee at the time of Julian, whom all worship as a divinity (*fr.* 1; cf. *fr.* 15). Eunapius places the blame for the massacre of Julian's relatives firmly on Constantius (*fr.* 20.3), adding that all of his family's property was stolen as well. We derive much of our information about Julian's teachers and associates, such as Maximus and the Christian sophist Prohaeresius, from Eunapius' *Lives of the Sophists*. We can thus imagine that Eunapius had provided some information about Julian's earlier life in his history, which has left a trace in Zosimus' summary of his work. In Zosimus, the imperial official Eusebius describes Julian as one who "has spent his whole life as a student" and who has no experience in worldly matters (3.1.3). Zosimus' claim that Julian excelled his teachers in every kind of learning may summarize a collection of anecdotes found in the original Eunapius (3.2.1).

While the brief works of Victor and Eutropius omit any reference to Julian's early years, they do provide interesting comments on the massacre of 337. Their version is perhaps that of the *KG* and represents the official imperial line, which absolved Constantius II and Constantine's other sons and blamed the killings on the soldiers acting on their own initiative. Both mention only Dalmatius, Constantine's nephew, as a victim of the massacre. Victor, writing at the time of Constantius, needed to be more circumspect, and he says that the instigator of the slaying was unknown (41.22). Previously he had mentioned that Constantine's appointment of Dalmatius as Caesar had angered the army, and the discerning reader is presumably intended to connect the comments and assign blame properly (41.15). Eutropius, writing later, was able to speak more freely. He also blames the killing of Dalmatius on the military, but adds that Constantius "allowed rather than ordered" the coup (10.9.1). Orosius also follows this tradition, saying that Dalmatius was "immediately destroyed by a military faction" (7.29.1).

The ecclesiastical historians provide the most details about the early life of Julian. Although Rufinus' abbreviated account contains no information, Socrates' account of the emperor is very full, and is surprisingly positive in comparison to the other Greek church historians (3.1.1–24). He attributes the killing of Dalmatius to the soldiers, but adds that Constantius' jealousy was an additional factor which endangered the lives of Gallus and Julian. Socrates points out that Constantius had required that all of Julian's teachers be Christian in an attempt to shield the boy from pagan influences. Julian's great skill at literature made Constantius worried that he might become emperor, Socrates implausibly suggests, and so the boy was sent away to Nicomedia for his further schooling. The historian frames his story as a conflict between Julian and Constantius centered upon religion. For example, certain orations of the renowned pagan orator Libanius suggest that Julian's teacher Hecebolius had insisted out of professional jealousy that the boy swear an oath not to attend the lectures of Libanius. Julian, sticking to the letter of the oath, had paid another student to attend and transcribe the lectures, which he read privately (Bowersock 1978: 27–8). Socrates, however, manipulates this story to claim that it had been Constantius who had forbidden Julian to attend Libanius' lectures because of the orator's paganism.

Socrates, like the other ecclesiastical historians, is particularly interested in Julian's conversion to paganism. He sees Maximus of Ephesus as primarily responsible for Julian's religious fervor as well as for his desire to rule the empire. While publicly pious and serving as an official in the church of Nicomedia, he shows Julian secretly studying philosophy and reassuring his friends that soon, when he has gained power, their position will be greatly improved. Accounts like the one found in Socrates, which suggest that a cabal of pagans had been working for or at least hoping for Julian's accession to the throne, have had some influence upon modern interpretations of his rise to power. John Drinkwater has, however, demonstrated that such an idea founders both on the ancient evidence and on common sense, since there was no reason to expect Julian's accession at that point, nor could his pagan friends provide any means to protect him (Drinkwater 1983). Socrates' account instead serves to blend Julian's revolutionary political activity with his religious deviance by closely linking his usurpation with his paganism.

Sozomen's account of Julian's youth focuses primarily upon his early devotion to Christianity. By narrating the early events of Julian's life in a flashback, after beginning with several anecdotes of Julian's anti-Christian activities, the historian deftly highlights the contrast between the persecuting emperor and the pious child. Julian's parents were Christian, he had been baptized, he had received biblical instruction, and he was raised by bishops (5.2.7).

Sozomen's account of the massacre is taken from Socrates, and he skips Julian's early schooling to go directly to his exile at Macellum (5.2.9). In this beautiful place, Sozomen claims, Julian and his brother had the perfect Christian upbringing, where they studied the Bible, went to church, and showed proper devotion to the cult of the martyrs. Sozomen provides an anecdote, missing from Socrates, which he found in the work of Julian's contemporary Gregory Nazianzen. Julian and Gallus worked together to build an edifice to house the remains of the martyr St Mamas (5.2.12–13). Julian struggled to build up his side of the monument, but each piece was thrust away as he tried to set it up. The message that Mamas was sending only became apparent later, however. While Sozomen is dependent upon Socrates for many of the details of Julian's advanced education, he shows himself to be more psychologically insightful in his account of the young Julian's attraction to Maximus of Ephesus (5.2.16–17). He concurs with Socrates that Maximus both encouraged Julian to hate Christianity and assured him that he would be emperor one day. Julian was susceptible to favorable prophecies and divination in general, Sozomen suggests, because his uncertain relationship with Constantius cast a constant pall of fear over his mind. Constantius wavered several times between executing Julian to prevent the risk of usurpation and elevating him to imperial power as a colleague. It thus seems not unlikely that this uncertainty predisposed him to find particular solace in the theurgic power to control the doings of the gods.

Theodoret provides an abbreviated account of Julian's early life. After a brief mention of Julian's pious early years and his inability to build the martyr's shrine (3.2), Theodoret moves forward to 351. With the emperor Constantius in the west and the pious Christian Gallus appointed Caesar, Julian, Theodoret says, decided to seize power for himself. Socrates had attempted to link Julian's desire to rule with his conversion to paganism in the person of Maximus, who was portrayed as both treasonous and blasphemous. Theodoret has taken this linkage even further. His Julian, driven by lust for power, decided to learn the magical arts which will ensure his victory (3.3). He traveled through Greece on a tour of magicians and seers who might predict the future for him. An anecdote which Theodoret drew from Gregory Nazianzen suggests that Julian did not so much undergo a conversion from Christianity as willed himself to be blind to its truth. A seer whom Julian met in Greece brought forth certain demons inside a temple for divinatory purposes, but when Julian instinctively made the sign of the cross, the demons fled. Julian questioned the man, who claimed the demons had left not from fear, but rather from simple displeasure at the tactlessness of Julian's behavior. Julian, tricked by this explanation, was initiated into idolatry, "so lust for power stripped the wretched man of piety" (3.3.5). Theodoret paints the picture of a Faustian Julian who sold his soul in order to rule the empire. His Julian is also the most cruel and the least learned, and Theodoret provides none of the complexity or contradictions of the man which Socrates and Ammianus give.

Victory in Gaul and the accession in Paris

As war threatened on the Persian frontier, Constantius decided to risk the elevation to power of Julian, his only surviving nephew. In November 355 Julian was appointed Caesar and was married to Constantius' sister in order to further cement their alliance. In order to defeat the usurper Magnentius in Gaul in 351, Constantius had encouraged various barbarians against him. Magnentius was now gone, but serious disturbances continued in the province. It was expected that Julian would serve merely as a figurehead in Gaul, while Constantius himself and his generals restored order (Athanassiadi 1981/92: 52–88; Bowersock 1978: 33–45; Blockley 1972a).

Julian, despite his complete lack of military training, took to the soldier's life. His forces had great success in restoring order in Gaul, most notably at the Battle of Strasbourg (357), which was the subject of a monograph by Julian himself (Eun. *fr.* 17). It seems that Julian's advisors, men appointed by Constantius, made many of the key decisions. Julian often quarreled over power with these advisors, and he maintained later that Constantius had purposely set up his Caesar in Gaul without resources in the hope that the emperor would rid himself of a rival.

After Julian was credited with the victory at Strasbourg, Constantius, who had faced numerous crises of usurpation during his reign, began to look upon his Caesar with some trepidation. Julian and others, it seems, began to entertain thoughts of Julian coming to power one day by various possible routes. A letter written by Julian to his close friend and advisor Oribasius suggests as much (*ep.* 14). Julian recounted, probably in 359, that he had had a dream in which a tall tree collapsed while a fresh new shoot grew alongside it. Julian's dream, of course, implies only that he would succeed Constantius, not that he planned an active conspiracy to overthrow the emperor (Baldwin 1975: 91).

In February 360, Constantius demanded that more than half of Julian's soldiers be sent to him in the east, where a Persian offensive was expected. Some felt that he envied Julian's successes in Gaul and wished to contain the Caesar's ability to challenge him. Julian publicly acquiesced and encouraged his troops to do so, despite unrest among his soldiers and the circulation of an anonymous broadsheet protesting the order. The Gallic troops, who would have been compelled to travel thousands of miles from their homes and families, were particularly exercised by the transfer. Later that night, soldiers surrounded Julian's quarters and demanded his appearance, whereupon he was crowned as Augustus.

Few events in late antiquity have inspired more modern debate than the circumstances surrounding Julian's revolt, and in partic- ular the question of Julian's own responsibility, if any, for his elevation. It has been suggested that he aimed at supreme power years before his elevation, with evidence drawn from his military operations in 359, which were said to be timid in order to amass strength for a revolt (Müller-Seidl 1955). More broadly, many scholars have doubted the version presented by Ammianus and by Julian himself, of a Caesar reluctantly forced into revolt, and have presented evidence either of premeditation or of backroom machina- tions which led up to the seizure of power (Barnes 1998: 153–5; Drinkwater 1983: 370–83; Bowersock 1978: 46–54).

After the proclamation, some months passed, during which Julian corresponded with Constantius in increasingly bitter tones in an attempt to be recognized as the emperor's equal without war. Finally, in 361, Julian formally broke with Constantius and moved his army swiftly through northern Italy to occupy the Balkans. Constantius began to move his army west to confront Julian in civil war when he caught a fever and died in Cilicia on 3 November 361, leaving Julian as sole ruler of the Roman world.

Ammianus presents a detailed account of the debate among Constantius, his wife Eusebia, and his advisors, as to the advis- ability of Julian's elevation to Caesar, and adds an elaborate description of his presentation to the soldiers and Constantius' speech of introduction (15.8). Ammianus artfully provides an intro- duction of Julian which is simultaneously directed to the soldiers and to the reader himself. The soldiers examine Julian's face care- fully for signs of what sort of emperor he might prove to be, and then break out into sustained applause, claiming that Julian's selection was not the act of Constantius but rather of the divine will. The moment is marked by Julian's wry quote of Homer, that he is seized by "purple death" (15.8.17), a reference to the royal color, which is matched by Ammianus' triumphant quote of Vergil, "I am undertaking a greater task" (15.9.1). In addition to preparing the reader for Julian's future military successes in Gaul, Ammianus foreshadows his future religious policies, quoting a blind old woman in Vienna who heard his name and exclaimed, "This man will restore the temples of the gods!" (15.8.22).

After a short digression on the Gauls, Ammianus begins his sixteenth book with a formal praise of the Caesar, telling the reader that what follows may read like a panegyric but is in fact entirely truthful. He compares Julian to the greatest of emperors, Titus, Trajan, Antoninus Pius, and Marcus Aurelius. He adds that the young Julian's successes in Gaul are all the more outstanding and deserving of praise because of his inexperience and the surprise with which his successes were met (16.1). Later in this book, Ammianus provides a more detailed section of praise of the Caesar (16.5). His ascetic and "philosophic" nature are particularly highlighted. Julian ate only the common food of the soldiers, and on the rare occasions when he slept he did so in rough blankets. In addition to studying philosophy, he was conversant in poetry, rhetoric, and literature. Ammianus adds some administrative anecdotes which demonstrate Julian's wit and his sense of justice, and concludes by mentioning his tremendous success in the reduction of the burden of taxation upon the Gauls. Despite these moments of idealization, however, Ammianus frequently portrays Julian in the course of the narrative as fearful or uncertain and prone to human emotions and inclinations. The portrayal of this complexity of character has long been admired as one of Ammianus' greatest accomplishments (Fontaine 1978).

Ammianus provides us with by far the most detailed description of Julian's activities in Gaul in the 350s (Matthews 1989: 87–93; Blockley 1972a). While Ammianus' account is biased, he provides enough information to deconstruct the story he tells. His Julian in Gaul is a military genius who must constantly struggle against the interference of Constantius' generals. The generals are not so much incompetent but rather are working toward the Caesar's failure for sinister reasons, and Constantius himself continually works to undermine Julian's success out of jealousy. Throughout the narrative, details of Constantius' pompous display (16.10) and military failure (18.7–10, 19.1–8) contrast with Julian's simplicity and success. Closer investigation, however, might encourage the reader to sympathize with Constantius' professional generals, who often gave good advice and who were undoubtedly annoyed by the interference of a novice and a figurehead. Constantius also was clearly responsive to Julian's concerns. For example, after Marcellus failed to support Julian militarily in 356, he was dismissed by the emperor, and Marcellus' attempt to denounce Julian at court before Constantius was unsuccessful (16.4, 7). Ammianus relates these facts with enough innuendo to cloud the matter, by pointing out that Constantius' ears were open to every slander. In 357 Julian had his greatest success at the Battle of Strasbourg, which made his military reputation. The battle was the subject of a lengthy rhetorical set piece in Ammianus, which derives in part from Julian's own account of the battle (16.12; Blockley 1977). Again the glory of the presentation of the battle is undercut by a stray detail which Ammianus includes, revealing that at a key moment Florentius, one of Constantius' generals, ensured a Roman victory by overruling a decision of the Caesar (16.12.14; Barnes 1998: 152–3; Matthews 1989: 91–2).

Ammianus' full account of the events at Paris in February 360 leading up to Julian's acclamation sharply rejects any conspiracy. His account can be considered a reflection of the "official" version insofar as many, though not all, of the details are present in two other important sources friendly to Julian: Libanius' *Funeral Oration for Julian* (*or.* 18) and Julian's own *Letter to the Athenians*, written not long after the acclamation in the hope of winning allies for the looming civil war with Constantius.

Ammianus claims that Constantius used the supposed need for troops in the east as a pretext for the withdrawal of Julian's troops, when in reality the emperor simply envied his Caesar's success and growing reputation. Julian's anxiety at Constantius' orders was derived not from thoughts of his own safety or power, but from public-minded fear for the future security of Gaul after the sharp diminishment of his troop strength (20.4). It was not Julian's idea, writes Ammianus, but that of the notary Decentius, that the troops should all gather in Paris before their departure. Julian spoke pleasantly to the soldiers he knew, arranged for the transport of their families to the east, and even entertained the officers at dinner. Throughout this period, however, "he encouraged them with gentle words to hasten cheerfully to the emperor," and assured them that Constantius would amply reward them (20.4.12). That evening, of their own accord, the soldiers revolted, acclaiming him as Augustus all night. Although he gave a speech refusing the honor, fear eventually compelled Julian to accept, and he promised that he would reward his men for their service.

Critics of Ammianus' account have often focused on his mention of the officers' dinner, which Julian conspicuously fails to mention in his own account of the evening. The existence of such a dinner is certainly compatible with several more conspiratorial accounts of the acclamation. Julian himself may have instructed some officers to support him, or others may have taken advantage of the situation to orchestrate the "spontaneous" uprising of the soldiers. Nothing in Ammianus' account, however, demands such an interpretation (Matthews 1989: 93–100).

The theories of conspiracy behind Julian's elevation usually rely most heavily upon certain fragments of Eunapius, whose approach to this period of Julian's life must therefore be carefully investigated. Eunapius, in a manner more blunt and crude than that of Ammianus, claims that Constantius continually sought to undermine Julian out of envy and anger (*fr.* 20). Eunapius declines to discuss the details of the Battle of Strasbourg, saying that he was unwilling to try to rival Julian's own work, although his own ignorance of military matters probably played a role in this decision as well (*fr.* 17). Eunapius' Julian nobly restrains his troops from plunder and teaches them virtue (*fr.* 18.1). He negotiates brilliantly with the Chamavi, who respect him as a god (*fr.* 18.6).

There can be no question that Eunapius presented Julian as completely justified in his revolt against Constantius. Zosimus describes Constantius' attempt to transfer troops to the east as part of a plot by the emperor to gradually remove all power from Julian, whom he envied (3.8.3–4). Did Eunapius go further and provide evidence of a conspiracy, instigated by pagans, to gain the throne for Julian? Two passages from Eunapius' *Lives of the Sophists* have often been misread to suggest this, but David F. Buck has clearly demonstrated the difficulties with such an interpretation (Buck 1993). The fragments are as follows. "Having summoned the priest from Greece and having performed with him certain things known only to themselves, he was roused for the destruction of the tyranny of Constantius. Oribasius of Pergamum and a certain Euhemerus from Libya joined him in these activities" (*fr.* 21.1). Compare this further comment on Oribasius: "he excelled in other virtues so much that he even made Julian emperor" (*fr.* 21.2).

Buck convincingly argues that both of these fragments refer, not to the evening of the elevation, when the possibility of manipulating the troops remained, but to some time after Julian's acclamation, as he prepared to meet Constantius in civil war. Ammianus remarks that Julian several times performed secret rites which reassured him that Constantius would soon die (21.1.6–7). Common sense suggests that even if Eunapius were aware of such a conspiracy of pagans behind Julian's usurpation, he would refrain from discussing such a discreditable fact about his hero in a laudatory history. If Eunapius had recounted such a conspiracy, it would certainly have been reported by Zosimus. Zosimus, however, provides an account similar to that of Ammianus, where Julian is obedient toward Constantius and distressed at being compelled to accept the crown. If Zosimus for some reason had suppressed Eunapius' account, then certainly one of the many sources hostile to Julian and to paganism would have recorded these details. Thus, although it remains possible that some conspiracy lay behind Julian's elevation to the throne, Eunapius did not in fact write about one in his *Histories*.

The *breviaria* are quite laudatory of Julian's early success in Gaul. Victor, writing under Constantius, praises the success of Julian in Gaul but hastens to add that this success was due to the planning and fortune of the senior emperor. He adduces the examples of Tiberius and Galerius, who had been successful generals when subordinate to superior emperors, but were not so successful when they themselves ruled (41.17–19). This curious didactic lesson seems to be good evidence for the existence of a general perception that Constantius might be jealous or sensitive about the attribution of credit for any military success of his Caesar. Eutropius preserves a more straightforward account of Julian's success, saying that Julian had come to Gaul with a small force in the face of great devastation, and had won many outstanding victories (10.14). Festus, more succinctly, merely describes Julian as "a man of proven fortune against barbarians" when he set out for Persia (28.1). Victor and Festus have no information about Julian's acclamation, but Eutropius' account is clear and implies no skullduggery: "when the German armies were being removed from the defense of the Gauls, Julian was made Augustus by the consent of the soldiers" (10.15.1).

Rufinus' brief account of Julian's accession omits the context and simply claims that he took upon himself the power of Augustus (10.27). His Greek ecclesiastical successors provide more details of Julian's actions in Gaul and in Paris. Socrates, for example, further demonstrates his unusually positive attitude toward Julian (3.1.25–36). His laudatory account echoes many of the points found in Ammianus and in Julian's own writings. He describes the generals who had been set over Julian in Gaul as lax and abandoned to luxury, but Julian as bold and energetic. By offering a bounty for killing a barbarian, Socrates claims, Julian weakened the enemy and improved his standing with the troops. Julian is credited with brilliant successes on the battlefield, and Socrates even relates an anecdote of a time when a crown happened to fall on the head of the Caesar, which was widely seen as an omen of his future rule. Socrates adds that "some" have written that Constantius had sent young Julian against the barbarians in the hope that he would perish. The historian, while stating that the idea seems implausible for several reasons, leaves it to the reader to judge. His description of the acclamation at Paris is positive and hints at no controversy: "Having had this success [at Strasbourg,] he was proclaimed emperor by the soldiers." Only after this praise does Socrates hint at the dangers to come: "Julian became emperor in this way, but whether he ruled thereafter as a philosopher, let my audience decide."

Sozomen's account of Julian in Gaul is drawn directly from Socrates (5.2.20–3). The changes he introduces serve mainly to soften the positive tone: Julian no longer is brilliant, nor does Sozomen relate the omen of the crown. Sozomen, too, poses Socrates' question about Constantius' motive for sending Julian to Gaul, but answers it with considerably more certainty and with several more arguments explaining the improbability of Constantius' malicious intent. Sozomen also does not connect Julian's elevation to his military success, as Socrates did, but simply states that Julian was proclaimed emperor without Constantius' sanction.

Theodoret is considerably less interested in secular affairs, and considerably more hostile to Julian than the other church historians. In his few comments, Theodoret describes Julian as "Caesar of Europe," and says simply that he sought power and raised an army against Constantius (2.32.6). Orosius also claims that Julian "usurped the dignity of Augustus" without providing details (7.29.16). Julian's success in Gaul, he suggests, drove him toward usurpation (7.29.15–16). Orosius, seeking providential meaning in history as always, explains Constantius' death and the constant civil wars he was forced to undertake as the product of his fierce support for Arianism, which had "torn to pieces the limbs of the Church" (7.29.18).

Religious policies

Julian had privately abjured Christianity almost a decade before he came to the throne, and upon gaining sole power he sacrificed to the gods and began to work toward the reinstatement of paganism. Julian refrained from suppressing Christianity entirely, but pursued numerous strategies to marginalize the religion and to encourage participation in pagan cult. In the winter of 361 he proclaimed the freedom to worship for all in the empire, allowing exiled Christians such as Athanasius to return to their home. The emperor apparently hoped that this would increase discord among different Christian sects. He also revoked certain exemptions from service on town councils, and restored certain properties to the cities from which they had been seized. Each of these laws had the important secular aim of strengthening the councils and local government. The exemptions would have been claimed often by clergy, however, and the property would have been in some cases seized by the church, and thus each struck indirectly at the privileges that the church had managed to secure for itself in the several decades since its establishment. The most devastating such blow, at least from the perspective of the educated class who wrote histories, was the law of 17 June 362, which denied the privileges of an official teaching position to all who were not of good character (Banchich 1993; Hardy 1968). A letter of Julian explained "good character": how could one teach Homer and the classics honestly without worshipping the gods who are integral to the works (*ep.* 42)? Even pagans like Ammianus tended to deplore this exclusion of qualified Christians from the classroom.

Julian refrained from the actual persecution of Christians on all but a few occasions, in an attempt perhaps to prevent the creation of martyrs. When pagans throughout the empire took matters into their own hands and inflicted violence against their Christian neighbors, however, it became clear that the emperor was unlikely to interfere. Very early in his reign, Julian's old teacher George, the bishop of Alexandria, was beaten to death by a pagan mob (Barcellona 1995: 61–3; Haas 1991). Julian decried the violence and disorder, but primarily on the grounds that, although George deserved to be killed, worshippers of the gods ought not stain their hands with blood. Julian's anti-Christian measures seem to have increased as he prepared to leave on his Persian expedition. In 363, for example, in a letter to Christians of the Mesopotamian town of Edessa, he explained sardonically that he was confiscating all of their church's possessions, to help the Edessans comply with the

Christian belief that the poor will more easily pass into the Kingdom of Heaven than the rich (Jul. *ep.* 115; Bowersock 1978: 92).

Julian sought to revitalize paganism through imperial patronage, and as he traveled east to Constantinople and then to Antioch, he devoted himself to the restoration of abandoned shrines and temples and sought the renewal of moribund sacrifices and rituals. His most dramatic attempt of this kind was his unsuccessful attempt to rebuild the Jewish Temple in Jerusalem (Blanchetière 1980; Drijvers 1992; Levenson 1990a). Such a restoration would not only have returned to the Jews the ability to sacrifice, but would have rendered impossible the realization of Jesus' prophecy that the temple would never be rebuilt, and thus struck a blow against the Christians. The project was a failure, however, whether through accident, sabotage, or supernatural intervention. Perhaps Julian's most ambitious stratagem to revive paganism was his plan for an imperial pagan priesthood that would emulate many features of the Christian church. It would be hierarchically arranged and priests would be required to be pious and ascetic. This pagan church would dispense charity and provide hostels in every city (Nicholson 1994; Koch 1927/8).

The brevity of Julian's reign has served to obscure certain aspects of his religious program. The ultimate goals he held out for his measures, and the chances that his program could succeed, remain contested issues. Thus many writers at the time and in following generations have been able to impose upon the figure of Julian their hopes and nightmares about the future course of Christianity and paganism in the empire.

Ammianus was a pagan and a staunch supporter of Julian. He was, nevertheless, quite critical of a number of aspects of Julian's religious program. Often in Ammianus we seem to hear the voice of an older and wiser man, looking back upon a moment pregnant with possibility and trying to explain where things went wrong, and why Julian's reign, with all of its promise, was in the end such a failure.

Ammianus claims that Julian received courage in his struggle against Constantius by the help of divinatory magic, which informed him that Constantius would soon die (21.1). Ammianus explains the science of divination in a defensive digression in which he is careful to refute charges that Julian was engaged in something improper or illegal, a tone which will recur in Ammianus' later discussion of Julian's activities.

Book 22 of Ammianus is largely devoted to the innovations Julian introduced at Constantinople. After a discussion of reforms of the court and of the military, Ammianus passes to Julian's pagan program, which he summarizes in a three-part phrase: "the temples should be opened, sacrifices be offered on their altars, and the worship of the gods be restored" (22.5.2). Ammianus attributes a somewhat devious motive to the proclamation of religious freedom. The emperor, he says, summoned Christian bishops to the palace and politely told them to allow each man to propound his belief without harm. This was done, claims the historian, with the knowledge that toleration would intensify their divisions and he would no longer have to face their united front, for "no beasts are as savage to men as most Christians are to each other" (22.5.4).

Ammianus carefully absolves Julian of the charges of persecution which are prevalent in the church historians, except for a stern condemnation of Julian's school law which forbade Christians to teach rhetoric. This law he denounces twice, as "inappropriate" and "deserving to be covered in eternal silence" (25.4, 22.10). Ammianus also recognizes that it was improper for Julian to ask the religion of various litigants in court cases before him, but claims that this nevertheless had no impact upon his ruling, and Julian could "never be accused of having deviated from the straight path of justice because of religion or anything else" (22.10).

Ammianus' account of the murder of the bishop George in Alexandria differs markedly from the versions in the Christian sources (22.11; Matthews 1989: 442–4). George is described as an informer to Constantius, and Ammianus claims that he suggested to the emperor that all of the buildings "erected by Alexander at great public expense" in Alexandria ought to be taxed. Although this presumably refers to temples, and thus was an anti-pagan measure, Ammianus has framed it as a question of unpopular fiscal policy. After the mob killed George and those suspected of being in league with him, Ammianus says that his confederates might have been saved by other Christians, had not the whole population universally hated George. Thus he once again frames the event as more than a simple conflict between Christians and pagans. Ammianus concludes by claiming that Julian was outraged and would have sought the execution of those responsible, but his advisors restrained him.

The necessity of sacrifice to the gods was an essential element of Julian's religion (Smith 1995: 198), but Ammianus seems to find Julian's excesses in this regard distasteful. The sacrifices were too expensive, Ammianus says, and they led to the unpleasant scene of soldiers, drunk and gorged on sacrificial meat, causing trouble throughout the city (22.12.6). In his obituary notice of Julian the historian repeats the criticism: the emperor sacrificed innumerable victims without regard to expense, and it was believed that there would have been a cattle shortage had he been victorious over the Persians (25.4.17). Julian's own dignity was also at risk, in Ammianus' view, for he was "justly" criticized for taking such obvious delight in carrying sacred objects himself, and he received the nickname "butcher" rather than priest because of his love of sacrifice (22.14.3). The emperor, concludes Ammianus, was "super-stitious rather than truly religious" (25.4.17).

Julian's attempts to reestablish cult and temple sites receive prominent notice in Ammianus. He mentions, for example, Julian's detour on the way to Antioch to visit the shrine of the Great Mother at Pessinus, where he sacrificed and prayed (22.9.5–8). Julian had previously undergone initiation into the cult of the Mother, and had written a hymn to her (Smith 1995: 137–8, 171–6). The emperor also sought to reopen the Castalian fountain, an oracular site associated with the ancient temple of Apollo at Daphne, a suburb of Antioch. Ammianus says that Hadrian had closed the fountain, which had prophesied his rise to imperial power, in order to prevent others from receiving a similar message. He adds that Julian found it necessary to remove some bodies buried around the spring and to purify the area in the ancient manner pioneered by the Athenians at Delphi (22.12.8). This bland version of events must surely have been designed by Ammianus to avoid any mention of Christianity. John Chrysostom is the first of many Christian sources to tell us, in his speech *On Saint Babylas against Julian*, that the body buried near the spring was the remains of Saint Babylas. Babylas had been transferred there by Julian's brother Gallus, and the martyr's presence was credited with preventing the "demon" in the spring from prophesying (Lieu 1986: 44–86; Matthews 1989: 439–40; Barnes 1998: 85). Shortly after the removal of the body, the temple of Apollo was destroyed by fire. Ammianus reports that Julian launched a major investiga-tion since he suspected Christians were to blame, but Ammianus himself suggests that an accident caused by a philosopher, Asclepiades, may have been the cause. While he disassociates himself from the anti-Christian theory of Julian, he also ignores the Christian theory which held that God destroyed the temple as revenge for the transfer of the relics.

The most audacious of Julian's temple restorations was his plan to rebuild the Jewish Temple in Jerusalem. Ammianus reports his motive as "to extend the memory of his reign by the greatness of his public works" (23.1.2). While it has been argued that this is the most accurate description of Julian's intentions (Drijvers 1992), most contemporary sources understood the reconstruction as an attempt to discredit Christianity. Once again, it seems, Ammianus has underplayed the anti-Christian elements of Julian's program. The project had to be halted due to the frequent appearance of fireballs which burned several workmen to death and made the site unapproachable. Ammianus gives no explanation for this bizarre phenomenon, although Christian sources attribute it to divine anger.

Eutropius presents a succinct judgement on Julian's religious policy: "he persecuted the Christians excessively, but nevertheless he avoided bloodshed" (10.16.3). This is the same way in which the ecclesiastical historians tend to frame their accounts (Penella 1993; Barcellona 1995; Thélamon 1981: 281–309). Each presents a few examples of actual Christian martyrs under Julian's reign. All stress as well that the lack of martyrs is evidence of the insidious cleverness of Julian, who tried through tricks and rewards rather than violence to turn Christians from the true faith.

Rufinus' account of Julian's religious program is short, but features many themes upon which later church historians elaborated. In particular, Rufinus' Julian is a clever persecutor, who learned that Christians were strengthened by martyrdom and thus attacked them more subtly. These attacks, Rufinus is careful to point out, were nevertheless as dangerous and as malicious as those of earlier persecutors: "a persecutor more clever than others, he won over nearly a majority of the people as if he had struck them violently, not by force or tortures but by prizes, honors, flattery, and persuasion" (10.33). Rufinus provides a list of positions forbidden to Christians and then several examples of the brave behavior of Christians under pressure. He claims that Christians were excluded from major positions in the bureaucracy and the army, and that the study of literature was forbidden to Christians (10.33). This last misrepresentation of Julian's school law, which actually forbade Christians to teach, but not to study, was repeated by most of his successor historians.

In his brief account of Julian's visit to the Castalian spring, Rufinus claims that the priests blamed the martyr Babylas for his inability to receive a prophetic response. In a rage, Julian ordered the remains removed, and a procession of psalm-singing Christians took them away (10.36). Rufinus claims that Julian, maddened with rage, ordered that Christians be arrested and tortured at random, and he reports one example of a victim of this supposed order. A young man named Theodore, with whom Rufinus himself spoke, was tortured for hours without breaking (10.37). Theodore later claimed that he was without pain and was able to calmly sing hymns because he felt that a boy was standing next to him, soothing his pain with cool water and a white cloth. Rufinus devotes particular attention to Julian's attempt to rebuild the Jewish Temple (10.38). The reconstruction is framed as a showdown between Judeo-pagan arrogance and Christian truth, and when a series of disasters destroyed the building site Julian's own coming downfall is proleptically announced.

Socrates' account of Julian's program is much fuller than that of Rufinus. He emphasizes Julian's cleverness and his ability to manipulate different factions in society (3.1.43–8). He is also eager to show that, despite Julian's claim to be a philosopher, the emperor did not in fact act in accordance with true philosophy during his reign. The recall of bishops, most of them orthodox, from exile, was a policy which would seem favorable to orthodox readers, and thus the historians are careful to emphasize Julian's hidden purposes. Socrates says that the recall was ordered to make Constantius appear to have been cruel toward his subjects in comparison with his successor (3.1.48). Socrates later repeats the charge, arguing that although Julian had readily agreed to Christian requests when they reflected poorly on the policies of Constantius, his normal instinct was to be contemptuous toward them (3.11.1–2).

Socrates draws from Rufinus the contention that the new incentives which a pagan emperor provided quickly separated true Christians from nominal ones. As evidence, he provides the case of the sophist Hecebolius, who was a Christian under Constantius, a pagan under Julian, and then a Christian again after Julian's death (3.13.5–6). Socrates presents a long digression inspired by Julian's school law (3.12.7, 3.16). In response to the law, Socrates relates, two Christian rhetoricians, the younger and elder Apollinaris, created a wholly Christian curriculum. The elder Apollinaris translated the five books of Moses into epic verse and put some other books of the Hebrew Bible into the form of tragedies. His son rewrote the New Testament in the form of Platonic dialogues. This fascinating expedient was not necessary for long, of course, since Julian soon died and the law was rescinded. Socrates uses this episode as an opportunity to discuss the broader issues of Christian education which it raised. He argues both that truth is to be found in the works of the ancients, even if it is not the full truth of Christianity, and, in a more instrumental way, he argues that Christians have need of the tools of rhetoric in order to effectively make their case against pagans. Julian's reign must surely have inspired many similar reflections on the relationship between Christian and secular education, which clearly remained a matter for serious discussion in Socrates' own day.

Socrates provides three examples of violent persecution during Julian's reign. He takes from Rufinus the case of Theodore and the miraculous brow-wiper (3.19). He also presents the case of the Phrygians Macedonius, Theodulus, and Tatian, who, disgusted at the reopening of a temple by the governor Amachius, broke into the temple at night and demolished the idols (3.15). Given a chance to avoid punishment by sacrificing, they obstinately refused, and as a result were tortured and roasted to death on a grill. Socrates describes the killing of George at Alexandria in far greater detail than Ammianus had (3.2). In his version, Constantius had granted to George the right to build a church over a Mithraeum, a subterranean temple to the eastern god Mithras. In cleaning out the shrine, numerous human skulls were discovered, which were said to be the remains of persons of all ages who had been sacrificed for divinatory purposes. The Christians paraded these skulls through the streets of Alexandria, whereupon the insulted pagans launched an attack which resulted in casualties on both sides. In connection with these disturbances, Socrates claims, George was killed, having been tied to a camel, torn to pieces, and then burned (along with the camel). The method of execution seems to have pagan ritual overtones, and the burning was a way of preventing the preservation of George's bones for later veneration. Socrates' account agrees with that of Ammianus in the suggestion that George was widely disliked by people of all classes. Some had claimed that George, a homoiousian, was killed by supporters of Athanasius, but Socrates disagrees, and as proof that pagans were to blame he reprints the letter which Julian wrote to the citizens on the occasion (3.3). The emperor blames the attack on pagans, who, he says, should not have engaged in such violence, even though he feels that George probably deserved even worse.

Sozomen draws upon Socrates for much of his narrative of Julian's religious policies, but he seems to have felt that Socrates was not critical enough of the emperor. Both through arrangement of material and through the introduction of supplementary material, Sozomen leaves the impression of a more malevolent emperor and a more frightening reign. Unlike Socrates' account, which proceeds through Julian's life in chronological order, Sozomen begins with several accounts of the emperor's paganism before sketching his childhood in flashback (5.1–2). This helps place Julian's evil in the foreground. We are told that the emperor so openly apostatized, and so frequently bathed himself in the blood of sacrificed animals, that he underwent a kind of reverse baptism. Sozomen also evokes the state of mind of the Christians of the empire at Julian's accession. He suggests that the fear Christians felt at the possibility of a true persecution was more painful than an actual persecution would have been (5.2.1). This is a recurrent theme in Sozomen, who, like other church historians, frequently reminds the reader that Julian's abstention from full-blown persecution was merely a device to forward his aim of conversion. When Maris, the bishop of Chalcedon, rebuked Julian for his atheism, Julian mocked his blindness, saying that Jesus would never cure him. Maris responded that he was glad to be blind, so that he would not have to gaze upon an apostate face. Julian made no reply, according to Sozomen, because he thought the display of "forbearance and gentleness" toward Christians would be more beneficial for paganism (5.4.9). Even after narrating the emperor's death, Sozomen returns to this idea, arguing that Julian's lack of overt persecution was only strategic and that he had threatened to launch a full-scale assault on Christianity on his return from Persia (6.2.9).

Sozomen's presentation of Julian's subtle persecution may be divided into two sorts of material. First, the historian provides examples of laws and policies of the emperor which were prejudicial, even if not openly persecutory, toward Christians, and second, he provides examples of actions taken by Julian's subordinates or by local officials which the emperor failed to prevent. Julian's school law is an example of the first sort. Unlike Socrates, Sozomen is not at all convinced of the value of the classics, stating that the writings of Apollinaris would undoubtedly be considered as good as the classics if it were not for the extreme love for antiquity by which men are possessed (5.18.4). Sozomen also provides numerous details about how the emperor manipulated financial and urban policy to benefit pagans. For example, Caesarea, the metropolis of Cappadocia, was removed from the list of independent cities because it was so strongly Christian. He adds that the property of the church of Caesarea was looted and the clergy forced to serve in the governor's bodyguard (5.4.1–5). Julian's removal of the exemptions and privileges which Constantine had granted to the clergy might not be self-evidently discriminatory, but Sozomen details the hardship that it caused (5.5.1–4). Churches were forced to pay back the funds they had raised from a tax which had been specially earmarked for them during the reign of Constantine. These back-dated demands required church property to be sold, and Sozomen claims that money was even demanded from nuns who had taken vows of poverty. Clergy were also held responsible for rebuilding temples which had been destroyed, and failure to pay led to torture and imprisonment.

To the short list of martyrs which Socrates had provided, Sozomen adds many more stories, drawn often from Gregory Nazianzen or from his own personal experience. These stories bear much similarity to the story of George. In most cases, pagans, encouraged by the example of their emperor, took advantage of the new order to attack Christians or drive them away. The murders of Eusebius, Nestabus, and Zeno in Gaza may serve as examples of this sort of event (5.9). The inhabitants of Gaza beat and imprisoned the three, and then assembled in the theater, where they accused the Christians of committing sacrilege in the temple and generally demeaning the gods. The prisoners were then killed in a gruesome fashion. It was reported, says Sozomen, that the emperor was enraged about these events, but this was untrue and merely an expression of the guilty feelings of the perpetrators. In fact, Julian did not even bother to write a letter, as he did after George's death, and when the governor of the province arrested some of the perpetrators, Sozomen claims, the emperor removed him from power and threatened him with death (5.9.11–13). Sozomen returns to the theme of the emperor's failure to act repeatedly. After recounting more similar stories, he remarks that even if the emperor did not commit these acts, nevertheless there were many martyrs (5.11.12). Later Sozomen describes how his own grandfather was one of many Christians who were forced to flee for fear of mob violence, repeating his contention that blame ought to be fixed upon the emperor, who did not apply the law to perpetrators (5.15.13–14). Sozomen also accuses Julian of appointing subordinates who persecuted Christians in violation of the emperor's explicit wishes. One such subordinate was Julian's uncle, also named Julian, who served as prefect of the east. When Julian was looting the church of Antioch and torturing a priest, he mocked the sacred church vessels by performing lewd acts upon them. In the case of this Julian, divine wrath functioned with appalling swiftness, as his genitals and rectum were immediately afflicted with an incurable worm infestation, which killed him (5.8).

Sozomen catalogues some of the means by which the emperor sought to stealthily induce his subjects to worship the gods (5.17). The emperor placed pictures of Zeus and Ares next to pictures of himself, in the hope, Sozomen suggests, of tricking Romans who were simply offering the respect due to an emperor into simultaneously worshipping pagan gods. The emperor also presented Roman soldiers who had come to receive their pay with incense and fire for a sacrifice. Many obeyed out of greed or habit, says Sozomen, although he does add a tale of several soldiers who realized too late what they had done, and then ran screaming through the streets in horror until they were able to return their pay to the emperor.

Sozomen relates, following Rufinus and Socrates, the stories of the temple of Apollo at Daphne and the Temple in Jerusalem. His account of the suburb of Daphne is particularly full, as he adds details about the discreditable and erotic nature of the place which he perhaps derived from his personal experience (5.19–20). Sozomen's account of the rebuilding of the temple is expanded from that of Socrates with the addition of more colorful details and of his own reflective comments on the lessons to be drawn from the events (5.22). Despite his reliance on Socrates, Sozomen claims to have learned the story from eyewitnesses, and he directs disbelieving readers to go and track down witnesses themselves.

Theodoret provides less detail and more atmosphere than Socrates or Sozomen, as is his wont. Like Sozomen, he is most critical of Julian's refusal to protect Christians under assault by their neighbors and by his entrusting of "civil and military offices to the most savage and impious men" (3.6.5). Theodoret provides quick sketches of martyrdoms and persecutions similar to those offered by Sozomen (3.7, 11, 15, 18). He expands on Sozomen's story of the blasphemy and ensuing disease of Julian's uncle Julian by adding that Felix and Elpidius, two other high government officials, were present as well (3.12–13). Shortly after Julian's horrible death, Felix too died, although he is silent on Elpidius' fate.

Theodoret follows the other ecclesiastical historians in depicting Julian as a cunning persecutor, "wearing a mask of reasonableness, but preparing traps and snares" to trick men into apostasy (3.15.1). The emperor, he says, polluted the well water and the food for sale in Antioch by the admixture of sacrificial meat (3.15.2). He also relates the story of the repentant soldiers, who sprinted through the city alarmed at their unwitting engagement in sacrifice. In his version, the soldiers are not let off so easily. Instead of simple dismissal, they were spared from execution only at the last minute and sent to a distant outpost of the empire (3.17). Their fate is similar to that suffered by Valentinian, who would later become emperor and then had the rank of tribune (3.16). Theodoret says that he was sprinkled by purifying water as he walked by a religious procession led by the emperor. In disgust, Valentinian punched the priest, and as a result was condemned to a desert outpost. Theodoret sees his elevation to emperor a year later as a sign of divine providence.

Orosius' short passage on Julian's religious policies may serve as a summary of some of the important themes of the church historians. Julian attacked Christianity "by subterfuge rather than by force," and sought to convert men to paganism "by honors, rather than by tortures" (7.30). The only legal measure Orosius mentions is the school law, in face of which, he reassures his readers, Christians preferred to resign rather than to convert. Sozomen believed that Julian would have begun to openly persecute Christians, had he returned victorious from Persia, and Orosius provides an elaborated version of this forecast, claiming that Julian had ordered the construction of an amphitheater in Jerusalem where bishops, monks, and saints would be fed to the beasts upon his return. The prevention of these evil plans by Julian's death is deemed further evidence of God's providence.

Secular policy

While Julian's religious policies set him apart most strikingly from the other emperors of late antiquity, his secular policies inspired a great deal of contemporary comment as well. Historians frequently evaluate his legal policies and practices. The good Roman emperor spent a large amount of his time hearing cases, and the quality of the emperor as a judge served as a traditional yardstick of the success of his rule. Julian's reign began with an exceptional tribunal. Shortly after the death of Constantius, the new emperor conducted treason trials, in which several of Constantius' former courtiers were condemned to exile or death. The trials were dominated by the military, whose support Julian needed to cement as quickly as possible (Bowersock 1978: 66–9; Thompson 1947a: 73–9). The historians also discuss his judging practices and philosophy in more mundane cases.

Other policies of Julian have been seen as deliberately archaizing, and part of a general attempt by the emperor to rule as a philosopher-king. Julian's dismissal of eunuchs, cooks, and barbers from his staff was believed to reflect a "philosophical" orientation, and he offered positions in the imperial bureaucracy to intellectuals and writers. He restored certain privileges to the senate at Constantinople, and in his dealings with senators, he attempted to revive the forms and attitudes of the early imperial and republican period in Rome's history. These revivals were seen alternately as inspired or affected by observers and historians.

Julian's fiscal and legal policies seem to have been part of an attempt to restore wealth and autonomy to the local councils, or *curiae*, of the cities and towns of the Greek east (Pack 1986). The independent city had been central to classical civilization for centuries, but the sprawling imperial bureaucracy had made possible the evasion of curial responsibilities, and encouraged powerful men to pursue careers at the imperial rather than the local level. In response to these trends, Julian removed exemptions which had allowed the powerful to avoid service on city councils. He also restored property which had been taken into private or church hands to the control of the councils and attempted to lower taxes on the cities. These moves were often criticized, both because they interfered with the vested interests and privileges of the powerful, and also because they were seen, perhaps correctly, as veiled attacks on ecclesiastical power and on Christianity in general.

Ammianus reserves some of his most extravagant praise for Julian in his role as judge. The historian is willing to see at least some merit in the emperor's suggestion that during his reign, it seemed that Justice herself had descended to earth (22.10.6, 25.4.19). Knowing that he was somewhat excitable, Ammianus tells us, Julian allowed himself to be corrected by his associates, and freely admitted when he had made a mistake. Julian is also praised for his careful judgement and willingness to closely examine all of the relevant facts (22.10.1). For Ammianus, however, the preeminent quality a judge should have is mercy, and he tells numerous anecdotes in which Julian displays this quality. Julian gave a sentence of exile rather than death to a rapist, and when the victim's parents complained, he explained that an emperor's mercy must be beyond the law (16.5.12). In a similar vein, he refrained from hearing a case in which a personal enemy of his would be a defendant until he had reconciled with the man (22.9.16–17). The sparing of the Alexandrians who had killed the bishop George could be seen as an example of mercy rather than of Christian persecution (22.11.11). It is common knowledge that Julian was merciful even toward enemies who had conspired against him, says Ammianus, preferring the threat of the sword to its actual use (25.4.8–9).

Ammianus considered the trials held at Chalcedon shortly after Julian's accession, at which various of Constantius' adherents were unfairly punished, to be an exception to Julian's general mildness (22.3). Instead, the trials, held in the presence of military officials, were examples more of prejudice than of impartiality. Certain of Constantius' most notorious courtiers were properly punished with death, Ammianus felt, including the chamberlain Eusebius, the investigator Apodemius, and the notorious Paul "the Chain," so named for his practice of stringing together series of accusations to prosecute the innocent. But others were condemned on little or no evidence, and the financial official Ursulus, who had been supportive of Julian when he was still Caesar, was condemned to death solely because he had earlier offended the generals with a stray comment. Julian tried to disassociate himself from this execution, but Ammianus refers to it as an "inexcusable crime." The historian further condemns Julian for allowing Arbitio, who had been one of Constantius' main henchmen and consistently inimical to Julian himself, to sit in judgement of others. This grievous misjudgement is blamed by Ammianus on Julian's "timidity, or his ignorance of what is proper" in the early days of his reign (22.3.9).

After the trials, Julian purged the court of staff and attendants. Ammianus uses this purge as an opportunity for a digression on the corruptions of the palace staff, and the thirst for luxury and hatred for discipline that had accompanied the growth in personnel (cf. Libanius *or.* 18.130–41). Despite the corruption, Ammianus still criticizes the emperor's actions, and complains that he ought to have kept a few attendants, "at least those known for good character and integrity" (22.4.2). Ammianus' judgement reflects the general favor he felt toward the proper display of imperial dignity, which Julian sometimes lacked (Matthews 1989: 231–8).

Ammianus is also critical of Julian's occasional lack of decorum in his public behavior. At the inauguration of the new consuls for the year 362, Julian attended on foot, which "some criticized as affected and tasteless" (22.7.1). Julian frequently sat in the senate house at Constantinople to hear cases, but once, when he heard that his old teacher, the philosopher Maximus of Ephesus, had arrived, he leapt up and escorted him in with a kiss. Ammianus saw this "improper display" as evidence that Julian was "excessively seeking after empty glory" (22.7.3). Ammianus disliked and distrusted Maximus, one of the theurgists whom he portrays as responsible for encouraging Julian to ignore the omens and embark on the Persian campaign.

Ammianus consistently describes Julian as a tax cutter. He inspired "joyful dancing" in Gaul when he lowered tax rates from twenty-five to seven gold pieces per person (16.5). He clashed with Constantius' men in Gaul not only over military policy but also over fiscal policy, most notably when he refused the plan of Florentius to impose an additional tax on the Gauls, who were already suffering under barbarian invasion (17.3). When Julian was given a province of his own to administer, he forbade officials to pressure the inhabitants to pay, with the unlikely result, according to Ammianus, that taxes were paid in full and in advance (17.3). In general, Julian's support of lower taxation is seen as a personal virtue, the result of his lack of greediness (25.4.15; Matthews 1989: 239–41).

Ammianus is guardedly critical of some of Julian's actions in his home town of Antioch. He feels that the emperor imposed price regulations during a food shortage simply to court popularity (22.14.1). These regulations were promulgated in the face of opposition from the powerful members of the council of Antioch. Ammianus does not support local authority, however, when it comes to granting additional power to councils to ensure that the wealthy and powerful serve. He objects vehemently no less than three times to Julian's policy that removed exemptions from service from those who had special privileges, or had served in the army, or were not residents of the town in question (21.12.23, 22.9.12, 25.4.21). The frequent repetition suggests that Ammianus or those close to him were negatively affected by the policy.

Little from Eunapius survives on Julian's policies beyond non-specific panegyric. An excerpt from the *Suda*, which may be Eunapian in origin, praises Julian as a good judge whom criminals feared (*fr.* 25.1). It contains the interesting detail that Julian was a particularly effective judge because his pleasant nature and his habit of appearing frequently in public allowed citizens free access to speak to him regularly. Zosimus' account is confused and may not provide reliable insight into Eunapius' work, but certain features are suggestive (3.11.3). Zosimus credits Julian with the building of a harbor, a colonnade, and a library, to which he donated his own books. His claim that Julian showed great favor to Constantinople by allowing many new people to serve on the *curia* may indicate another point of difference between Eunapius and Ammianus. The positive tone given to the description of this policy contrasts with Ammianus' repeated denunciation of Julian's removal of exemptions from potential members of the *curia*. Eunapius' perspective is decidedly more local and urban than that of the imperial and cosmopolitan Ammianus.

Eutropius is very favorable toward Julian, whom he deems "an outstanding man who would have governed the state nobly if the fates had allowed" (10.16.2). Eutropius cites his erudition in both Greek and Latin. Julian's fiscal responsibility and tax reductions receive particular praise. Eutropius also describes him as generous toward his friends, but less discriminating than an emperor ought to be, for some friends damaged his reputation. This cryptic notice may remind the reader of the scene recorded by Ammianus of Julian's embrace of Maximus, who was blamed by Ammianus for the failure of Julian's Persian invasion. Alternatively, Eutropius may have in mind subordinates like the emperor's uncle Julian, whom Sozomen and Theodoret blamed for violence toward Christians.

While Rufinus is uninterested in Julian as a secular leader, Socrates presents several evaluations of his policies outside the religious sphere (3.1.48–60). As part of Julian's courting of favor early in his reign, Socrates says, he had Eusebius, the chief eunuch, executed, and property that had been stolen by eunuchs was returned to the people. This event is separated from any account of the trials at Chalcedon, where it belongs, but instead is linked to Julian's dismissal of eunuchs, cooks, and barbers from the palace. Socrates comments, as had Ammianus, that many criticized these dismissals as insufficiently respectful of the need for imperial pomp and dignity. The historian further remarks upon Julian's archaic manner of governing, claiming that the emperor remained up all night writing speeches which he personally delivered in the senate, the first ruler since Julius Caesar to behave in this fashion. Socrates also mentions Julian's reformation of the imperial courier service, which Ammianus had criticized as overburdened by church personnel shuttling between synods (21.16.18). In general Socrates finds this behavior affected and pretentious. He recapitulates the complaint of Ammianus and Eutropius that the emperor too often consorted with unworthy companions. For Socrates these are the professional philosophers, "many of whom were more to be identified by their worn out cloaks than by their learnedness," who replaced the functionaries who were dismissed by Julian (3.1.56). Throughout this passage Socrates presents a running commentary on the relationship between philosophy and Julian's behavior, arguing both that Julian's behavior was not truly philosophical and that true philosophy and imperial rule cannot coexist. Rather than praising the emperor for reducing taxes, as other historians had done, Socrates several times criticizes him both for special levies directed against the church and for turning a blind eye toward overzealous tax collection when the subjects of the taxman were Christian (3.13.8–10, 3.14.7–8). Socrates is also critical of Julian's price edict in Antioch, the flaws of which he explains in fairly sophisticated terms (3.17.1–3).

Sozomen, in sharp contrast with Socrates, has completely removed any reference to Julian's secular policies and accomplishments and focuses entirely on his religious policies and beliefs. One must speculate that Sozomen thought that the inclusion of such material in an ecclesiastical history was either inappropriate to the genre or was too favorable toward the Apostate. Theodoret too avoids any mention of Julian's non-religious policies, although it is less surprising in his decidedly non-secular history.

Persian invasion and death

Julian planned an invasion of Persia from early in his reign (Blockley 1992: 24–30; Matthews 1989: 130–83; Marcone 1979; Bowersock 1978: 106–19; Ridley 1973). His military successes in Gaul and his victory over Constantius left him and his contemporaries with a high estimation of his skill and good fortune. The ultimate goals of an invasion of Persia have been debated (Seager 1997; Blockley 1992; Lane Fox 1997). At the very least, Julian hoped to demonstrate his superiority to Constantius, strengthen his position at home, and retaliate against the Persians for their recent successes. Julian may have had more expansive goals, including the overthrow of the Persian emperor Shapur or even the annexation of the entire Persian empire.

Historians report opposition, both human and divine, to the expedition. In March 363 Julian crossed the Euphrates with his army and then marched south, sending a portion of the army east as a diversion. In early April the army moved through Persian territory, receiving the surrender of several fortified towns. Julian and his army then approached Ctesiphon and halted on the west bank of the Tigris. Because the reinforcements had not yet arrived and the army of Shapur was near, Julian abandoned the idea of besieging Ctesiphon. As his army began to retreat, he ordered the entire fleet of ships to be destroyed by fire. Ancient historians as well as modern scholars have provided various explanations for this action.

The Roman army retreated by land, pursued by Shapur, pressed by guerrilla warfare, and threatened by hunger due to the scorched-earth tactics of the Persians. On 26 June in a minor skirmish Julian was fatally struck by a spear. Some attributed the blow to a Persian, but others blamed a disgruntled Roman or Christians in the Roman ranks. Julian is said to have ended his life in emulation of Socrates, calmly discussing philosophy with friends as he died. The army quickly named as emperor Jovian, who salvaged the situation as best he could by suing for peace on difficult terms with Shapur to ensure the safety of the Roman army (Lenski 2000; Heather 1999a; Matthews 1989: 183–8; Scheda 1966; Conduché 1965).

Ammianus is surprisingly vague about the purpose of Julian's invasion. He attributes to Julian love of war, a desire for revenge, and hope of receiving the title "Parthicus" (22.12.1–2). The broader strategic goals, like Ammianus' narration of the campaign itself, remain hazy and filtered through a mythical lens. Ammianus was an eyewitness to the expedition, and his historical, tactical, and geographical details have been generally judged favorably by modern historians. Nevertheless, Ammianus created a narrative which impresses the reader more for its emotional power than for its detailed accuracy.

The importance of Julian's Persian war to Ammianus, and the strangeness and difficulty of Ammianus' narrative of the events, are the subject of a powerful article by Rowland Smith (1999; cf. also Matthews 1989: 130–79; Meulder 1991; Austin 1979: 92–101). Ammianus had warned the reader that his account of Julian will approach panegyric, and the emperor's heroic longing for war against Persia moved the narrative into epic territory. Along the way, Ammianus underlines the magnitude of the task ahead and the audacity of Julian by reference to great heroes of the Roman past. The emperor died like a Homeric hero, and passed his last evening conversing as if in a Platonic dialogue. The epic nature of the story is magnified by the heavy foreshadowing of failure. Even while Julian was still in Antioch, numerous portents and omens made it clear that the expedition should not be undertaken. As the army moved south, further unfavorable signs occurred, and Ammianus tells us that the philosophers advising Julian were misunderstanding and misinterpreting these negative omens. Julian is absolved of blame for ordinary mistakes in strategy or tactics, and instead Ammianus portrays him as a doomed but glorious leader, whose faults are the heroic ones of aiming "beyond mortal aspirations" (22.9.1).

At Antioch, Ammianus claims, Julian first became excessive in his ambitions (22.9.1). It was a bad omen that the emperor entered the city during the celebration of the Adoneia, when the population was sunk in ritual wailing and mourning (22.9.15). The failure of the rebuilding of the Temple in Jerusalem also boded poorly for the future of the expedition (23.1.3). The twenty-third book is littered with evil signs: the death of fifty men in a hay accident (23.2.6), the death of a lion, the royal animal (23.5.8), the death of a soldier named Jovian by a lightning strike (23.5.12–14). While traditional interpreters of signs told Julian that this lightning strike portended evil for the campaign, the philosophers who advised Julian claimed that lightning was nothing but an atmospheric phenomenon, and that the death was therefore without significance.

As the army neared Ctesiphon, Ammianus downplayed the ill omens, and praised the heroic exploits of emperor and his men as they besieged and sacked several cities. But before the walls of Ctesiphon, a sacrifice of bulls to Mars was unsuccessful, and Julian's angry promise that he would never sacrifice to Mars again proved prophetic (24.6.17). The army could not successfully lay siege to Ctesiphon, but the discussion which followed this decision is missing from our manuscripts. When the narrative picks up, Julian has given the order to march toward the interior and to burn the ships (24.7). Ammianus says that the ships were burned to deny their use to the enemy and to free up the men who were responsible for transporting the ships for combat. In retrospect, however, he says that it was as if the goddess of battle frenzy herself had lit the deadly fire (24.7.4).

The army was forced to retreat, pursued by Persian troops, and the omens became hopelessly bad (24.8.4). At night, Ammianus tells us, Julian watched his guardian spirit depart sadly from his tent (25.2.4). The next day, hastening without a breastplate to support the rear of the army against a Persian attack, Julian was pierced in the liver by a spear. Dying in his tent, Julian reassured his companions that he believed that the soul outlives the body, and that he found death in battle to be the most honorable way to die. After further philosophical talk, Julian died (25.3). Ammianus follows this affecting scene immediately with an obituary of the emperor. The historian is unstinting in his praise of Julian's virtues, but does not refrain from criticism. Ammianus remarks that some critics would claim that Julian had provoked war with Persia to the detriment of the Roman state, but that, in fact, it was not Julian but Constantine who was to blame for hostilities between the two parties (25.4.23; Warmington 1981). After Jovian was chosen to succeed Julian, Ammianus unfairly blames him for the mess which Julian left behind (25.5–7; Heather 1999a).

We know Eunapius' version of the war largely through the outline of Zosimus. Eunapius tells us that he had at his disposal the memoirs of Oribasius, the doctor who had been a close advisor to Julian during the campaign (*fr.* 15). For these events, then, we would expect Eunapius to have been more accurate than usual, and in general Zosimus' account is quite similar to that of Ammianus (3.12–30). Zosimus' account of the fighting before Ctesiphon is, however, hopelessly confused (3.26), and it is impossible to tell how Eunapius had explained Julian's burning of the ships and withdrawal. It seems clear that Eunapius did not cast blame on the emperor, since in one fragment the historian criticizes the carping soldiers who did not recognize the brilliance of Julian's plan to march back to Roman territory (*fr.* 27.6). In another fragment he expresses concern that the soldiers might be corrupted by the great abundance of booty around Ctesiphon, so perhaps Eunapius portrayed Julian's decisions as necessary because of the greed of the soldiers (*fr.* 27.5).

Zosimus says that Julian was wounded by a sword and remained alive until midnight, which suggests that Eunapius preserved the deathbed philosophizing found in Ammianus (3.29.4). Most likely Eunapius did not offer any conclusions as to the identity of Julian's killer (*fr.* 28.1). It is likely that Eunapius portrayed the Persian invasion as a success, since Zosimus claims that at the time of his death, Julian had almost completely destroyed the Persian empire (3.29.4). The harsh treatment of Jovian by Zosimus and by the author of a *Suda* entry perhaps drawn from Eunapius suggests that he, like Ammianus, blamed Jovian for squandering the "victory" which Julian had won.

Eutropius, like Ammianus, was present on the expedition, and he, too, favors Julian and condemns Jovian (10.16–17). He writes that Julian captured several towns and forts, "laid waste to Assyria, and for a while set up camp before Ctesiphon. Returning home as victor ... he was killed by an enemy's hand" (10.16.1). Eutropius thus asserts as strongly as Eunapius that Julian had actually won the war against the Persians. Perhaps his statement that Julian was killed by an enemy is meant to rebut those who believed that the emperor was a victim of one of his own men.

Festus provides a taste of the sense of doom familiar from Ammianus' account, saying that Julian led "cursed standards" against the Persians (28.1). He describes the movement of the army to the gates of Ctesiphon and then a daring movement by sea. This attack, Festus claims in an echo of Eunapius, would have resulted in the taking of Ctesiphon if only the soldiers had not been distracted by booty (28.2). Festus, therefore, unlike Eutropius, does not claim that Julian had been victorious, although he absolves the emperor of complete blame. Festus' comment on the burning of the ships is of interest: "Despite his companions warning him to return, he had more faith in his own plan, and after he burned the ships, he was led by a deserter who had come for deception" (28.2). Although the connection is not clearly made, Festus seems to suggest that the burning was inspired by the deserter. In any case, he highlights Julian's error.

Festus' account of the death of Julian contains a few more details than might have been expected in his abbreviated history (28.3). The fatal wound, he says, penetrated Julian's hip to the groin, and he pins the blame on an enemy horseman. Festus also alludes to the philosophical end of the emperor, who "emits his delaying soul" after speaking of many things to his companions. Festus, like Eutropius, criticizes Jovian for failing despite his possession of an army "superior in battle" (29.1). This positive portrayal of Julian is surprising coming from a Christian like Festus who was so hated by Eunapius and Ammianus. Since Festus writes to support the coming Persian invasion by Valens, it is important for propaganda purposes to portray Julian's expedition as wise and successful, and to emphasize the ignominy of Jovian's surrender and cession of territory.

Rufinus gives few details about Julian's Persian invasion. The emperor "set out indeed, but never returned," killed by either his own men or by the enemy (10.37). The accession of Jovian to power marks the return of "legitimate government," and as soon as he becomes emperor, God's providence is manifest (11.1). Persians provide food and supplies to the hungry army, and Jovian triumphantly restores peace to the eastern frontier and to the empire as a whole. Orosius, too, is sparing in his discussion of the invasion. He claims that the failure of the expedition occurred when Julian was misled by a traitor to move from Ctesiphon to the desert (7.30.6). Wandering carelessly through the wasteland, the emperor found death at the hands of an enemy. Jovian's ensuing peace treaty was "not very worthy, but necessary enough" (7.31.1).

Socrates' version is more complete. He claims that Julian had invaded Persia in early spring because he had heard that Persians are naturally sluggish and indolent during the winter (3.21). He describes the invasion as initially so successful that the Romans succeeded in besieging Ctesiphon and causing the Persian king to sue for peace. At this point, however, Julian refused to negotiate, Socrates claims, because he had become convinced that he was the reincarnation of Alexander the Great and could be satisfied with nothing less than complete victory. In full battle the Romans again defeated the Persians, but Julian was killed. In the version presented by Socrates, Julian is even more successful in war than the most partisan pagan historians had claimed. The result is to pin the final blame for the failure not on the army or on his successor but on Julian's own megalomania.

After Julian's death, Socrates says, the army blamed the emperor's intemperance for their defeat, and in particular they blamed his foolishness in listening to a Persian deserter, who convinced him to burn the ships (3.22.9). Julian's delusion and hubris cause him, in Socrates' account, to continue to fight despite the Persian willingness to submit, and similar conceit leads to his death (3.21.11). In Ammianus' account, Julian entered his final battle with a shield but no breastplate owing to the suddenness of the attack, but Socrates' Julian wears no armor simply because of his delusional self-confidence. The historian gives various possible accounts of Julian's slayer. He is inclined to agree with those who say that he was killed by his own men, although some say that a Persian was to blame. As an alternative theory, he adds that an epic poem by a certain Callistus on the war attributes the killing to a demon (3.21.14–15). While Socrates thinks that this is possible, he recognizes that Callistus may be simply writing poetically.

Sozomen continues to focus on religious aspects of Julian's reign which Socrates had overlooked or downplayed (6.1). To prepare for the invasion of Persia, he reports that Julian wrote an arrogant letter to Arsaces, the Christian king of Armenia, in which he abused Constantius, blasphemed Christ, and demanded that he support the invasion. Sozomen also accuses Julian of planning his route east to avoid cities which are overtly Christian, and notes that the emperor stopped at Carrhae to sacrifice at the temple of Zeus. Recognizing that the failure of the expedition resulted from the threat of starvation which the army faced under Jovian, Sozomen builds his critical account of Julian's leadership around his failure to properly supply his army. As the Romans marched south through Assyria and took many cities, Sozomen maintains that Julian foolishly destroyed storehouses and granaries without considering that he would have to retrace his steps to return to Rome (6.1.4). This mistake becomes clear when the emperor, camped with the army at Ctesiphon, recognized that he was in danger of being trapped between the Tigris and the Euphrates, yet was unable to return by his original path which he had destroyed. Julian again showed his lack of foresight when he ordered all the provisions to be thrown off the ship, thinking that the soldiers would fight more boldly from necessity. A Persian who had resolved to die for his country struck the final blow against the army when he led them for three days through a wasteland. In Sozomen's account, this deserter was not responsible for the burning of the ships, which was carried out to free up the men guarding them for combat (6.1.9). Nevertheless, the repeated lack of foresight by Julian left the army worn out from the journey and weakened by the lack of supplies.

Sozomen provides a striking description of the emperor's death. A gust of wind threw up a cloud of dust, and in the moment of darkness which resulted, a horseman with a spear killed the emperor and rode off (6.1.13). At the moment of his wounding, Sozomen says that Julian threw some of his blood in the air, either to reproach Jesus, whom he blamed for the blow, or in anger at the sun god, who he felt had favored the Persians (6.2.10–11). Like Socrates, Sozomen offers the reader several possible identities for the unknown assailant. While he may have been a Persian or a Saracen, Sozomen thinks that it is most likely that the killer was a Roman Christian. Sozomen, unlike Socrates, spends several lines defending the murder, explaining that the Greeks have a long and healthy tradition of tyrannicide, and of standing by their families, their country, and their God (6.2.1–2). Whatever the nationality of the killer, the real cause, Sozomen argues, was divine wrath, as several omens had demonstrated. Sozomen is more confident than Socrates in attributing Jovian's unfavorable peace treaty to the danger and disruption which Julian's strategy had caused (6.3.2). As an epilogue to Julian's reign, Sozomen mentions certain catastrophes, such as droughts and earthquakes, which reveal the awful state of the empire during the emperor's rule (6.2.13–16). He even blames a tidal wave in Egypt which occurred during the reign of Valentinian and Valens on Julian.

Theodoret writes from Antioch, the city that served as a staging ground for Persian campaigns. Perhaps his Antiochene perspective explains why he is the only ecclesiastical historian to provide Julian with a creditable reason for his Persian campaign. At Constantius' death, he claims, the Persian army invaded the empire, and thus Julian justly plotted revenge. Unfortunately, his godless army was unable to have success (3.21). Theodoret, like Sozomen, focuses on the failure of Julian to properly provision his army (3.25). He accuses Julian of burning the ships to inspire his troops to fight harder, and he charges that he neither brought ample supplies from Rome, nor plundered the enemy's territory. Instead, Julian forced his army to march without food or drink through the desert. Theodoret does not claim the killing of Julian for the Christians, but instead suggests that the slayer could have been a Persian, a Saracen, or a soldier who could not endure his hunger. Theodoret provides a dramatic scene of the fatal wounding, as Sozomen had, with Julian flinging a handful of his blood in the air and crying out, "You have won, Galilean!" (3.25.7).

Theodoret paints a sinister picture of the aftermath of Julian's rule. In the temple at Carrhae where Julian had sacrificed, a woman's body was discovered, cut open for the evil divinatory purposes of the emperor and his philosopher friends (3.26). Many boxes filled with human heads were found at Antioch (3.27). Not only does Theodoret attempt to defend Jovian against the partisan histories of Julian's adherents, but he brazenly denies that such a controversy existed. Following the account of Rufinus, he claims that as soon as the Persian king learned that Jovian, not Julian, was emperor, he sent envoys to discuss peace and established a market-place to feed the Roman soldiers in the desert. Then the army came home safely, and peace was established for the next thirty years (4.2).

Conclusion

Their representation of Julian provided late antique historians with a way to explore numerous issues of religion, the role of the emperor, and foreign policy. While the split between pagan and Christian images of Julian was, of course, particularly sharp, it was not absolute. Ammianus, Socrates, and Festus, for example, in different ways, analyze the emperor with results that transcend expectations based on religious loyalties. Modern scholars no less than ancient historians are divided in their evaluation of this complex, revolutionary figure. Although late antique histories must serve as one of the major sources for the information we have about Julian, the sharp differences between them serve as a reminder of how hesitantly and carefully we must use the information they provide to reconstruct the past.

19

THE EMPEROR
THEODOSIUS I
(THE GREAT)

As the last emperor to rule an undivided emperor, Theodosius' reign appears particularly important in retrospect (Williams and Friell 1994; Matthews 1975; King 1960). After his death in 395, the empire would never be so united again. Upon assuming power after the military disaster at Adrianople, he rebuilt the army, but then presided over its decline in several civil wars. Theodosius also played a part in putting an end to the Trinitarian struggles of the fourth century by repeated legislation against heresy, helping to establish what has been considered orthodoxy ever since. His reign also saw significant steps toward the outlawing and destruction of paganism. His submission to the powerful bishop Ambrose signaled a new relationship between church and emperor. Late antique historians provide us with insight into the nature of the changes and conflicts of the age of Theodosius.

Accession

The emperor's father, also named Theodosius, was a general during the reign of Valentinian who fought in Britain, Gaul, and Africa. Ammianus provides us with many details of the elder Theodosius' campaigns, stressing the general's excellence and courage (27.8, 28.3, 28.5.15, 29.5). Because Ammianus writes during Theodosius' reign, he undoubtedly felt compelled to praise the emperor's father, whom he refers to as the "general with a famous name" (28.3.1). A close reading of Ammianus, however, reveals unflattering details in the accounts of some of the campaigns which Theodosius the elder led, as well as great emphasis on the harshness of his military discipline. This suggests that Ammianus was not a supporter of the general or his son, despite the fulsome praise which the requirements of contemporary politics demanded (Thompson 1947a: 89–91).

Theodosius the Elder was executed in 375 after Valentinian's death, under circumstances which remain unclear (Errington 1996). Orosius tells us that "envy" was responsible for his demise, and that he accepted his death in a manly and Christian manner after being baptized (7.33). Ammianus does not discuss the execution. His history stretches to 378 in his discussion of the eastern empire, but only to 374 in the west. While there may have been good structural reasons for arranging the history in this way (Matthews 1989: 382; Blockley 1975: 95–6), Ammianus may also have wished to avoid treating an event that must have been politically delicate (Thompson 1947a: 92–5). Ammianus subtly refers to the general's fate when he likens his bravery to that of "Domitius Corbulo and Lusius" [Quietus], both of whom died as a result of court intrigues (29.5.4).

Ammianus gives us a glimpse of the young Theodosius at age 27, "afterwards a most outstanding emperor" (29.6.15), but his narrative does not describe his forced retirement back to his estates in Spain around the time of his father's execution, nor his recall to power after Adrianople. While in Spain, Theodosius married Aelia Flaccilla and had two children, including the future emperor Arcadius. After Valens' death in 378, Gratian summoned Theodosius to the east, and he was proclaimed emperor on 19 January 379 in Sirmium in northern Italy. Ammianus refers obliquely to Theodosius' accession in his account of the trial of Patricius and Hilarius, who sought by magic to determine who would succeed Valens. They stopped after learning the first letters of the next emperor's name – Theod – which they saw as clearly referring to one Theodorus (29.1.28–33; cf. Soc. 4.19; Soz. 6.35). The story emphasizes the obscurity of Theodosius to contemporaries and the perceived unlikelihood of his rise to power.

Socrates and Sozomen present a favorable view of Theodosius' accession, claiming that he was so renowned for his excellence in war that he was considered by all to be worthy (5.2; cf. Soz. 7.2.1). Orosius even deems Theodosius better than Trajan (7.34.2–4). In Theodoret's detailed account, which has often been relied upon for modern reconstructions of the event, he claims that Theodosius was an obvious choice because of his aristocratic birth and military skill (5.5). The inconsistencies in Theodoret's account, however, make it clear that he has invented much of it. In particular, he credits Theodosius with a non-existent victory over the Goths, which so impresses Gratian that he is promoted to emperor. Theodoret, working with a few facts, in this case the existence of a military victory and Theodosius' retirement in Spain, has constructed a credible though inaccurate narrative (Errington 1996). Before Theodosius' accession but after his recall, Theodoret adds, the general dreamed that he had been granted imperial robes and a crown by Meletius, the bishop of Antioch (5.6.1–2). In this way Theodoret presents the emperor as having received his position from God and from an Antiochene bishop, before it was granted by Gratian's secular power.

Against heresy

The attitudes of historians toward Theodosius and his reign are closely correlated with their attitudes toward Christianity. Shortly after Theodosius' accession he became gravely ill and received baptism. After his recovery, his already strong Christian faith may well have become stronger. In his first wave of Christianizing laws in 380 and 381, Theodosius moved to make the Nicene Creed official and purged homoiousians and other unorthodox Christians from bishoprics and churches.

Rufinus portrays Theodosius as a second Constantine, who was completing the work of the first Christian emperor. Thus "the worship of idols, which according to the policy of Constantine had begun to be neglected and destroyed, collapsed while he ruled" (11.19). Rufinus emphasizes that Theodosius was moderate and peaceful in his transfer of churches from Arian to Catholic control, and he praises his piety and his lack of pretension in his relationships with the clergy (11.19).

Socrates provides more details than does Rufinus about Theodosius' religious policies, although the piety and moderation of the emperor remain the primary themes. His piety was apparent early on. While on his sickbed, Socrates writes, the emperor first ascertained that the bishop Ascholius was a firm adherent to the Nicene Creed before he allowed the baptism to proceed (5.6). Since Theodosius had lived in Ascholius' see for a year and a half before his baptism, he must certainly have known his religious beliefs, but the anecdote serves to underline Theodosius' orthodox commitment. Theodosius' greatest achievement, for Socrates, was the imposition of unity upon a fractured church. Socrates argues that this unity was achieved through persuasion rather than force. He claims, for example, that with the exception of exiling Eunomius, Theodosius allowed all heretics to meet and preach in churches which were outside of the city walls (5.20). The emperor gave

Demophilus, the homoiousian bishop of Constantinople, the opportunity to accept the Nicene Creed and thereby "to welcome peace and unity." Demophilus' refusal and the ensuing general expulsion of Arians were the consequence of Arian rejection of harmony and peace (5.7). Socrates' Theodosius consistently argues for unanimity and reason in the face of bishops who trust solely in clever arguments (5.10).

Sozomen, in comparison with Socrates, does not put as much stress on celebrating the emperor's restraint toward heretics. In Sozomen's version, for example, Theodosius' dismissal of the Arian Demophilus from the bishopric is less apologetic (7.5.5–7). Sozomen is also more inclined to favor clerical power over imperial power, as the following anecdote demonstrates. An old priest treated the emperor with reverence, but then patted the emperor's son on the head in a familiar way, causing the emperor to become enraged at this lack of respect toward his heir. The priest, however, explained that his actions had a theological point. How much more enraged ought the emperor be toward Arians, said the priest, who show disrespect to the Son of God as unequal to the Father. Not only did Theodosius apologize to the priest for his anger, Sozomen tells us, but he also became less willing to meet with heretics. He also passed a law forbidding the public discussion of the nature of God, which Sozomen portrays in a positive light (7.6.4–7; cf. Theod. 5.16.5). In general the lawyer Sozomen, unlike any other of the ecclesiastical historians, demonstrates a familiarity with Theodosius' laws which survive for us in the compilation of the Theodosian Code (Errington 1997). On seven occasions he refers to such laws, which he sometimes relies upon to correct or augment claims by Socrates. Sozomen corrects Socrates' claim, for example, that the only unorthodox Christian to be exiled was Eunomius. Instead, he writes that "some" were exiled and "others" were deprived of privileges. The punishments meted out against heretics according to the law, says Sozomen, were great, but they were tempered by the emperor's mercy, since "he was not eager to persecute" (7.12.12).

Theodoret, like Socrates, sees concord as an important virtue in the church, and after Theodosius is appointed emperor he is said to have immediately moved to restore harmony among the clergy (5.6.3). Like Sozomen, Theodoret favors the power of the church over the power of the state, and in several elaborate set pieces Theodoret demonstrates what he sees as Theodosius' admirable submission to bishops and his awareness of the superior power of the church. This is symbolically revealed when Theodosius kisses the bishop Meletius like a pious son would approach his father (5.7.3).

Against pagans

Early in Theodosius' reign, he did not legislate overtly against paganism, except to reiterate the bans on blood sacrifice which had been standard since Constantine. But despite the tolerant approach from above, local mobs and monks sometimes took matters into their own hands, killing pagans or destroying temples. These attacks often went unpunished by the emperor, and they increased in frequency with the support of the zealous Maternus Cynegius, whom Theodosius appointed as prefect of the East in 384 (Williams and Friell 1994: 47–60; Matthews 1975: 139–44; King 1960: 76–7). Despite the increase in violent acts by Christians, Theodosius maintained the status quo with regard to paganism throughout the 380s and even appointed pagans to high offices, including two historians who had previously served under Julian. Eutropius was prefect of Illyricum in 380 and 381, and was consul in 387, sharing the honor with the emperor Valentinian II. Aurelius Victor was appointed prefect of Rome in late 388.

Beginning in 391, however, Theodosius promulgated a series of anti-pagan laws far stronger than anything the Roman world had previously seen (Williams and Friell 1994: 119–33; King 1960: 77–86). First Theodosius passed a ban on entering shrines and temples, and forbade the worship of idols in Rome and Egypt. Late in 392 he passed an even stronger law, which banned all sorts of minor charms and divinations that could be associated with paganism. In between these decrees, the anti-pagan fervor of the monks continued to boil over, and both pagans and Christians recognized that the destruction of the Serapeum, the temple of Serapis which had stood in Alexandria, marked a major escalation in religious warfare in the empire. Even though Theodosius allowed and sometimes encouraged the destruction of temples, it seems most likely that he did not pass laws that actively required such demolition, although this remains a debated question.

Eunapius' history is contemptuous of Christians and, therefore, of Theodosius. While Eunapius probably showed little interest in Theodosius' policies concerning non-orthodox Christians, some information on the emperor's anti-pagan policies does remain. Eunapius' depiction of the destruction of the Serapeum does not survive from his *History*, but he provides some insight on the pagan view of events in a summary from his *Lives of the Sophists* (*fr.* 56). He sneers at the destruction of the temples in Alexandria, describing the events as a mock battle against stones and statues which offer no defense. Eunapius describes the seizing of idols as "grave robbery" and suggests that the Christians are motivated by greed. Eunapius' great contempt for monks undoubtedly was fueled by their destructive activities, which went unpunished by the emperor.

It has never been entirely clear what role Theodosius played in the destruction of the temples and perhaps was not entirely clear at the time. Rufinus attempts to associate Theodosius with the "beneficial" side of temple destruction while avoiding the attribution of blame for the mob violence which often accompanied such actions. The ambiguity is clear in the case of a decree presented by Rufinus concerning a temple in Alexandria. A conflict between pagans and Christians over the possession of a basilica led to rioting and deaths, and local officials were unable to dislodge the pagans who had fortified the building. Rufinus says that the emperor's order written in response to this riot declined to punish those responsible for the deaths in the earlier street fighting "because of his natural clemency." On the other hand, Theodosius then called for the elimination of the idols which were "the roots of the discord" (11.22). This led, in Rufinus' account, to the final destruction of the Serapeum (11.23–30).

Socrates' description of the events in Alexandria differs in several ways from that of Rufinus. Socrates must have received some information about the attacks from his grammar teachers Helladius and Ammonius, pagans who participated in the violence and then fled to Constantinople. Socrates claims that Theodosius ordered the demolition of the temples unbidden. Violence erupted, according to Socrates, because the pagans, "especially philosophers," were angered by the mocking display of sacred ritual objects and statues. Thus Socrates' version removes Rufinus' description of the struggle over the control of property and presents the dispute in directly ideological and religious terms. After the temple was destroyed, Socrates adds, the emperor ordered temple statues to be melted down to make utensils for distribution to the poor (5.16).

Sozomen's account of the conflict in Alexandria mixes elements of the accounts of Rufinus and Socrates with other original material (7.15.2–10). In Sozomen, the pagans have shut themselves up in the Serapeum itself, and he provides details of the tortures and murders they committed against Christians. Theodosius himself, Sozomen says, did not give the orders to begin the demolition, and in fact his clemency was apparent when, after the rioting, he pardoned pagans in the hope that they might more readily be converted. The emperor's actions are thus portrayed as a reaction to the sedition of the pagans, as it was only after the riots that he demanded the demolition of the temples. Clergy and monks receive more credit in Sozomen for forwarding the anti-pagan crusade, and the emperor's role is reduced to simply allowing the events to unfold.

Theodoret claims that Theodosius issued general laws ordering the destruction of all temples, but his characteristic vagueness makes his use of details unreliable. He provides a detailed account of one such event, the demolition of the temple of Zeus at Apamea led by the bishop Marcellus with the aid of imperial officials (5.21). By contrast, his account of the destruction of the Serapeum is much less detailed than that of Rufinus and the other ecclesiastical historians. No account of the violence at Alexandria is given. Instead, he focuses closely on presenting a vivid picture of the pagan crowd watching an axe fall on the cult statue of Serapis. When the blow caused no earthquake, but instead sent forth a family of mice who had lived in the statue's wooden head, the folly of paganism was revealed to all (5.22). Theodoret describes these events without context, but he provides a symbolic image of the overthrow of temple cult during Theodosius' reign.

Church and state

In addition to Theodosius' innovations in the relationship between the state and the heretic or pagan, his reign marked the beginning of a new relationship between emperor and church in the view of later writers (McLynn 1994: 291–330). In 388 a mob in Callinicum near the Persian border had rioted and destroyed a Jewish synagogue. The emperor demanded that the bishop or at least the townspeople pay restitution for this illegal act, but Ambrose, the powerful bishop of Milan, intervened, suggesting that if the Roman military should take the side of the Jews, the Romans would suffer the same fate that the Jewish people had suffered (Ambrose *epp.* 40, 41). Theodosius heeded the bishop's advice.

Theodosius' capitulation to Ambrose over the destruction of the synagogue proved to be a harbinger of his reaction to the bishop's demands after a more celebrated and more significant event in late 390. A popular charioteer tried to rape a Gothic soldier, Butheric, in the city of Thessalonica, and was imprisoned. The people demanded his release, in order that he be able to participate in the games, but were denied. Rioting then broke out, and Butheric and some other Gothic soldiers were killed and their bodies dragged through the city. Neil McLynn has argued that Theodosius' revenge was ineptly carried out by his soldiers (McLynn 1994: 315–30; cf. Williams and Friell 1994: 67–8; King 1960: 77–86). Although the soldiers were authorized to find and kill those responsible, the slaughter spiralled out of control and became an indiscriminate attack against the entire city. Theodoret claims that seven thousand people were killed (5.17.3). Theodosius was faced with a difficult situation, which Ambrose helped to solve. Likening the emperor to King David, Ambrose demanded public penitence before he could receive the eucharist. Reliable details of the penance are lacking, although fifth-century historians claim that Theodosius spent several months as a penitent at Ambrose's church in Milan, dressed in civilian clothes, until he was readmitted to communion at Christmas 390. Rather than admit that he had lost control of his subordinates, the emperor won back the affections of his subjects by a dramatic acceptance of responsibility. The story was then framed by the church historians as an example of redemption, rather than cruelty. The immediate effect of the episode was to strengthen Theodosius' position as emperor. The episode was remembered, however, as marking a new era in the relationship between church and state with the subordination of the emperor to a bishop.

Rufinus describes the massacre quickly but critically, accusing the emperor of satisfying "not justice but madness" (11.18). He claims that the massacre took place in the Hippodrome, probably mistakenly transposing the scene of the original crime with the place of Theodosius' vengeance (McLynn 1994: 320). Rufinus attributes the chastisement of Theodosius not to Ambrose specifically but to "the priests of Italy," the church as a whole, thereby strengthening the archetypal nature of the scene. Rufinus also stresses that something "wonderful" came from the massacre, a law which required thirty days for reflection before the sentence of the emperor would be carried out.

The story is absent from Eunapius and Zosimus, perhaps because the Christian elements could not be easily incorporated into a classicizing frame. Socrates, too, omits the story, which contradicts the message of his history that strong emperors and weak bishops work together to ensure peace in the church.

Theodoret tells the story of Theodosius' penance with far greater detail than any other historical source. First he provides a preface to the story by musing on the propensity of humans to exceed proper boundaries due to their passions, explaining that it is therefore unsurprising to learn that Theodosius committed an act of extreme cruelty. Nevertheless, he promises that the story will be profitable for the reader, and that the details in the end will prove more beneficial than detrimental to Theodosius' reputation (5.16.6–7). The massacre itself is treated cursorily, and he omits the names of those involved, the purpose of the rioting, and even the setting of the events. Theodoret emphasizes only the violence and lack of discrimination in the killing (5.17). He tells the rest of the story with considerable amounts of first-person narration and with an eye toward the dramatic tableau. Theodosius is confronted at the door of the church by Ambrose, who speaks rhetorically and at length: "How could you stretch forth in prayer hands still dripping with the blood of unjust murder?" Theodoret then claims that the emperor spent eight months in the palace weeping and explaining to Rufinus, his pagan master of offices, that his exclusion from the church is nevertheless just. Rufinus attempted to intercede with Ambrose, but the bishop rebuffed him, saying, "Rufinus, you are as shameless as a dog" (5.18.10). Finally the emperor repented for his sins, throwing himself on the floor of the church and tearing his hair. Theodoret particularly highlights Theodosius' submission to Ambrose by claiming that, when the bishop asked the emperor what form his repentence will take, the emperor responded that it is the business of the bishop to command, and the emperor to obey. Theodoret further suggests that the bishop's power over the emperor extended to his ability to demand the promulgation of specific laws, since he claims that Ambrose imposed as a condition of penance the passing of the law which required thirty days' consideration before carrying out a capital sentence. The usefulness of the law, Theodoret claims, was soon revealed during riots in Antioch, after which Theodosius' immediate desire to punish harshly was constrained by the "thirty days" law (5.20.3). In fact, these riots took place in 387, preceding the passage of the law by years. Theodoret's version of the events surrounding the massacre at Thessalonica, then, manipulates chronology and invents dialogue and details to recast the incident as a morality lesson which emphasizes the proper dominance of church over state.

Sozomen's account of the massacre is less pointed and less coherent. He has Ambrose confront Theodosius outside the church in Milan in 394, years after the event. Sozomen places emphasis upon the pathos of the slaughter, providing several anecdotes of brave behavior by the victims, including a faithful slave who chose to die on behalf of his master and a father who saw two of his sons die because of his inability to choose a favorite. Sozomen is less didactic than Theodoret in his account, which is presented as one of several examples of Ambrose's outstanding deeds, and of his boldness when confronting the powerful on behalf of God (7.25).

Magnus Maximus

In addition to information on Theodosius' religious activities, historians provide conflicting information and judgements on the military activities of the emperor. After Theodosius' accession, he fought a series of wars against the Goths which are poorly recorded in our sources. These wars ended in 382 with a treaty of peace and a triumphal procession for Theodosius in Constantinople. While Theodosius was occasionally occupied keeping peace on the frontiers during the rest of his reign, his primary military accomplishment was the suppression of two usurpers in the west. The first usurper was the Spanish general Magnus Maximus, who revolted for reasons unknown in spring 383 and killed the emperor Gratian in Gaul. Maximus tried to come to terms with Theodosius, but the legitimate emperor remained non-committal for several years. The position of the boy emperor Valentinian II at Milan, whose affairs were managed by his mother, Justina, was precarious. Eventually, after Maximus invaded Italy and caused Valentinian to flee, Theodosius marched to northern Italy, where he defeated and killed the usurper in August 388. Theodosius arrived in triumph in Rome the next year and remained in the west until spring 391.

Photius says that Eunapius offered slander and ill will toward every Christian emperor (*cod.* 77), and Eunapius' discussion of Theodosius' campaigns provides good evidence for his assertion. In his criticisms Eunapius tends to recycle the same accusations he had made earlier against Constantine, blaming Theodosius' failures upon an excess of luxury and indolence and condemning the military innovations which he introduced (Buck 1988: 41–2). He states bluntly that during Theodosius' reign "the barbarians gradually ravaged Thrace" (*fr.* 47.2). Eunapius is also critical of Theodosius' policy of recruiting barbarians into the army, and he includes several stories which demonstrate the fundamental untrustworthiness of barbarian soldiers, who are said to have pledged eternal treachery against the Romans (*fr.* 59; Buck 1988: 42–4). Theodosius' success in his western wars serves as an opportunity to lament the wasting of resources that could have been better used for foreign expansion. Eunapius claims that when Theodosius mustered troops for the campaign against Magnus Maximus, the barbarians fled in fear and hid in the marshes. This demonstrated, he argues, that if only Theodosius and the Romans were less concerned with pleasure and ease, they would easily conquer the entire world (*fr.* 55). Eunapius' criticism of the delay between the death of Gratian and the retaliatory invasion by Theodosius is particularly unfair, since in order to protect his eastern flank Theodosius needed sufficient time both to build up the badly depleted army and to conclude negotiations with Persia over the status of Armenia.

Christian authors tend to present a more idealized picture of the emperor's military exploits. Rufinus' history was written to raise the spirits of those discouraged by recent barbarian invasions. Thus he seeks to portray Theodosius as a second Constantine, who does not merely conquer usurpers or enemies, but rather scores victories for the triumph of the true faith over heresy and paganism (Consolino 1994: 264–8; Thélamon 1981: 311–21). For example, Rufinus describes the defeat of Magnus Maximus as a victory not only because "a tyranny had been suppressed," but also because Theodosius restored to Valentinian II "the Catholic faith which his mother," the Arian Justina, "had violated" (11.17).

Socrates provides a more detailed account of Theodosius' military activities than the one we find in Rufinus. He describes the battle with Maximus as a bloodless one, claiming that the soldiers of the usurper were so overawed by Theodosius' preparations that they surrendered their leader to him. In an aside in a discussion of Theodosius' triumphal procession through Rome, Socrates says that the intellectual pagan senator Symmachus had performed an oration before the usurper, and, fearing for his life after Maximus' fall, had sought sanctuary in a church (5.14.4–6). The anecdote allows Socrates to emphasize Theodosius' mercy and to cast a glancing blow against a prominent pagan. Sozomen reveals that Maximus publicly claimed to be moving into Italy on behalf of orthodox Christianity and in opposition to the Arianism of Valentinian's court. The historian rejects this claim as simply a ruse by a power-hungry general. Maximus was an orthodox Christian, and Sozomen here must be reporting traces of the propaganda and counter-propaganda issued by the various courts in the period leading up to the war. Sozomen's information on the battle itself, however, replicates that of Socrates (7.13–14).

For Theodoret, the extreme youth of Valentinian II encouraged Magnus Maximus to invade Italy (5.12). Like Sozomen, he is eager to rebut Maximus' claim to be the upholder of orthodoxy against the Arian Valentinian. The historian thus reproduces the usurper's appeal to the young emperor to return to orthodoxy or face invasion, which must have been publicized by the usurper (5.14). Maximus' arguments appear to have won him some adherents, for Theodoret then provides details he claims to derive from a rebuttal letter of Theodosius, in which the legitimate emperor chastises Valentinian for his heresy and explains that it has led to the dangerous situation which he now faces (5.15). The battle itself takes up only a sentence in Theodoret: Valentinian first was returned to orthodoxy, and then the usurper was executed.

While Orosius does not provide information about church history, he does stress the importance of Theodosius' orthodoxy in guaranteeing his military victories. Theodosius is described as equal in military skills to Trajan, and superior in piety. Because of this superior piety, Orosius argues, Theodosius enjoyed bloodless victories over his enemies, and he also surpassed Trajan, who was without male children, in dynastic creation, since the offspring of Theodosius continued to rule the empire up to Orosius' day (7.34.2–4). In contrast to the Greek ecclesiastical historians, Orosius lauds the military successes of Theodosius which followed immediately upon his accession to the throne. By trust in Christ, Orosius says, Theodosius was able to overcome "Scythian" tribes which had even struck fear in Alexander the Great. Orosius further adds that Theodosius received the submission of all of the Goths and made a peace with the Persians which still lasted in Orosius' day (7.34.5–8). To a greater extent than other historians, Orosius emphasizes the power and nobility of Theodosius' enemies to better demonstrate the role of fervent piety in his success. He emphasizes that Theodosius' forces were inferior to Maximus', and that victory was therefore only possible through religious faith. Orosius similarly claims that Maximus was "strong and honorable and worthy to be Augustus," if only he had not revolted (7.34.9). Orosius draws a lengthy lesson from Theodosius' bloodless victory. "Under Christian kings and in Christian times," when civil wars must be fought, they are concluded without violence (7.35.6).

The Battle of the Frigidus

Theodosius' preparations to return to the East after the defeat of Maximus included placing his general, Arbogast, in control of the west. For several years, Arbogast was the power behind the throne, issuing orders in the name of the teenaged emperor Valentinian II, who committed suicide under suspicious circumstances in May 392 (Croke 1976). After several months of strained relations between Arbogast and Theodosius, Arbogast, who as a barbarian could not aspire to rule the empire, named his own emperor, Eugenius, an obscure former teacher of rhetoric. Although Eugenius was a Christian, under his brief reign pagan ritual was revived. Thus when Arbogast and Eugenius were defeated by Theodosius at the Frigidus river in September 394, it was widely seen as a victory for Christianity. The battle began with an attack by Theodosius' Gothic troops, which was repulsed. Theodosius' army was ultimately victorious, however, thanks to a heavy wind which suddenly blew against the army of the usurper and was widely held among Christians to be a miracle.

Eunapius' partisan approach to Theodosius is most clear in his treatment of the Battle of the Frigidus (Buck 1988: 47–50; *fr.* 60.1). He removes almost every hint of pagan sympathies from the defeated army, such as the Jupiter and Hercules banners under which they fought. Other sources agree that the turning point was a hard, cold wind that blew against the forces of Eugenius and Arbogast. This wind, which other versions attributed to the intercession of the Christian deity, Eunapius replaced with a non-existent eclipse. Theodosius' forces win in a very unheroic fashion, by falling upon the western forces while they slept and killing the majority in their beds.

In Rufinus, the Battle of the Frigidus is set forth as a conflict between Christianity and paganism, the military equivalent of the destruction of the Serapeum (11.33). To further this picture, Rufinus highlights the contrast between Theodosius and the aggressive pagan Nicomachus Flavianus, while mentioning Eugenius and Arbogast only infrequently (Thélamon 1981: 311–21). Theodosius' preparations are religious, not military: he arms himself "not so much with the aid of weapons and arms as with fasts and prayers," he prostrates himself before reliquaries, and he holds nightly vigils before the battle. These preparations contrast with those of the pagans, who explore the entrails of sheep and are reassured by Flavianus that the divination predicts victory for Eugenius. After the first clash of armies, Theodosius' barbarian troops are routed, but this, Rufinus assures us, was arranged by God to ensure that the battle would be won by Romans and not by Goths. At this point in the battle Theodosius prostrates himself and prays to God, and a heavy wind frustrates the forces of Eugenius.

Rufinus is particularly keen to make the victory at the Frigidus psychological and ideological rather than simply military. When Nicomachus Flavianus committed suicide at the end of the battle, he was despondent, Rufinus says, more over the failure of divination than the failure of the usurpation. Similarly, Rufinus concludes his account of the battle with the comment that the victory was glorious more because of the failed prophecies and hopes of the pagans than because of the death of the usurper (11.33).

Socrates gives a much more straightforward account of the Battle of the Frigidus than Rufinus, and he provides almost no religious content. In Socrates, Arbogast and Eugenius plot together to kill Valentinian II out of simple lust for power. There is no suggestion that the battle is a conflict between Christianity and paganism. While Theodosius does pray, and a hard wind does blow, Socrates does not draw an explicit lesson from the events. On the whole, Socrates' treatment provides evidence for the claim that he is less concerned about paganism than are the other church historians (5.25; Urbainczyk 1997b: 156–9).

Sozomen reintegrates religious material into his treatment of the conflict (7.24). He shows Theodosius preparing to head west by praying at the church he had erected to hold the recently discovered head of John the Baptist. As the armies meet in battle, Sozomen describes the familiar story of the emperor prostrating himself and praying for help. In Sozomen's version, however, the prayer has an immediate effect when some of Eugenius' officers, who had been stationed in ambush, agree to defect in return for high posts in Theodosius' army. Sozomen omits the information on Nicomachus Flavianus which Rufinus provided, and he does not explicitly represent the battle as a clash between paganism and Christianity. An anecdote he provides does, however, allude to this idea. At the very time that the battle was being won in the west, a demon appeared in the church where Theodosius had prayed. After pausing to taunt John the Baptist for being decapitated, the demon announced that he, presumably as a stand-in for paganism, had been conquered.

Theodoret's account of the battle is more artfully constructed but less accurate than the other ecclesiastical historians' accounts (5.24). In his version, Theodosius points out the contrast between the Cross of Christ, which was the standard of his army, and the image of Hercules put forward by the enemy. The emperor also has a dream in which John the Baptist and the Apostle Philip promise their aid, and to prove its significance, one of his soldiers has the same dream. As in other Christian versions, the wind blinded the army of the usurpers, who in Theodoret's account surrendered when they realized that God opposes them. When Eugenius is brought before him, Theodosius rebuked him first for his usurpation, and then for his trust in Hercules. Thus Theodoret portrays the purpose of the war more as the suppression of a usurpation than as the upholding of Christianity. While the Christian God is essential to the story, the moral is primarily that Theodosius "always sought divine aid, and always received it" (5.24.17).

Just as Orosius had underlined the virtues of Maximus to further glorify Theodosius' victory, he also portrays Arbogast as a veritable superman, "outstanding in courage, foresight, boldness, and power" (7.35.11). In both cases, Orosius asserts, it is the power of God which overcame the evil plans of men. Orosius describes at length the hard wind, which alternately ripped the shields out of the enemies' hands and crushed the shields too tightly against them. Hurled javelins were blown back to transfix the throwers. Again Orosius emphasizes the lack of bloodshed, although he mentions in passing the death of Theodosius' auxiliary troops, ten thousand Goths, which he sees as a benefit rather than a loss. Orosius ends his account with a challenge to pagans to provide a single example from all of Roman history of a war ending so pleasantly and easily. This demonstrates, he asserts, that heaven prefers the side trusting in God to the side trusting in itself and its idols (7.35.22).

Conclusion

Theodosius died suddenly in 395. He left behind two sons, Honorius and Arcadius, who were weak emperors with undistinguished reigns. Arcadius' son Theodosius II had a long but equally undistinguished reign. In retrospect, the emperor seemed unusually strong and successful in war when compared to emperors who did not personally take the field. Theodosius' posthumous reputation increased substantially at the hands of Christians of the next generation. He was the last emperor to rule the entire Christian empire, and thus remained an important symbol for generations to come. The ruinous civil wars and religious intolerance which the pagan historians deplored were soon overlooked. Late antique Christian historians gathered diverse elements of his reign to create a portrait of an ideal emperor, who was strong enough to crush paganism and heresy, yet submissive to clerical authority.

BIBLIOGRAPHY

Allen, P. (1987) "Some Aspects of Hellenism in the Early Greek Church Historians," *Traditio* 43: 368–81.

—— (1990) "The Use of Heretics and Heresies in the Greek Church Historians: Studies in Socrates and Theodoret," in G. Clarke, B. Croke, A.E. Nobbs, and R. Mortley, eds, *Reading the Past in Late Antiquity*, Rushcutters Bay, Australia: Australian National University Press, 266–89.

Amidon, P.R. (1997) *The* Church History *of Rufinus of Aquileia: Books 10 and 11*, New York: Oxford University Press.

Anderson, G. (1993) *The Second Sophistic*, London: Routledge.

Angliviel de la Beaumelle, L. (1992) "La Torture dans les Res Gestae d'Ammien Marcellin," in M. Christol, ed., *Institutions, société et vie politique dans l'Empire romain au IVe siècle après J.-C.*, Rome: Ecole française de Rome, 91–113.

Arnaud-Lindet, M.-P. (1990) *Orose: Histoire contre les païens*, Paris: Les Belles Lettres.

—— (1994) *Festus: Abrégé des hauts faits du peuple romain*, Paris: Les Belles Lettres.

Arnheim, M.T.W. (1972) *The Senatorial Aristocracy in the Later Roman Empire*, Oxford: Clarendon Press.

Asmussen, J.P. (1983) "Christians in Iran," in *Cambridge History of Iran*, vol. 3, pt. 2, Cambridge: Cambridge University Press.

Athanassiadi, P. (1981/92) *Julian and Hellenism: An Intellectual Biography*, Oxford: Oxford University Press. Second edition (1992) *Julian: An Intellectual Biography*, London: Routledge.

Auerbach, E. (1957) [1946] *Mimesis: The Representation of Reality in Western Literature*, W. Trask, tr., Garden City, N.Y.: Doubleday.

Austin, N.J.E. (1979) *Ammianus on Warfare: An Investigation into Ammianus' Military Knowledge*, Brussels: Latomus.

Avery, W.K. (1940) "The Adoratio Purpurae and the Importance of the Imperial Purple in the Fourth Century of the Christian Era," *Memoirs of the American Academy in Rome* 17: 66–80.

Azema, Y. (1984) "Sur la date de la mort de Théodoret de Cyr," *Pallas* 31: 137–55.

Baldini, A. (1984) *Ricerche sulla Storia di Eunapio di Sardi: problemi di storiografia tardopagana*, Bologna: CLUEB.

Balducci, C. (1947) "La ribellione del generale Silvano nelle Gallie (355)," *Rendiconti dell' Accademia dei Lincei* 8: 423–8.

Baldwin, B. (1975) "The Career of Oribasius," *Acta Classica* 18: 85–97.

—— (1978) "Festus the Historian," *Historia* 27: 197–218.

—— (1980a) "Olympiodorus of Thebes," *L'Antiquité Classique* 49: 212–31.

—— (1980b) "Priscus of Panium," *Byzantion* 50: 18–61.

—— (1981) "Greek Historiography in Late Rome and Early Byzantium," *Hellenika* 33: 51–65.

—— (1990) "The Language and Style of Eunapius," *Byzantinoslavica* 51: 1–19.

Balsdon, J.P.V.D. (1979) *Romans and Aliens*, London: Duckworth.

Banchich, T.M. (1984) "The Date of Eunapius' *Vitae Sophistarum*," *Greek, Roman, and Byzantine Studies* 25: 183–92.

—— (1987) "On Goulet's Chronology of Eunapius' Life and Works," *Journal of Hellenic Studies* 107: 164–7.

—— (1988) "*Vit. Soph.* X.2.3 and the Terminus of the First Edition of Eunapius' *History*," *Rheinisches Museum* 131: 375–80.

—— (1993) "Julian's School Laws: Cod. Theod. 13.5.5 and Ep. 42," *Ancient World* 24: 5–14.

Barcellona, F.S. (1995) "Martiri e confessori dell'età di Giuliano l'Apostata: dalla storia alla leggenda," in F.E. Consolino, ed., *Pagani e Cristiani da Giuliano l'Apostata al Sacco di Roma*, Messina: Rubbetino, 53–83.

Bardy, G. (1946) "Théodoret," in *Dictionnaire de théologie Catholique* 15.1: 299–325.

Barnes, T.D. (1970) "The Lost *Kaisergeschichte* and the Latin Historical Tradition," *Bonner Historia–Augusta–Colloquium 1968/69*: 13–43.

—— (1976) "The *Epitome de Caesaribus* and Its Sources," *Classical Philology* 71: 258–68.

—— (1978) *The Sources of the Historia Augusta*, Brussels: Latomus.

—— (1981) *Constantine and Eusebius*, Cambridge, Mass.: Harvard University Press.

—— (1985) "Constantine and the Christians of Persia," *Journal of Roman Studies* 75: 126–36.

—— (1993a) "Ammianus Marcellinus and His World," *Classical Philology* 88: 55–70.

—— (1993b) *Athanasius and Constantius: Theology and Politics in the Constantinian Empire*, Cambridge, Mass.: Harvard University Press.

—— (1998) *Ammianus Marcellinus and the Representation of Historical Reality*, Ithaca, N.Y.: Cornell University Press.

Bartalucci, A. (1976) "Lingua e Stile in Paolo Orosio," *Studi classici e orientali* 25: 213–56.

Bartelink, G.J.M. (1969) "Eunape et le vocabulaire chrétien," *Vigiliae Christianae* 23: 293–303.

Bell, H.I. (1924) *Jews and Christians in Egypt: The Jewish Troubles in Alexandria and the Athanasian Controversy*, London: British Museum.

Bihain, E. (1962a) "Le 'Contre Eunome' de Théodore de Mopsueste, source d'un passage de Sozomène et d'un passage de Théodoret concernant Cyrille de Jérusalem," *Le Muséon* 75: 331–55.

—— (1962b) "La source d'un texte de Socrate (HE 2.38.3) relatif à Cyrille de Jérusalem," *Byzantion* 32: 81–91.

Bird, H.W. (1973) "Further Observations on the Dating of Enmann's Kaisergeschichte," *Classical Quarterly* 23: 375–7.

—— (1975) "A Reconstruction of the Life and Career of S. Aurelius Victor," *Classical Journal* 70: 49–54.

—— (1984) *Sextus Aurelius Victor: A Historiographical Study*, Liverpool: Francis Cairns.

—— (1986) "Eutropius on Numa Pompilius and the Senate," *Classical Journal* 81: 243–8.

—— (1987) "The Roman Emperors: Eutropius' Perspective," *Ancient History Bulletin* 1: 139–51.

—— (1988a) "Eutropius: His Life and Career," *Échos du monde classique* 32: 51–60.

—— (1998b) "Eutropius: In Defence of the Senate," *Cahiers des études anciennes* 20: 63–72

—— (1989) "A Strange Aggregate of Errors for A.D. 193," *Classical Bulletin* 65: 95–8.

—— (1990) "Structure and Themes in Eutropius' Breviarium," *Classical Bulletin* 66: 87–92.

—— (1992) *Eutropius: Breviarium ab Urbe Condita*, Liverpool: Liverpool University Press.

—— (1994) *Aurelius Victor: De Caesaribus*, Liverpool: Liverpool University Press.

Blanchetière, F. (1980) "Julien. Philhellène, Philosémite, Antichrétien. L'affaire du Temple de Jérusalem (363)," *Journal of Jewish Studies* 31: 61–81.

Blockley, R.C. (1969) "Internal Self-Policing in the Late Roman Administration. Some Evidence from Ammianus Marcellinus," *Classica et Medievalia* 30: 403–19.

—— (1971) "Dexippus of Athens and Eunapius of Sardis," *Latomus* 30: 710–15.

—— (1972a) "Constantius Gallus and Julian as Caesars of Constantius II," *Latomus* 32: 63–78.

—— (1972b) "Dexippus and Priscus and the Thucydidean Account of the Siege of Plataea," *Phoenix* 26: 18–27.

—— (1975) *Ammianus Marcellinus. A Study of His Historiography and Political Thought*, Brussels: Latomus.

—— (1977) "Ammianus Marcellinus on the Battle of Strasbourg: Art and Analysis in the History," *Phoenix* 31: 218–31.

—— (1980a) "Constantius II and his Generals," in C. Deroux, ed., *Studies in Latin Literature and Roman History II*, Brussels: Latomus, 467–86.

—— (1980b) "The Ending of Eunapius' History," *Antichthon* 14: 170–6.

—— (1981) *The Fragmentary Classicising Historians of the Later Roman Empire: Eunapius, Olympiodorus, Priscus and Malchus*, vol. 1. Liverpool: Francis Cairns.

—— (1983) *The Fragmentary Classicising Historians of the Later Roman Empire: Eunapius, Olympiodorus, Priscus and Malchus*, vol. 2. Liverpool: Francis Cairns.

—— (1986) "The Coded Message in Ammianus Marcellinus 18.6.17–29," *Échos du monde classique* 30: 63–5.

—— (1992) *East Roman Foreign Policy: Formation and Conduct from Diocletian to Anastasius*, Leeds: Francis Cairns.

—— (1998) "Ammianus and Cicero: The Epilogue of the History as a Literary Statement," *Phoenix* 52: 305–14.

Bonamente, G. (1986) *Giuliano l'Apostata e il Breviario di Eutropio*, Rome: Giorgio Bretschneider.

Bonanni, S. (1981) "Ammiano Marcellino e i Barbari," *Rivista di Cultura Classica e Medioevale* 23: 125–42.

Bornmann, F. (1974) "Osservazioni sul testo dei Frammenti di Prisco," *Maia* 26: 111–20.

—— (1979) *Prisci Panitae Fragmenta*, Firenze: Le Monnier.

Bouffartigue, J. (1992) *L'Empereur Julien et la culture de son temps*, Paris: Institut d'études augustiniennes.

Bowersock, G.W. (1978) *Julian the Apostate*, Cambridge, Mass.: Harvard University Press.

—— (1986) "From Emperor to Bishop: The Self-Conscious Transformation of Political Power in the Fourth Century A.D.," *Classical Philology* 81: 298–307.

—— (1990a) *Hellenism in Late Antiquity*, Ann Arbor: University of Michigan Press.

—— (1990b) Review of Matthews (1989), *Journal of Roman Studies* 80: 244–50.

Bowersock, G.W., P. Brown, and O. Grabar, eds (1999) *Late Antiquity: A Guide to the Postclassical World*, Cambridge, Mass.: Harvard University Press.

Braun, R. and J. Richer (1978) *L'Empereur Julien de l'histoire à la légende (331–1715)*, Paris: Les Belles Lettres.

Braund, D. (1994) *Georgia in Antiquity: A History of Colchis and Transcaucasian Iberia 550 BC–AD 562*, Oxford: Clarendon Press.

Breebaart, A.B. (1979) "Eunapius of Sardis and the Writing of History," *Mnemosyne* 32: 360–75.

Brock, S.P. (1982) "Christians in the Sasanian Empire: A Case of Divided Loyalties," *Studies in Church History* 18: 1–19.

—— (1994) "Greek and Syriac in Late Antique Syria," in A.K. Bowman and G. Woolf, eds, *Literacy and Power in the Ancient World*, Cambridge: Cambridge University Press, 149–60.

Brok, M.F.A. (1976/7) "Un Maletendu tenace (Les rapports entre Hérodien et Ammien Marcellin," *Revue des études anciennes* 78/9: 199–207.

Brown, P. (1971) *The World of Late Antiquity AD 150–750*, New York: W.W. Norton.

—— (1972) *Religion and Society in the Age of Saint Augustine*, New York: Harper & Row.

—— (1988) *The Body and Society: Men, Women and Sexual Renunciation in Early Christianity*, New York: Columbia University Press.

Browning, R. (1975) *The Emperor Julian*, London: Weidenfeld & Nicolson.

Buchheit, V. (1958) "Rufinus von Aquileia als Fälscher des Adamantiosdialogs," *Byzantinische Zeitschrift* 51: 314–28.

Buck, D.F. (1987) "Dexippus, Eunapius, Olympiodorus: Continuation and Imitation," *Ancient History Bulletin* 1: 48–50.

—— (1988) "Eunapius of Sardis and Theodosius the Great," *Byzantion* 58: 36–53.

—— (1993) "Eunapius on Julian's Acclamation as Augustus," *Ancient History Bulletin* 7: 73–80.

Burgess, R.W. (1993) "*Principes cum Tyrannis*: Two Studies on the *Kaisergeschichte* and its Tradition," *Classical Quarterly* 43: 491–500.

Burrus, V. (1995) *The Making of a Heretic: Gender, Authority, and the Priscillianist Controversy*, Berkeley: University of California Press.

Cameron, A. (1993a) *The Later Roman Empire: AD 284–430*, Cambridge, Mass.: Harvard University Press.

—— (1993b) *The Mediterranean World in Late Antiquity: AD 395–600*, London: Routledge.

Cameron, A.D.E. (1964) "The Roman Friends of Ammianus," *Journal of Roman Studies* 54: 15–28.

—— (1965) "Wandering Poets. A Literary Movement in Byzantine Egypt," *Historia* 14: 470–509.

—— (1982) "The Empress and the Poet: Paganism and Politics at the Court of Theodosius II," *Yale Classical Studies* 27: 217–89.

—— (1985) "Polyonymy in the Late Roman Aristocracy: The Case of Petronius Probus," *Journal of Roman Studies* 75: 164–82.

Canivet, P. (1958) *Thérapeutique des maladies helléniques*, Paris: Editions du Cerf.

Canivet, P. and A. Leroy-Molinghen, eds (1977) *Théodoret de Cyr: Histoire des Moines de Syrie*, Paris: Editions du Cerf.

Capozza, M. (1962/3) "Nota sulle fonti di Eutropio per l'età regia," *Mem. Acc. Patav. Cl. Scienze mor. Lett. Arti* 75: 349–85.

—— (1973) *Roma fra monarchia e decemvirato nell'interpretazione di Eutropio*, Rome: Università di Padova.

Chadwick, H. (1976) *Priscillian of Avila: The Occult and the Charismatic in the Early Church*, Oxford: Clarendon Press.

Chalmers, W.R. (1953) "The *Nea Ekdosis* of Eunapius' *Histories*," *Classical Quarterly* 3: 165–70.

—— (1960) "Eunapius, Ammianus Marcellinus and Zosimus on Julian's Persian Expedition," *Classical Quarterly* 10: 152–60.

Chauvot, A. (1992) "Parthes et Perses dans les sources du IVe siècle," in M. Christol, ed., *Institutions, société et vie politique dans l'Empire romain au IVe siècle après J.-C.*, Rome: Ecole française de Rome, 115–25.

—— (1998) *Opinions Romaines face aux Barbares au IVe siècle ap. J.-C.*, Paris: De Boccard.

Chesnut, G.F. (1975) "Kairos and Cosmic Sympathy in the Church Historian Socrates Scholasticus," *Church History* 44: 161–6.

—— (1986) *The First Christian Histories: Eusebius, Socrates, Sozomen, Theodoret, and Evagrius*, Macon, GA: Mercer University Press.

Chitty, D.J. (1966) *The Desert a City: An Introduction to the Study of Egyptian and Palestinian Monasticism under the Christian Empire*, Oxford: Basil Blackwell.

Christensen, T. (1989) *Rufinus of Aquileia and the Historia ecclesiastica, Lib. VIII–IX, of Eusebius*, Copenhagen: Kongelige Danske videnskabernes selskab.

Chuvin, P. (1990) *A Chronicle of the Last Pagans*, Cambridge, Mass.: Harvard University Press.

Cichocka, H. (1975) "Die Konzeption des Exkurses im Geschichtswerk des Ammianus Marcellinus," *Eos* 63: 329–40.

Cizek, E. (1989) "L'image de l'autre et les mentalités romaines du Ier au IVe siècle de notre ère," *Latomus* 48: 360–71.

Clark, E.A. (1992) *The Origenist Controversy*, Princeton: Princeton University Press.

Classen, C.J. (1972) "Greek and Roman in Ammianus Marcellinus' History," *Museum Africum* 1: 39–47.

—— (1988) "'Nec spuens, aut os aut nasum tergens vel fricans' (Amm. Marc. XVI 10,10)," *Rheinisches Museum für Philologie* 131: 177–86.

Clover, F.M. (1983) "Olympiodorus of Thebes and the Historia Augusta," *Bonner Historia–Augusta–Colloquium 1979/1981* 15: 127–56.

Cohn, A. (1884) "Quibus ex fontibus Sex. Aurelii Victoris et libri de Caesaribus et Epitomes undecim capita priora fluxerint," Diss. Berlin: Adolf Cohn.

Conduché, D. (1965) "Ammien Marcellin et la mort de Julien," *Latomus* 24: 359–80.

Consolino, F.E. (1994) "Teodosio e il ruolo del principe cristiano dal *De obitu* di Ambrogio alle storie ecclesiastiche," *Cristianesimo nella storia* 15: 257–77.

Corsini, E. (1968) *Introduzione alle "Storie" di Orosio*, Turin: G. Giappichelli.

Courcelle, P. (1969) "Jugements de Rufin et de Saint Augustin sur les empereurs du IVe siècle et la défaite suprême du paganisme," *Revue des études anciennes* 71: 100–30.

Croke, B. (1976) "Arbogast and the Death of Valentinian II," *Historia* 25: 235–44.

—— (1983) "The Context and Date of Priscus Fragment 6," *Classical Philology* 78: 297–308.

Crouzel, H. (1998) *Origen*, A.S. Worrall, tr., Edinburgh: T. & T. Clark.

Crump, G.A. (1975) *Ammianus Marcellinus as a Military Historian*, Wiesbaden: Steiner.

Dauge, Y.A. (1981) *Le Barbare: Recherches sur la conception romaine de la barbarie et de la civilisation*, Brussels: Latomus.

de Jonge, P. (1948) "Scarcity of Corn and Corn-Prices in Ammianus Marcellinus," *Mnemosyne* 4: 238–45.

den Boeft, J. (1992) "Ammianus graecissans?," in J. den Boeft, D. den Hengst, and H.C. Teitler, eds, *Cognitio Gestorum: The Historographic Art of Ammianus Marcellinus*, Amsterdam: Royal Netherlands Academy of Arts and Sciences, 9–18.

—— (1999) "Pure Rites: Ammianus Marcellinus on the Magi," in J.W. Drijvers and D. Hunt, eds, *The Late Roman World and its Historian: Interpreting Ammianus Marcellinus*, London: Routledge, 207–15.

den Boeft, J., J.W. Drijvers, D. den Hengst, and H.C. Teitler (1998) *Philological and Historical Commentary on Ammianus Marcellinus XXIII*, Groningen: Egbert Forsten.

den Boer, W. (1960) "The Emperor Silvanus and His Army," *Acta Classica* 3: 105–9.

—— (1972) *Some Minor Roman Historians*, Leiden: E.J. Brill.

den Hengst, D. (1992) "The Scientific Digressions in Ammianus' Res Gestae," in J. den Boeft, D. den Hengst, and H.C. Teitler, eds, *Cognitio Gestorum: The Historiographic Art of Ammianus Marcellinus*, Amsterdam: Royal Netherlands Academy of Arts and Sciences, 39–46.

—— (1999) "Preparing the Reader for War: Ammianus' digression on siege engines," in J.W. Drijvers and D. Hunt, eds, *The Late Roman World and its Historian: Interpreting Ammianus Marcellinus*, London: Routledge, 29–39.

DiMaio, M. and W. Arnold (1992) *"Per vim, per caedem, per bellum*: A Study of Murder and Ecclesiastical Politics in the Year 337 AD," *Byzantion* 62: 158–91.

Downey, G. (1951) "The Economic Crisis at Antioch Under Julian the Apostate," in P.R. Coleman-Norton, ed., *Studies in Roman Economic and Social History in Honor of Allan Chester Johnson*, Freeport, N.Y.: Books for Libraries Press, 312–21.

—— (1965) "The Perspective of the Early Church Historians," *Greek, Roman, and Byzantine Studies* 6: 57–70.

Drijvers, J.W. (1992) "Ammianus Marcellinus 23.1.2–3: The Rebuilding of the Temple in Jerusalem," in J. den Boeft, D. den Hengst, and H.C. Teitler, eds, *Cognitio Gestorum: The Historiographic Art of Ammianus Marcellinus*, Amsterdam: Royal Netherlands Academy of Arts and Sciences, 19–26.

—— (1999) "Ammianus Marcellinus' Image of Arsaces and Early Parthian History," in J.W. Drijvers and D. Hunt, eds, *The Late Roman World and its Historian: Interpreting Ammianus Marcellinus*, London: Routledge, 193–206.

Drinkwater, J.F. (1983) "The 'Pagan Underground,' Constantius II's 'Secret Service', and the Survival, and the Usurpation, of Julian the Apostate," in C. Deroux, ed., *Studies in Latin Literature and Roman History III*, Brussels: Latomus, 348–87.

—— (1994) "Silvanus, Ursicinus and Ammianus Marcellinus: fact or fiction?", in C. Deroux, ed., *Studies in Latin Literature and Roman History VII*, Brussels: Latomus, 568–76.

—— (1997) "Julian and the Franks and Valentinian I and the Alamanni: Ammianus on Romano-German relations," *Francia* 24: 1–15.

—— (1999) "Ammianus, Valentinian and the Rhine Germans," in J.W. Drijvers and D. Hunt, eds, *The Late Roman World and its Historian: Interpreting Ammianus Marcellinus*, London: Routledge, 127–37.

Dufraigne, P. (1975) *Aurelius Victor: Livre de Césars*, Paris: Les Belles Lettres.

Duval, Y.-M. (1970) "La venue à Rome de l'empereur Constance II en 357, d'après Ammien Marcellin (XVI, 10, 1–20)," *Caesarodunum* 5: 299–304.

Eadie, J.W. (1967) *The* Breviarium *of Festus*, London: The Athlone Press.

Elliott, T.G. (1983) *Ammianus Marcellinus and Fourth Century History*, Sarasota, FL: Samuel Stevens & Company.

Emmett, A. (1981) "Introductions and Conclusions to Digressions in Ammianus Marcellinus," *Museum Philologum Londiniense* 5: 15–33.

Enmann, A. (1884) "Eine verlorene Geschichte der römischen Kaiser und das Buch de viris illustribus urbis Romae," *Philologus* supp. 4: 337–501.

Errington, R.M. (1996) "The Accession of Theodosius I," *Klio* 78: 438–53.

—— (1997) "Christian Accounts of the Religious Legislation of Theodosius I," *Klio* 79: 398–443.

Ettlinger, G.H. (1975) *Eranistes*, Oxford: Clarendon Press.

Evans, R.F. (1968) *Pelagius: Inquiries and Reappraisals*, New York: Seabury Press.

Fabbrini, F. (1979) *Paolo Orosio uno storico*, Rome: Edizione di storia e letteratura.

Fedalto, G. (1992) "Rufino di Concordia. Elementi di una biografia," *Antichità altoadriatiche* 39: 19–44.

Feldman, L. (1993) *Jew and Gentile in the Ancient World: Attitudes and Interactions from Alexander to Justinian*, Princeton: Princeton University Press.

Fontaine, J. (1978) "Le Julien d'Ammien," in R. Braun and J. Riché, eds, *L'Empereur Julien, de l'histoire à la légende 331–1715*, Paris: Les Belles Lettres, 31–65.

—— (1992) "Le style d'Ammien Marcellin et l'esthétique théodosienne," in J. den Boeft, D. den Hengst, and H.C. Teitler, eds, *Cognitio Gestorum:*

The Historiographic Art of Ammianus Marcellinus, Amsterdam: Royal Netherlands Academy of Arts and Sciences, 27–38.

Fornara, C.W. (1983) *The Nature of History in Ancient Greece and Rome*, Berkeley: University of California Press.

—— (1990) "The Prefaces of Ammianus Marcellinus," in M. Griffith and D.J. Mastronarde, eds, *The Cabinet of the Muses*, Atlanta: Scholars Press, 163–72.

—— (1991) "Julian's Persian Expedition in Ammianus and Zosimus," *Journal of Hellenic Studies* 111: 1–15.

—— (1992a) "Studies in Ammianus Marcellinus I: The Letter of Libanius and Ammianus' Connection with Antioch," *Historia* 41: 328–44.

—— (1992b) "Studies in Ammianus Marcellinus II: Ammianus' Knowledge and Use of Greek and Latin Literature," *Historia* 41: 420–38.

Frakes, R.M. (1995) "Cross-References to the Lost Books of Ammianus Marcellinus," *Phoenix* 49: 232–46.

Frank, R.I. (1972) "Ammianus on Roman Taxation," *American Journal of Philology* 93: 69–89.

Frend, W.H.C. (1970) "The Missions of the Early Church 180–700 A.D.," in *Miscellanea Historiae Ecclesiasticae 3*, Louvain: Publications Universitaires de Louvan, 2–23.

—— (1984) *The Rise of Christianity*, Philadelphia: Fortress Press.

—— (1989) "Augustine and Orosius on the End of the Ancient World," *Augustinian Studies* 20: 1–38.

Frézouls, E. (1962) "La mission du 'magister equitum' Ursicin en Gaule (355–357) d'après Ammien Marcellin," in M. Renard, ed., *Hommages à Albert Grenier II*, Brussels: Latomus, 673–88.

Funke, H. (1967) "Majestäts- und Magieprozesse bei Ammianus Marcellinus," *Jahrbuch für Antike und Christentum* 10: 145–75.

Geiger, J. (1979) "Ammianus Marcellinus and the Jewish Revolt under Gallus: A Note," *Liverpool Classical Monthly* 4: 77.

—— (1979/80) "The Last Jewish Revolt against Rome: A Reconsideration," *Scripta Classica Israelica* 5: 250–7.

Geppert, F. (1898) *Die Quellen des Kirchenhistorikers Socrates Scholasticus*, Leipzig: Theodor Weicher.

Giangrande, G. (1956) "Caratteri stilistici delle *Vitae Sophistarum* di Eunapio," *Bolletino del Comitato per la preparazione dell'edizione nazionale dei classici greci e latini* 4: 59–70.

Gillett, A. (1992) "The Date and Circumstances of Olympiodorus of Thebes," *Traditio* 48: 1–29.

Gilliam, J.F. (1972) "Ammianus and the Historia Augusta: The Lost Books and the Period 117–285," *Bonner Historia–Augusta–Colloquium 1970*, Bonn: 125–47.

Gimazane, J. (1889) *Ammien Marcellin, sa vie et son oeuvre*, Toulouse: Edouard Privat.

Glas, Anton (1914) *Die Kirchengeschichte des Gelasios von Kaisareia*, Leipzig: Teubner.

Gordon, C.D. (1960) *The Age of Attila: Fifth-Century Byzantium and the Barbarians*, Ann Arbor: University of Michigan Press.

Goulet, R. (1980) "Sur la chronologie de la vie et des oeuvres d'Eunape de Sardes," *Journal of Hellenic Studies* 100: 60–72.

Grant, R.M. (1980) *Eusebius as Church Historian*, Oxford: Clarendon Press.

Gregory, T.E. (1975) "Novatianism: A Rigorist Sect in the Christian Roman Empire," *Byzantine Studies* 2: 1–18.

Grillet, B., G. Sabbah, and A.-J. Festugière (1983) *Sozomène: histoire ecclési-astique, livres I–II*, Paris: Editions du Cerf.

Guinot, J.-N. (1984) "Un évêque exégète: Théodoret de Cyr," in C. Mondésert, ed., *Le monde grec ancien et la Bible*, Paris: Beauchesne, 335–60.

—— (1995) *L'Exégèse de Théodoret de Cyr*, Paris: Beauchesne.

Güldenpenning, A. (1889) *Die Kirchengeschichte des Theodore von Kyrrhos. Eine Untersuchung ihrer quellen*, Halle: Max Niemeyer.

Guyot, P. (1980) *Eunuchen als Sklaven und Freigelassene in der griechisch-römis-chen Antike*, Stuttgart: Klett-Cotta.

Haas, C.J. (1991) "The Alexandrian Riots of 356 and George of Cappadocia," *Greek, Roman, and Byzantine Studies* 32: 281–301.

Halton, T. (1988) *Theodoret of Cyrus: On Divine Providence*, New York: Newman Press.

Hammond, C.P. (1977) "The Last Ten Years of Rufinus' Life and the Date of his Move South from Aquileia," *Journal of Theological Studies* 28: 372–429.

Hanson, R.P.G. (1988) *The Search for the Christian Doctrine of God*, Edin-burgh: T. & T. Clark.

Hardy, B.C. (1968) "The Emperor Julian and his School Law," *Church History* 37: 131–43.

Harries, J. (1991) "Patristic Historiography," in I. Hazett, ed., *Early Chris-tianity: Origins and Evolution to AD 600 in Honour of W.H.C. Frend*, Nashville: Abingdon Press, 269–80.

—— (1999) *Law and Empire in Late Antiquity*, Cambridge: Cambridge University Press.

Harrison, T. (1999) "*Templum Mundi Totius*: Ammianus and a religious idea of Rome," in J.W. Drijvers and D. Hunt, eds, *The Late Roman World and its Historian: Interpreting Ammianus Marcellinus*, London: Routledge, 178–90.

Heather, P.J. (1986) "The Crossing of the Danube and the Gothic Conver-sion," *Greek, Roman, and Byzantine Studies* 27: 289–318.

—— (1991) *Goths and Romans 332–489*, Oxford: Clarendon Press.

—— (1995) "The Huns and the End of the Roman Empire in Western Europe," *English Historical Review* 110: 4–41.

—— (1996) *The Goths*, Oxford: Blackwell.

—— (1999a) "Ammianus on Jovian," in J.W. Drijvers and D. Hunt, eds, *The Late Roman World and its Historian: Interpreting Ammianus Marcellinus*, London: Routledge, 105–16.

—— (1999b) "The Barbarian in Late Antiquity: Image, reality, and transformation," in R. Miles, ed., *Constructing Identities in Late Antiquity*, London: Routledge, 234–57.

Hellegouarc'h, J. (1999) *Eutrope: abrégé d'histoire romaine*, Paris: Les Belles Lettres.

Heyen, J. (1968) "A propos de la conception historique d'Ammien Marcellin (*Ut miles quondam et Graecus*, 21.16.9)," *Latomus* 27: 191–6.

Hill, R.C. (2000) *Theodoret of Cyrus: Commentary on the Psalms, Psalms 1–72*, Washington, D.C.: The Catholic University of America Press.

Holum, K.G. (1982) *Theodosian Empresses: Women and Dominion in Late Antiquity*, Berkeley: University of California Press.

Honoré, T. (1998) *Law in the Crisis of Empire, 379–455 AD*, Oxford: Clarendon Press.

Hopwood, K. (1978) "The Political Power of Eunuchs," in *Conquerors and Slaves: Sociological Studies in Roman History Volume I*, Cambridge: Cambridge University Press, 172–96.

Humphreys, M. (1999) "*Nec Metu Nec Adulandi Foeditate Constricta*: The Image of Valentinian I from Symmachus to Ammianus," in J.W. Drijvers and D. Hunt, eds, *The Late Roman World and its Historian: Interpreting Ammianus Marcellinus*, London: Routledge, 117–26.

Hunt, E.D. (1982) *Holy Land Pilgrimage in the Later Roman Empire AD 312–460*, Oxford: Clarendon Press.

—— (1985) "Christians and Christianity in Ammianus Marcellinus," *Classical Quarterly* 35: 186–200.

—— (1993) "Christianity in Ammianus Marcellinus Revisited," *Studia Patristica* 24: 108–13.

—— (1999) "The Outsider Inside: Ammianus on the rebellion of Silvanus," in J.W. Drijvers and D. Hunt, eds, *The Late Roman World and its Historian: Interpreting Ammianus Marcellinus*, London: Routledge, 51–63.

Inglebert, H. (1996) *Les Romains chrétiens face à l'histoire de Rome: histoire, christianisme et romanités en Occident dans l'Antiquité tardive (IIIe–Ve siècles)*, Paris: Institut d'études augustiniennes.

Janvier, Y. (1982) *La géographie d'Orose*, Paris: Les Belles Lettres.

Jones, A.H.M. (1964) *The Later Roman Empire, 284–602: A Social, Economic, and Administrative Survey*, Norman, OK: University of Oklahoma Press.

—— (1966) *The Decline of the Ancient World*, New York: Longman.

Kelly, C. (1998) "Emperors, Government and Bureaucracy," in A.Cameron and P. Garnsey, eds, *Cambridge Ancient History vol. 13, The Late Empire: A.D. 337–425*, Cambridge: Cambridge University Press, 138–83.

Kelly, J.N.D. (1959) *Early Christian Doctrines*, New York: Harper & Brothers.

—— (1975) *Jerome: His Life, Writings, and Controversies*, New York: Harper & Row.

—— (1995) *Golden Mouth: The Story of John Chrysostom – Ascetic, Preacher, Bishop*, London: Duckworth.

King, C. (1987) "The Veracity of Ammianus Marcellinus' Description of the Huns," *American Journal of Ancient History* 12: 77–95.

King, N.Q. (1960) *The Emperor Theodosius and the Establishment of Christianity*, Philadelphia: Westminster Press.

Klein, R. (1979) "Der Rombesuch des Kaisers Konstantius II. im Jahre 357," *Athenaeum* 57: 98–115.

Koch, W. (1927/8) "Comment l'empereur Julien tacha de fonder une église païenne," *Revue belge de philologie et d'histoire* 6: 123–46; 7: 49–82, 511–50, 1363–85.

Kohns, H. (1975) "Die Zeitkritik in den Romexkursen des Ammianus Marcellinus," *Chiron* 5: 485–91.

La Croix, B. (1965) *Orose et ses Idées*, Montréal: Institut d'Études Médiévales.

Ladner, G.B. (1976) "On Roman Attitudes Toward Barbarians in Late Antiquity," *Viator* 7: 1–26.

Lane Fox, R. J. (1987) *Pagans and Christians*, New York: Knopf.

—— (1997) "The Itinerary of Alexander: Constantius to Julian," *Classical Quarterly* 47: 239–52.

Lenski, N. (1995) "The Gothic Civil War and the Date of the Gothic Conversion," *Greek, Roman, and Byzantine Studies* 36: 51–87.

—— (1997) "*Initium mali Romano imperio*: Contemporary Reactions to the Battle of Adrianople," *Transactions and Proceedings of the American Philological Society* 127: 129–68.

—— (2000) "The Election of Jovian and the Role of the Late Imperial Guards," *Klio* 82: 492–515.

Leroy-Molinghen, A. (1980) "Naissance et enfance de Théodoret," in A. Théodoridès, P. Naster, and J. Ries, eds, *L'enfant dans les civilisations orientales*, Louvain: Peeters, 153–8.

Levenson, D. (1972) *Antioch: City and Imperial Administration in the Later Roman Empire*, Oxford: Oxford University Press.

—— (1990a) "Julian's Attempt to Rebuild the Temple: An Inventory of Ancient and Medieval Sources," in H.W. Attridge, J.J. Collins, and T.H. Tobin, eds, *Of Scribes and Scrolls. Studies on the Hebrew Bible, Intertestamental Judaism, and Christian Origins Presented to John Strugnell on the Occasion of his Sixtieth Birthday*, Lanham, University Press of America, 261–79.

—— (1990b) *Barbarians and Bishops: Army, Church, and State in the Age of Arcadius and Chrysostom*, Oxford: Clarendon Press.

Liebeschuetz, J.H.W.G. (1972) *Antioch: City and Imperial Administration in the Later Roman Empire*, Oxford: Oxford University Press.

—— (1990) *Barbarians and Bishops: Army, Church, and State in the Age of Arcadius and Chrysostom*, Oxford: Clarendon Press.

Lieu, S.N.C. (1986) *The Emperor Julian: Panegyric and Polemic*, Liverpool: Liverpool University Press.

Livrea, E. (1978) *Anonymi fortasse Olimpiodori Thebani Blemyomachia (P. Berol. 5003)*, Meisenheim am Glan: A. Hain.

Luiselli, B. (1984/5) "L'idea romana di Barbari nell'età delle grandi invasioni germaniche," *Romanobarbarica* 8: 33–61.

MacMullen, R. (1964) "Some Pictures in Ammianus Marcellinus," *Art Bulletin* 46: 435–55.

—— (1981) *Paganism in the Roman Empire*, New Haven: Yale University Press.

Maenchen-Helfen, J.O. (1973) *The World of the Huns: Studies in their History and culture*, Berkeley: University of California Press.

Malcovati, E. (1942) "I Breviari del IV secolo," *Annali della Facoltà di Lettere, Filosofia, e Magistero dell'Università di Cagliari Bari Università* 21: 23–42.

Marchetta, A. (1987) *Orosio e Ataulfo nell'Ideologia dei Rapporti Romano-Barbarici*, Rome: Istituto Storico Italiano per il Medio Evo.

Marcone, A. (1979) "Il Significato della Spedizione di Giuliano contro la Persia," *Athenaeum* 57: 334–56.

Marincola, J. (1997) *Authority and Tradition in Ancient Historiography*, Cambridge: Cambridge University Press.

Markus, R.A. (1975) "Church History and the Early Church Historians," *Studies in Church History* 11: 1–17.

—— (1990) *The End of Ancient Christianity*, Cambridge: Cambridge University Press.

Matthews, J. (1970) "Olympiodorus of Thebes and the History of the West (A.D. 407–425)," *Journal of Roman Studies* 60: 79–97.

—— (1975) *Western Aristocracies and Imperial Court, A.D. 364–425*, Oxford: Clarendon Press.

—— (1986) "Ammianus and the Eternity of Rome," in C. Holdsworth and T.P. Wiseman, eds, *The Inheritance of Historiography, 350–900*, Exeter: University of Exeter Press.

—— (1987) "Peter Valvomeres, Re-arrested," in J.C. Bramble, M. Whitby, P.R. Hardie, and M. Whitby, eds, *Homo Viator: Classical Essays for John Bramble*, Bristol: Bristol Classical Press, 277–84.

—— (1989) *The Roman Empire of Ammianus*, Baltimore: The Johns Hopkins University Press.

—— (1992) "Ammianus on Roman Law and Lawyers," in J. den Boeft, D. den Hengst, and H.C. Teitler, eds, *Cognitio Gestorum: The Historiographic Art of Ammianus Marcellinus*, Amsterdam: Royal Netherlands Academy of Arts and Sciences, 47–58.

—— (1994) "The Origin of Ammianus," *Classical Quarterly* 44: 252–69.

—— (2000) *Laying Down the Law: A Study of the Theodosian Code*, New Haven: Yale University Press.

Mayer, W. and P. Allen (2000) *John Chrysostom*, London: Routledge.

Mazza, M. (1980) "Sulla teoria della storiografia cristiana: osservazioni sui proemi degli storici ecclesiastici," in S. Calderone, ed., *La storiografia ecclesiastica nella tarda antichità*, Messina: Centro di studi umanistici, 335–89.

McCoy, M.B. (1985) "Corruption in the Western Empire: The Career of Sextus Petronius Probus," *Ancient World* 11: 101–6.

McLynn, N. (1994) *Ambrose of Milan: Church and Court in a Christian Capital*, Berkeley: University of California Press.

Meulder, M. (1991) "Julien l'Apostat contre les Parthes: un guerrier impie," *Byzantion* 61: 458–95.

Millar, F. (1969) "P. Herennius Dexippus: The Greek World and the Third-Century Invasions," *Journal of Roman Studies* 59: 12–29.

Momigliano, A. (1963) "Pagan and Christian Historiography in the Fourth Century A.D.," in A. Momigliano, ed., *The Conflict Between Paganism and Christianity in the Fourth Century*, Oxford: Clarendon Press, 79–99.

—— (1990) "The Origins of Ecclesiastical Historiography," in A. Momigliano, ed., *The Classical Foundations of Modern Historiography*, Berkeley: University of California Press, 132–52.

Mommsen, T.E. (1959) "Orosius and Augustine," in *Medieval and Renaissance Studies*, Ithaca, N.Y.: Cornell University Press, 325–48.

Mortley, R. (1990) "The Hellenistic Foundations of Ecclesiastical Historiography," in G. Clarke, B. Croke, A.E. Nobbs, and R. Mortley, eds, *Reading the Past in Late Antiquity*, Rushcutters Bay, Australia: Australian National University Press, 225–50.

Müller-Seidl, I. (1955) "Die Usurpation Julians des Abtrünnigen im Lichte seiner Germanenpolitik," *Historische Zeitschrift* 180: 225–44.

Munro-Hay, S. (1988) *Aksum: An African Civilisation of Late Antiquity*, Edinburgh: Edinburgh University Press.

Murphy, F.X. (1945) *Rufinus of Aquileia (345–411): His Life and Works*, Washington, D.C.: Catholic University Press.

—— (1956) "Rufinus of Aquileia and Paulinus of Nola," *Revue des études augustiniennes* 2: 79–93.

Nicholson, O. (1994) "The 'Pagan Churches' of Maximinus Daia and Julian the Apostate," *Journal of Ecclesiastical History* 45: 1–10.

Nixon, C.E.V. (1971) "An Historiographical Study of the *Caesares* of Sextus Aurelius Victor," Diss. University of Michigan.

Oberhelman, S.M. (1987) "The Provenance of the Style of Ammianus Marcellinus," *Quaderni Urbinati di Cultura Classica* 56: 79–89.

O'Flynn, J.M. (1983) *Generalissimos of the Western Roman Empire*, Edmonton, Alberta: University of Alberta Press.

Oulton, J.E.L. (1928) "Rufinus's Translation of the Church History of Eusebius," *Journal of Theological Studies* 30 (1929): 150–74.

Pack, E. (1986) *Städte und Steuern in der Politik Julians*, Brussels: Latomus.

Pack, R. (1953) "The Roman Digressions of Ammianus Marcellinus," *Transactions of the American Philological Association* 84: 181–9.

Paschoud, F. (1980a) "La polemica provvidenzialistica di Orosio," in S. Calderone, ed., *La storiografia ecclesiastica nella tarda antichità*, Messina: Centro di studi umanistici, 113–34.

—— (1980b) "Quand parut la première edition de l'histoire d'Eunape?" *Bonner Historia–Augusta–Colloquium* 14: 149–62.

—— (1985a) "Le Début de l'Ouvrage Historique d'Olympiodore," in *Studia in honorem Iiro Kajanto*, Helsinki: Classical Association of Finland, 185–96.

—— (1985b) "Eunapiana," *Bonner Historia–Augusta–Colloquium* 17: 239–303.

—— (1989a) "La préface de l'ouvrage historique d'Eunape," *Historia* 38: 198–223.

—— (1989b) "'Se non è vero, è ben trovato': tradition littéraire et vérité historique chez Ammien Marcellin," *Chiron* 19: 37–54.

—— (1989c) "Zosime, Eunape et Olympiodore, Témoins des Invasions Barbares," in E. Chrysos and A. Schwarcz, eds, *Das Reich und die Barbaren*, Wien: Böhlau, 181–201.

—— (1992) "Valentinien travesti, ou: de la malignité d'Ammien," in J. den Boeft, D. den Hengst, and H.C. Teitler, eds, *Cognitio Gestorum: The Historiographic Art of Ammianus Marcellinus*, Amsterdam: Royal Netherlands Academy of Arts and Sciences, 67–84.

Peachin, M. (1985) "The Purpose of Festus' Breviary," *Mnemosyne* 38: 158–60.

Penella, R.J. (1990) *Greek Philosophers and Sophists in the Fourth Century A.D.: Studies in Eunapius of Sardis*, Leeds: Francis Cairns.

—— (1993) "Julian the Persecutor in Fifth Century Church Historians," *Ancient World* 24: 31–43.

Price, R.M. (1985) *A History of the Monks of Syria by Theodoret of Cyrrhus*, Kalamazoo, Mich.: Cistercian Publications.

Ratti, S. (1996) *Les empereurs romains d'Auguste à Dioclétien dans le Bréviaire d'Eutrope*, Paris: Les Belles Lettres.

Rees, B.R. (1988) *Pelagius, a Reluctant Heretic*, Woodbridge, Suffolk: Boydell Press.

Rees, R. (1999) "Ammianus Satiricus," in J.W. Drijvers and D. Hunt, eds, *The Late Roman World and its Historian: Interpreting Ammianus Marcellinus*, London: Routledge, 141–55.

Ridley, R.T. (1969/70) "Eunapius and Zosimus," *Helikon* 9–10: 574–92.

—— (1973) "Notes on Julian's Persian Expedition," *Historia* 22: 317–30.

Rike, R.L. (1987) *Apex Omnium: Religion in the Res Gestae of Ammianus*, Berkeley: University of California Press.

Roberts, M. (1988) "The Treatment of Narrative in Late Antique Literature: Ammianus Marcellinus (16.10), Rutilius Namatianus and Paulinus of Pella," *Philologus* 132: 181–95.

Roueché, C. (1986) "Theodosius II, the Cities, and the Date of the 'Church History' of Sozomen," *Journal of Theological Studies* 37: 130–2.

Rousseau, P. (1985) *Pachomius*, Berkeley: University of California Press.

Rubin, Z. (1986) "Diplomacy and War in the Relations between Byzantium and the Sassanids in the Fifth Century A.D.," in P. Freeman and D. Kennedy, eds, *The Defence of the Roman and Byzantine East*, Oxford: B.A.R., 677–95.

Sabbah, G. (1978) *La méthode d'Ammien Marcellin. Recherches sur la construction du discours historique dans les Res Gestae*, Paris: Les Belles Lettres.

—— (1997) "Ammien Marcellin, Libanius, Antioche et la date des derniers livres des *Res gestae*," *Cassiodorus* 3: 89–116.

Sacks, K.S. (1986) "The Meaning of Eunapius' History," *History and Theory* 25: 52–67.

Salemme, C. (1987) "Tecnica della Comparazione e Presitio Stilistico in Ammiano Marcellino 28,4," *Civiltà classica e cristiana* 8: 353–78.

Santini, C. (1979) "Per una caratterizzazione stilistica del 'Breviarium' di Eutropio," *Giornale Italiano Filologia* 31: 1–16.

Schamp, J. (1987a) "Gélase ou Rufin: un fait nouveau," *Byzantion* 57: 360–90.

—— (1987b) "The Lost Ecclesiastical History of Gelasius of Caesarea (CPG, 3521): Towards a Reconsideration," *The Patristic and Byzantine Review* 6: 146–52.

Scheda, D. (1966) "Die Todesstunde Kaiser Julians," *Historia* 15: 380–3.

Schoo, G. (1911) *Die Quellen des Kirchenhistorikers Sozomenos*, Berlin: Trowitzsch & Sohn.

Scivoletto, N. (1970) "La civilitas del IV secolo e il significato del Breviarium di Eutropio," *Giornale Italiano di Filologia* 22: 14–45.

Seager, R. (1986) *Ammianus Marcellinus: Seven Studies in his Language and Thought*, Columbia, Mo.: University of Missouri Press.

—— (1996) "*Ut Dux Cunctator et Tutus*: The Caution of Valentinian (Ammianus 27.10)," *Papers of the Leeds International Latin Seminar* 9: 191–6.

—— (1997) "Perceptions of Eastern Frontier Policy in Ammianus, Libanius, and Julian (337–363)," *Classical Quarterly* 47: 253–68.

Seeck, O. (1883/1984) *Q. Aurelii Symmachi quae supersunt*, Berlin: Weidman.

Simon, M. (1964/86) *Verus Israel: A Study of the Relations Between Christians and Jews in the Roman Empire, 135–425*, New York: Oxford University Press.

Sirago, V.A. (1970) "Olimpiodoro di Tebe e la sua Opera Storica," in L. de Rosa, ed., *Richerche storiche ed economiche in memoria di Corrado Barbagallo*, Naples: Edizioni Scientifiche Italiane, 3–25.

Smith, R. (1995) *Julian's Gods: Religion and Philosophy in the Thought and Action of Julian the Apostate*, London: Routledge.

—— (1999) "Telling Tales: Ammianus' Narrative of the Persian Expedition of Julian," in J.W. Drijvers and D. Hunt, eds, *The Late Roman World and its Historian: Interpreting Ammianus Marcellinus*, London: Routledge, 89–104.

Stertz, S.A. (1980) "Ammianus Marcellinus' Attitudes Toward Earlier Emperors," in C. Deroux, ed., *Studies in Latin Literature and Roman History II*, Brussels: Latomus, 487–514.

—— (1998) "Pagan Historians on Judaism in Ancient Times," in J. Neusner, ed., *Approaches to Ancient Judaism, Volume 14*, Atlanta: Scholars Press, 21–57.

Stoian, I. (1967) "A propos de la conception historique d'Ammien Marcellin (*Ut miles quondam et Graecus*)," *Latomus* 26: 73–81.

Teillet, S. (1984) *Des Goths à la Nation Gothique: Les origines de l'idée de nation en Occident du Ve au VIIe siècle*, Paris: Les Belles Lettres.

Teitler, H.C. (1985) *Notarii and Exceptores: An Inquiry into the Role and Significance of Shorthand Writers in the Imperial and Ecclesiastical Bureaucracy of the Roman Empire*, Amsterdam: J.C. Gieben.

—— (1999) "*Visa Vel Lecta*? Ammianus on Persia and the Persians," in J.W. Drijvers and D. Hunt, eds, *The Late Roman World and its Historian: Interpreting Ammianus Marcellinus*, London: Routledge, 216–23.

Thélamon, F. (1970) "L'Empereur idéal d'après l'*Histoire ecclésiastique* de Rufin d'Aquilée," *Studia Patristica* 10: 310–14.

—— (1979) "L'histoire de l'Église comme 'histoire sainte,'" *Revue des études augustiniennes* 25: 184–91.

—— (1981) *Païens et chrétiens au IVe siècle*, Paris: Etudes augustiniennes.

—— (1992) "Apôtres et prophètes de notre temps," *Antichità altoadriatiche* 39: 171–98.

Thompson, E.A. (1944) "Olympiodorus of Thebes," *Classical Quarterly* 38: 43–52.

—— (1947a) *The Historical Work of Ammianus Marcellinus*, Cambridge: Cambridge University Press.

—— (1947b) "Notes on Priscus Panites," *Classical Quarterly* 41: 61–5.

—— (1963) "Christianity and the Northern Barbarians," in A. Momigliano, ed., *The Conflict between Paganism and Christianity in the Fourth Century*, Oxford: Clarendon Press, 56–78.

—— (1996) *The Huns*, Oxford: Blackwell.

Todd, M. (1975) *The Northern Barbarians, 100 BC–AD 300*, London: Hutchinson.

Tougher, S. (1999) "Ammianus and the Eunuchs," in J.W. Drijvers and D. Hunt, eds, *The Late Roman World and its Historian: Interpreting Ammianus Marcellinus*, London: Routledge, 64–73.

Tränkle, H. (1972) "Ammianus Marcellinus als römischer Geschichtsschreiber," *Antike und Abendland* 11: 21–33.

Trigg, J.W. (1998) *Origen*, London: Routledge.

Tritle, L.A. (1994) "Whose Tool? Ammianus Marcellinus on the Emperor Valens," *American History Bulletin* 8: 141–53.

Trombley, F. (1999) "Ammianus Marcellinus and Fourth-Century Warfare: A Protector's Approach to Historical Narrative," in J.W. Drijvers and D. Hunt, eds, *The Late Roman World and its Historian: Interpreting Ammianus Marcellinus*, London: Routledge, 17–28.

Turcan, R. (1966) "L'abandon de Nisibe et l'opinion publique (363 ap. J.C.)," in R. Chevallier, ed., *Mélanges d'archéologie et d'histoire offerts à André Piganiol* 2, Paris: 875–90.

Urbainczyk, T. (1997a) "Observations on the Differences between the Church Histories of Socrates and Sozomen," *Historia* 46: 355–73.

—— (1997b) *Socrates of Constantinople*, Ann Arbor: University of Michigan Press.

—— (1998) "Vice and Advice in Socrates and Sozomen," in M. Whitby, ed., *The Propaganda of Power: The Role of Panegyric in Late Antiquity*, Leiden: Brill, 299–319.

Ventura, C.M. (1992) *Principi Fanciulli: Legittimismo Constituzionale e Storiografia Cristiana nella Tarda Antichità*, Catania: Edizioni del Prisma.

Warmington, B. (1956) "The Career of Romanus, *Comes Africae*," *Byzantinische Zeitschrift* 49: 55–64.

—— (1981) "Ammianus Marcellinus and the Lies of Metrodorus," *Classical Quarterly* 31: 464–8.

Whitby, M. (1999) "Images of Constantius," in J.W. Drijvers and D. Hunt, eds, *The Late Roman World and its Historian: Interpreting Ammianus Marcellinus*, London: Routledge, 77–88.

Wiedemann, T.E.J. (1986) "Between Man and Beasts. Barbarians in Ammianus Marcellinus," in I.S. Moxon, J.D. Smart, and A.J. Woodman, eds, *Past Perspectives: Studies in Greek and Roman Historical Writing*, Cambridge: Cambridge University Press, 189–211.

Williams, R. (1983) "The Logic of Arianism," *Journal of Theological Studies* 34: 56–81.

—— (1987) *Arius: Heresy and Tradition*, London: Darton, Longman, & Todd.

Williams, S. and G. Friell (1994) *Theodosius: The Empire at Bay*, New Haven: Yale University Press.

Wölfflin, E. (1904) "Das Breviarium des Festus," *Archiv für lateinische Lexikographie und Grammatik* 13: 69–97 and 173–80.

Wolfram, H. (1988) *History of the Goths*, Berkeley: University of California Press.

Woodman, A.J. (1988) *Rhetoric in Classical Historiography: Four Studies*, London: Croom Helm.

Young, F. (1983) *From Nicaea to Chalcedon: A Guide to the Literature and its Background*, Philadelphia: Fortress Press.

Zawadski, T. (1989) "Les Procès politiques de l'an 371–372 (Amm. Marc. XXIX 1, 29–33; Eunapius, Vitae Soph. VII 6, 3–4; D 480)," in H.E. Herzig and R. Frei-Stolba, eds, *Labor Omnibus Unus. Festschrift Gerold Walser*, Stuttgart: F. Steiner Verlag Wiesbaden, 274–87.

Zuccali, C. (1993) "Sulla cronologia dei Materiali per una storia di Olimpiodoro di Tebe," *Historia* 42: 252–6.

Zuckerman, C. (1994) "L'Empire d'Orient et les Huns: notes sur Priscus," *Travaux et mémoires* 12: 159–82.

INDEX